Knowledge in Risk Assessment and Management

Knowledge in Risk Assessment and Management

Edited by

Terje Aven and Enrico Zio

Registered Offices
John Wiley & Sons, Inc., 111 River Street, Hoboken, NJ 07030, USA
John Wiley & Sons Ltd, The Atrium, Southern Gate, Chichester, West Sussex, PO19 8SQ, UK

Editorial Office
9600 Garsington Road, Oxford, OX4 2DQ, UK

For details of our global editorial offices, customer services, and more information about Wiley products visit us at www.wiley.com.

Wiley also publishes its books in a variety of electronic formats and by print-on-demand. Some content that appears in standard print versions of this book may not be available in other formats.

Library of Congress Cataloging-in-Publication Data

Names: Aven, Terje, editor. | Zio, Enrico, editor.
Title: Knowledge in risk assessment and management / edited by Terje Aven, University of Stavanger, Norway, Enrico Zio, Politecnico di Milano, Italy.
Description: Hoboken, NJ : John Wiley & Sons, Inc., [2018] | Includes bibliographical references and index. |
Identifiers: LCCN 2017044669 (print) | LCCN 2017051142 (ebook) | ISBN 9781119317883 (pdf) | ISBN 9781119317937 (epub) | ISBN 9781119317890 (cloth)
Subjects: LCSH: Risk assessment. | Risk management. | System analysis.
Classification: LCC HD61 (ebook) | LCC HD61 .K596 2018 (print) | DDC 658.15/5—dc23
LC record available at https://lccn.loc.gov/2017044669

Cover design by Wiley
Cover Images: (Top and bottom: Lines and oil gas industry)
© KTSDESIGN/SCIENCE PHOTO LIBRARY/Gettyimages;
© Golf_Chalermchai Karasopha/Gettyimages

Set in 10/12pt Warnock by SPi Global, Pondicherry, India
Printed and bound in Malaysia by Vivar Printing Sdn Bhd

10 9 8 7 6 5 4 3 2 1

Contents

List of Contributors

Eirik Bjorheim Abrahamsen
University of Stavanger, Norway

Terje Aven
University of Stavanger, Norway

Christine L. Berner
DNV GL, Norway

Torbjørn Bjerga
University of Stavanger
Norway

Kevin Coyne
Office of Nuclear Regulatory
Research, US Nuclear Regulatory
Commission, Washington, DC

Ivan Damnjanovic
Texas A&M University

Roger Flage
University of Stavanger
Norway

Sven Ove Hansson
KTH, Sweden

Bjørnar Heide
Petroleum Safety Authority Norway
Norway

Nicola Pedroni
Laboratoire Genie Industriel
CentraleSupélec
Université Paris-Saclay, France

Jon Tømmerås Selvik
University of Stavanger, Norway

Nathan Siu
Office of Nuclear Regulatory
Research
U.S. Nuclear Regulatory
Commission
Washington, DC

Shital Thekdi
University of Richmond, USA

Vegard L. Tuft
Safetec Nordic AS, Trondheim
Norway

Pietro Turati
Laboratoire Genie Industriel
CentraleSupélec
Université Paris-Saclay, France

Jan Erik Vinnem
Norwegian University of Science and
Technology, Norway

Beate R. Wagnild
Safetec Nordic AS, Trondheim
Norway

Olga M. Slyngstad
Safetec Nordic AS, Trondheim
Norway

Marja Ylönen
VTT Technical Research Centre of
Finland

Enrico Zio
Systems Science and the Energetic
Challenge Chair
Foundation Electricite' de France
Laboratoire de Genie Industriel (LGI)
CentraleSupélec
Universite' Paris-Saclay
France
and
Department of Energy
Politecnico di Milano, Italy

Preface

This book is about knowledge in risk assessment and management. Why a book on this subject? It is because the assessment and management of risk is fundamentally based on the knowledge and information available. Paradoxically, recognizing this simple fact is an important step forward. Indeed, recently the need has arisen of explicitly specifying the concept that risk is conditioned on knowledge (K). Then, the methodologies and approaches for risk assessment and management are to be seen as the supports for incorporating knowledge into a systematic, rigorous and transparent framework. In other words, risk assessment and management is a way of producing, representing and presenting knowledge about phenomena and the future, and then informing decision makers. This is achieved by developing models, representing and expressing uncertainties, propagating the uncertainties and using probabilities or other measures to describe risk. The description of risk is conditional on the knowledge K, as for example a probability is a judgement of uncertainty given some knowledge of the uncertain process or event. Knowledge is typically based on data and information, and takes the form of justified beliefs – often stated as assumptions in the risk model and characterization.

The value of the risk assessment and management, then, stands on the quality of the methodologies and approaches adopted, and on the strength of the knowledge K on which these are built. Whereas procedures of quality assurance have been developed for the former, how to deal with the latter – knowledge K – is still an open issue and a research challenge in risk assessment and management. How should it be described and evaluated in the risk assessment? How should it be reflected and taken into account in the decision-making process of risk management? This book aims to make some contributions to clarifying the problem, answering some of the questions and meeting the related practical challenges.

The book comprises 12 chapters on the fundamental concepts, ideas, principles and approaches involved (Part I), risk assessment and decision-making methods and issues (Part II) and applications (Part III).

Part I

Chapter 1 sets the stage by looking into the fundamental issues and principles related to knowledge characterization in risk assessment and management. An example is used to drive the illustration. The example is simple but sufficiently complete to allow clear discussions of critical aspects of the process, including risk conceptualization and measurements, treatment of uncertainties, characterization of the knowledge available, accounting for potential surprises, consideration of vulnerability, and robustness and resilience.

Chapter 2 follows up by providing a deep look into the concept of knowledge. The chapter reflects on how the knowledge concept used in risk assessment matches the wealth of studies on knowledge that we find in philosophy and sociology. It is questioned how the risk field can learn from these studies, for further developing the knowledge dimension of risk assessment and management.

Chapter 3 discusses the treatment and communication of uncertain assumptions in relation to risk assessments. The chapter describes a formal setup that connects the risk concept, the risk description, risk indices, and the knowledge dimension, including the assumptions in particular. Then, it presents a scheme for systematizing uncertain assumptions, and it is shown how it can be used to provide recommendations on strategies for the treatment of such assumptions from both a risk analyst's and risk manager's perspectives. The setup and scheme build on recent advances in uncertainty-based risk conceptualizations, including, in particular, the concept of assumption deviation risk: the so-called NUSAP notational scheme for uncertainty and quality in science for policy, and the assumption-based planning framework.

Chapter 4 presents a general framework that can provide information about the validity of the assumptions made in a risk model about a system's future behavior, in order to provide early warnings. This is highly relevant for risk assessment and management, as any model-based risk description is strongly dependent on the underlying modeling assumptions and the validity of these assumptions is difficult to express. This question needs to be addressed to adequately understand, assess and manage risk, in particular the risk related to potential surprises and unforeseen events. The framework described in the chapter is based on a signal-processing approach that monitors for signals associated with a trend change in the system's behavior.

Chapter 5 provides an in-depth analysis of uncertainty analysis in a risk assessment and management context. Given the relevance of uncertainty in risk assessment and management – and indeed the importance of what is not known just as much as what is, the chapter presents a general framework for uncertainty analysis, building on what we are uncertain about, who is uncertain and how we should represent or express the uncertainties. The framework has two distinct features:

- a clear distinction between uncertainty as a concept and the way uncertainty is measured or described
- a distinction between the uncertainty of the analysts and that of the decision makers.

Chapter 6 addresses the concept of completeness uncertainty. The interpretations found in the literature of this term are ambiguous, and its treatment appears difficult. The chapter aims at clarifying what the concept is about and it shows that in essence it can be treated as model uncertainty.

Chapter 7 reflects on issues related to the quality of a risk assessment, addressing both "scientific criteria" and "being useful" in a decision-making context. New insights are gained by considering two novel aspects:

- the perspective of risk assessment, which shifts the focus from the accurate risk estimation to the characterization of knowledge and lack of knowledge
- the recognition that decision makers need to go beyond the conditional risk as described and assessed by the risk analysts and experts, to consider unconditional risk.

The quality of risk assessment is then discussed in this context, highlighting the questions of what it depends on, how it can be ensured and checked.

Chapter 8 puts forward modeling and simulation as ways to explore and understand system behavior, for identifying critical scenarios and avoiding surprises. Recognizing that for complex systems, the simulation models can be:

- high-dimensional
- black-boxes
- dynamic
- computationally expensive

the chapter presents adaptive strategies for guiding the simulations so as to increase knowledge of the critical system behavior in a reasonable computational time. Two simulation frameworks for hazard identification are proposed: one focusing on the search for extreme unknown consequences associated with a given set of scenarios and the other focusing on the exploration of those scenarios, potentially leading the system to critical consequences and the retrieval of the corresponding root causes.

Part II

Chapter 9 presents a decision-support prioritization method that incorporates uncertainty through strength-of-knowledge (SoK) and target-sensitivity assessments. Current thinking for assessing these uncertainties and their importance in the decision-making process is based on a probabilistic perspective and decision analysis. The chapter presents a new method for prioritizing investments with consideration of the most influential uncertainties from the decision-making point of view, thereby allowing for systematic SoK considerations. The method is demonstrated on an emergency management system that is vulnerable to future economic, environmental, and political factors.

Chapter 10 addresses the issue of structuring decisions in the process of risk management. When the decision procedure starts, it is often unsettled or unknown exactly:

- what issues are going to be decided upon
- whether a single decision is going to be made about all of them or the decision will be subdivided and in that case how
- when the decision(s) should be made
- what options are open to the decision-maker(s)
- the criteria for a successful decision.

In the chapter, the structuring of decisions is systematized by dividing it into ten major components. Conceptual tools are introduced that can be used for the analysis and management of each of these components. Careful investigation of the consequences of different ways of structuring decisions can provide decision makers with the knowledge needed to ensure the efficiency and transparency of the risk management decision process.

Part III

Chapter 11 presents a practical approach to risk assessment – quantitative risk analysis (QRA) – of offshore oil and gas installations from design to operation, highlighting the importance of knowledge and related assumptions. A QRA is a powerful decision-support tool, used in many industries exposed to major accident risk. QRAs are often large and comprehensive, and are sometimes criticized for providing results too late, being too costly and not adequately addressing uncertainty and possible deviations in input parameters.

Chapter 12 outlines another way to show how knowledge can be incorporated in risk assessment and management practice. An extension of the method currently used by the Norwegian Petroleum Safety Authority to express the level of risk and to detect trends in risks in the Norwegian petroleum industry is suggested. This extension incorporates specific robustness and knowledge assessments.

Chapter 13 illustrates the risk-related knowledge management challenges faced by a safety authority (specifically, the United States Nuclear Regulatory Commission), but also by the risk assessment and management community as a whole. It explains the use of risk information and knowledge in the practice of regulatory decision-making, highlighting its multi-faceted character, which leads to challenges for knowledge engineering and the development of information systems supporting knowledge management. Approaches to improving the management of risk information for increased knowledge are also described.

Acknowledgements

The work has been partly funded by the Norwegian Research Council – as a part of the Petromaks 2 program (grant number 228335/E30). The support is gratefully acknowledged.

Part I

Fundamental Ideas, Principles and Approaches

1

Risk Assessment with Broad Uncertainty and Knowledge Characterisation: An Illustrating Case Study

Terje Aven and Roger Flage

University of Stavanger, Norway

This chapter presents a risk assessment of a master's degree programme in risk management. The assessment is to support decision-making on how to best develop the programme in the coming years. The aim of the chapter is to perform this case study to show how a risk assessment can be conducted and used when risk perspectives are adopted that highlight knowledge and uncertainty characterisations that go beyond the standard approach based on consequence and probability estimation. Such perspectives have been given considerable attention recently, and real-life examples have been sought, showing the practical implications of these perspectives. The example is simple and allows for clarifying discussions of critical aspects of the analysis process, including risk conceptualisation and measurement, treatment of uncertainties, characterisation of the knowledge available, accounting for potential surprises, as well as vulnerability, robustness and resilience considerations. It is concluded that with integration of the new ideas from the early planning stages, the risk assessment is not more difficult to run than with the traditional approach; the decision process is, however, in our view substantially improved because the decision makers are better informed on many of the aspects important for the decisions to be made.

1.1 Introduction

The Petroleum Safety Authority Norway (PSA-N), which is an independent government regulator with responsibility for safety, emergency preparedness and the working environment in the Norwegian petroleum industry, has recently introduced a new definition of risk, which states that risk represents the consequences of an activity along with the associated uncertainty (PSA-N 2015). The previous

Knowledge in Risk Assessment and Management, First Edition. Edited by Terje Aven and Enrico Zio.

definition was based on a traditional consequence and probability perspective in line with the triplet of Kaplan and Garrick (1981), covering scenarios, consequences and probabilities. Work has been initiated in the industry to understand the practical meaning and implications of this new definition from PSA-N.

The Society for Risk Analysis (SRA) has just issued a new glossary on key risk concepts (SRA 2015), which allows for several definitions of risk. However, in all the definitions referred to, events/consequences and uncertainty are key components, and the issues about practical meaning and implications are also relevant. As a third example, we would like to mention the ISO 31000 standard on risk management (ISO 2009), which has also built the definition of risk on uncertainty and not probability. In the standard, risk is defined as the effect of uncertainty on objectives.

When it comes to the risk description in a risk assessment, it is necessary to use a measure of the uncertainties, and the question is then what the alternatives are and what measure should be used. Uncertainties are related to knowledge and, hence, describing uncertainties is about describing not only the knowledge itself but also the quality of this knowledge.

Considerable theoretical work has been conducted on this topic, aimed at clarifying the understanding of the key concepts and providing recommendations on how to best describe risk; see for example Aven (2012) and Flage *et al.* (2014).

Experience from practical risk assessment work has shown that many people struggle to see the difference between the old consequence–probability-based risk perspective and the new ideas; for example, what is the difference between uncertainty and probability? Also, there is a concern that the new way of thinking will lead to more complicated assessments, emphasising uncertainties too much, with the result that communication between analysts and decision makers will be made unnecessarily difficult.

To meet these challenges, there is a need for work that can contribute to clarifying the difference between the traditional perspectives and the new ones, pointing to the differences and demonstrating what these new ideas add to current practice.

In our view, the best way of doing so is to present and discuss simple, easily understandable examples (case studies), which make it possible to highlight the ideas without being disturbed by a lot of technical details. The present chapter aims to do precisely this. We present parts of a risk assessment, including the planning and use stages, of a master's degree programme in risk management, in which the assessment is based on the new ideas about risk. The assessment is to be used to support decision-making at the university, and in this chapter we discuss the main process stages and findings, highlighting issues linked to differences in risk perspectives and what the new way of thinking adds to current practice. In an appendix, we present an overview of the key features of the new perspectives that were required to adapt the existing theoretical work to a more practical context. The case study considered has a qualitative analysis focus.

The remainder of the chapter is organised as follows. Firstly, in Section 1.2, we present the case study in more detail. Then, in Sections 1.3 and 1.4, we look into the planning of the risk assessment and the execution of the assessment, respectively. Section 1.5 covers the use of the assessment, having a focus on risk management and related decision-making. Section 1.6 discusses the analysis process and findings, and, finally, Section 1.7 provides some conclusions.

1.2 The Case Study

The University of Stavanger officially became a university in 2005, after a review process showing that certain quality requirements were met. However, it has offered risk and safety-related programmes at master's level (two-year programmes, building on a bachelor's degree of three years duration) for about 30 years. During the first 10 years, these programmes were based on petroleum and offshore engineering study programmes; later, they were also oriented towards societal safety. Gradually, the offshore and petroleum-based programmes have been made more general, and now the master's programmes offered are run with a wider risk management and societal safety focus. Still, the applications are to a large extent related to oil and gas, and one of the specialisations of the risk management programme is in offshore safety.

The trend in recent years has been towards an increase in international students and a corresponding reduction in Norwegian students. Student recruitment has always been an issue, as the competition related to getting the best students from the bachelor's engineering programmes is tough. The oil and gas industry has attracted many talented students, but the industry's need for candidates varies greatly, along with the oil price. Environmental concerns are also factors in this respect, when looking into the future of the programme.

To support decision-making on how to best develop the master's programme in risk management in the coming years, the risk assessment presented in this chapter was been carried out. As explained in Section 1.1, we have sought to do this in the most "current way"; that is, in line with the new perspectives on risk.

1.3 Planning of the Risk Assessment

The main activities of the planning stage of the risk assessment are:

- clarification and specification of the decisions to be supported by the risk assessment
- the development of the objectives of the assessment
- establishing the scope of the assessment – clarifying what aspects and features to include and not include in the work.

Other activities, such as organisation of the work, will not be further discussed here.

As mentioned in Section 1.1, the overall main objective of the risk assessment is to support the decision-making process on how to best develop the master's programme in risk management in the coming years. As a first step, the main stakeholders involved are identified: students, academic staff (professors), administration, potential employers (industry, public sector...) and society as a whole. For each of these stakeholders, we identify a set of ideal goals/criteria; see Table 1.1.

From this, the following aims of the risk assessment are formulated:

a) Identify gaps between these goals/criteria and the current status.
b) Identify events and factors that could have strong effects on the achievement of the above goals/criteria, or other issues of importance for the development of the programme in coming years.
c) Suggest a set of measures that is considered necessary to bridge the gap and meet these goals/criteria and avoid potential negative consequences and surprises.
d) Assess the risk associated with implementing or not implementing these measures, as well as costs and benefits in a wider sense, highlighting all relevant pros and cons.
e) For the risk judgements, follow the approach presented in the appendix, which in brief means that the following tasks should be carried out in this case:
   - Identify events that could result in goals/criteria being/not being met.
   - Identify underlying events/factors/sources/threats that could be of importance in this regard.
   - Assess the probabilities of these events using a suitable interval probability scale.
   - Assess the strength of knowledge supporting these judgements. Identify assumptions on which these probability judgements are based. Assess possible deviations from these assumptions. Consider ways of improving relevant knowledge.
   - Scrutinise the assessments by letting others in the organisation check the assessments, in particular for knowledge gaps and signals and warnings.
   - Assess the robustness and resilience if something unlikely/surprising should occur.
   - Consider measures to improve the robustness and resilience.
   - Carry out an ALARP (As Low As Reasonably Practicable) process to further reduce risk.
f) Derive a priority list of the measures for implementation, based on different potential policies.

Table 1.1 Ideal goals/criteria specified for each stakeholder category.

Stakeholders	Ideal goals/criteria				
Students	An education that provides good opportunities for relevant jobs	Highly qualified staff (professors and administration)	Exciting and stimulating scientific environment	A good social environment	Driving force for further developments
Academic staff (professors)	Recruiting good students	High international research and development level supporting the programme	Use of modern teaching and communication means	Highly motivated as lecturers and supervisors	
Administration	Professional service for the students	Professional service for the academic staff	Driving force for further developments		
Potential employers	Perceive and find candidates from the programme highly competent and motivated	Good contact with academic staff	A significant need for candidates from the programme		
Society	Candidates add value to the society with their competence and skills	Scientific staff add value to society			

The assessment was carried out by core academic staff in the Risk Management group at the Department of Industrial Economics, Risk Management and Planning at the University of Stavanger. The implementation of the suggested measures will depend on decision processes at the department and school levels, managed by the head of department and the Dean, respectively.

1.4 Execution of the Risk Assessment

Brainstorming sessions were conducted to carry out the activities associated with aims (a)–(c): identify gaps, events and factors, and measures to bridge the gaps.

A list of gaps was identified and divided into two categories: those judged as the most important, and others. Table 1.2 summarises the results for two such gaps, where the first gap is considered the most critical one. We focus our discussion on this gap. It states that to meet the goals formulated in Table 1.1, a main challenge is recruitment of good students. The current requirement to enter the Risk Management programme is an average grade of C or better from an engineering (or similar) bachelor's programme, and the number of applications has been fairly stable in recent years: slightly above the minimum level to fill the study programmes with qualified students. At the same time, we see that the master's programme in industrial economics has a large number of applications, which results in higher bachelor's grade point averages requirements. Two obvious explanations for this are that economics and business are well known to students at high school level and the master's programme in industrial economics is well known in Norway and internationally: it is a prestigious programme and the salary and career prospects are very good. Risk management, on the other hand, is a new field and not so well known to many students.

To recruit better students to the risk management area, it is suggested that a specialisation in risk management be established under the industrial economics master's programme. The programme already offers courses in risk management, and the suggestion could be seen as a further development of an already established link between these two areas. Another measure being considered is to apply to become a "centre of excellence", a prestigious research centre, supported by the Research Council of Norway. The idea would be that such a centre would make the risk management programme better known, both nationally and internationally, attracting more students. As a third measure, initiatives are considered for making risk management a subject at high school level. Realising this aim would, however, be a long process, but it could strongly influence recruitment success.

The next task is to conduct a risk assessment of these measures. We restrict attention to the measure M1, and the base case, i.e. doing nothing and

Table 1.2 Examples of identified gaps, important events and factors, and measures to bridge the gaps.

Identified gaps	Events and factors (risk sources, threats)				Measures		
Recruitment of more good students	Labour market Oil-price volatility	Programme judged as attractive for future careers Highly recognised programme	Risk and safety group obtains Centre of Excellence status	Risk management not a subject in schools, nor in the bachelor's programmes at the university	Develop a specialisation in risk management as part of master's programme in industrial economics (M1)	Apply to obtain Centre of Excellence status for the research group	Apply to obtain Centre of Excellence status for the research group
Limited use of modern teaching and communication means	Professors up to date on these means and motivated	Quality of tools is good	Sufficient resources made available		Recording of lectures	Use of short videos highlighting key topics in each course	

proceeding as today. We then go systematically through the issues listed in the guideline presented in the previous section and in the appendix. Tables 1.3 and 1.4 summarise some key points in these assessments for the base case and M1, respectively.

We see from Table 1.3 that the analysis group judges that, proceeding as today, it is quite likely that we will see a reduction in the recruitment of good students. This judgement is based on several assumptions, including that the master's programme is perceived among students as being strongly oriented towards petroleum applications. Although the programme has a generic risk assessment and management focus, it has a history linked to oil and gas, it offers a specialisation in offshore safety and the scientific staff work closely with the petroleum industry. The petroleum industry is currently under pressure: it is subject to intervention by governments, driven by climate change policies, and this may strongly affect young people in their choice of education. Fewer students will look for petroleum-oriented programmes. This may also affect student applications to the risk management programme. If the oil price remains low, the recruitment to petroleum-related programmes is likely to be further weakened. The analysis group has based its probability judgements on a fluctuating oil price, bringing a better incentive to invest in the industry, and more optimism. However, they judge it unlikely that a high oil price will lead to much higher interest in the study programme, given the current "green societal change". If the oil price increases, we may see improvements in recruitment, but we have previous experience that a very high oil price causes many candidates to end their studies after finishing their bachelor's degree, since in those circumstances the industry's demand for new employees is so high that they can easily get a job without a master's degree.

The assumption that competition to get the best students is increasing is prompted by the fact that universities and colleges offer an increasing number of master's programmes, and the marketing for these is more and more intense. The value of good students is very high in a university system, as these students represent a key recruitment base for PhD programmes.

The competition assumption is given a low assumption deviation risk score, because the analysis group considers it very likely that this assumption will hold. The two other assumption risks in Table 1.3 are judged as medium assumption deviation risk. This is based on an overall evaluation of the probability of deviations from the assumptions, the implications from these deviations, and the strength of knowledge supporting these judgements.

To assess the strength of knowledge supporting the probability assignments, the assumptions' deviation risks are taken into account, as are the availability and amount of data/information, different views among experts, and judgements of the basic understanding of the phenomena and processes being studied, in line with the approach outlined in the appendix. The events considered are unique future events, and the data and information available are more or

Table 1.3 Summary of risk judgements* for the base case: no specific measures implemented.

Events that could result in goals/criteria not being met	Events that could be of importance in this regard	Assessed probabilities for these events	Key assumptions made	Assessment of deviation risk	Assessment of the strength of knowledge supporting the probabilities assigned
A reduction is seen in the recruitment of good students (A_{1a})	Low/high oil price	$0.25 \leq P(A_{1a}) \leq 0.50$	The competition to get the best students is increasing	Low	Medium
	The risk and safety group at the university obtains centre of excellence status		The masters programme in risk is perceived as strongly oriented towards petroleum applications	Medium	
			The oil price continues to fluctuate	Medium	

*As defined in the list at the end of Section 1.4.

Table 1.4 Summary of risk judgements* for the measure M1.

Events that could result in goals/criteria not being met	Events that could be of importance in this regard	Assessed probabilities for these events	Key assumptions made	Assessment of deviation risk	Assessment of the strength of knowledge supporting the probabilities assigned
The specialisation is not approved (A_1)	New head of department	$P(A_1) \leq 0.10$	No change in head of department	Low	Strong
A very low number of students in industrial economics choose the specialisation in risk management (A_2)	The students find the specialisation unattractive (e.g. because of too much safety focus)	$0.25 \leq P(A_2) \leq 0.50$	People in the industrial economics group accept the risk management specialisation The specialisation continues to have a risk focus more than a safety focus	Low	Medium
The students in industrial economics following the risk management specialisation are weak (A_3)	The weak students choose the risk management specialisation Recruitment to the industrial economics programme is significantly weakened	$P(A_1) \leq 0.10$	The recruitment to the industrial economics programme continues to be strong	Low	Strong

*As defined in the list at the end of Section 1.3.

less relevant for making judgements about the probability of them occurring. The link between oil prices and student recruitment is not trivial, and in the analysis group there were different views on the importance of the various assumptions.

The probability judgements reflect the uncertainties as to whether the Risk Management Group will become a centre of excellence or not. The analysis group views the probability of the group being awarded the status in the coming years to be less than 0.1, given that the success rate among such applications is less than 10 %. If, however, the group should succeed and become such a centre, the probabilities in Table 1.3 would change dramatically. It is concluded that improvement would very likely be seen in the recruitment of good students: the assigned probability would change to at least 0.90; that is, $P(A_{1b}) \geq 0.90$. Furthermore, such an event would lead to $P(A_{1a}) \leq 0.05$.

Table 1.4 is analogous to Table 1.3 but relates to the case when measure M1 is implemented; in other words, the department develops a specialisation (module) in risk management as a part of the master's programme in industrial economics. We will comment on the event that the specialisation is not approved (A_1). This event is not considered likely; a probability of maximum 0.10 is assigned. This value is based on the assumption that there will be no change of head of department in the coming years. The current head is positively disposed towards introducing such a specialisation. The assumption risk is judged to be low, due to a judgement that there is a high probability of the assumption being true and strong knowledge supporting this judgement. Overall, strong knowledge is judged for this probability assignment, on the basis of judgements of the assumptions, as well as judgements linked to the availability and amount of data/information, different views among experts and understanding of the phenomena and processes being studied. The analysis group finds that the knowledge supporting the probability judgement is strong, as the group has good insight into the processes leading to the approval of the specialisation and has support from key persons at the department in establishing this specialisation.

Table 1.5 gives further details about the risk judgements (e) for the measure M1. To simplify, we restrict attention to the event that the specialisation is not approved (A_1). The first point covers a scrutiny of the assessments by letting others in the organisation check the assessments, in particular for knowledge gaps and signals. One of the interesting outcomes of these judgements was the fact that it was revealed that not all members of staff in the industrial economics department were enthusiastic about the proposal. The problem noted was that the inclusion of risk management as a specialisation could influence the programme in an unfortunate way and also lead to increased competition within the department for the best students.

As regards robustness/resilience, think about a situation in which a central person in the industrial economics group changes view and becomes negative

Table 1.5 Summary of additional risk judgements* for the measure M1 and event A_1.

Events that could result in goals/criteria not being met	Scrutinise the assessments by letting others in the organisation check the assessments, in particular for knowledge gaps	Assess the robustness and resilience if something unlikely/surprising should occur	Consider measures to improve the robustness and resilience	Are there relevant signals and warnings?	Carry out an ALARP process to further reduce risk
The specialisation is not approved (A_1)	Revealed that not all members of the staff in industrial economics were enthusiastic about the proposal	If a central person in the industrial economics group changes view and becomes negative to the proposal, it could complicate the approval process	Inform and motivate key people in the department about the plans	The observation that there was some resistance in the department	Reduce risk, by informing and motivating key people

*As defined in the list at the end of Section 1.3.

about the proposal. What would the effect be for the proposal? Clearly, it could jeopardise the plans, and suitable measures should therefore be implemented to reduce the vulnerabilities and reduce the risk. In line with ALARP thinking (HSE 2001), and to strengthen the robustness/resilience, initiatives should be taken to inform and motivate key people in the department about the plans, arguing that they would mean a stronger master's programme in industrial economics and an even stronger recruitment base, as well as additional supervision resources. Observing that there is resistance among some members of staff provides a strong signal that some action is required.

A ranking of the risks of specific events can be made in line with the guidelines in the appendix. For the event "a reduction is seen in the recruitment of good students (A_{1a})", a very high risk (category 4) is assigned, as the analyst group assigns a high score to the potential for extreme consequences and a relatively large associated probability of such consequences. Of course, what is an "extreme" consequence is a relative concept. The event: "the specialisation is not approved (A_1)" is assigned a moderate risk (category 2), as the analysis group assigns high scores, based on the potential for large consequences but a relatively small associated probability, as well as strong background knowledge.

This list does not provide clear guidance on what to do. For that purpose, we also need to address issues of costs and benefits in a broader sense. Firstly, we ask, what is the manageability of the risk? How difficult is it to reduce the risk?

For the A_{1a} event, measures that are strongly believed to reduce the risk can be implemented, improving the current situation and leading to the recruitment of good students. The most effective measure is considered to be the establishment of a specialisation in risk management as part of the master's programme in industrial economics, at least from a longer perspective. The costs are considered rather small compared to the benefits gained. Also, other measures were considered effective relative to the costs, for example a dedicated campaign for recruiting more students from the bachelor's level.

Different analysis tools can be used to model links between the different events and conditions addressed above, for example Bayesian belief networks (influence diagrams). As a simple illustration, we could have modelled three events (nodes): a parent event, "reduction in recruitment", and two child events, "study programme perceived as oil and gas oriented" and "low oil price". The network can be used in a semi-quantitative analysis, using probabilities and strength-of-knowledge judgements, but in this case a qualitative analysis to increase understanding of the phenomena studied is the main purpose.

1.4.1 Emerging Events (Risks)

The analysis group performed a brainstorming activity to reveal emerging risk events, and the most important one identified was "one or more young professors offered position at other university/institution". One of the members of the analysis group had identified some signals supporting the reality of this event, but the knowledge basis was considered very weak. The event is classified as an emerging event: an event that requires due attention. The risk management group is rather small but it has grown in recent years and now has a staff that makes it less vulnerable to this type of risk. Yet it would be a serious loss if one of these people should leave the group, as the number of people with the competence required is small.

1.5 Use of the Risk Assessment

The risk assessment has two main objectives: to provide insights about the risks linked to the operation of the master's programme and how various measures can influence these risks, and in this way to provide support for decisions on how to further develop the programme. The assessment does not prescribe what to do, but provides decision support. In this case, the main findings from the assessment were:

- The recruitment of more good students is the number one issue.
- A specialisation in risk management as a part of the master's programme in industrial economics is considered an effective means to this end.
- In addition, other means should be implemented, including a campaign among bachelor's students, who can be potential applicants to the risk management programme.
- In the longer term, risk management should be developed as a subject at high school level.

The assessment also underlined the need for effective communication to ensure that everybody understands the implications of a specialisation in risk management as a part of the master's programme in industrial economics.

1.6 Discussion

A traditional qualitative risk assessment typically covers the following points: hazard/threat identification, assessment of the consequences of these hazards/threats, probability judgements and a summarising risk metric, typically a risk matrix. The problems with using such metrics in describing risk are well known; see for example Cox (2008) and Flage and Røed (2012). Some of the main issues are:

- Often the events plotted are not well defined
- The consequences of the events are in many cases not well represented by a single point in the matrix but by several, with different probabilities. If we

restrict attention to one point, we will often think of this value as being the "expected value"; the centre of gravity of the probability distribution for the appropriate consequences. In most cases, this value is not very informative in showing the consequence dimension.

- The meaning of the concept of probability is often not explained. Is probability a tool for expressing the analyst's degree of belief or uncertainty, or is it used to reflect variation?
- Two events can have the same location in the risk matrix, but the knowledge supporting these judgements could be completely different: in one case, the knowledge is very strong; in another case it is very weak. This is not shown in the matrix, and the risk description could be misleading. It is static, and cannot reflect changes in knowledge.
- Colours are often used in the matrix, indicating that the risk is, say, unacceptable, acceptable, or should be reduced. Such a scheme should be avoided, as mechanical conclusions on the basis of likelihood and consequences could be rather arbitrary, not taking into account important aspects of the decision problem, such as the knowledge dimension.

If risk matrices are to be used to summarise the risk description, they need to be supplemented with strength-of-knowledge judgements, for example as illustrated by the approach presented in the appendix. For this analysis, we have not considered risk matrices at all; rather, we have sought to highlight a broader information and knowledge basis, capturing aspects such as assumption deviation risk, strength of knowledge and robustness.

Table 1.6 summarises key differences between a traditional approach and the one adopted in this chapter, which focuses on showing the difference in risk descriptions. However, the conceptual foundations for the two approaches are also different. Whereas the traditional approach is based on probability, the new approach has a risk perspective, which highlights uncertainties, as mentioned in Section 1.1. We shall not discuss this difference in further detail in this chapter, as this has been done previously in other works; see for example Aven (2014, 2015). The point made here is simply that the differences in risk descriptions is also linked to differences in the foundations of the approaches. In addition, the differences in risk understanding and risk description affect the way the risk assessments are used in decision-making. The traditional approach has a more narrow perspective, in the sense that the probabilities, to a large extent, are judged to represent or express the risks, whereas the alternative approach acknowledges that risk is more than these probabilities and no quantitative metric can fully describe risk. The alternative approach, therefore, normally leads to a humbler way of thinking, with due consideration of knowledge and lack of knowledge dimensions using qualitative assessments method. These dimensions may also be included in the traditional approach, but it is more difficult, as the framework lacks the concepts needed.

Table 1.6 Differences between a traditional approach and the one adopted in this chapter.

Approach aspect	Traditional	New approach presented in this chapter	Comments
Probability concept	The meaning is often not clarified	A subjective probability, interpreted as explained in the appendix	To ensure the quality of an analysis, all key concepts need to be properly defined and interpreted
Risk concept	Combination of loss/consequences and probability, sometimes even the product of these (the expected value)	Combination of consequences and associated uncertainties, and risk is described by specified consequences, a measure of uncertainty, and the background knowledge	In the alternative approach, a clear distinction is made between the risk concept and how it is measured
Risk description (characterisation)	Risk matrix focus (likelihood and consequence)	A broad spectrum covering consequences, probability, judgement of the strength of knowledge, etc. (see the appendix)	The chapter provides an illustration of how risk is described using the alternative approach
Use of models	Common	Common	Models are used in both approaches
Use of risk description	Often mechanical procedures based on the results of the risk analysis, for example conclusions about unacceptable or acceptable risk based on a placing in a risk matrix	The risk results inform the decision maker. The decision maker must see beyond the risk description to make a proper decision	Risk-informed decision-making can also be the result when adopting a traditional approach, but experience shows that this approach often leads to more mechanical risk-based decision procedures

Models are used in both approaches to improve understanding of the risks and to reveal how different factors relate to others. The models can be of different types. A main category is models of the phenomena, such as fault trees, event trees and Bayesian networks. Another category is probability models, modelling variation in populations of similar situations or units. We have not addressed probability models in this chapter because the activity we are examining does not allow for such modelling. Such models have an important role to play, but consideration needs to be given to the justification of these models and their limitations for practical use in a risk decision-making context.

The risk assessment carried out in this chapter has focused on the overall ideas, using simple analysis methods. For example, to identify hazards/threats, brainstorming meetings were conducted, with simple guidewords commonly used for such tasks; see for example Card *et al.* (2012) and Meyer and Reniers (2013). The details are omitted here, because these aspects of the assessment are considered standard and not a key part of the new approach presented here. A huge number of such methods for hazard/threat identification exist and we think that in general more work should be devoted to this important part of the risk assessment. An interesting approach that deserves more focus is the anticipatory failure determination (AFD) method (Kaplan *et al.* 1999; Aven 2014).

We view probability as a key concept in any risk assessment. We need to express in some way the uncertainties and the degrees of belief we, as analysts, have in relation to whether or not an event will occur. However, we acknowledge that a (subjective) probability alone is not sufficient to characterise the uncertainties and the degrees of belief. We need to add judgements about the strength of knowledge supporting the probability assignment. This is thoroughly discussed in Aven (2013) and Flage *et al.* (2014) and has also been addressed at the beginning of this section.

We also see the use of interval probabilities as attractive in the qualitative or semi-qualitative settings used here. These intervals mean that the assessor is not willing to be more precise in their assessment than the interval describes, given the knowledge available. Some may think that the use of such intervals makes the strength-of-knowledge judgement superfluous, but this is not the case. Intervals are also based on some background knowledge, including assumptions, and it is essential to also include this dimension in the total description informing decision makers.

If we focus on the hazards/threats and the measures needed to meet these, it may seem unnecessary to describe risk using probabilities; the numbers seem so arbitrary anyway. To this it can be argued that we need to prioritise between different risks and measures, and the issue is how to be best informed. We may conclude that some risks need to be reduced and given top priority, but such a conclusion is in most cases better supported if a judgement about the probability can be made. An interval scale commonly meets the need for accuracy without being arbitrary. In the example, we did not use pre-defined probability scales, but this is common. For example, a scale might be as follows: unlikely (≤ 0.05), less likely ($0.05 - 0.20$), likely ($0.20 - 0.50$) and very likely (> 0.50).

The setup used allows both positive and negative consequences to be studied, although risk assessments often have a focus on undesirable outcomes. In many cases, as in this example, the key issue is to develop the study programme in the best possible way, and we are not only concerned about hazards and threats; equally important are the opportunities and possibilities for obtaining positive results. Not including the upside part when assessing risk is a general challenge for the risk field, and it is not solved by the proposed approach. However, the framework introduced highlights both positive and negative consequences, and in this way it can stimulate broad processes and perspectives, avoiding placing too much focus on failures of and compliance with specified goals, compared to new developments and innovative solutions and measures.

1.7 Conclusions

We have looked into the planning, execution and use of a risk assessment for a university master's programme in risk management. The assessment is to be seen as a case study, showing how a qualitative or semi-quantitative risk assessment can be conducted underpinned by a risk perspective that highlights knowledge and uncertainty characterisations that go beyond the standard approach based on consequence and probability estimation.

We conclude that the new approach gives a different focus for such analyses. The risk is not summarised in a risk matrix, using probability and consequence categories. A much broader risk picture is established, capturing aspects of uncertainties and knowledge that are not common in current approaches. Using the checklist in the appendix, analysts can go systematically through a set of issues judged important for the risk, their assessment and their treatment. The new aspects provide the decision makers with a stronger and more informative decision basis, because the assessments are not limited to risk descriptions based on consequences (losses) and probability, an approach which in fact ignores key aspects of risk. By integration of the new ideas from the early planning stages, the risk assessment is not more difficult to run than the traditional approach. The new risk description has more items to be addressed, but not all are relevant in all cases, and with experience it should be possible to carry out the assessment as quickly as for a traditional analysis. However, even if the new approach should require some additional time on specific issues, we consider it a valuable use of resources. A proper informative risk description requires that the knowledge and lack of knowledge aspects of risk are given due attention; current practice needs to improve on this point.

Acknowledgements

The work has been partly funded by the Norwegian Research Council – as a part of the Petromaks 2 program (grant number 228335/E30). The support is gratefully acknowledged.

References

Aven, T. (2012) The risk concept – historical and recent development trends. *Reliability Engineering & System Safety*, 99, 33–44.

Aven, T. (2013) Probabilities and background knowledge as a tool to reflect uncertainties in relation to intentional acts. *Reliability Engineering & System Safety*, 119, 229–234.

Aven, T. (2014) *Risk, Surprises and Black Swans: Fundamental Ideas and Concepts in Risk Assessment and Risk Management.* London: Routledge.

Aven, T. (2015) On the allegations that small risks are treated out of proportion to their importance. *Reliability Engineering & System Safety*, 140, 116–121.

Card, A.J., Ward, J.R. and Clarkson, P.J. (2012) Beyond FMEA: the structured what-if technique (SWIFT). *Journal of Healthcare Risk Management*, 31, 23–29.

Cox, T. (2008) What's wrong with risk matrices? *Risk Analysis*, 28(2), 497–512.

Flage, R. and Aven, T. (2009) Expressing and communicating uncertainty in relation to quantitative risk analysis (QRA). *Reliability and Risk Analysis: Theory and Applications*, 2(13), 9–18.

Flage, R. and Aven, T. (2015) Emerging risk – conceptual definition and a relation to black swan type of events. *Reliability Engineering & System Safety*, 144, 61–67.

Flage, R., Aven, T., Baraldi, P. and Zio, E. (2014) Concerns, challenges and directions of development for the issue of representing uncertainty in risk assessment. *Risk Analysis*, 34(7), 1196–1207.

Flage, R. and Røed, W. (2012) A reflection on some practices in the use of risk matrices. In: *Proceedings of the 11th International Probabilistic Safety Assessment and Management Conference and the Annual European Safety and Reliability Conference 2012*, 25–29 June 2012, Helsinki, Finland. Curran Associates, Inc. ISBN 978-1-62276-436-5.

HSE (2001) *Reducing Risk, Protecting People.* HSE Books. ISBN 0 7176 2151 0.

Kaplan, S., Visnepolschi, S., Zlotin, B. and Zusman, A. (1999) *New Tools for Failure and Risk Analysis: Anticipatory Failure Determination (AFD) and the Theory of Scenario Structuring.* Southfield, MI: Ideation International Inc.

Lindley, D.V. (2006) *Understanding Uncertainty.* Hoboken, NJ: Wiley.

Meyer, T. and Reniers, G. (2013) *Engineering Risk Management.* Berlin: De Gruyter Graduate.

Appendix

A1.1   Summary of Risk Assessment Approach

A distinction is made between an overall risk description for all activities and a description for a specific project. There is also a distinction between familiar, well-defined events (hazards/threats/opportunities) and emerging events (risks). We consider that we face emerging risk (related to an activity) when we have weak background knowledge but this knowledge contains indications/justified beliefs that some new type of event (at least new in the context of the activity in question) might occur and then potentially have severe consequences in terms of something humans value (Flage and Aven 2015).

When assigning a probability of an event occurring, it should be noted that this probability is conditional on some background knowledge K. This knowledge can be more or less strong. A method is described below that can be used to assess this strength.

The setup is based on an understanding of risk by capturing two dimensions:

- values at stake: the consequences of the activity with respect to something that humans value (could be deviations from a goal)
- the associated uncertainties.

In the risk assessment we specify the consequences, typically by referring to risk sources (threats, hazards, risk factors) and events and their effects. For the uncertainties, we use probability judgements together with strength-of-knowledge judgements, as will be described in the following.

A1.2   Hazards/threats (Known Types)

A list of such hazards/threats is identified. These are events in the future and they must be clearly defined, for example in relation to the relevant time period. For each hazard/threat, the following aspects are assessed (to the extent that they are relevant):

a) probability that it will occur (some predefined interval categories may be used)
b) consequences of these hazards/threats, for example by addressing the extent to which goals/criteria/plans are not met, using a 90 % prediction interval (an interval that one is 90 % sure contains the consequence) or a probability distribution for different outcomes
c) assumptions on which the assessments in (a) and (b) are based and the risk associated with possible deviations from these (Could changes in assumptions happen? What will then be the consequences?)

d) availability and amount of data/information
e) different views among experts
f) the basic understanding of the phenomena and processes being studied
g) overall assessment of the strength of the knowledge on which (a) and (b) are based, using the assessments made under (c)–(f) as input (see method below).

In connection with these points, the following issues are considered:

- knowledge gaps
- steps that can be taken to increase the knowledge
- existence of relevant signals and warnings
- changes of knowledge over time
- possibility of unknown knowns (others have the knowledge, but not the analysis group)
- possibility that events are disregarded because of very low probabilities, but these probabilities are based on critical assumptions.

An overall assessment of the risk is made, based on these points. A categorisation that follows can be useful to rank the events in terms of degree of (judged) risk:

- *Very high risk:* potential for extreme consequences, relatively large associated probability of such consequences and/or significant uncertainty (relatively weak background knowledge)
- *High risk:* potential for extreme consequences, relatively small associated probability of such consequences, and moderate or weak background knowledge
- *Moderate risk:* between small and high risk; for example, a potential for moderate consequences, and weak background knowledge
- *Low risk:* not a potential for serious consequences.

The use of risk matrices is in general not recommended because it is difficult to establish sufficiently informative risk characterisations using them; see the discussion in Section 1.6. However, if such matrices are to be used, they should cover events, related probability assignments (using intervals), consequence assignments (for example a 90% prediction interval for the consequences given the occurrence of the event), strength-of-knowledge judgements (for example represented by colours reflecting strong, medium or weak strength of knowledge), and a list of critical assumptions and risk factors (risk sources).

The criticality of the assumptions can be based on crude qualitative risk judgements of deviations from the assumptions (covering deviations, effects of these deviations, probability and strength-of-knowledge judgements). High level of criticality (high judged deviation risk) is coloured red; medium yellow and low green. Many red and yellow assumptions mean low strength of knowledge.

Risk factors (sources) are listed and a crude qualitative importance analysis can be conducted in the following way. How sensitive is the risk for changes in the risk factor (source)? And to what extent is the risk factor present (degree of exposure, probability)? In addition, we need to consider the strength of knowledge on which these judgements are based.

Risk management can use these assessments of assumptions and risk factors (sources) as a starting point. What can be done to reduce the risk related to deviations in assumptions? And how can risk factors (sources) be made less critical? Measures are suggested and they are evaluated based on considerations of costs and benefits; see suggested approach below. As a part of this evaluation, a crude qualitative assessment can be conducted for two dimensions: manageability and effect of the measure:

- The manageability is how difficult it is to reduce the risk, and depends on technical feasibility, time aspects, costs, and so on.
- The effect of the measure is how large the effect of the measure on risk: consequence, robustness/resilience, probability and strength of knowledge.

A crude matrix can be presented with, for example, three categories (high, medium, low) based on these two dimensions of manageability and effect on risk.

In the above analysis, a probability is interpreted as follows: the probability $P(A) = 0.1$ (say) means that the assessor compares their uncertainty (degree of belief) about the occurrence of the event A with the standard event of drawing at random a specific ball from an urn that contains 10 balls (Lindley 2006). An interval probability, say $[0.05, 0.3]$, is interpreted as follows: the assigner states that their assigned degree of belief is greater than an urn chance of 0.045 (the degree of belief of drawing one red ball out of an urn containing 1000 balls where 45 are red) and less than an urn chance of 0.34. The analyst is not willing to make any further judgements.

A1.3 Opportunities (Known Type)

The method is the same as for hazards/threats, but the consequences are positive.

A1.4 Emerging Events (Risks)

As mentioned above, we face emerging risk when we have weak background knowledge but this knowledge contains indications/justified beliefs that some new type of event might occur and then potentially have severe consequences. Here, we give a rough assessment of risk by addressing:

- the potential for large consequences
- uncertainties (strength of knowledge)
- knowledge gaps
- what can be done to increase the knowledge
- signals and warnings
- changes of knowledge over time
- the possibility of unknown knowns
- the possibility that events are disregarded because of very low probabilities, but these probabilities are based on some critical assumptions
- how robust/vulnerable the systems are (how the systems are affected by the occurrence of the hazards/threats)
- how resilient the systems are (how the systems are able to cope with the hazards/threats, also surprising forms of such events).

An overall assessment is made, and the risks are classified as "Requires due attention" and "Other emerging events".

A1.5   Methods for Assessing the Strength of Knowledge

This section is based on Flage and Aven 2009 and Aven 2014. The knowledge is judged as weak if one or more of these conditions is true:

W1. The assumptions made represent strong simplifications.
W2. Data/information are/is non-existent or highly unreliable/irrelevant.
W3. There is strong disagreement among experts.
W4. The phenomena involved are poorly understood; models are non-existent or known/believed to give poor predictions.

If, on the other hand, all (whenever they are relevant) of the following conditions are met, the knowledge is considered strong:

S1. The assumptions made are seen as very reasonable.
S2. Large amounts of reliable and relevant data/information are available.
S3. There is broad agreement among experts.
S4. The phenomena involved are well understood; the models used are known to give predictions with the required accuracy.

Cases in between are classified as having a medium strength of knowledge. To obtain a wider strong knowledge category, the requirement that all of the criteria (S1)–(S4) need to be fulfilled (whenever they are relevant) could, for example, be replaced by a criterion saying that at least one (or two, or three) of the criteria (S1)–(S4) need to be fulfilled and, at the same time, none of the criteria (W1)–(W4) may be fulfilled.

A simplified version of these criteria is obtained by using the same score for strong but giving the medium and weak scores if a suitable number of conditions are not met. For example a medium score can be given if one or two of the conditions (S1)–(S4) are not met and a weak score otherwise; that is, when three or four of the conditions are not met.

The strength of knowledge may be illustrated in a risk matrix, with events given a colour, say red, yellow or green, depending on whether the background knowledge is considered to be weak, medium or strong, respectively.

Possible extensions of this system can be developed. One idea is to add a fifth criterion stressing further the "potential surprise" dimension, reflecting the degree to which the knowledge K (comprising data, information and justified beliefs) has been scrutinised. Aspects then to consider could be checks of knowledge gaps, unknown knowns and signals and warnings (see the second list at the start of Section A1.2). This leads to fifth criteria W5 and S5 as follows:

W5. The knowledge K has not been scrutinised.
S5. The knowledge K has been thoroughly scrutinised.

A1.6 Cost–benefit Assessment Approaches

To assess whether a measure should be implemented or not, there is a need for an assessment of its pros and cons. There are basically two methods used in practice:

- Economic cost–benefit analysis on the basis of calculations of the expected present value.
- Broad assessment processes on the basis of assessments of pros and cons of implementing the measure.

The first method can be used in relation to situations where the uncertainties are minimal, which means that one can make accurate predictions of what will happen in the future: the variation in the outcome is known, and the project/ activity portfolio is very large.

For implementation of measures to manage the risks related to extreme events, the second method is used.

The following basic approach is recommended for measures that are suggested to meet some specific goals or overall objectives:

1) If the costs are small, implement the measure if it is considered to have a positive effect on these goals or objectives.
2) If the costs are significant, make an assessment of all relevant pros and cons of the measure. If the expected present value (or corresponding indices) can be meaningfully calculated, implement the measure if this value is positive.
3) Also consider implementing the measure if it generates a considerable positive effect on the risk and/or other conditions, seen in relation to the goals or objectives, for example in the safety/security context:
   - reducing uncertainty, strengthening knowledge
   - strengthening the robustness in case of hazards/threats, strengthening the resilience.

2

The Enigma of Knowledge in the Risk Field

Terje Aven[1] and Marja Ylönen[2]

[1] *University of Stavanger, Norway*
[2] *VTT Technical Research Centre of Finland*

In recent years we have seen a growing interest in the knowledge dimension in risk analysis settings. The interest has been motivated by developments within the fields of risk assessment and risk management, which have highlighted the relevance of uncertainties and the need to look beyond and behind the probabilities, towards knowledge aspects. Schemes for characterizations of strong and weak knowledge for the probabilities have been suggested. In this chapter we reflect on how the knowledge concept used in this context matches the wealth of studies on knowledge that we find in philosophy and sociology. We ask whether the risk field can learn from these studies and further develop the knowledge dimension in risk assessment and management. The aim of the chapter is to provide new insights on these issues and in this way strengthen the foundation of risk analysis and improve its practice. The chapter will address both epistemological and ontological issues related to knowledge, and provide reflections of the suitability/unsuitability of various conceptualizations of the knowledge concept in a risk analysis context.

2.1 Introduction

For more than 30 years the consequence–probability perspective has been the dominant risk perspective, at least in the engineering environment. The Kaplan and Garrick (1981) so-called "triplet" definition of risk is one of the most common interpretations of this perspective, with its inclusion of events/hazards, their consequences and their associated probabilities. Here probability is either a frequentist or a subjective probability. To describe or measure risk, the probabilities are estimated or assigned, based on data, models and expert judgments.

Knowledge in Risk Assessment and Management, First Edition. Edited by Terje Aven and Enrico Zio.
© 2018 John Wiley & Sons Ltd. Published 2018 by John Wiley & Sons Ltd.

There are, however, broader risk perspectives, which highlight uncertainties and the knowledge dimension more strongly than the consequence–probability perspective; see examples provided by the new Society for Risk Analysis (SRA) glossary (SRA 2015a) and ISO 31000 (ISO 2009). One of the examples covered by the SRA refers to the definition adopted by the Petroleum Safety Authority of Norway (PSA-N 2015), which defines risk as the consequences of the activity considered and the associated uncertainties. To describe the risk in line with such a definition, one is naturally led to a triplet covering specified events and consequences, a measure of uncertainty, and the knowledge on which this specification and this measure is based. An example of a measure of uncertainty is subjective probability; another is the combination of subjective probability and strength of knowledge (SoK) judgments.

To explain these concepts in more detail, consider two situations: one where the background knowledge supporting the assigned probabilities is strong (for example, as the result of a lot of relevant reliable data, good understanding of the phenomena studied, assumptions made being considered reasonable, and so on) and the other where the background knowledge is considered weaker. According to the consequence–probability perspective, the risk does not directly reflect this difference in state of knowledge, although it could and should, of course, influence the decision making related to the treatment of the risk. A risk description based on consequence and probability can be viewed as a conditional risk given the background knowledge. For broader risk perspectives, the knowledge aspects are more explicitly covered by the risk description. Thus, regardless of the perspective, the meaning of the concept of knowledge becomes an important issue. This is the topic of this chapter.

In the new SRA glossary, two types of knowledge are referred to:

> …know-how (skill) and know-that of propositional knowledge (justified beliefs). Knowledge is gained through for example scientific methodology and peer-review, experience and testing.

In the scientific literature on knowledge, the common perspective is, however, not justified beliefs but justified *true* beliefs. This is the point of departure for most textbooks on knowledge. The SRA (2015a) glossary challenges this definition. Aven (2014) provides some examples of this view: a risk analysis group may have strong knowledge (insights) about how a system works and can provide strong arguments as to why it will not fail over the next year, but it cannot know for sure whether or not it will in fact fail. Nobody can. The group's beliefs can, for example, be expressed through a probability. The knowledge is considered to be reflected partly in the probability, partly in the background knowledge on which this probability is based. As another example, consider a case where a group of experts believe that a system will not be able to withstand a specific load. Their belief is based on data and information, modelling and analysis, but they can be wrong. It is difficult to find a place for a "truth requirement" in these examples. Do we then not have knowledge?

We will provide a thorough discussion of this issue in this chapter. We bring new insights into the discussion by examining the literature on knowledge, from the fields of philosophy, sociology and management. We look for alternative ways of defining (propositional) knowledge, the hypothesis being that there are ways of understanding knowledge that are more in line with the justified belief definition than the justified true belief one, and which are relevant for the risk analysis field.

The rest of the chapter is organized as follows. Firstly, in Section 2.2 we present two simple case studies to illustrate the discussion and link the conceptual analysis to the practice of risk analysis and decision making. Then in Section 2.3 we provide a review of existing definitions and perspectives on knowledge and knowledge generation in the philosophy, sociology and management literature. From this review, we discuss in Section 2.4 how we can utilize this insight in a risk analysis context. In Section 2.5 we present some conclusions.

2.2 Introduction to Case Studies

2.2.1 An Offshore Example

This first example relates to a hydrocarbon leak at the Heimdal installation on 26 May 2012 (PSA-N 2012). During the testing of two emergency shutdown valves, a hydrocarbon leak of an estimated 3500 kg, with an initial leak rate of 16.9 kg/s occurred. Gas was detected in a large area of the installation. The pipe section of interest was based on an older design, where there is a change of pipeline specifications (a "spec break") to a lower pressure class, upstream of the last valve before the flare. With such a design, the order in which the three valves are operated is critical: if the last valve before the flare is opened last, the pipe will be subjected to higher pressure than it was designed to withstand. Such a design is not in accordance with recent standard design practice.

The criticality of the order in which the three valves are operated was not clear to the personnel who performed the test. It was, however, well known in other organizational units of the company.

2.2.2 Swine Flu Vaccination

The second example relates to the occurrence of swine flu in 2009. The World Health Organization declared that the flu had developed into a full-scale world epidemic, and a vaccine was quickly developed. In some countries

(Iceland, Finland, Norway and Sweden), the authorities explicitly set the goal of vaccinating the whole population. The illness turned out to be quite mild, but it had some severe side effects that were previously unknown. Based on similar types of situations, one could say that it was likely that there would be some side effects, but in advance no one could say with confidence what these would be. The vaccination was carried out because the authorities believed that the flu itself would cause serious illness and problems, at a much higher level than the side effects. Normally there is time for fairly thorough testing of the vaccine, enabling the authorities to control the risk related to side effects, but in 2009 this was not the case. The uncertainties were large. The problem was that the decision concerning vaccination had to be taken quickly. There was no time for thorough research and testing, and adaptive management. The authorities also had to balance the need for good risk characterization and a desire to get the population vaccinated. In the Nordic countries mentioned above, the authorities initiated "moral persuasion" campaigns: solidarity became the slogan: "get vaccinated to protect your fellow citizens".

2.3 Perspectives on Knowledge

This section is in two parts. Firstly, we review existing definitions of knowledge using the examples from Section 2.2 as illustrations. Then we look at ways of generating knowledge and how we can make strength of knowledge (SoK) judgments.

2.3.1 Definitions of Knowledge

Often it is argued that defining the concept of knowledge is futile because of its complicated nature. Already in medieval Islam the concept of knowledge was seen as so difficult that it would not be verbally defined (Rosenthal 2007, p. 48). However, the world has a wealth of concepts that are ambiguous and contested, such as democracy, morality and power. That does not mean that they should remain undefined. And in fact, in the literature we find several ways of defining the concept of knowledge. We have already looked into two: justified true beliefs and justified beliefs. The remainder of this section examines some other suggestions that have been presented in the philosophical, sociological and management literature.

Acknowledging the long history of discussions on the concept of knowledge, we will focus on some selected sets of definitions, which we consider to have the potential to add insights to the risk-analysis field; see Table 2.1. To establish these definitions we have reviewed the philosophical, sociological and management literature on knowledge (e.g. Dant 1991; Toulmin 1999; Tsoukas and Vladimirou 2001; Audi 2003; Pojman 2003; Dalkir 2011).

Table 2.1 Different definitions of knowledge with a summary of the authors' comments.

Definitions of knowledge	Comments made by the authors of this chapter
"Knowledge is the construal of relations between abstract entities that are taken to represent the world of human experience, that can be used by them both to understand their experience of the world and to guide their actions." (Dant 1991, p. 5)	This definition is in accordance with justified beliefs. It specifies beliefs as relations between abstract entities, defined by knowers. Knowledge guides human action.
"Knowledge is the individual ability to draw distinctions within a collective domain of action, based on appreciation of context or theory of both." (Tsoukas and Vladimirou 2001, p. 983, based on Bell 1999, p. lxiv)	This definition is in line with justified beliefs. It emphasizes the individual ability to draw distinctions. Knowledge is seen as a possession of the individual, but it is affected by context and theory.
"Knowledge is subjective and valuable information that has been validated and that has been organized in to a model (mental model); used to make sense of our world; typically originates from accumulated experience; incorporates perceptions, believes and values." (Dalkir 2011)	This definition also follows justified beliefs. Knowledge is subjective, but it needs to be validated and shared by other members in society so that it works as a mental model through which one senses the world. Knowledge is based on experience and combined perceptions.
"Knowledge is a flux mix of framed experiences, values, contextual information, and expert insight that provides a framework for evaluating and incorporating new experiences and information. It originates and is applied in the minds of knowers. In organisations, it often becomes embedded not only in documents or repositories but also in organizational routines, processes, practices and norms." (Davenport and Prusak 1998, p. 5)	This definition provides a more complex picture of knowledge. It has been criticized for including too many things, such as values, experiences and contexts, and for not providing specifications of their relationships, risking making knowledge an all-encompassing concept (Tsoukas and Vladimirou 2001). Yet, it provides insights into how, in order to become powerful, knowledge needs to be incorporated in organisations' everyday practices.
"Knowledge is true judgment." (Brown 2015, p. 67: Dewey 1969–1991) "Knowledge as assurance, or as fulfilment which confirms and validates." (Dewey 1906, p. 301)	Knowledge is not seen as justified beliefs but true judgments, which refer to the final outcome of scientific inquiry. A judgment is seen as true if it resolves a problematic situation. Action is a realization of knowledge, because action verifies, validates knowledge or provides tests of truth.

The first definition is by Dant (1991, p. 5) and states that knowledge is:

> ...the construal of relations between abstract entities that are taken to represent the world of human experience, that can be used by them both to understand their experience of the world and to guide their actions.

This definition emphasizes the construal of relations between abstract entities, such as the relations between the swine flu and the vaccination that should prevent people from getting the flu, or, in the offshore example, the link between the hydrocarbon leak and the operations of the valves.

Dant's definition is in line with *justified beliefs*, but it is more concrete in that it is specific about what these beliefs concern, namely the relations between these entities. The "construal" – explanatory – part refers to knowers that have defined the relations between abstract entities. These defined relations then correspond to the "justified beliefs". The beliefs are related to how a leakage may occur as a result of different operating schemes, and the effectiveness of the vaccination. In the vaccine case, the justification of the relationship between abstract entities was rather poor; it was difficult to link the vaccine with some type of effectiveness rate of the vaccination. Because of this, relationships were created but based on poor justifications. We may even say that there was a lack of knowledge as regards the formation of the relations between the vaccination and its effect. In the offshore case, we can talk about wrong or deficient knowledge among the operating personnel but not among the other people in the organization, who were aware about the design basis and who could have explained the critical order of the operation of valves. Those people possessed adequate information for justifying the relationships between the abstract entities; "strong knowledge", we may prefer to say.

The second part of Dant's definition is about the use of knowledge and the role of subject (agent) that knowledge plays in a society, in the sense that knowledge affects human thinking and steers action and thus has societal consequences. However, Dant does not explicitly mention the consequences of knowledge. Established construal relations between abstract entities will guide the decision making, for example the policy decision to start vaccinations.

The second definition, from Tsoukas and Vladimirou (2001, p. 983, based on Bell 1999, p. lxiv) entails the idea that:

> ...knowledge is the individual ability to draw distinctions within a collective domain of action, based on appreciation of context or theory of both.

This definition of knowledge highlights the individual possession of knowledge and the capacity to draw distinctions. People who performed the test in the offshore case did not draw distinctions as regards new and old designs of the system. This distinction was key to understanding the system. Especially in a high-risk industry, the individual's negligence in failing to investigate the context, such as the design basis, before starting to work, is an indication of irresponsibility and weak knowledge. However, weak knowledge does not relate solely to an individual's capability to draw distinctions, but also to weakness of theory or to organization-level features, such as deficiencies in the flow of information, communication; transfer of experience and knowledge building. Hence the strength of the knowledge is circumscribed by individual- and organization-level aspects, as well as by theory.

The third definition, from Dalkir (2011), refers to knowledge as:

> ...subjective and valuable information that has been validated and that has been organized into a model (mental model); used to make sense of our world; typically originates from accumulated experience; incorporates perceptions, believes and values.

With regard to the swine flu case, the World Health Organisation had obviously adopted a mental model as regards the possibility of a worldwide pandemic with serious consequences. This was based on health experts' accumulated experience on epidemics but also on a belief that vaccination itself would not have large side effects. In addition, values concerning the willingness to protect humans from serious flu were included in their model. However, the validation aspect of the side effects was lacking and therefore the authorities' knowledge was incomplete according to this understanding of the knowledge concept.

The fourth definition, from Davenport and Prusak (1998, p. 5), refers to knowledge as a:

> ...flux mix of framed experiences, values, contextual information, and expert insight that provides a framework for evaluating and incorporating new experiences and information. It originates and is applied in the minds of knowers. In organizations, it often becomes embedded not only in documents or repositories but also in organizational routines, processes, practices and norms.

This definition highlights the exploratory and heuristic function of knowledge: current knowledge is a kind of framework through which new ideas are examined. For instance, an already known pandemic with negative consequences provided a framework to drive prompt intervention in the swine flu epidemic. Knowledge derives from different sources and consists of different elements, such as values, experiences and scientific or expert understanding. Moreover, the definition refers to the process and means by which specific beliefs become institutionalized; that means more stable, taken-for-granted and shared by a wider audience. Institutionalization of knowledge may, for example, happen through the reporting or adoption of good practices. When institutionalized, knowledge has a strong position and is difficult to defeat.

In the swine flu case, several framed experiences, values and information and expert knowledge were integrated. Earlier information and experiences of epidemics to a large extent framed the understanding of the swine flu case and the need for vaccination. This type of institutionalized knowledge was difficult to argue against.

The fourth definition broadens the understanding of knowledge by taking into consideration several elements that constitute the knowledge. However, that also makes it more messy and difficult to grasp because the relationships between the elements remain obscure. Yet even this definition provides relevant insight into the knowledge by emphasizing the institutionalization aspect; that is, how knowledge can become effective when it is incorporated into the organization's practices and routines.

The fifth definition of knowledge is based on pragmatism, a philosophical strand that aims to go beyond the dualism between action and knowledge (Kilpinen *et al.* 2008). Knowledge cannot be seen as separate from action and human practices but as dependent on them. In John Dewey's philosophy of science, knowledge does not refer to beliefs but "true judgments" (Brown 2015). For Dewey, all judgments are judgments of practice that means that "they propose a course of action and not just describe a state of affairs". The term "true" must here be carefully interpreted; not as a claim for the judgments to be true in the sense that the outcome will be the reality – the correct one in the real world – as is the case for the "true justified belief" interpretation of knowledge. A judgment is seen as true if action verifies, or validates it, as will be explained in the following. From a pragmatic viewpoint, one can have prior knowledge about a matter, whether swine flu vaccination or emergency shutdown valves, but it is through action that knowledge as a true judgment can be verified. In the offshore case, the critical order of closure for valves based on an older design became evident for the testing personnel only after testing the emergency shutdown valves. The prior knowledge turned out to be wrong after the action. Similarly, in the vaccination case, the prior knowledge of the vaccine was hypothetical, and lacking assurance. Proper knowledge about the vaccine was obtained through action: vaccination and its effective fulfilment. Even though pragmatism would suggest that only through action can one verify prior knowledge, it is an ethical and political question as to whether actions should be taken at all.

The following distinctions, related to belief and acceptance, and holding, adopting and endorsing as cognitive attitudes, provide further ideas about knowledge as true justification.

Belief here refers to (Brown 2015; McKaughan and Elliot 2015):

> ...disposition to feel that a statement p is true or to regard it as true without necessarily being willing to act on, assert, or reason with it. Instead acceptance refers to taking p as a premise in negotiation or action. Hence belief and acceptance represent different epistemic attitudes, and different values will be appropriated. Belief is more a state of affair whilst acceptance refers more clearly to action.

Belief and acceptance are cognitive attitudes, belief being the more passive one and acceptance being the more active one because it requires judgments. Acceptance means that one has adopted "a policy of deeming" in terms of scientific claims, whether related to hypotheses, theories, data, models or results.

Following these ideas, we need to relate the concept of justified beliefs to acceptance, as this concept also means making some active efforts to clarify whether some hypotheses, data, theories, ways of conducting research, results and appliance of results can be accepted. In this view, justified beliefs are analogous to "true judgments" as defined in John Dewey's philosophy of science (Brown 2015).

Other distinctions of cognitive attitudes also exist, for example based on holding, adopting and endorsing (Lacey 2015). Holding requires that all lines of research that could produce outcomes that would lead to discarding p have been studied. Also, all objections related to the sufficiency of the available data need to have been considered. Adoption and endorsing are weaker forms of justification. Endorsed claims do not belong to the stock of established scientific knowledge and they can be more easily discarded. Endorsing p requires making judgments about the strengths of evidence.

The above ideas can be seen as being in line with the definition of science given by Hansson (2013; see also Hansson and Aven 2014):

> Science (in the broad sense) is the practice that provides us with the most epistemically warranted statements that can be made, at the time being, on subject matter covered by the community of knowledge disciplines, i.e. on nature, ourselves as human beings, our societies, our physical constructions, and our thought constructions.

The key aspect here is the "most epistemically warranted statements", a phrase that resembles the concept of justified beliefs and accepted beliefs discussed above.

2.3.2 How to Generate Knowledge

Knowledge can be generated in different ways. It is common to distinguish between five approaches.

The first one relates to empiricism, which considers knowledge as objective facts that can be gained from the external world "out there" by gathering observations through systematic scientific methods. Those methods play an important role as regards gathering an evidence base (Gourlay 2001). Empirical facts and statistics about the spread of swine flu and comparisons with earlier pandemics will provide knowledge from the empiricist viewpoint.

The second approach is rationalism: the understanding that through reasoning we can know. We may use some rational criteria on the basis of which beliefs can be evaluated. For instance, reasoning about how earlier pandemics have spread and behaved provides a knowledge base for thinking about the dangerous nature of swine flu.

The third approach is social constructionism, which regards beliefs (knowledge) and agreements about them as an outcome of negotiations. In this view knowledge is never fixed but is under a constant construction process (Lincoln and Guba 2000, p. 177). Swine flu was defined as a problem by several experts, and the vaccination decision in the Nordic countries was the result of the authorities' beliefs about its dangerous nature. The experts' discussions about swine flu and vaccination provided a basis for the knowledge.

Knowledge based on dialogue may be affected by power aspects too. Power and knowledge are intrinsically interwoven, as illustrated by, for example, Pierre Bourdieu's theory of social fields (Bourdieu and Wacquant 1992). The basic idea is that each scientific domain consists of relatively strong knowledge that is based on institutionalized beliefs, assumptions, methods and approaches. These dominate the field. There are continuous fights over the control of the field. "Orthodoxes" define what is acceptable, right and valued knowledge in the field, whilst "heretics" try to challenge the doxa: what are taken for granted, unquestioned rules, assumptions, methods and practices (Grenfell 2012). If the heretics succeed in challenging the doxa and the orthodoxes who maintain the doxa, then the power equilibrium in the field is shaken. If the orthodoxes are not able to fight back, the rules of the field will be also changed. Power relationships may have an impact on the emphasis of certain kinds of knowledge over others. In the swine flu vaccination case, the development of a vaccine has been in the interest of medical companies and in the interest of public health authorities. So knowledge is not free from power relationships.

The fourth approach states that knowledge and beliefs are circumscribed by specific historical, economic and social conditions (e.g. Scheler 1980; Mannheim 1979). Knowers are not seen as separate from some objective reality but as carriers of beliefs that are formed in specific historical and cultural situations (Lincoln and Guba 2000). There can be degrees of adequacy of beliefs. Even though the belief would correspond to reality in the sense that it allows social action, it might not be adequate (Hall 1983). As an example, in the case of swine flu vaccination, the decision to vaccinate had to be made quickly and, due to lack of time, sufficient testing was not carried out. The authorities' willingness to get people vaccinated was based on inadequate beliefs, in the sense that they were based on uncertainties and they obscured the contradictions related to different understandings of the suitability of vaccination. Hence there are degrees of adequacy of knowledge, and a tendency to think in a certain way is also dependent on people's social background (Mannheim 1979; Hofstede 1991; Gurvitch 1971). Acknowledging that knowledge is circumscribed by specific historical, economic and social conditions would suggest that it would be important to gather knowledge from several sources and from people from different backgrounds, as only in this way would a sufficiently broad knowledge base be achieved.

The fifth approach is pragmatism, according to which justified beliefs and judgments are validated by their consequences. Scientific inquiry is seen as a systematized problem-solving process, as a mode of knowledge production. The consequences of the judgments will reveal whether the judgments are true or false (Brown 2015). As previously mentioned, pragmatism aims to exceed the dualism between action and knowledge. According to Dewey (1906), action is a realization of knowledge, as action alone verifies or validates knowledge or supplies tests of truth. In the offshore case, the testing personnel had an assumption about the way valves should work (even though the assumption was wrong). It was only after action that they understood how things are. If knowledge is seen as guiding the action, action itself also provides new knowledge. Action tests the correctness of earlier assumptions and may trigger changes in them if action based on earlier knowledge turns out to be wrong. So knowledge is tested in action and feedback from action may force one to change the background assumptions and knowledge.

Pragmatist ideas resemble the plan–do–check–act or plan–do–check–adjust loops in quality management. The "check" part presumes that there is a possibility of observing the results of an action. For risk analysis, the issue is often that decisions have to be made when there is no possibility of waiting to see the outcome, as our two examples both demonstrate.

All these approaches involve different directions from which knowledge can be generated, whether from observations, reasoning, dialogue, social and historical conditions or action. Consequently, evaluations of the strength of knowledge can be based on these approaches. For instance, the empiricist perspective would be that the evidence base for the beliefs is strong (Gourlay 2001). From the rationalist viewpoint, it is reasoning and logic which provide the basis for making a judgment about strong knowledge. Similarly, from the viewpoint of social constructionism, it is through dialogue and negotiations that strong knowledge can be obtained. In the fourth approach, it is the historical, cultural and economic situation that validates the strength of the knowledge. And from the pragmatist perspective, it is the consequences of action that show whether the knowledge was correct and strong or incorrect and weak.

Expert consensus may be considered a criterion in relation to the social constructionist approach. However, consensus can be the result of similar values, for example on how strongly a statement needs to be supported by empirical evidence. Hence it is essential that one does not misread the consensus of technical experts for knowledge (Lacey 2015). A means for avoiding this problem is of course to include broad participants in the assessments. Only if experts represent different areas/disciplines and values, and are able to reach consensus, does it make sense to talk about a knowledge-based consensus (Miller 2013). However, the requirement for diversity may face many obstacles in practice, such as lack of time and money to gather different experts.

Often consensus between experts representing a narrow expert base would be interpreted as strong knowledge, even though the criterion of social diversity is not met. For complex issues, dissensus among experts representing different disciplines/areas and values is likely and in many cases could represent more valuable knowledge for decision makers than a consensus of experts from the same background.

2.4 Discussion – New Insights for the Risk Analysis Field

Knowledge is a key concept within the field of risk assessment and risk management. In this section we will explore how the theory discussed in the previous section can be used in this field. We have identified areas for which we see some potential added value:

1) In a risk assessment context, assessment of uncertainties and likelihoods needs to be based on some knowledge, and it is of interest to evaluate the strength of this knowledge in some way.
2) The risk field is about generating risk related knowledge, in relation to:
   - specific activities, phenomena, processes, events, and so on, for example the health effects of smoking and drug use or how a blowout can occur on an oil and gas producing platform
   - concepts, theories, frameworks, approaches, principles and methods for being able to understand, assess and manage (in a wide sense) risk (Aven and Zio 2014; SRA 2015b).

The next three sections consider these three areas in turn.

2.4.1 Knowledge on which Uncertainty Assessments and Likelihoods are Based

In risk assessments, we need to assess the uncertainties of the assessors in relation to the occurrence of specific events and unknown quantities, for example the number of fatalities in a period of time. Different methods are used for this purpose. The most common is probability (subjective, judgmental, knowledge-based). If the assessor assigns the probability $P(A|K) = 0.1$ (say), on the basis of their background knowledge K, they are equating their uncertainty (degree of belief) about the occurrence event A with a standard of drawing at random a specific ball from an urn that contains ten balls (Lindley 2006). If such probabilities are used, we also need to reflect on the knowledge K that supports the assignment of the probabilities. Think of a situation where a risk analyst arrives at a probability P; in one case the background knowledge is strong, in the other, weak, but the probabilities are the same. To meet this challenge, considerable work has recently been carried out to systematise and establish methods for classifying the strength of this knowledge to inform the decision makers. The results are then summarised in the pair (P,SoK), where SoK provides a qualitative measure of the strength of the knowledge supporting P. We refer to Flage and Aven (2009), with criteria related to aspects like justification of assumptions made, amount of reliable and relevant data/information, agreement among experts and understanding of the phenomena involved. See also the related NUSAP system ("numeral, unit, spread, assessment, and pedigree") (Funtowicz and Ravetz 1990, 1993; Kloprogge *et al.* 2005,2011; Laes *et al.* 2011; van der Sluijs *et al.* 2005a,2005b), which is based on similar ideas.

The review and discussion in Section 2.3, and in particular in Section 2.3.2, provide some ideas about knowledge that could have potential for application in relation to the challenge of classifying and measuring this strength of knowledge, SoK. In Table 2.2 we have compared the four criteria used in Flage and Aven (2009) and the five approaches for generating knowledge summarised in Section 2.3.2.

Table 2.2 shows that observations and reasoning are to a large extent covered by the existing scheme for SoK judgments. "Empiricism and observations" correspond to "Amount of reliable and relevant data/information", and "Rationalism and reasoning" are covered by "Justification of assumptions made" and "Understanding of the phenomena involved". "Social constructionism" and "Dialogue" have links to "Agreement among experts", but, as discussed in Section 2.3.2, care should in general be taken when considering consensus among experts to be a way of measuring strength of knowledge. Only if experts represent different areas/disciplines and values, does it make sense to talk about a "knowledge-based" consensus. "Social and historical conditions" have no clear correspondence in the existing scheme for SoK judgments. A possible way to include this aspect of knowledge generation is obtained by defining a fifth criterion in this scheme: "Social and historical justification". The point here is to reflect the degree to which the justified beliefs have obtained justification through the social and institutional structures that are relevant for the issues addressed, for example approval by appropriate scientific committees, such as national committees on health or food.

Table 2.2 Matches between strength of knowledge and epistemological approaches.

	Aspects of strength of knowledge judgments			
	Justification of assumptions made	Amount of reliable and relevant data/ information	Agreement among experts	Understanding of the phenomena involved
Epistemological approach				
Empiricism, observations		x		
Rationalism	x			x
Reasoning				
Social constructionism			x	
Dialogue				
Social and historical conditions				
Pragmatism				

An "x" indicates good matches between the strength of knowledge score (Flage and Aven 2009) and the epistemological approaches per Section 2.3.2.

It is acknowledged that such justification can maintain specific "truths" that some "heretics" may question. If we adopt Bourdieu's understanding of power and knowledge as intrinsically interwoven, it is desirable that there are continuous battles related to knowledge. Similar comments can be made for some of the other criteria for the strength of knowledge, for example, "understanding of the phenomena involved". The score of the criteria reflects justifications with a specific basis; there is always a potential for surprises relative to this knowledge as it is someone's knowledge, someone's justified beliefs. In this view, there is a need for a sixth criterion related to possible surprises and aspects not foreseen using the other criteria. Such a criterion needs to address the degree to which the knowledge basis has been subject to scrutiny with respect to potential surprises. One important aspect here would be to check for unknown knowns: insights that some have but not others. See also discussion in Aven (2016). Table 2.3 summarises the extended set of criteria used to assess the strength of knowledge.

The last approach for knowledge generation, pragmatism, links knowledge to action and the results of the actions. As a way of measuring the strength of knowledge, this approach is thus problematic in a risk assessment context: the probability and risk judgments relate to the future and we cannot wait for the

Table 2.3 Extended set of criteria to assess the strength of knowledge.

Criteria	Comments
Justification of assumptions made	
Amount of reliable and relevant data/information	
Agreement among experts	Diversity in expert background and competences is needed
Understanding of the phenomena involved	
Social and historical justification	The criterion reflects the degree to which the justified beliefs have obtained justification through the social structures and institutions that are relevant for the issues addressed
Scrutiny of knowledge-basis with respect to potential surprises	The criterion reflects the degree to which the knowledge basis has been subject to scrutiny with respect to potential surprises, for example covering checks for unknown knowns

The last two criteria are not covered by the scheme of Flage and Aven (2009).

observations. However, pragmatism encourages adaptive risk management, trial and error and learning by doing, and so on, which are common ways of managing risks, particularly in the case of large uncertainties (Cox 2012; Aven 2013). In high-risk contexts, there are in most cases practical and also often ethical limitations to following a learning-by-doing approach, yet it is often used, in particular when the benefits are large. See also Section 2.4.3.

2.4.2   Knowledge about Specific Activities

Risk assessments are used to obtain knowledge about specific activities, such as phenomena or processes. The insights are provided by experts from the relevant fields and disciplines, for example medicine and health, with support from risk analysis experts. The assessments are about generating knowledge, and hence the approaches and discussion in Section 2.3.2 apply. This knowledge relates to the following key components: risk sources and events, their consequences, barriers and uncertainties. The links between risk sources/events and the consequences are of special interest when it comes to answering questions such as the extent to which the use of a drug is dangerous.

The risk field offers concepts, principles and methods for providing this type of risk knowledge, using statistical analysis and risk assessment methods such as event trees, fault trees and Bayesian belief networks. Probability is the common tool to represent and express the uncertainties, but other approaches are also used, as discussed above, such as probabilities combined with strength of knowledge judgments. In this way, the discussion in this chapter, and in particular the analysis and suggestions made in Section 2.4.1, also add new insights to specific activities, phenomena, processes etc., refer the introduction of Section 2.4). To describe risk related to a specific activity, the combined uncertainty expression (P,SoK) represents a suitable tool in many cases, and the suggested approach for the SoK judgments in Section 2.4.1 enhances the current methods used for this purpose.

2.4.3 Knowledge on Development of Generic Concepts and Theories

Risk assessments produce a risk description or characterization conditional on some background knowledge K. Current practice provides guidelines on how to conduct these assessments. At the same time, the risk field scrutinizes this practice and searches for improvements. The use of SoK judgments supplementing probabilistic analyses can be seen as an example of this process. In the same way, the discussion in Section 2.3 provides a basis for challenging and enhancing some of the established thinking in the field. A key point is the substance of this background knowledge K. Following Aven (2016), K covers data, information and justified beliefs, and we see that we are back to the fundamental discussion about what knowledge is. We acknowledge that data and information per se are not knowledge, as formulated by Hansson (2002); knowledge extends beyond this information as the information needs to be cognitively assimilated to qualify as knowledge. The basic question relates to the understanding of beliefs, the justification of these beliefs and their link to the specific historical and social contexts, where the "truths" are defined and contested (Miller 2013; Bourdieu and Wacquant 1992).

The common definition of a belief, as we find in any dictionary, is that a belief is the state of mind in which a person thinks something to be the case. In a professional risk assessment context, such a belief is commonly interpreted as a judgment, as for example when expressing the degree of belief that an event will occur, using a subjective probability. There is no place for feelings in such a judgment, although some interpretations of belief also allow for this, as was noted in Section 2.3.1 when discussing the fifth definition of knowledge based on John Dewey's philosophy of science (Brown 2015). Here a belief refers to the *disposition to feel that a statement p is true or to regard it as true*. From a professional risk-assessment point of view, it is essential to make the distinction between professional judgments about uncertainties and how one feels about them. The latter dimension is normally captured by terms such as 'perception' and 'risk perception' (Aven and Renn 2010).

In the offshore example of Section 2.2.1, the operations personnel had a belief that the system was a standard one. They had a state of mind that it was a "normal" system. When conducting a risk assessment, these judgments become, to varying degrees, justified beliefs, as some principles and methods are used to generate these beliefs. The approaches discussed in Section 2.3.2 provide examples of such principles and methods.

This leads us to the link between justification and the reality and the "truth". As was noted in Section 2.1, restricting knowledge to justified *true* beliefs is not meaningful and useful in risk-assessment contexts. The term "justified"' then becomes the critical one. In this context, we interpret a justification as being the result of a trustworthy process according to some defined rules. It applies to the justification of a specific statement by an individual, and broad justifications of scientific theses. The specific field and science determine what is trustworthy and what are the rules, and there will always be a discussion on what these are.

Boltanski and Thévenot (1991) distinguish between different types of justifications, which work in different contexts and are based on so-called "common good (high)" principles. These principles relate to aspects such as "economic", "efficient", "safe", "healthy", "familiar", and so on. When science and politics are intertwined then different justifications are also mixed. For example "trustworthy scientific methods" may become entangled with "willingness to promote public health and reduce costs of a pandemic", as in the swine flu case.

In the offshore example, the knowledge-generating process was not trustworthy, as key personnel in the company were not included in the judgments; only the operating personnel. Consensus was achieved among a very narrow group of people.

According to the pragmatic perspective (fifth approach), the justification of the judgments needs to be seen in relation to a problem or situation at hand. What is "good" is determined by reference to this problem but also to what can be seen as high values, such as the authorities' willingness to promote public health in the swine flu case.

As was noted in relation to pragmatism in Section 2.4.1, this perspective and approach encourage adaptive risk management; alternatives are dynamically tracked to gain information and knowledge about the effects of different courses of action. One chooses an action based on broad considerations of risk and other aspects, monitors the effect, and adjusts the action based on the monitored results (Linkov *et al.* 2006).

There is not much written about knowledge in the generic risk analysis literature. If one makes a search for "justified beliefs" in this literature, one does not obtain many hits. In our view, this demonstrates that knowledge as a concept is given far too little attention in the scientific literature on risk. The current risk analysis practice presumes to a large extent that knowledge has been captured by the probabilities and related risk metrics. This is, however, not the case, and we are led to ways of adding SoK judgments to the probabilities and risk metrics used. Then we need to have a clear understanding of what the concept of "knowledge" actually expresses.

2.5 Conclusions

In this chapter we have explored how definitions and understandings of the knowledge concept in the philosophical, sociological and management literature can be used to enhance the risk field, for both theory and practice. The definitions of knowledge examined provide support for the perspective of seeing knowledge as justified beliefs, and add additional insights that are useful for risk assessment and management. An existing method for assessing the strength of knowledge in risk assessments is improved using these insights, by adding an assessment criterion linked to the process and a means by which specific beliefs become institutionalized; the justification is obtained through the social and institutional structures that are relevant for the issues addressed, for example through approval by appropriate scientific committees. In addition, a criterion "scrutinizing the knowledge basis for potential surprises" is suggested, motivated by the fact that the scoring of the criteria reflects justifications with a specific knowledge basis. Generic insights about fundamental risk concepts have also been obtained.

Acknowledgements

This work was partly funded by the Research Council of Norway through the PETROMAKS2 programme (grant number grant number 228335/E30). This support is gratefully acknowledged.

References

Audi, R. (2003) *A Contemporary Introduction to the Theory of Knowledge.* New York: Routledge.

Aven, T. (2013) On how to deal with deep uncertainties in a risk assessment and management context. *Risk Analysis*, 33(12), 2082–91.

Aven, T. (2014) What is safety science? *Safety Science*, 67, 15–20.

Aven, T. (2016) Supplementing quantitative risk assessments with a stage addressing the risk understanding of the decision maker. *Reliability Engineering & System Safety*, 152, 51–57.

Aven, T. and Renn, O. (2010) *Risk Management and Risk Governance.* Berlin: Springer Verlag.

Aven, T. and Zio, E. (2014) Foundational issues in risk analysis. *Risk Analysis*, 34(7), 1164–1172.

Bell, D. (1999) The axial age of technology. In: *The Coming of Post-industrial Society* (special anniversary edn). New York: Basic Books.

Boltanski, L. and Thévenot L. (1991) *On Justification. Economics of Worth.* Princeton: Princeton University Press.

Bourdieu, P. and Wacquant, L.J.D. (1992) *An Invitation to Reflexive Sociology.* Chicago: University of Chicago Press.

Brown, M.J. (2015) John Dewey's pragmatist alternative to the belief-acceptance dichotomy. *Studies in History and Philosophy of Science*, 53, 62–70.

Cox, L.A.T. (2012) Confronting deep uncertainties in risk analysis. *Risk Analysis*, 32, 1607–1629.

Dalkir, K. 2011. *Knowledge Management in Theory and Practice* (2nd edn). London: The MIT Press.

Dant, T. (1991) *Knowledge, Ideology and Discourse: A Sociological Perspective.* London: Routledge.

Davenport, T.H. and Prusak, L. (1998) *Working Knowledge.* Cambridge, MA: Harvard University Press.

Dewey, J. (1906) The experimental theory of knowledge, *Mind. New Series*, 15(59), 293–307.

Dewey, J. (1969–1991) *The Collected Works of John Dewey, 1882–1953* (37 volumes). J.A. Boydston (ed.) Carbondale: Southern Illinois UP.

Flage, R. and Aven, T. (2009) Expressing and communicating uncertainty in relation to quantitative risk analysis (QRA). *Reliability and Risk Analysis: Theory and Applications*, 2(13), 9–18.

Funtowicz, S.O. and Ravetz, J.R. (1990) *Uncertainty and Quality in Science for Policy.* Dordrecht: Kluwer Academic Publishers.

Funtowicz, S.O. and Ravetz, J.R. (1993) Science for the post-normal age. *Futures*, 25, 735–755.

Gourlay, S. (2001) Knowledge management and HRD. *Human Resource Development International*, 4(1), 27–46.

Grenfell, M. (ed.) (2012) *Pierre Bourdieu: Key Concepts* (2nd edn). Oxford: Routledge.

Gurvitch, G. (1971) *The Sociological Frameworks of Knowledge.* New York: Harper & Row.

Hall, S. (1983) The problem of ideology – Marxism without guarantees. In Matthews, B. (ed.) *Marx – A Hundred Years On.* London: Lawrence and Wishart.

Hansson, S.O. (2002) Uncertainties in the knowledge society. International Social Science Journal, 54(171), 39–46.

Hansson, S.O. (2013) Defining pseudoscience and science. In: Pigliucci, M., Boudry, M. (eds) *Philosophy of Pseudoscience.* Chicago: University of Chicago Press.

Hansson, S.O. and Aven, T. (2014) Is risk analysis scientific? *Risk Analysis*, 34(7), 1173–1183.

Hofstede, G. (1991) *Culture and Organisations: Software of the Mind.* Maidenhead: McGraw Hill.

ISO (2009) Risk Management – Vocabulary. Guide 73:2009.

Kaplan, S. and Garrick, B.J. (1981) On the quantitative definition of risk. *Risk Analysis*, 1, 11–27.

Kilpinen, E., Kivinen, O., Pihlström, S. (2008) Johdanto (Introduction). In: Kilpinen, E., Kivinen, O., Pihlström, S. (eds) Pragmatismi filosofiassa ja yhteiskuntatieteissä. [Pragmatism in Philosophy and Social Sciences.] Helsinki: Gaudeamus.

Kloprogge, P., van der Sluijs, J. and Petersen, A. (2005) *A Method for the Analysis of Assumptions in Assessments*. Bilthoven, The Netherlands: Netherlands Environmental Assessment Agency (MNP).

Kloprogge, P., van der Sluijs, J.P. and Petersen, A.C. (2011) A method for the analysis of assumptions in model-based environmental assessments. *Environmental Modelling and Software*, 26, 289–301.

Laes, E., Meskens, G. and van der Sluijs, J.P. (2011) On the contribution of external cost calculations to energy system governance: The case of a potential large-scale nuclear accident. *Energy Policy*, 39, 5664–5673.

Lacey, H. (2015) 'Holding' and 'endorsing' claims in the course of scientific activities. *Studies in History and Philosophy of Science*, 50, 89–95.

Lincoln, Y.S. and Guba E.G. (2000) Paradigmatic controversies, contradictions, and emerging confluences. In: Denzin, N.K. and Lincoln, Y.S. (eds) *Handbook of Qualitative Research* (2nd edn). California: Sage Publications.

Lindley, D.V. (2006) *Understanding Uncertainty*. Hoboken, NJ: Wiley.

Linkov, I., Satterstrom, F., Kiker, G., *et al.* (2006) From comparative risk assessment to multi-criteria decision analysis and adaptive management: Recent developments and applications. *Environment International*, 32, 1072–1093.

Mannheim, K. (1979) *Ideology and Utopia: An Introduction to the Sociology of Knowledge*. London: Routledge and Kegan Paul. Original (1936).

McKaughan, D.J. and Elliott, K.C. (2015) Introduction: Cognitive attitudes and values in science. *Studies in History and Philosophy of Science*. Part A, 50, 57–6.

Miller, B. (2013) When is consensus knowledge-based? Distinguishing shared knowledge from mere agreement. *Synthese*, 190, 1293–1316.

Pojman, L.P. (2003) *The Theory of Knowledge: Classic and Contemporary Readings* (3rd edn). Belmont, CA: Wadsworth/Thomson.

PSA-N (2012) Rapport etter gransking av hydrokarbonlekkasje på Heimdal 26.5.2012 (in Norwegian). Stavanger: Petroleum Safety Authority Norway.

PSA-N (2015) Petroleum Safety Authority Norway. http://www.psa.no/framework/category408.html#_Toc407544820. Accessed 28 May 2016.

Rosenthal, F. (2007) *Knowledge Triumphant: The Concept of Knowledge in Medieval Islam*. Leiden, Boston: Brill.

Scheler, M. (1980) [1926]. *Problems of a Sociology of Knowledge*. London: Routledge.

SRA (2015a) Glossary Society for Risk Analysis. www.sra.com/resources. Accessed 28 May 2016.

SRA (2015b) Foundations of risk analysis, discussion document www.sra.com/ resources. Accessed 28 May 2016.

Toulmin, S. (1999) Knowledge as shared procedures. In: Engeström, Y., Miettinen, R. and Punamäki, R-L. (eds) *Perspectives on Activity Theory*. Cambridge: Cambridge University Press.

Tsoukas, H. and Vladimirou, E. (2001) What is organizational knowledge? *Journal of Management Studies*, 38(7), 973–993.

van der Sluijs, J., Craye, M., Futowicz, S., *et al.* (2005a) Combining quantitative and qualitative measures of uncertainty in model-based environmental assessment. *Risk Analysis*, 25(2), 481–492.

van der Sluijs, J., Craye, M., Funtowicz, S., *et al.* (2005b) Experiences with the NUSAP system for multidimensional uncertainty assessment in model based foresight studies. *Water Science and Technology*, 52(6), 133–144.

3

Treatment and Communication of Uncertain Assumptions in (Semi-)quantitative Risk Assessments

Roger Flage[1] and Christine L. Berner[2]

[1] *University of Stavanger, Norway*
[2] *DNV GL, Norway*

This chapter addresses uncertain assumptions in (semi-)quantitative risk assessment. We first describe a formal setup that connects the risk concept, the risk description, risk indices, and the knowledge dimension, including assumptions in particular. We then present a scheme for systematising uncertain assumptions, and show how it can be used to provide recommendations about strategies for the treatment of such assumptions from both from a risk analyst and risk manager perspective. The setup and scheme build on:

- recent advances in uncertainty-based risk conceptualisations, including and in particular the concept of assumption deviation risk
- the so-called "NUSAP" notational scheme for uncertainty and quality in science for policy
- the assumption-based planning framework.

An example is used to highlight concepts and ideas.

3.1 Introduction

Assumptions are an inevitable part of any quantitative risk assessment (QRA). Some examples of assumptions that could be made in a QRA of an offshore petroleum production platform are:

- The number of personnel on board the platform will at any time be 50.
- The platform will be able to withstand a collision impact energy of 14 MJ.
- The blowout rate in case of an uncontrolled blowout will be 9000 Sm^3/day.

Knowledge in Risk Assessment and Management, First Edition. Edited by Terje Aven and Enrico Zio.
© 2018 John Wiley & Sons Ltd. Published 2018 by John Wiley & Sons Ltd.

The Meriam-Webster dictionary defines an assumption as "a fact or statement (such as a proposition, axiom [...], postulate, or notion) taken for granted". In this chapter, focused on the risk assessment and management setting, we take the view that assumptions are "conditions/inputs that are fixed in the assessment but which are acknowledged or known to possibly deviate to greater or lesser extent in reality" (Berner and Flage 2016a, 46). Although the term is superfluous based on the preceding definition, to highlight the acknowledged deviation potential, in this chapter we will still sometimes use the term *uncertain* assumptions. This deviation potential is clear from the example assumptions above. For example, it is unlikely that the blowout rate will be exactly $9000\,Sm^3/day$. If the actual blowout rate deviates from the assumed one, the assessed risk level may to greater or lesser extent remain valid, depending in particular on the magnitude of the deviation and the sensitivity of the relevant risk index. Note that it is tacitly understood that deviations here refer to *unfavourable* deviations, in the sense of deviations that increase the assessed risk.

An assumption may be made as a simplification, to avoid spending time and resources on assessing (quantifying) uncertainty. An assumption may also be made due to lack of knowledge, as a result of difficulty assessing (quantifying) the uncertainty. Intuitively, making a simplifying assumption will be strongly justified if there is both a low degree of belief that the actual conditions will deviate from what has been assumed, and if a deviation will have a low impact on the assessed risk level. However, such a conclusion does not account for the knowledge dimension. The low belief in deviation may be based on a weak knowledge basis, and the assessed risk level may reflect the use of a crude model. On the other hand, if there is a high degree of belief in deviation from an assumption that has been made, and a deviation in that assumption substantially influences the assessed risk, the obvious solution would be to not make such an assumption. Instead, the risk analyst would establish a probability distribution on the quantity that the assumption would have been made in terms of, and then integrate that uncertainty assessment into the uncertainty assessment of the overall quantity of interest using the law of total expectation/probability. Again, however, the knowledge dimension is not considered. The probability distribution established on the assumption quantity could be based on weak knowledge. For example, the probability distribution may require new assumptions to be made, for which the deviation potential is assessed as high.

The above type of considerations indicate a need to explicitly consider the knowledge dimension when deciding on strategies for handling uncertain assumptions in the risk assessment. Another consideration is resource use. Different methods can be used to handle uncertain assumptions, including qualitative categorisations, so-called "assumption deviation risk assessments", the law of total expectation/probability (as described above), and interval probability. These methods require different levels of effort and it is desirable to find a balance between the requirements for coherent quantitative uncertainty characterisation on the one hand, and practical limitations such as resource use on the other (Berner and Flage 2016a). The more important or critical an uncertain assumption is, the more justifiable it is to spend resources on characterising the uncertainty and assessing the effects of potential deviations from the base-case assumption.

Assumptions can be seen as part of the background knowledge on which the risk assessment is based (e.g. Aven 2013; see also Section 3.2). This background knowledge forms part of the risk description according to some risk description conceptualisation (SRA 2015), and several authors have argued for the importance of describing and communicating to the decision maker (here also referred to as the risk manager) not only the background knowledge itself, but also the *strength* (goodness, quality, and so on) of the knowledge underlying the risk assessment (Aven 2013; Funtowitz and Ravetz 1990; Aven 2014; Beard 2004; Pender 1999; Schofield 1998). This is also the case outside the field of risk assessment. For example, the so-called NUSAP notational scheme, developed to address uncertainty and quality in science for policy, has been shown to have strong parallels with the semi-quantitative risk description associated with an uncertainty-based risk perspective (Berner and Flage 2016b). Semi-quantitative here refers to a quantitative risk description supplemented by qualitative characterisations of the strength of knowledge that the former is based on. In other words, it does not refer to the use of risk matrices or similar risk characterisations, as is sometimes the case in the literature.

After treatment in the risk assessment and communication to the risk manager, and once a decision has been made to carry out an activity, uncertain assumptions need to be followed up as part of risk management to ensure that the premises underlying the decision to judge the risk level as acceptable remain valid. The so-called "assumption-based planning" framework (Dewar 2002) has been shown to provide a useful framework for developing strategies to follow up risk assessment assumptions (Berner and Flage 2017).

In this chapter, which is based on and summarises as well as extends the works of Berner and Flage (2016a; 2016b; 2017), we address uncertain assumptions in (semi-)quantitative risk assessment (S-QRA). We first describe a formal setup that connects the risk concept, the risk description, risk indices, and the knowledge dimension, including assumptions in particular. We then present a scheme for systematising uncertain assumptions, and show how it can be used to provide recommendations about strategies for the handling of such assumptions from both a risk analyst and risk manager perspective. The setup, scheme and strategies build on:

- recent advances in uncertainty-based risk conceptualisations, including and in particular the concept of assumption deviation risk (Aven 2013)
- the NUSAP notational scheme (Funtowicz and Ravetz, 1990)
- the assumption-based planning framework (Dewar 2002).

An example is used to highlight concepts and ideas.

The remainder of the chapter is organised as follows. In Section 3.2, we describe the formal setup. Then, in Section 3.3, we introduce the example and, in Section 3.4, we present the scheme for systemising uncertain assumptions. Sections 3.5, 3.6 and 3.7 provide recommendations about the handling of uncertain assumptions in risk assessment, on the communication of uncertain assumptions, and on the treatment of uncertain assumptions in risk management, respectively. A discussion and some concluding remarks are offered in Section 3.8.

3.2   A Formal Setup Connecting Risk and Related Concepts

The recently published Society for Risk Analysis glossary (SRA 2015) distinguishes between the concept of risk and the description of risk. Seven definitions of risk as a concept are provided, including (SRA 2015, 3):

- "Risk is the possibility of an unfortunate occurrence".
- "Risk is the potential for realization of unwanted, negative consequences of an event".
- "Risk is the consequences of the activity and associated uncertainties".

A key commonality of these and the remaining definitions in the glossary is that they are not formulated in terms of probability or any other specific measure of uncertainty. Rather, they are formulated in terms of uncertainty (or using other terms that indicate a state of uncertainty, such as "possibility" or "potential", as seen above). In line with the distinction between risk as a concept and the description of risk, specific uncertainty measures such as probability enter only as part of the risk description. The SRA glossary gives six examples of risk descriptions/metrics (SRA 2015, 3–4):

1) The combination of probability and magnitude/severity of consequences
2) The combination of the probability of a hazard occurring and a vulnerability metric given the occurrence of the hazard
3) The triplet (s_i, p_i, c_i), where s_i is the ith scenario, p_i is the probability of that scenario, and c_i is the consequence of the ith scenario, $i = 1,2, ...N$.
4) The triplet (C',Q,K), where C' is some specified consequences, Q a measure of uncertainty associated with C' (typically probability), and K the background knowledge that supports C' and Q (which includes a judgment of the strength of this knowledge)
5) Expected consequences (damage, loss)
   [...]
6) A possibility distribution for the damage (for example a triangular possibility distribution).

These risk descriptions have different levels of generality. For example, according to description 5, risk is described as the product of probabilities and consequences. Description 1, on the other hand, says that the risk description covers the combination (not necessarily the product) of these two dimensions. Compared to description 1, description 3 adds scenarios, while description 4 introduces a general measure Q of uncertainty (not necessarily probability) and includes the knowledge dimension K as part of the risk description. The latter can be understood as justified beliefs, established based on data and information, testing, argumentation, modelling, and so on, and is in risk assessments often expressed in the form of assumptions (Aven 2014). In description 4, the specified consequences C' are to be understood in a broad sense, to cover both specified events/scenarios and quantities characterising the consequences. Of course, description 5 can be seen as a risk metric/index used within a more general overall risk description, as we will do.

In this chapter, we adopt risk concept 3 and risk description 4 as the overall risk description. Using probability P as the quantitative measure of uncertainty and letting Y denote some quantity characterising the consequences (that is, letting C' = Y), we introduce $R(x_0)$ as a (possibly normalised) expected value-based risk metric, defined as (Berner and Flage 2016a):

$$R(x_0) = c\, E\big[Y \mid X = x_0, K\big] \tag{3.1}$$

where c is a normalising constant and X an uncertain quantity fixed at the (base case) value x_0. Strictly speaking, the condition $X = x_0$ is part of K but these terms are split in (3.1) for illustration purposes. The class covered by (3.1) includes a broad range of well-known risk metrics, such as (Aven 2015):

- individual risk, defined as the probability of death by a randomly selected person within a specified time period, typically a year
- potential loss of life, defined as the expected number of fatalities within a specified time period, also typically a year
- fatal accident rate, defined as the expected number of fatalities per 100 million hours of exposure
- frequency-number of fatalities curve (f-N curves), defined as the expected number of occurrences of events leading to N or more fatalities.

3.3 Example

The following example is inspired by a QRA carried out to evaluate the risk related to bunkering of LNG (liquified natural gas) at a ferry terminal in Norway (DNV 2013a). The QRA assesses and expresses first- and second-party risk using individual risk as the risk index, and third-party risk using f-N curves. In the example, we do not focus on the risk assessment itself

(DNV 2013a) – the hazard identification, frequency assessment, consequence analysis, and so on – but rather on the assumptions made as part of the risk assessment and thus on the associated assumptions register (DNV 2013b), which contains a structured overview and evaluation of the assumptions made in the QRA. These assumptions relate to the following subjects (DNV 2013b):

- Description and background data
  - manning levels
  - meteorological data
  - meteorological parameters
  - ignition sources: equipment/traffic/people/hot work
  - bunkering installation: base case design and inventory
  - escape and evacuation of passengers and personnel
- LNG accidents
  - representative scenario assumptions: release location/height, release sizes
  - frequency analysis assumptions: leak frequencies
  - event tree modelling assumptions: detection and isolation times, isolation failure, immediate ignition probability, event tree framework, event tree probabilities
- Consequence modelling assumptions: dispersion parameters, consequence modelling parameters
- Storage and loading – Specific: bunkering frequency
- Impact criteria: end point (impact) and vulnerability (fatality) criteria.

In this chapter, we focus on a subset of concrete assumptions related to the above subjects, namely assumptions related to the following quantities:

- the amount of hot work in the bunkering area
- the probability of ignition due to people as a source
- the solar flux
- representative hole sizes for different leak size categories
- the number of people directly involved in the bunkering operation
- the number of people in different categories (LNG plant employees, neighbours, ferry terminal employees, ferry passengers, hikers, and so on) exposed to increased risk
- the wind speed and direction
- the time to detection and isolation of a leak.

In the remainder of the chapter, we address the treatment of these quantities in the risk assessment phase (Section 3.5), in the risk communication phase (Section 3.6), and in the risk management phase (Section 3.7). First, however, we present a scheme for systematising uncertain assumptions related to quantities like these.

3.4   Systematising Uncertain Assumptions

In the introduction, we pointed to the need to consider the knowledge dimension – in addition to the belief in deviation from the (base case) assumption, and the sensitivity of the relevant risk index with respect to such deviations – when assessing the importance or criticality of an assumption. By labelling both the belief in deviation and the sensitivity as either "low" or "moderate/high", and the strength of knowledge as either "strong" or "moderate/weak", a scheme comprising eight assumption settings arises (Berner and Flage 2016a; 2017), as shown in Table 3.1. Assumptions in these settings have an increasing criticality when moving both in the direction from setting I though setting III to setting V, as well as when moving from either of these settings to the corresponding setting characterised by moderate/weak knowledge, say from setting I to setting II.

The classification scheme in Table 3.1 is intended primarily as a qualitative screening scheme. Classifying the belief in deviation or the sensitivity as low or moderate/high is thus not intended to be based on strict quantitative criteria. It could be envisaged defining the belief in deviation as low if, for some value d, the probability $P(X - x_0 > d)$ is lower than some threshold, or if the expected value $E[X - x_0]$ is above or below some threshold. Similarly, the sensitivity would be low if some selected importance measure were lower than some threshold. The intention is, however, to design a scheme that, based on some crude judgements by the analyst, allows for a ranking of assumptions as a guide to how much effort to spend on further analytical treatment of these in the risk assessment. Detailed and precise quantification of these probabilities and expected values could draw attention and resources from this subsequent process. If used, such threshold values should be understood as reference points and not as absolutes, especially for the settings where the knowledge is not judged as strong and where the level of precision in the assigned probabilities

Table 3.1 Settings faced when making assumptions in a risk assessment.

		Strength of knowledge	
Belief in deviation from x_0	Sensitivity of $R(x_0)$ wrt x_0	Strong	Moderate/weak
Low	Low	Setting I	Setting II
	Moderate/high	Setting IIIa	Setting IVa
Moderate/High	Low	Setting IIIb	Setting IVb
	Moderate/high	Setting V	Setting VI

Source: Berner and Flage 2016b. Reproduced with permission of Elsevier.

and expected values may be low. Furthermore, while the latter type of (sensitivity/importance) criterion should be more straightforward to implement, considering that the assumption is implemented as a parameter x_0 of the function $R(x_0)$, it would be difficult to give context- and case-independent guidelines on which importance measure or threshold value to use. The same goes for the specification of the threshold values for the belief in deviation.

The strength of knowledge assessment lends itself more easily to implementation using qualitative criteria. For example, Flage and Aven (2009, 14) suggest judging the knowledge as strong ("minor uncertainty" is the term used by Flage and Aven (2009), but strong knowledge is considered a more precise term and is therefore preferred here) if all the following conditions are met (whenever they are relevant):

- "The phenomena involved are well understood; the models used are known to give predictions with the required accuracy.
- The assumptions made are seen as very reasonable.
- Much reliable data is available.
- There is broad agreement among experts."

When these criteria are used to assess the strength of knowledge related to an assumption $X = x_0$, the first, third and fourth criteria must be understood as having to do with the phenomenon generating the outcome of X. Furthermore, the second criterion related to the reasonability of assumptions must be understood as relating to supplementary assumptions, i.e. other assumptions that follow from the assumption being assessed. For example, if a specific barrier failure frequency is assumed to be equal to some fixed value, based on historical data, then a supplementary assumption would be that the historical data/performance is also applicable to future situations.

In the next section, we use the assumption-setting scheme above to address the treatment of uncertain assumptions in (semi-)quantitative risk assessment (S-QRA).

3.5 Uncertain Assumptions in Risk Assessments: The Risk Analyst Perspective

In this section, we present and illustrate the implementation of a set of guidelines for treating uncertain assumptions in S-QRA, using the assumptions-settings scheme introduced in Section 3.4 as a starting point and a set of concrete assumptions related to the quantities in the list at the end of Section 3.3 as examples. The concrete assumptions considered are:

A) There will be no hot work in the bunkering area during bunkering: $X = x_0 = 0$, where X is the duration of hot work performed during bunkering.

B) The contribution to the frequency of ignition from sources associated with people (per person per second of cloud exposure) is 1.68E-4: that is, $X = x_0 = 1.68E\text{-}4$, where X is the said frequency.

C) The number of people directly involved in the bunkering operation will be four: $X = x_0 = 4$, where X is the said number of people.

D) The number of people in different categories (LNG plant employees, neighbours, ferry terminal employees, ferry passengers, hikers and so on) exposed to increased risk due to the bunkering will be as specified in Table 2 in DNV (2013a): $X = x_0 = y$, where y is a vector of quantities specifying the number of people in different categories exposed to increased risk.

E) The solar flux in case of a leak will be $100\,\text{W/m}^2$: $X = x_0 = 100$, where X is the solar flux when a leak occurs.

F) Representative hole sizes for small (<10 mm), medium (10–50 mm) and large (>50 mm) leaks are y_1, y_2 and y_3, respectively, as calculated by the LEAK software tool: $X = x_0 = (y_1, y_2, y_3)$, where X is a vector of hole sizes considered "representative" for the said leak sizes.

G) The wind speed and direction in case of a leak will be 6 m/s and 67.5–112.5°, respectively, which is equal to the most likely combination of these parameters: $X = x_0 = (6, 67.5\text{–}112.5)$, where X is a vector specifying the wind speed and direction.

H) The time to detection and isolation of a leak will be 90 s: $X = x_0 = 90$, where X is the time to detection and isolation of a leak, in seconds.

Table 3.2 summarises the proposed guidelines for the different assumption settings. The details of and rationale for these guidelines, as well as their application to the above assumptions, is given and shown in the following. This section is based on Berner and Flage (2016a).

Assumptions in Setting I are characterised by a low degree of belief in deviation and a low sensitivity of the relevant risk metric to changes in the (base case) assumption, and these judgements (related to the belief in deviation and the sensitivity) are made based on a strong knowledge. In this setting, ignoring the uncertainty related to X by setting $X = x_0$ and reporting just $R(x_0)$ is strongly justified. The assumption $X = x_0$ of course needs to be documented, but it can be listed as a non-critical assumption.

Assumption A can be argued to be an example of a Setting I assumption. Table A3.1 in the appendix gives the justification underlying such a classification. Accordingly, beyond being documented and listed as non-critical in the assumptions register, this assumption receives no further attention in the risk assessment (but some follow-up is warranted in the subsequent risk management; see Section 3.7).

An assumption in Setting II is also characterised by both a low belief in deviation and low sensitivity (strictly speaking, it is the risk metric that is characterised by low sensitivity, but for brevity we will here and later on refer to the assumption

Table 3.2 Guidelines for treatment of uncertain assumptions in S-QRA.

Belief in deviation from x_0	Sensitivity of $R(x_0)$ to x_0	Strength of knowledge	
		Strong	**Moderate/weak**
Low	Low	Setting I: Report $R(x_0)$ List the assumption $X = x_0$ as non-critical	Setting II: Report $R(x_0)$ Highlight qualitative strength of knowledge assessment of assumption $X = x_0$
	Moderate/ high	Setting III: Report $R(x_0)$	Setting IV: Report $R(x_0)$
Moderate/ high	Low	Highlight assumption deviation risk assessment for assumption $X = x_0$, based on probability *or* As for Setting V	Highlight assumption deviation risk assessment for assumption $X = x_0$, based on probability or interval/imprecise probability. *or* As for Setting VI
	Moderate/ high	Setting V: Assign $F(x|z_0,K)$ and determine $E[R(X)|z_0,K]$ wrt F using law of total expectation. List assumption $Z = z_0$ as non-critical	Setting VI: Assign $F(x|z_0,K)$ and determine $E[R(X)|z_0,K]$ wrt F using law of total expectation. Highlight assumption deviation risk assessment for assumption $Z = z_0$, based on probability or interval/imprecise probability *or* Assign interval/imprecise probability distribution on X and determine resulting interval for $E[R(X)|K]$

Source: Berner and Flage 2016a. Reproduced with permission of Elsevier.

as being characterised by low sensitivity). However, these judgements are not based on strong knowledge. The assumption $X = x_0$ is the best judgement and there is no basis for assessing a different risk level than $R(x_0)$, although the decision maker should be made aware of the weaker knowledge basis. Assumption B can be argued to be an example of a Setting II assumption; see Table A3.1.

Assumptions in Setting V are characterised by a moderate or high belief in deviation and a moderate or high sensitivity, where these judgements are made based on strong knowledge. An assumption with these characteristics would be highly critical. At the same time, the strong knowledge means that a well-founded probability distribution $F(x|z_0,K) = P(X x|Z = z_0,K)$ can be established and used to determine the (unconditional) risk index $E[R(X)]$. For these two reasons, Setting V type assumptions are not often made. Here $Z = z_0$ represents (additional) assumptions that are introduced when establishing the distribution F, and which, due to the strong knowledge involved, are judged as strongly justified and can thus be listed as non-critical.

Assumption G can be argued to be an example of a Setting V assumption; see Table A3.1. This specific assumption is not actually made in the QRA that has inspired assumptions A–H. Instead, a joint probability distribution is established for the wind speed and direction, based on weather statistics, and this is then integrated into the overall risk indices. An additional assumption introduced here is that the weather statistics used are relevant for the location of the future ferry bunkering activity.

Assumptions in Setting VI have the same belief in deviation and sensitivity characteristics as assumptions in Setting V, but the knowledge basis for these judgements is not strong. Establishing a probability distribution on X may be difficult or require weakly justified assumptions $Z = z_0$. If an interval/imprecise probability distribution can be established on X, one solution is to determine the resulting interval for the overall risk index. For example, if it is possible to establish a strongly justified conditional distribution $F(x|Z,K)$ and a strongly justified interval $[z_{min},z_{max}]$ within which Z will be with certainty (say due to physical constraints), then an interval for the (unconditional) risk index $E[R(X)|K]$ can be determined by integration with respect to $F(x|Z = z_{min},K)$ and $F(x|Z = z_{max},K)$. Alternatively, the (conditional) risk index $E[R(X)|z_0,K]$ can be determined by integration with respect to $F(x|Z = z_0,K)$, where $Z = z_0$ is a "best judgement" assumption. An assumption deviation risk assessment related to $Z = z_0$, based on probability or interval/imprecise probability, can then be highlighted along with the risk metric value.

Assumption H can be argued to be an example of a Setting VI assumption; see Table A3.1. A detection and isolation time of 90 s is the best judgement of the risk analyst; however, there is disagreement between different stakeholders, with some arguing that the assumed time will be considerably shorter (36 s, close to a factor of three less than the analyst's best judgement), and the analyst does not consider a substantially longer time to be unlikely. By assigning an interval for the detection and isolation time, say [36, 300], where 36 s corresponds to a minimum time comprised of a detection time of 30 s (assuming the use of fast responsive gas detectors) and an isolation time of 6 s (assuming immediate automatic closure of emergency shutdown valve upon detection), and 300 s corresponds to a 5 minute combined detection and isolation time, which is considered somewhat arbitrary but nonetheless a time that is highly unlikely to be exceeded.

Assumptions in Setting III are characterised by a low belief in deviation and a moderate or high sensitivity, or vice versa, where these judgements are based on a strong knowledge. These assumptions can be treated in the same way as Setting V assumptions. Alternatively, a so-called "assumption deviation risk assessment" can be performed. This requires less effort but at the same time does not give the comprehensive and integrated level of quantitative insights as a Setting V approach.

The term "assumption deviation risk" was coined by Aven (2013) and refers to the assessment of the "risk" related to a deviation between what has been assumed and what actually occurs. An assumption deviation risk assessment consists in assessing (Aven 2013 p. 139):

- the deviation from the assumptions made with associated consequences
- a measure of uncertainty of this deviation and consequences
- the knowledge that these are based on.

In terms of the notational framework of this chapter, an assumption deviation risk assessment may thus consist in first defining different potential values $d = (d_1,...,d_n)$ of the deviation $D = X - x_0$; next assessing the associated probabilities $p = (p_1,...,p_n)$ and effects $s = (s_1,...,s_n)$, where $p_i = P(D = d_i|K)$ and $s_i = R(x_0) - R(x_0 + d_i)$, $i = 1,...,n$; and finally making a strength of knowledge assessment (SoK) of the knowledge underlying the resulting triplet (d,p,s). The assessment of the probabilities and effects in an assumption deviation risk assessment may be qualitative, for example using score categories such as "high", "medium" or "low" (Aven 2013).

Assumptions C and D can be argued to be examples of Setting IIIa and IIIb assumptions, respectively; see Table A3.1. In Section 3.6, Assumption C is used as an example to illustrate how uncertain assumptions can be assessed and communicated to the decision maker using a combination of the NUSAP notational scheme and assumption deviation risk, as well as through visualisation of their knowledge basis.

Assumptions in Setting IV have the same belief in deviation and sensitivity characteristics as assumptions in Setting III, but the knowledge basis for these judgements is not strong. The recommendation here is analogous to that for Setting III: either handle as a Setting VI assumption or perform an assumption deviation risk assessment, with the latter possibly based on an interval probability considering the weaker knowledge involved compared to Setting III.

Assumptions E and F can be argued to be examples of Setting IVa and IVb assumptions, respectively; see Table A3.1. In Section 3.6, Assumption E is used as an example to illustrate how uncertain assumptions can be assessed and communicated to the decision maker/risk manager using a combination of the

NUSAP notational scheme and assumption deviation risk, as well as through visualisation of their knowledge basis.

In the following section, we examine the NUSAP notational scheme and consider its parallels with S-QRA as well as how NUSAP can be used to improve S-QRA. For the latter purpose, we specifically consider the visualisation of the strength of knowledge related to an assumption, as well as combining the NUSAP notational scheme with assumption deviation risk assessment.

3.6 Communicating Uncertain Assumptions

The NUSAP notational scheme for uncertainty and quality in science for policy (Funtowicz and Ravetz 1990) was developed to improve the process for making policy decisions informed by science. When introduced, it was intended to address a new type of policy problem referred to as "post-normal" decision problems, where "facts are uncertain, values in dispute, stakes high and decisions urgent" (Funtowicz and Ravetz 1991, 137).

The name NUSAP is an acronym made up of the first letters of the five so-called "qualifiers" of the scheme (Funtowicz and Ravetz 1990; van der Sluijs *et al.* 2005a, van der Sluijs 2006):

- Numeral refers to some quantity of interest.
- Unit refers to the unit in which the numeral qualifier is expressed.
- Spread refers to a quantitative representation (say, an interval) of the uncertainty/inexactness/variability of the numeral qualifier.
- Assessment refers to "qualitative judgements about the information" (van der Sluijs *et al.* 2005a, 482) provided by the numeral, unit and spread qualifiers, based on significance levels, subjective probabilities or qualitative categories such as high, low, optimistic, pessimistic, and so on. (van der Sluijs *et al.* 2005a).
- Pedigree refers to a qualitative evaluation of the information provided by the numeral, unit, spread and assessment qualifiers.

Assessing the pedigree qualifier involves the use of a so-called pedigree matrix. The design of the pedigree matrix can vary depending on the situation and context. An example of such a matrix is shown in Table 3.3. To assess the pedigree, the foundation of the information provided by the other NUSAP qualifiers is evaluated against certain criteria in various categories. A pedigree score may be introduced to code the evaluations made on a numerical scale, as shown in the first column of Table 3.3.

The NUSAP scheme has also been linked to the concept of assumptions, as Kloprogge *et al.* (2011) extend the use of the pedigree matrix to assess the value-ladenness of assumptions. Here, value-laden assumptions are understood as assumptions that can lead to a biased assessment

Table 3.3 Pedigree matrix.

Score	Theoretical structure	Data input	Peer acceptance	Colleague consensus
4	Established theory	Experimental data	Total	All but cranks
3	Theoretically based model	Historic/field data	High	All but rebels
2	Computational model	Calculated data	Medium	Competing schools
1	Statistical processing	Educated guesses	Low	Embryonic field
0	Definitions	Uneducated guesses	None	No opinion

Source: as suggested by Funtowicz and Ravetz (1990, 140 and 196).

Table 3.4 Correspondence between the NUSAP scheme components, the risk description components of an S-QRA, and assumption deviation risk assessment.

NUSAP	S-QRA risk description	Assumption deviation risk assessment
Numeral	Y^*	x_0
Unit	—	—
Spread	Y'	D
Assessment	$Q(Y \in Y')$	$Q(D = d)$, e.g. p
Pedigree	SoK	SoK
—	K	s

Source: Table based on and extended from Berner and Flage (2016b). Reproduced with permission of Elsevier.

Berner and Flage (2016b) compare the NUSAP notational scheme and the uncertainty-based risk perspective described in Section 3.2. Let Y^* denote a prediction of the quantity of interest Y, and Y' a set or interval of potential outcomes (values) of Y. Table 3.4 summarises the findings of this comparison in terms of parallels between the NUSAP notational scheme, the S-QRA risk description, and assumption deviation risk assessment.

As can be seen in Table 3.4, the numeral and unit qualifiers correspond to either the prediction Y^* or the assumption $X = x_0$, depending on whether the reference is the S-QRA risk description or an assumption deviation risk assessment. Next, the spread qualifier corresponds to the sets Y' or d, and the assessment qualifier corresponds to the associated uncertainty measures. Finally, the pedigree qualifier corresponds to the strength of knowledge assessment (SoK) in both S-QRA and an assumption deviation risk assessment, exemplified by the categories strong, moderate and weak in Sections 3.4 and 3.5.

As an example, if Y denotes the number of fatalities resulting from some specified accident, then:

- Y^* would be the predicted number of fatalities if the accident were to occur, say $Y^* = 4$
- Y' would be an interval or set of intervals, say the intervals 1–2, 3–5, 6–10 and >10
- the measure $Q(Y \in Y')$ would be the associated probabilities, say 0.4, 0.4, 0.15 and 0.05
- SoK would be an assessment of the strength of the knowledge K supporting the assigned prediction and probabilities.

The knowledge component K of the S-QRA risk description and the effect component s in assumption deviation risk assessment do not correspond to any of the five NUSAP qualifiers. However, one of the further developments of the NUSAP notational scheme relates to the visualisation of the pedigree assessment. Some of the tools developed for this purpose are to some extent extensions of the so-called NUSAP diagnostics diagram introduced by Funtowicz and Ravetz (1990). This is a two-dimensional diagram, intended to communicate pedigree strength and the sensitivity of a particular input/ parameter with regards to the model output. These two dimensions are closely related to the strength of knowledge and sensitivity/effect components of the uncertain assumptions scheme described in this chapter.

More recent visualisation tools studied in light of the NUSAP notational scheme include radar diagrams (Schneider and Moss 1999; van der Sluijs *et al.* 2004, 2005b), snowflake charts (Schneider and Moss 1999), kite diagrams (Risbey *et al.* 2001; van der Slujis *et al.* 2004, 2005a, 2005b; Boone *et al.* 2010) and pedigree charts (Wardekker *et al.* 2008). Figure 3.1 shows a set of radar diagrams expressing the strength of knowledge related to Assumptions C and E (see Section 3.5). These diagrams are based on use of the pedigree matrix in Table 3.5, which is built from the strength of knowledge criteria described by Flage and Aven (2009); see Section 3.4. The evaluation related to the relevant pedigree scores for Assumptions C and E is presented in Table 3.6.

Berner and Flage (2016b) propose a presentation format for communicating uncertain assumptions. This is based on a combination of the NUSAP scheme and assumption deviation risk assessment. As promised in Section 3.5, the combined format is illustrated for the example assumptions C and E in Table 3.6. Both of these assumptions are based on relatively strong knowledge, as illustrated in Figure 3.1. The area covered by the thick black lines illustrate that the overall background knowledge is strong for Assumption C. For Assumption E the area covered by the thick black line is smaller, indicating a

Table 3.5 Pedigree matrix based on the strength of knowledge criteria of Flage and Aven (2009).

Score	SoK label	Phenomena/model	Data	Expert agreement	Realism of assumption
3	Strong	The phenomena involved are well understood; the models used are known to give predictions with the required accuracy.	Much reliable data is available.	There is broad agreement among experts.	The assumption made is seen as very reasonable.
2	Moderate	Conditions in between strong and weak: say the phenomena involved are well understood, but the models used are considered simple/crude.	Conditions in between strong and weak; say some reliable data are available.	Conditions in between strong and weak.	Conditions in between strong and weak.
1	Weak	The phenomena involved are not well understood; models are non-existent or known/believed to give poor predictions.	Data are not available or are unreliable.	There is lack of agreement/ consensus among experts.	The assumption made represent a strong simplification.

Table 3.6 Combination of the NUSAP scheme and assumption deviation risk assessment.

ID	Assumed value (x_0) / Numeral	Unit	SoK/ Pedigree	Magnitudes of deviation (d)	Probabilities of deviations (p)	Sensitivity (s)
C	4	Number of people directly involved in bunkering operation	(3, 3, 3, 3)	−1	Low	Low
				+2	Low	High
E	100	W/m^2	(3, 3, 2, 2)	+500	High	Low
				+1000	Moderate	Low

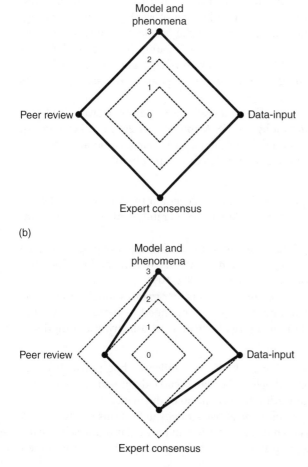

(a)

(b)

Figure 3.1 Radar diagrams: (a) for Assumption C; (b) for Assumption E.

more moderate strength of knowledge. The combination of high phenomeno-logical understanding and availability of data, in combination with a lower score on expert consensus and peer review, may indicate that there is some disagreement on how to use the relevant input.

3.7 Uncertain Assumptions in Risk Management: The Risk Manager Perspective

Assumptions constitute a key set of premises for a risk assessment. Deviations from, or "failures" of these assumptions could invalidate the results of a risk assessment to greater or lesser extent. To ensure that the conclusions of the risk assessment and the judgements and decisions informed by it remain valid (such as the judgement that the activity in question can be performed with an acceptable level of risk), uncertain assumptions need to be followed up to ensure that they remain valid too. One way of doing so is to make use of the so-called "assumption-based planning" framework (Dewar 2002) which, according to Berner and Flage (2017), is a useful framework for managing uncertain risk assessment assumptions, as shown in the following.

Assumption-based planning is a framework developed by Dewar and Levin as a tool for strategic planning by the US Army (Dewar 2002). A key concept within this framework is that of the so-called load-bearing, vulnerable assumptions underlying a plan. These assumptions can be met by the following set of strategies:

- signposts, where a signpost is defined as "an event or threshold that indicates an important change in the validity or vulnerability of an assumption" (Dewar 2002, 92)
- Shaping actions, where "a shaping action is an organizational action to be taken in the current planning cycle and is intended to control the vulnerability of a load-bearing assumption" (Dewar 2002, 109).
- Hedging actions, where "a hedging action is an organizational action to be taken in the current planning cycle and is intended to better prepare the organization for the potential failure of one of its load-bearing assumptions" (Dewar 2002, 123).

In addition, contingency actions, which are similar to but unlike hedging actions – which are performed *before* the plan is carried out – are performed *if and when* deviations occur during the execution of the plan.

Berner and Flage (2017) modify the above strategy definitions to adapt them to the risk assessment and management setting, in particular to the scheme for systemizing uncertain assumptions presented in Section 3.4. The modified definitions are as follows:

- A signpost is an event or threshold that indicates an important change in the belief in deviation from original assumptions or the sensitivity of such a deviation (with regard to the risk index used).
- A shaping action is an action to be taken, intended to avoid significant (and unwanted) deviations from an original assumption on which a risk assessment is based.
- A hedging action is an action to be taken, intended to better prepare the organization/system for the potential failure of one of its critical assumptions.

Table 3.7 presents guidelines about which type or types of strategies are applicable to manage uncertain risk assessment assumptions, depending on which assumption setting the assumption belongs to. The rationale of these guidelines is given in the following, before the example assumptions A–H are considered in light of these guidelines.

Setting I and II assumptions are characterised by a low belief in deviation and a low sensitivity. In Setting I, the knowledge supporting these

Table 3.7 Primary (secondary) assumption management strategies.

Belief in deviation from x_0	Sensitivity of $R(x_0)$ to x_0	Strength of knowledge	
		Strong	Moderate/weak
Low	Low	Setting I: Verify SoK	Setting II: Signpost
	Moderate/high	Setting IIIa: Verify SoK (Singpost) (Hedging) (Contingency)	Setting IVa: Signpost (Shaping) (Hedging) (Contingency)
Moderate/high	Low	Setting IIIb: Verify SoK (Shaping)	Setting IVb: Shaping (Hedging) (Contingency)
	Moderate/high	Setting V: Shaping Hedging Contingency	Setting VI: Shaping Hedging Contingency (Signpost)

Source: Berner and Flage (2017). Reproduced with permission of Elsevier.

classifications is judged as strong. Verifying this judgement helps increase the confidence in a decision to not follow up assumptions in this setting any further. On the other hand, in Setting II the knowledge supporting the belief in deviation and sensitivity judgements is not judged as strong. This can be understood as an acknowledgement that, based on the current knowledge, there are no indications to justify additional follow-up of the assumption compared to Setting I assumptions. However, the less-than-strong knowledge could result in surprises. Establishing one or more signposts to monitor factors indicating that a deviation of the assumption has or is about to occur ensures that the assumption is not entirely forgotten. Any actual or potential deviations will then be handled on a case-by-case basis upon the triggering of a signpost.

Setting IIIa and IVa assumptions are characterised by a low belief in deviation and a moderate or high sensitivity. In Setting IIIa, the knowledge supporting these classifications is judged as strong. Verifying this judgement – in particular for the belief in deviation classification – will increase the confidence that deviations are unlikely to occur during the considered situation. However, should the situation change, the belief in deviation can change too, and a signpost can be used in such settings to warn of changing conditions. Based on cautionary thinking, and as secondary strategies, the moderate or high sensitivity present for assumptions in Setting IIIa can be seen as indicating hedging and contingency actions. On the other hand, in Setting IVa the knowledge supporting the belief in deviation and sensitivity classifications is judged as moderate or weak. Based on a cautionary thinking, at least signposts but possibly also shaping actions (the latter as a secondary action) can then be seen as justified, because a potential for surprises relative to the low belief in deviation is acknowledged. This type of consideration in light of the moderate or high sensitivity can also be seen as justifying hedging and contingency actions (as secondary actions).

Setting IIIb and IVb assumptions are characterized by a moderate or high belief in deviation and low sensitivity. In Setting IIIb, the knowledge supporting these classifications is judged as strong. Verifying this judgement – in particular for the sensitivity classification – will build confidence that the effect of an assumption deviation will be limited. Shaping actions are relevant secondary actions if the assumption deviation under certain circumstances could have more than a small effect. On the other hand, in Setting IVb the knowledge supporting the belief in deviation and sensitivity judgements is not judged as strong. The state of the knowledge base opens up for questioning both the belief in deviation and sensitivity classifications. Again, based on cautionary thinking and to potentially err on the side of safety, taking the belief in deviation classification for granted while questioning the sensitivity classification leads to the conclusion that both shaping as well as hedging and contingency actions are relevant, with the former to be preferred since, at least based on the current knowledge, actions related to the occurrence of an assumption will be more effective than actions related to the effect of an assumption.

Setting V and VI assumptions are characterised by a moderate or high belief in deviation and a moderate or high sensitivity. In Setting V, the knowledge supporting these classifications is judged as strong. Both shaping as well as hedging and contingency actions are thus appropriate. As deviations are expected and prepared for, signposts would be superfluous (unless the shaping actions implemented depend on an early warning that a deviation is about to occur, using signposts). On the other hand, in Setting VI the knowledge supporting the belief in deviation and sensitivity classifications is judged as moderate or weak. Then signposts are a relevant secondary strategy, in addition to primary strategies as recommended for Setting V, if only to collect data on assumption deviations that occur and thereby strengthen the knowledge supporting the belief in deviation classification. Of course, strengthening the knowledge will be an appropriate strategy for all assumptions characterized by moderate or weak knowledge.

Table 3.8 shows how risk management strategies can be assigned to the assumptions A–H introduced in Section 3.5.

3.8 Discussion and Concluding Remarks

In this chapter, we have addressed uncertain assumptions in the context of a semi-quantitative risk assessment (S-QRA), where the latter is understood as quantitative risk assessment supplemented by qualitative strength-of-knowledge assessments. The focus has been on frameworks, schemes and methods for the treatment of these assumptions in the risk assessment, on the communication of the risk description – uncertain assumptions in particular – from the risk analyst to the decision maker/risk manager, and on the development of management strategies to follow up uncertain assumptions after the risk assessment has been performed. In the following, we first discuss selected aspects of the presented frameworks, schemes and methods, before ending with some concluding remarks.

A main benefit of the set of schemes described in this chapter is that they provide a systematic and unified way of handling uncertain assumptions, from the risk assessment, through the risk communication, to the risk management. Essentially the same scheme as for systematising uncertain assumptions applies to the treatment of the assumptions in both the risk assessment and the risk management. The only difference in terms of the assumption settings is that for the risk assessment context only Settings III and IV are distinguished,

Table 3.8 Management strategies for example assumptions.

ID	Assumption subject	Assumption specification	Assumed value	Setting	Strategies
A	Ignition sources: hot work	Duration of hot work performed during bunkering	0	I	Verify SoK: verify that hot work ban is being implemented in plant operating procedures.
B	Ignition sources: people	Default frequency of ignition from sources associated with people (per person per second of cloud exposure)	1.68E-4	II	Signpost: Monitor plant incident reporting system, and plan to check for reports of violation of no smoking policy (or similar incidents) in the next revision of the risk assessment.
C	Manning level and distribution	Number of people directly involved in the bunkering operation	4	IIIa	Verify SoK: Verify that actual manning during operation matches planned manning. (Signpost: Reorganisation, or revision of manning plans.) (Hedging: Instruct bunkering personnel to immediately dismiss any excess personnel from the area during bunkering.) (Contingency: Stop bunkering operation unless excess exposed personnel are removed from the bunkering area immediately.)
D	Manning level and distribution	Number of people in different categories (LNG plant employees, neighbours, ferry terminal employees, ferry passengers, hikers) exposed to increased risk due to the bunkering	Ref. Table 2 in DNV (2013a)	IVa	Signpost: Changes in ferry type (to a ferry with larger passenger capacity), or changes to the use or zoning of the surrounding areas. (Shaping: None identified.) (Hedging: None identified.) (Contingency: Stop or avoid initiating bunkering operation if an unusual crowding of people is observed in the vicinity of the LNG plant, say a demonstration or a concert)

E	Meteorological data	Solar flux in case of a leak (W/m²)	100	IIIb	Verify SoK: Verify through measurement the solar flux variation over time at plant location. (Shaping: None identified.)
F	Release sizes	Representative hole sizes for small (<10 mm), medium (10–50 mm) and large (>50 mm) leak sizes	"To be calculated by LEAK [software tool]" (i.e. not specified in assumption register)	IVb	Shaping: Consider using the upper limits of the small and medium categories as their respective hole sizes. (Hedging: If suggested shaping action is not implemented as base case, run sensitivity scenarios.) (Contingency: None identified.)
G	No Setting V assumptions made in QRA	-	-	V	Shaping: - Hedging: - Contingency: -
H	Detection and isolation times	Time to detection and isolation of a leak (seconds)	90	VI	Shaping: Use assumed response times as requirements for selection of designer/vendors. Hedging: None identified. Contingency: None identified. (Signpost: Exceedance of the assumed values during emergency preparedness exercises and isolation valve tests.)

Source: Berner and Flage (2017). Reproduced with permission of Elsevier.

whereas for the risk management context more nuance is introduced by distinguishing settings IIIa, IIIb, IVa and IVb. Moreover, as the scheme for systematising uncertain assumptions builds on the concept of assumption deviation risk, it fits well with the presentation format for uncertain assumptions described in Section 3.6, which is based on a merging of the NUSAP notational scheme and assumption deviation risk assessment.

While the described schemes do incur an additional "cost" (compared to a practice of just documenting and perhaps making some sensitivity evaluations for the assumptions made), in terms of the information and effort needed to identify, classify, analyse and mitigate the uncertain assumptions, much of the information required to classify assumptions according to the scheme described in Section 3.4 may already exist in quantitative risk assessments as performed today. This point is illustrated by the classification of the example assumptions A–H in the appendix. The QRA (DNV 2013a) that inspired the example assumptions contains an assumptions register (DNV 2013b), which documents and evaluates assumptions made in the QRA. The sensitivity classifications of the assumptions A–H are informed by sensitivity evaluations already existing in the assumptions register. However, the proposed scheme includes consideration of the belief in deviation as well as the knowledge dimension (as motivated in the introduction), which means that it goes beyond the practice described above.

One limitation of the scheme for systematising uncertain assumptions presented in Section 3.4, as addressed in Section 3.5, is the lack of context- and case-independent quantitative thresholds to define when to classify the belief in deviation and the sensitivity as either high, moderate or low. The assessments related to the example assumptions A–G show, however, that if a pragmatic approach is taken, acknowledging the qualitative nature of the scheme, it can be implemented without specific quantitative thresholds.

Another limitation related to the setup, schemes and examples used in this chapter is that these are geared towards considering a single assumption at a time; that is, simultaneous assumption deviations and in particular dependencies between assumptions are not considered. In terms of the setup and risk metric described in Section 3.2, addressing the issue of simultaneous assumption deviations would involve X to be considered a vector. While this is already done for assumptions D, F and G, for each of these assumptions X relates to attributes of the same subject or phenomenon, namely the number of people in different categories in Assumption D, different hole sizes in Assumption F, and the wind speed and direction in Assumption G. What is missing is the consideration of simultaneous deviations in assumptions related to different subjects; say, an increase in the manning level concurrently with an increase related to ignition sources. Further work is warranted to look into this issue.

Some of the secondary management strategies in Section 3.7 were justified with reference to cautionary thinking. Such thinking cannot of course be implemented without consideration of the costs and burdens of doing so. A less "cautiously biased" scheme can be obtained by merging the low and moderate belief in deviation and sensitivity categories, instead of the moderate and high categories as is done in this chapter, and by merging the moderate and strong knowledge categories instead of the weak and moderate categories as is done in this chapter. When it comes to the issue of costs and burdens, it is also relevant to point out that any proposed risk management strategies related to assumptions in the different settings need to be considered in light of both their benefits and burdens/costs, and a management review and judgement about whether they should be implemented or not. As an example, for the example Assumption E, related to the solar flux in case of a leak, it may be decided that on-site measurement of the solar flux should not actually be performed to verify the strength of knowledge related to the belief in deviation classification. The cost of such an action may be judged as grossly disproportionate to the benefits obtained.

As illustrated using a so-called bow-tie model (see, for example, Aven 2015) in Figure 3.2, the use of assumption-based planning strategies to manage assumption deviation risk related to risk assessment assumptions have

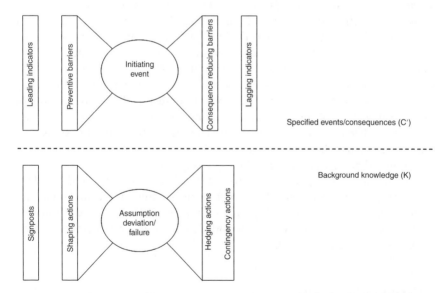

Figure 3.2 The bow-tie model used to illustrate the parallels between (top) the risk management of initiating events (hazards/threats) and (bottom) the assumption-based planning framework (Berner and Flage 2017). *Source:* Berner 2017. Reproduced with permission of Elsevier.

parallels in risk management measures related to initiating events (hazards/threats) studied in the same risk assessments:

- Leading risk indicators can be seen as analogous to signposts detecting changes in the belief that an assumption will deviate/fail.
- Preventive barriers can be seen as analogous to shaping actions implemented to avoid assumption deviation/failure.
- Consequence reducing barriers can be seen as analogous to hedging and contingency actions put in place to reduce the effect of assumption deviation/failure.

The difference is, as also indicated by the figure, that while the management of the initiating events (hazards/threats), using risk indicators and barriers, relates to the specified events/consequences (C') dimension of the risk description; the management of assumption deviations/failures, using the various assumption-based planning strategies, relates to the background knowledge (K) dimension of the risk description; see Section 3.2.

Making assumptions is inevitable when performing quantitative risk assessments, and cannot generally be avoided. However, uncertain assumptions need to be treated and communicated appropriately, and this chapter is intended to contribute to meeting such an objective by describing frameworks, schemes and methods through which this can be done. One of the aims of the chapter has been to illustrate the importance and role of the knowledge dimension when dealing with uncertain assumptions. The schemes and examples in Sections 3.5 and 3.7 have shown that how the uncertainty related to an assumption should be treated in the risk assessment, as well as suitable strategies for following up the assumption during the execution of the activity in question, are determinable by the degree of belief in deviation of the (base case) assumption, the sensitivity of the relevant risk metric to changes in the (base case) assumption, and the strength of knowledge involved. Furthermore, the scheme and examples in Section 3.6 has shown that how risk is described in a semi-quantitative risk assessment (as understood in this paper) has strong parallels to, and can be improved by, an existing scheme originally developed to address uncertainty and quality in science for policy. One of the key parallels relates to the need to qualitatively assess and highlight the strength of knowledge on which information in an assessment or study is based.

Acknowledgements

The work on which the chapter is based was partly funded by the Norwegian Research Council, as a part of the PETROMAKS 2 program (grant number 228335/E30). This support is gratefully acknowledged.

References

Aven, T. (2013). Practical implications of the new risk perspectives. *Reliability Engineering and System Safety*, 115, 136–145.

Aven, T. (2014). *Risk, Surprises and Black Swans, Fundamental Ideas and Concepts in Risk Assessment and Risk Management*. New York, Routledge.

Aven, T. (2015). *Risk Analysis* (2nd edn). John Wiley & Sons.

Beard, A.N. (2004). Risk assessment assumptions. *Civil Engineering and Environmental Systems*, 21(1), 19–31.

Berner, C. and Flage, R. (2016a). Strengthening quantitative risk assessments by systematic treatment of uncertain assumptions. *Reliability Engineering and System Safety*, 151, 46–59.

Berner, C.L. and Flage, R. (2016b). Comparing and integrating the NUSAP notational scheme with an uncertainty based risk perspective. *Reliability Engineering and System Safety*, 156, 185–194.

Berner C.L. and Flage R. (2017) Creating risk management strategies based on uncertain assumptions and aspects from assumption based planning. *Reliability Engineering & System Safety*, 167, 10–19.

Boone, I., van der Stede, Y., Bollaerts, K., *et al.* (2009). NUSAP method for evaluating the data quality in a quantitative microbial risk assessment model for Salmonella in the pork production chain. *Risk Analysis*, 29(4), 502–517.

Dewar, J.A. (2002). *Assumption-Based Planning: A Tool for Reducing Avoidable Surprises*. Cambridge University Press. Cambridge UK.

DNV, (2013a). Report – QRA for Skangass LNG plant. Ferry bunkering project. Available from: http://dsbinfo.no/Global/3.%20QRA.pdf. Accessed 12 March 2017.

DNV, (2013b). Appendix A Assumption register. Available from: http://dsbinfo. no/Global/7%20Vedlegg%20A.pdf. Accessed 12 March 2017.

Flage, R. and Aven, T. (2009). Expressing and communicating uncertainty in relation to quantitative risk analysis. *Reliability and Risk Analysis: Theory and Application*, 2(13), 9–18.

Funtowicz, S.O. and Ravetz, J.R. (1990). *Uncertainty and Quality in Science for Policy* (Vol. 15). Springer Science & Business Media.

Funtowicz, S.O. and Ravetz, J.R. (1991). A new scientific method for global environmental issues. In: R. Costanza (ed.) *Ecological Economics: The Science and Management of Sustainability*. New York, Columbia University Press.

Kloprogge, P., van der Sluijs, J.P. and Petersen, A.C. (2011). An environmental modelling and software method for the analysis of assumptions in model-based environmental assessments. *Environmental Modelling and Software*, 26(3), 289–301.

Pender, S. (1999). Managing incomplete knowledge: Why risk management is not sufficient. *International Journal of Project Management*, 19, 79–87.

Risbey, J.S., van der Sluijs, J.P. and Ravetz, J.R. (2001). Protocol for assessment of uncertainty and strength of emission data. Report no. E-2001–10. Department of Science Technology and Society, Utrecht University, Utrecht. Available at: http://dspace.library.uu.nl/bitstream/handle/1874/7870/e2001–10. pdf?sequence=1. Accessed 9 February 2015.

Schofield, S. (1998). Offshore QRA and the ALARP principle. *Reliability Engineering and System Safety*, 61(1), 31–37.

Schneider, S.H. and Moss, R. (1999). Uncertainties in the IPCC TAR: Recommendations to lead authors for more consistent assessment and reporting. Unpublished document.

SRA (2015). SRA Glossary. Available at: http://www.sra.org/sites/default/files/ pdf/SRA-glossary-approved22june2015-x.pdf.

van der Sluijs, J.P., Janssen, P.H.M., Petersen, A.C., *et al.* (2004). RIVM/MNP guidance for uncertainty assessment and communication: tool catalogue for uncertainty assessment. Utrecht University. ISBN 90–393–3797–7 Available at: http://www.nusap.net/download.php?op=MostPopular&ratenum=50&ratetype =num. Accessed 9 February 2015.

van der Sluijs, J.P., Craye, M., Funtowicz, S., *et al.* (2005a). Combining quantitative and qualitative measures of uncertainty in model based environmental assessment: the NUSAP system. *Risk Analysis*, 25(2), 481–492.

van der Sluijs, J.P., Craye, M., Funtowicz S., Kloprogge, P. and Ravetz, J. (2005b). Experiences with the NUSAP system for multidimensional uncertainty assessment. *Water Science and Technology*, 52(6), 133–144.

van der Sluijs, J. (2006). Uncertainty, assumptions and value commitments in the knowledge base of complex environmental problems. *Interfaces between Science and Society*, 1(48), 64–81.

Wardekker, J.A., van der Sluijs, J.P., Janssen, P.H., Kloprogge, P. and Petersen, A.C. (2008). Uncertainty communication in environmental assessments: views from the Dutch science-policy interface. *Environmental Science and Policy*, 11(7), 627–641.

Appendix

Table A3.1 Assumption setting classification justifications for example assumptions.

ID	Assumption subject	Assumption specification	Assumed value	Setting	Setting classification justifications***
A	Ignition sources: hot work	Duration of hot work performed during bunkering	0	I	BiD (L): It is expected that personnel follow internal procedures. Also, potential hot work can easily be carried out either before or after bunkering of LNG, which takes place only once per day for a duration of 1.5h (according to the design). Sens. (L): "Overall effect is a key influence on the risks, but not sensitive to any particular ignition source." SoK (S): The design basis is considered a reliable source of information.
B	Ignition sources: people	Default frequency of ignition from sources associated with people [per person per second of cloud exposure]	1.68E-4	II	BiD (L): Assumed value is considered conservative (a factor 4 higher than that given in a joint industry project ignition study referred to in the assumption register). Sens. (L): "Overall effect is a key influence on the risks, but not sensitive to any particular ignition source." SoK (M/W): Probability value used is a "default" value within the software used, and not based on site-specific considerations.
C	Manning level and distribution	Number of people directly involved in the bunkering operation	4	IIIa	BiD (L): There is no reason to believe that the number of personnel involved in the bunkering operation will exceed the number of personnel designated to that task. Sens. (M/H): "Societal risks are directly influenced by the numbers of personnel exposed to hazardous events and hence the results are sensitive to the manning assumptions." SoK (S): Manning plans are considered a reliable source of information.

(Continued)

Table A3.1 (Continued)

ID	Assumption subject	Assumption specification	Assumed value	Setting	Setting classification justifications***
D	Manning level and distribution	Number of people in different categories (LNG plant employees, neighbours, ferry terminal employees, ferry passengers, hikers, etc.) exposed to increased risk due to the bunkering	Ref. Table 2 in DNV (2013a)	IVa	BiD (L): The number of people in different categories can deviate, but it is expected that the average over the different categories will remain more or less stable. Sens. (M/H): "Societal risks are directly influenced by the numbers of personnel exposed to hazardous events and hence the results are sensitive to the manning assumptions. Key influence on societal risk/FAR." SoK (M/W): Varying strength of knowledge base for specification of exposed individuals in the different categories.
E	Meteoro-logical data	Solar flux in case of a leak [W/m^2]	100	IIIb	BiD (M/H): Assumed value is considered a representative value, but the solar flux varies significant (e.g. "maximum solar flux (i.e. midday midsummer) is about 1320 W/m^2". Sens. (L): "Representative conditions used – relevant to consequences, with relatively minor influence on subsequent risks." SoK (S): Well-known phenomenon and recognized models used.

F	Release sizes	Representative hole sizes for small (<10 mm), medium (10–50 mm) and large (>50 mm) leak sizes	"To be calculated by LEAK [software tool]" (i.e. not specified in assumption register)	IVb	BiD (M/H): Some deviation potential present ("Nevertheless, the representative nature of each release size should be recognised."). Sens. (L): "The release size taken as representative is a key factor in the release parameters and subsequent consequences in each case. However, the use of representative releases is inherent in QRA and the frequencies are assigned according to each of the defined leak size ranges, such that the overall risks should not be sensitive to the specific values selected." SoK (M/W): Using three leak categories judged as a moderate simplification.
G	No assumptions made in the QRA	—	Setting V	V	BiD (M/H): — Sens. (M/H): — SoK (S): —
H	Detection and isolation times	Time to detection and isolation of a leak (seconds)	90	VI	BiD (M/H): Assumed values are considered realistic but there is judged to be a moderate potential for exceedance. Sens. (M/H): "The detection and isolation assumptions are key influences on the release duration and impact on the selection of representative release rates. On balance, any specific inventory assumption will have a limited influence on the overall risks, although the inventory is a key parameter with respect to the detailed modelling of each scenario." SoK (M/W): Disagreement between stakeholders on detection and isolation times to be used.

BiD, belief in deviation; Sens., sensitivity. SoK: strength of knowledge; L, low; M/H, moderate/high; S, strong; M/W, moderate/weak.

* Based on, or quotes taken from, DNV (2013b).

** Classifications performed by Berner and Flage (2017), based on the written sources (DNV 2013a; 2013b).

4

Critical Slowing-down Framework for Monitoring Early Warning Signs of Surprise and Unforeseen Events

Ivan Damnjanovic[1] and Terje Aven[2]

[1] *Texas A&M University*
[2] *University of Stavanger, Norway*

A description of risk is fundamentally linked to knowledge of system behavior and associated modeling assumptions. However, the validity of these assumptions is difficult to express. The validity needs to be addressed to adequately understand, assess, and manage risk, in particular the risk related to potential surprises and unforeseen events. This chapter presents a general framework to assess the validity of the assumptions about a system's future behavior, the aim being to provide early warnings. The framework is based on a signal processing approach that monitors for a statistical signature of a critical slowing down, a signal that is associated with a pending change in system behavior. Several examples are included to illustrate the framework and its analogy with the way humans and other living beings read warnings.

4.1   Introduction

Risk analysis is an essential part of the planning process. Regardless of whether we plan a summer vacation, the replacement of a valve on an offshore platform, or highly complex operations in projects such as the Mars Exploration Rover mission, we go through the same process of imagining the situations that can lead to damage, loss, and other forms of distress. We use data, information, and other available evidence to develop a model representation of the system and its environment. In fact, it is this model, conceptual and/or mathematical, upon which we build a description of risk (Covello and Mumpower 1985).

However, the model is only an approximation of reality. It is based on various assumptions and simplifications of the processes that govern the system behavior. Therefore, a description of risk is inherently conditioned on the

Knowledge in Risk Assessment and Management, First Edition. Edited by Terje Aven and Enrico Zio.
© 2018 John Wiley & Sons Ltd. Published 2018 by John Wiley & Sons Ltd.

model assumptions, which reflect the current state of knowledge (K). More formally, and in general terms, the risk description can be written as (A,C,Q|K), where, A represents the considered event, C the considered consequences, and Q is a measure of uncertainty in a broad sense (Beard 2004).

Consider a probability triple (outcome space, event set, and probability measure) that defines a risk description in a more narrow sense. Given that the model is just an approximation of the reality based on background knowledge, the sample space and the event set can never be defined with the absolute certainty. In other words, if the behavior is unpredictable, there is nothing to assure us that the list of outcomes/events is exhaustive, and that unforeseen events are not possible. Moreover, if the event set is incomplete, how confident are we in the probability judgments? Can we expect surprises? Clearly, the background knowledge is a source of risk, and consequently must be explicitly accounted for in a description of risk as schematically indicated by writing (A,C,Q,K) (Aven 2014).

However, explicitly defining the state of background knowledge in risk description is a challenging task. A recent study (Aven 2013a) aims to address this problem by providing a general data–information–knowledge–wisdom (DIKW) framework that requires an explicit account of the assumptions upon which the analysis is conducted. Flage and Aven (2009) proposed a direct method of grading the strength of knowledge on a scale from weak to strong, while Aven (2013b) introduced a score-based measure that captures deviations from the conditions or states used in the assumptions. Similarly, a "numeral, unit, spread, assessment and pedigree" (NUSAP) system initially developed by Funtowicz and Ravetz (1990) aims to represent the confidence in the background knowledge for the purpose of management and communication of uncertainty in science for policy.

The assessment of the strength of knowledge plays a critical role in robust and adaptive analysis of systems that are characterized by deep uncertainty (Linkov *et al.* 2006). Even though these analyses emphasize the dynamic nature of making decisions, they provide little or no contribution to assessment of the strength of knowledge and validity of the assumptions. Validation processes (Sornette *et al.* 2007) offer a basis for incorporating new information for the assessment of model assumptions. However, the focus is limited to the previously identified models and assumptions, and not the state of knowledge about the system's behavior and early warning signs. Alternatively, there are a number of methods developed to provide early warnings of failure (Weick *et al.* 1999), yet these do not provide a link between the observed signals and warnings on one side, and knowledge of the system's behavior on the other side. What is missing is a framework that will link observations and knowledge to early warning signs.

This chapter presents a framework to develop early warnings of surprising and unforeseen events (EWS-SUE), using a system's time-series data and signal-processing methods. The framework is based on the notion that the changes in the system's operating regime are often associated with unknown and unpredictable future behavior; in other words where there is a lack of confidence in the original assumptions and previous knowledge. The proposed approach does not define a dynamic measure of the strength of the knowledge directly, but rather focuses on capturing early warning signs (that is, abductive anomalies) that the system is about to undergo a critical transition. In other words, we focus on developing a monitoring process that can warn us about potentially unknown and unanticipated behavior.

The approach of critical transitioning is closely related to the method of statistical process control: both aim to capture early signs of anomalies in data that may be indicative of changes in the system behavior and the emergence of a new equilibrium. However, the proposed framework is more general, because it originates from the universal principles of dynamic system behavior and is free from assumptions such as exchangeability, which is a concept used in Bayesian analysis and reflects similarity of units.

Note also that the proposed method does not aim to replace traditional methods for accounting for new information to update probability judgements and select models (that is, Bayesian methods); rather, it aims to complement existing methods by providing a tool to detect early signs of surprising and unforeseen events. We suggest building on the Bayesian approach to update parameters and select models (Carlin and Louis 1997); the proposed critical transition framework is a high-level screening of the validity of the underlying assumptions.

In the next section we present an overview of the key dynamic properties of a system for which we want to define and monitor risk. We use a simple oscillator as an example of how to describe a system's phase space and potential function. This brief introduction to dynamic systems allows us then to present the concept that is fundamental to the proposed framework – the concept of critical slowing down.

4.2 System Dynamics and Critical Slowing-down Signals

All active systems generate data in the form of a time series, a sequence of data representing the time evolution of system's observations. While in the eyes of a layman these data appear to be random and insignificant, in reality they often provide important information about future behavior of the system (Katok and Hasselblatt 1997).

Consider a simple harmonic oscillator, such as a ball suspended on an elastic string, as an example of a system that generates time-series data (see Figure 4.1). Subjected to external force F (Figure 4.1a), the system will move away from the

(a)   (b)   (c)

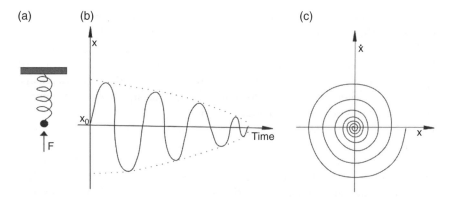

Figure 4.1 Damped harmonic oscillator: (a) oscillator, (b) original signal, (c) phase space.

initial equilibrium point x_0, generate a signal $x(t)$, and gradually settle back to the same point x_0 at time T (Figure 4.1b). Based on data in Figure 4.1b, we can (re)constitute a phase space of the system; that is, all possible states of a system (see Figure 4.1c). For example, the state of the oscillator is uniquely defined by its speed ($\dot{x}$) and position (x). If the system is in state ($\dot{x}, x$) then the phase space fully defines a unique trajectory of the system evolution from that point. In other words, if we know state ($\dot{x}, x$) then we can fully predict the future behavior.

One can also see from Figure 4.1-b that the system's trajectory can be bounded. Let us assume that lower and upper boundary can be represented by a function $V(t)$. If we rotate Figure 4.1b through 90° clockwise, and extend the representation to include a third dimension, then the system appears to behave as a ball rolling down on the surface of an upside-down cone defined by $V(t)$ rotated around the x-axis. In fact, if one knows this surface, then all possible states of the system are fully defined. For example, the system states could never go beyond the boundary set by $V(t)$ because the boundary is defined by the system configuration: the length of the string, its elastic properties and so on. We refer to this function as the system's potential function. In fact, the behavior of all dynamic systems can be characterized by such functions.

For generic dynamic systems one can visualize the potential function as a complex "spatial geography" of valleys, hills, and mountains, where the system moves on the path of the maximum decrease in potential energy (that is, the steepest descent), settling at the local minima, and then being perturbed by external forces to another hilltop. These valleys are often referred to as "orbits", and the lowest point in the orbit as an "attractor point". Guckenheimer and Holmes (1983) provide a more formal description of dynamic systems and potential functions.

Dynamic systems are constantly subject to random perturbations which make the process of determining the potential functions and locations of the attractor points difficult. In such situations, where one cannot fully describe the potential function along all possible states, we rely on the analysis of the neighborhood in which the system is currently operating. By using rolling-window time-series statistics, such as autocorrelation and variance, or spectral analysis in the frequency domain, one can, at best, approximate the potential function in the neighborhood in which the system is currently operating, and there look for the universal statistical signature of critical slowing down (Scheffer *et al.* 2012), to be explained in the following.

We explain the phenomenon of critical slowing down by focusing on the potential functions of two distinctively different systems: a system that is far from the transition and the system that is close to the transition. Figure 4.2 illustrates the potential functions of the two systems and the associated time-series metrics. In part (a) the system is characterized by a "deep basin" of attraction, with steep slopes around the equilibrium point. Such systems, subjected to stochastic perturbations, will promptly return to the equilibrium point. In other words, the system is resilient to perturbations. The time-series statistics (that is, variance and autocorrelation of lag 1) show behavior that is consistent with the system being in a stable orbit: the variance and correlation are constant and relatively low.

The system in part (b), however, is at an equilibrium point with a relatively flat basin of attraction. Subjected to stochastic perturbations, this system will slowly return to the equilibrium point. Therefore, even minor disturbances can take the system to the saddle point and into a new basin of attraction that may be associated with fundamentally different system behavior. Figure 4.2 also shows the statistical signatures of these two systems' topologies. Far away from the transition point, where the topology is characterized as a deep basin, the system exhibits lower autocorrelation and variance; close to transitions, where the topology is characterized as a shallow basin, the system shows an increase in variance and autocorrelation, as well as longer recovery times (Scheffer *et al.* 2009; Dakos *et al.* 2012).

In fact, some of the general principles of critical transitioning have already found applications in reliability analysis and safety engineering. For example, recovery-time models are often used in vibration analysis of rotary equipment to identify changed operating conditions (Eisenmann 1998). Similarly, acoustic monitoring devices are used to analyze pressure-relief valves and warn against potential failure (Fletcher 1993). Even though these and similar approaches (Ellestad 1986; Peria *et al.* 2001) are largely empirical, their development can be traced back the fundamental principles of dynamic systems and the critical slowing-down concept.

In summary, the phase space and the potential functions can provide a detailed structure of how systems change over time. This framework implies

(a)

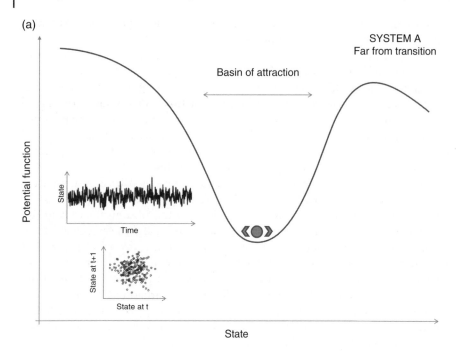

(b)

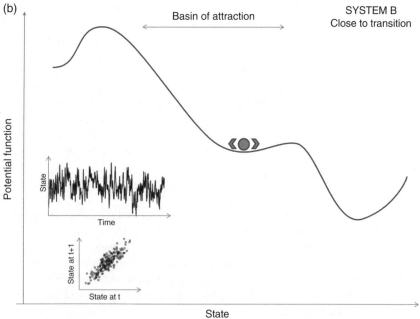

Figure 4.2 Statistical patterns of critical transitions: (a) system far from transition, (b) system close to transition.

the existence of universal pattern (the critical slowing down) as systems move away from the previous attractors and approach new ones. This is precisely the point where a link between system-wide observations, "abduction anomalies" in the form of critical slowing down, and knowledge of system behavior can be established. In other words, if the time-series metrics from the system observations indicate a pending transition to a new attractor that has not been previously accounted for or anticipated (that is, a signal anomaly) in the background knowledge, then such an event constitutes an abductive anomaly and provides an early warning sign that surprises may be about to occur.

4.2.1   Signal Anomalies as Early Warning Signs

To understand the general problem of developing early warning signs for surprise and unforeseen events (EWS-SUE) based on signal processing and critical slowing down, one first needs to consider the nature of the risk-description process itself. This process can be viewed in two modes – the prediction mode, where the initial description is developed, and the observation mode, where we use observations to assess the validity of the initial assumptions. In the prediction mode, we adopt assumptions based on the current state of knowledge, and then proceed to develop a model of the system behavior. The predicted system behavior represents the foundation upon which the risk description is built. Note that the term "system model" can be interpreted in a broad sense, encompassing both experts' mental constructs and mathematical formulations.

In the observation mode, on the other hand, we collect data signals and consequently gain or lose confidence that our "system model" is an accurate representation of the reality. Note that this is fundamentally in line with the Bayesian paradigm, where new information is used to update our prior beliefs. However, rather than applying it in a narrow context of the event probabilities or model selection, the analysis should be set in the context of the knowledge about the system's behavior. To do so, one first needs to understand what system observations contradict our belief (assumptions or model) of how the system should behave.

The scientific method provides a general framework for acquiring new and correcting previous knowledge from observations (Crowell 1937). Peirce (1935) defines the scientific method as spiral interplay among the methods of reasoning: deduction, induction, and abduction. The process starts with abduction: formation of a hypothesis about the observed phenomenon or anomaly. This is followed by a set of deductive inferences, and concluded with experimental observations to test the candidate hypothesis.

How can one then develop early-warning signs based on the scientific method? The answer to this question is hidden in the very first step of the scientific method: detecting an anomaly in the signal (that is, an abductive anomaly). The presence of an anomaly in the system signals challenges our knowledge. It makes us worried and shatters our confidence in our capacity to predict future system behavior. In fact, it is a warning sign that our knowledge is inconsistent with the observations and a warning sign of potential surprises and unforeseen events.

4.3   EWS-SUE Monitoring Framework

In this section we present the proposed framework, linking the system signals, time-series statistics, and the critical slowing-down pattern to the background knowledge. As a result, the risk description becomes time dependent, not only in a narrow context of updating probability judgments, but also in a larger context of using the system's signals to update our confidence in the background knowledge and provide early warning signs of surprises and unforeseen events (EWS-SUE).

Figure 4.3 illustrates the proposed monitoring framework. The first step of this process is to provide a high-level description of the situation. This includes identifying the system and specifying the signals that are to be monitored. Defining the knowledge about the underlying system is the next step. This is important to identify the discrepancy between the signal that is observed and the signal that is anticipated. Following this, we provide a formal description of the abductive anomaly as an inconsistency between the observed signal and the signal that is anticipated based on our knowledge. The risk description that

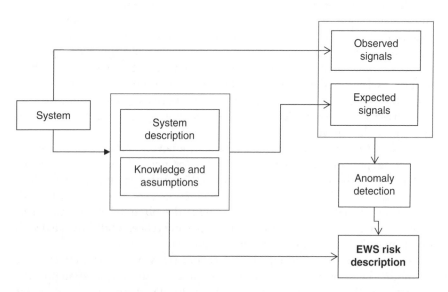

Figure 4.3 Overview of EWS-SUE monitoring framework.

specifies early warning signs of surprise and unforeseen events is presented next. This signal-dependent description of the risk is the central point of the proposed monitoring framework. It links the previous efforts in developing descriptions based on background knowledge (Aven 2014) to the signals, time series statistics, and the pattern of critical slowing down.

4.3.1 The System

Assume that the behavior of the larger system **S** is subjected to a risk assessment. For example, we would like to assess the risks associated with an offshore drilling unit. From the systems theory point of view, the behavior of system **S** is defined by its internal characteristics: the technical features of the unit, including the organizational processes, and their characteristics as developed to operate the unit. Therefore, the background knowledge K that supports a description of risk (A,C,Q,K) can be expressed in terms of the knowledge K about the system of interest.

Let us also assume that system **S** is an active operating system; in other words, the system **S** is engaged with its environment and generates response data. For example, the operating offshore drilling unit will generate a stream of observables, such as spatial movements, fluid flows, strains, stresses, and vibration measurements, as well as organizational and human behavior observables such as activities, events, and communication logs. We will refer to these as observed system signals $x(t)$.

4.3.2 System Description: Knowledge and Assumptions

Without loss of generality, we assume that the knowledge about the system behavior K can be expressed by a set of basic representations – such as logic, rules, frames, and nets – that enables inferences to be made about the system behavior (Brachman and Levesque 2004). This formulation of knowledge is adopted from the field of artificial intelligence and is flexible enough to account for various assumptions and model specifications.

Definition 4.1 (Knowledge representation): Knowledge K is a pair (B, I) where B is a set of basic representations (i.e. rules) of the system behavior and I is a set of sanctioned inferences over B.

To illustrate this, consider the behavior of the damped oscillator in Figure 4.1. How do we present the knowledge of such a relatively simple system? First, we need to derive the basic rules of behavior. The key behavioral rules of such system come from the basic laws of physics: Hook's law describes the relationship between weight of the ball, the perturbation force, and the characteristics of the spring and dampening mechanisms, and the position, speed, and acceleration of the oscillating ball. Given this set of behavioral rules and formulas one can now make inferences about the behavior of the oscillator in an open environment. For example, we can infer that upon an external perturbation the oscillator will return to equilibrium state if no additional force is applied to the system.

Consider now more complex system behavior, such as the structural behavior of a semi-submersible platform. Similar to the oscillator example, the basic set of rules for this system is derived from the laws of applied physics: fluid dynamics, system stability, hydrostatics, hydrodynamics, and others. In essence, this basic set of rules is directly related to the equations and models that were used to design the structure; in other words, during the design process we use a basic representation to simulate the behavior of a structure under different loading scenarios. Furthermore, the output of this simulation process is a sanctioned inference over the basic representation. The same logic can also be used for the human and organizational behavior – we use basic behavior models, such as responses to incentives or working in teams, to define the outcome of activities.

Now that we have defined the system knowledge K(B,I), which system signals are consistent with it, and which ones are not?

4.3.3 System Signals and Detecting Abductive Anomalies

To answer this question, we first need to provide definitions that are required to formally link the knowledge representation to the expected signal and the statistics used for detecting anomaly.

Definition 4.2 (Consistency of signal with background knowledge): A system signal $x(t)$ is said to be consistent with knowledge K if it can be inferred from the system's basic representation. We refer to this as the expected or anticipated signal given the current knowledge about the system K(B,I).

To explain this further, let us continue with the two previous examples: the oscillator and the offshore platform. After the oscillator is impacted by force F, it is expected to generate a sinusoidal damped signal in the position of the ball at time $x(t)$, as shown in Figure 4.1. If the signal follows the rules defined in K(B,I), then we say that it is consistent with what we know about how the oscillator should behave when subjected to force F.

Now consider an offshore platform. It generates a vector of system response signals $x(t)$. We say that the signal $x(t)$ is consistent with the knowledge K if these vibrations can be inferred from the defined rules; that is, the equations. For example, subjected to hydrodynamic loading the platform will produce vibrations within a specific range of amplitudes and frequencies similar to the output of the design simulations; if the observed signal confirms this, then we can claim that the signal is consistent with what we know about hydrodynamic vibrations in offshore structures.

Definition 4.3 (Abductive anomaly in signal): The observed signal over time interval $x(t)$, implies an abductive anomaly A if and only if it is inconsistent over K.

Inconsistency of the signal represents an instance of the failure of the background knowledge to fully explain the behavior of the system. In fact, such inconsistent observations define the first step in the scientific process, where the hypotheses, sometimes also referred to as abductables, are formulated and tested. The ultimate result of this process is new knowledge and a revised set of basic representations and inferences $K^*(B,I)$, now consistent with all observations including the newly detected anomaly.

For example, if the oscillator starts generating a non-cyclical signal, then we can say that the signal is not consistent with the knowledge representation and the rules derived from Hook's law. Similarly, if the vibrations in an offshore platform cannot be reproduced based on the laws used in its design, then we have an instance of a phenomenon that is not captured by the current rules $K(B,I)$. Hence, this phenomenon requires further investigation to enable us to update and/or revise what we know about the system behavior. In other words, we need to initiate the scientific method.

However, these changes in the system behavior are often associated with immediate adverse events. For example, the occurrence of severe vibrations is itself a sign of imminent structural failure, which is obviously too late to allow any meaningful mitigation measures. What is needed are early warnings that the system behavior has changed *before* we observe such severe vibrations. More specifically, we need system indicators that can capture hidden changes in the signals before they become inconsistent with the knowledge. The universal principle of critical slowing specifies such statistics and patterns (Scheffer *et al.* 2012).

Definition 4.4 (Abductive anomaly as early warning sign): Let $Y(x(t))$ be a vector of the time series statistics of a signal $x(t)$. Then $Y(x(t))$ represents an early warning abductive anomaly if it is in contradiction with the expected signal statistics $Y_{K(B,I)}(x(t))$ inferred from K.

First, it is important to distinguish between the signal $x(t)$ and the signal statistics $Y(x(t))$. The signal metrics represent the statistical properties of the signal, such as autocorrelation, mean, variance, and other higher-order moments of the time series given a rolling window interval. For example, if we consider the offshore platform example, the platform vibrations constitute the signal $x(t)$, while the mean, variance, and autocorrelation of the vibration signal represent the signal statistics $Y(x(t))$. Which signal statistics $Y(x(t))$ then represent an early warning abductive anomaly? In other words, when do these statistics contradict the expected signal statistics $Y_{K(B,I)}(x(t))$ inferred from K? In short, the early warning abductive anomaly occurs when the system shows an early sign of unanticipated transiency. In fact, before changing from one operating regime to another, the systems will show a specific "signature" in the signal statistics, such as increased autocorrelation and variance. If such a transition is not anticipated and is inconsistent with the background knowledge, then it represents an indicator of an unknown attractor and by extension an unknown behavior.

Consider the oscillator we used as an example in Figure 4.1. Assume we observe an abductive anomaly in its speed and position $(\dot{x}, x)$: the ball's signal shows a critical slowing-down sign when it is at the lowest point; that is, when the elastic string is fully extended. Certainly we do not expect to see this behavior based what is specified in K(B,I). While we may have thought that an event such as the failure of the elastic string could occur, we certainly would not think it very likely and therefore we did not include it on the list of the risks that require continuous monitoring. If the string fails and the ball falls down on the floor, the event might come to us a surprise; but was it really? Before the event occurred, one could have detected an abductive anomaly with the respect to what is defined in K(B,I). In other words, the abductive anomaly in the system's signal provides an early warning sign that surprises are possible.

Now we can update the risk description to include the early warning signs. Definition 4.5 provides such a description by explicitly accounting for the knowledge representation and abductive anomalies in signal observations.

Definition 4.5 (Risk description with early warning signs of surprises and unforeseen events): Let A be a set of events and C a set of consequences generated by the system S; also let K(B,I) represent the background knowledge about the system(s) behavior, and Q represent a measure of the uncertainty about A and C interpreted in a broad sense. Then, the description of risk at the time of observation of a signal $x(t)$ can be specified as $[A, C, Q, K(B,I), x(t), Y(x(t)), Y_{K(B,I)}(x(t))]$.

This description takes into account early warnings, in the context of observed and anticipated signal statistics $[Y(x(t)), Y_{K(B,I)}(x(t))]$. As new signals are observed, their time-series statistics are analyzed to detect the signature of critical slowing down. If such a signature is not expected from the background knowledge, then it represents an early warning sign of surprise and unforeseen events (EWS-SUE).

Next we show that this framework is intuitive and consistent with how living beings read and interpret signals. In fact, this chapter presents a more formal definition of reading signals in the context of risk assessment and monitoring using the analogy of human intuition.

4.4   Illustrative Examples

We provide three examples that illustrate the proposed framework of using system signals and the critical slowing-down signature statistics as early warning signs of surprises and unforeseen events. In the first example (Hans the hiker), we illustrate that the proposed approach is similar to situational awareness analyses used by hikers, among others, to monitor signals from the physical environment. In the second example (Lars the football player), we show that introspection techniques such as recovery-time to assess the potential for health surprises is based on the same principle. Finally, in the third example (Susan the engineer), we show that the application of situational awareness protocols could provide warning of unforeseen events.

4.4.1   Hans the Hiker and Avalanche Risk

Hans is an amateur hiker. He enjoys spending weekends out of the city, hiking in the Alps. For hikers and mountain climbers such as Hans, the risk of avalanches is understood.

Hans' pre-hike routine mimics a general risk assessment process. He starts the process by identifying potential risk events, and then proceeds to assign subjective judgements about their likelihood. The set of events included covers both internal system events such as equipment failure and external system events such as avalanches. However, Hans is more confident of some probability judgments than others. For example, he is quite confident in his judgement of the likelihood of equipment failure; on the other hand, he is unsure about the weather conditions and relies on the national weather services to provide this judgement. Before heading out to the mountains, Hans' risk description takes the form (A,C,Q,K), where A represents the events, C the consequences, Q is a general measure of uncertainty, and K is his knowledge supporting Q, A, and C, covering for example the responses of the important "systems", such as how he acts when he is tired, how snow and rock move under his feet, how wind affects his climbing, and so on.

In addition, Hans' training as a hiker and mountain climber includes the concept of situational awareness – the state of mind that emphasizes constant monitoring of the environment $x(t)$ using the senses, such as hearing, vision, and smell. Hence, Hans' description of the environment encompasses sounds, images, and scents that the environment generates over time. In other words, Hans' risk description includes constant monitoring of the signals and their validation against the expected signals, as derived from rules defined by his background knowledge K(B,I). For example, sounds of running mountain streams, images of peaceful snow-covered slopes, and fresh scents from pine forests fit his background knowledge and therefore are expected signals. If the signal shows a contradiction with his previous knowledge, then this makes him think twice about the situation. In fact, Hans' dynamic picture of risks while hiking is analogous to the formulation given in Definition 4.5.

Hans starts the hiking day early in the morning. The sun has just come out, and the sky is clear. It is not cold. In fact, the weather is just perfect for hiking. However, as he is putting his shoes on, he hears a remote humming sound. "Strange", he thinks, but the sound continues. Suddenly, Hans starts to feel uneasy about the situation. He moves around the area to locate the source of sound, but he sees nothing unusual. Nevertheless, he decides to get into the car and drive away. One hour later he comes back to the site to find it under snow. An unlikely local avalanche has occurred. If he had stayed, he would have died. However, his training in situational awareness prepared him to react to an unusual signal from the environment, and to abandon the location.

The avalanche is an event that stems from a change in system equilibrium. When the event is initialized, the flowing snow mass generates sound waves that lie in the infrasonic frequency range between 0.001 and 20 Hz (Bedard 1989). This frequency range is below audible limit of the human ear and can propagate over large distances. However, frequencies close to 20 Hz are sometimes detected as humming sounds, or by the impact they have on the human nervous system. Hans was lucky to have paid attention to this signal and to react to it. In practice, the human capacity to detect these signals is limited. The majority of the new early warning systems for avalanches are based on infrasound sensors, which detecting an increase in the density of the lower frequencies in the signal spectra (Thüring *et al.* 2015).

In summary, Hans' early warning system follows the same principles proposed in this chapter: a risk description that explicitly takes into account background knowledge, monitoring of system signals, and a method for detecting inconsistency – abductive anomalies in the signal. Note also that Hans didn't have a detailed risk monitoring model for avalanche risk, nor did he use data to update the probability of the event in a Bayesian manner. He relied on a macro-level monitoring of the system acoustic signals and inferred from an emerging pattern that the environment was changing – surprises were possible.

4.4.2 Lars the Football Player and Heart Attack Risk

Lars is a 60-year-old university professor. He has been in good health most of his life and is physically active. Lars plays a friendly game of soccer every Friday afternoon with his graduate students and fellow faculty. In fact, Lars is very passionate about soccer, as he used to play it professionally in his twenties.

Even though Lars' physician has recommended this activity, he has also warned him not to "chase every ball", as he (Lars) is "not in his twenties anymore". Lars understands this in general. After all, it takes him some time to recover after climbing four flights of stairs from the parking lot of his apartment building to the fourth floor where his flat is located.

Lars has an informal risk description of his everyday life activities. He thinks of the events that could cause him harm, injury, or any other type of distress, and then makes subjective judgments on the likelihood of these events. His assessment of risk is based on a set of rules derived from both experience and a formal learning process (from books, articles, conversation, and so on). In other words, Lars has a risk description that takes the form (A,C,Q,K). But, more importantly, Lars engages his senses, such as pains and his heart rate, and makes inferences from this information.

Recently, Lars has noticed that his heartbeat rate $x(t)$ increases even after "normal activities" such as walking up a hill. He attributes this to lack of more rigorous exercise. In fact, Lars remembers coming back from a summer vacation to his soccer team training camp in terrible condition. It took him a week or so to get back into shape. So, Lars decides to add a Wednesday run to his Friday soccer. However, after running about two laps around the stadium, Lars stops to catch his breath. Now, his heartbeat is very high and it takes him more than half an hour to recover. Lars realizes something is not right, so he calls the doctor who ultimately diagnoses a heart condition. This came as a big surprise to Lars.

Cardiac recovery time test is an effective method for measuring the general physical condition of a patient. It is part of a larger cardiac stress test, in which patients are subjected to an external stress in a controlled clinical environment (Ellestad 1986). The general premise of the test is that an increase in recovery time is associated with abnormalities in coronary circulation (that is, a change in the system's operating regime).

In summary, Lars, like all of us, is constantly monitoring signals from his body (his internal system). We do not run complex diagnostic tests on a continuous basis; rather, we monitor body signals such as heartbeat, pressure, temperature, pain, skin condition, and so on. We may not know what is wrong, but through this observation, an introspection process, we can get an early warning that the system operating regime is changing.

4.4.3 Susan the Engineer and Poisoning Risk

Susan is an engineer who works in an office building. In order to make the working environment more stimulating and engaging, the facility manager has started a program of distributing fruit and sparkling water to the offices. Susan loves this office perk and her productivity has increased ever since the program started, about two years ago.

Susan considers the supply of sparkling water as highly reliable and safe. In fact, she does not even think about it. Every morning around 9 am, an office staff member brings a bottle of sparkling water and a bowl of fruit to her desk.

It is 9 am on Monday morning. Susan is at the office after spending the weekend visiting friends from high school. Susan notices that the basket of fresh fruit and a bottle of sparkling water has been placed on the table. She feels happy about this, because recently the delivery of fruit and sparkling water has not been as reliable as in past. Susan drinks the water. Around 10 am a colleague from a nearby office finds Susan in excruciating pain, lying on the floor. By noon, Susan has been transferred to an emergency room and diagnosed with acute poisoning. This was not something Susan could have ever have anticipated or foreseen.

Susan's general knowledge about the system that governs office facility operations is based on her experience with it. It is this knowledge that she relied upon in evaluating potential risks. While Susan was aware that the environment and systems embedded in it could cause some harm (say falling objects, transmittable diseases such as flu, or poor indoor air quality), she did not foresee the possibility of being poisoned by drinking a glass of sparkling water.

Did Susan have a chance to do something about it? Were there any early warning signs that she could have acted upon?

Susan's office is embedded in an environment comprising multiple systems that serve as a support to the mission of her organization: there are janitorial staff, maintenance crew, administrative support staff, an IT office, engineers, accountants, and so on. In the past, the system for delivering water to her desk has performed perfectly. There was nothing to worry about when drinking from the bottle. In other words, her description of risk (A,C,Q,K) did not include the event that occurred.

The water bottles are distributed to the offices by a specific crew. The sparkling water is poured from a trusted source (a faucet on the second floor) by a crew member and then delivered by another person to all the offices. This crew has a number of additional tasks. In fact, water delivery is only a minor role of the crew, which also has a janitorial role, cleaning the offices and bathroom, vacuuming, and so on. The water supply system that operates in Susan's environment is therefore only a part of a larger janitorial system. This janitorial system operates under specific environmental conditions depending on weather patterns – for example, on rainy days when the janitorial staff have to work harder to clean mud that this brought into the building. This system is also subject to constant perturbations: small variations in procedures due, say, to someone being late, bottles being missing or dirty, and so on. Recently, due to management cost-cutting measures, the size of the office operations staff was reduced.

So how did this poisoning happen? Jack, a member of the janitorial staff, failed to show up for work Monday morning. During his last shift on Friday, Jack was in charge of cleaning toilets. Since there was a lack of containers for mixing bleach and water in the supply room, Jack had decided to use a water bottle that someone had left in the hallway. Halfway through this task, Jack received an emergency phone call from a family member and left work. Before leaving he dumped the bottle's content in the toilet bowl, and left the empty bottle in the bathroom sink. Note that Jack is also the person who is in charge of washing the bottles in the afternoon, so that in the morning all the bottles are clean and ready to be filled and distributed. This situation was due to most recent attempt to cut the cost of operations. On Monday morning, a staff member saw the bottle left in the sink (with bleach residue), assumed it was clean, filled it, and brought it to Susan. In retrospect, we can easily describe this incident, but beforehand it was hard to even imagine the chain of events that occurred.

Susan was observant of her surroundings. She was aware of the timing of the bottle delivery and its consistency from day to day, the cleanliness of the hallways and restrooms on her floor, as well as the amount of dirt on the rug and the trash in the bin in her office. All of these observations constituted the signal $x(t)$. In fact, Susan was concerned with increased variability of the signal: the unpredictability of the water delivery and the office cleaning services. In retrospect, this was the abductive anomaly that could have prompted her to rethink the risks associated with all the functions that the particular supply chain undertook. This is not to say she could have predicted the event, but she could have applied a precautionary principle and got the water herself.

Increased variability is one of the prime characteristics of supply chains operating on the edge of their capacity (Maglio *et al.* 2007). Lack of resources and improper work-loads and procedures are revealed in the shape of erratic signals coming from the supply chain. This is similar to statistical process control, where increased variance in a system's output is indicative of a change in the operating regime.

4.5   Some Reflections on Illustrative Examples

This section provides some reflections on the characteristics of risk description we used in the examples, as well as the key challenges that Hans, Lars, and Susan were facing when implementing their system of early warning of surprises and unforeseen events. Next, we discuss some generalizations of the key framework features.

In all the three examples, the systems that are being monitored by the protagonists are active; in other words, the systems (snow-packed slopes, the human body, and the supply chain) generate signals as they engage with their environment. This is in contrast to systems that not-continuously engaged with the environment and can generate signals only when they are activated. For example, many engineered safety devices are activated only if a specific condition is met. Therefore, early warnings signs of their failure are difficult to obtain; in fact, their performance becomes observable only at the instance when their function is required. To overcome this issue, we typically institute periodic testing of the equipment, but this process provides quite different indicators of risk than those outlined in this chapter.

From the statistical point-of-view, the protagonists' use of new information differs from the narrow context of Bayesian updating of event probabilities. The emphasis is instead given to the consistency of the signal with the background knowledge. Next, we reflect on two important challenges of practically applying the developed framework.

Time-scale (lead time) The time from the first appearance of the signal of critical slowing down to the change in the system's operating regime is referred to as the lead time and varies for different systems. To be of practical use, early warning signs should be identified with an appropriate event lead time. For example, Hans and Lars had enough lead time to act upon the signal as an early warning. Even though the signal received by Susan might have been too vague, it still arrived on a time scale that would have allowed her to act upon it. In many instances, the early warning signs arrive with a very short lead time. For example, earthquakes, tsunamis, and changes in currents occur suddenly, leaving no time to make decisions. However, recent advances in automated control allow for real-time monitoring and automatic execution of the mitigation actions when a pattern is detected. For example, some avalanche information centers are directly connected with early warning emergency communication systems. Similar systems are in place for tsunami and earthquake detection.

Systems on multiple scales Monitoring critical transitions in signals can be challenging if the phenomenon and the monitoring systems are on different scales. For example, consider the "perfect storm" scenario (Paté-Cornell 2012). A fishing boat is about to head to the ocean. The boat crew has very few signals from the local environment that a "perfect storm" is brewing. They could detect an upcoming storm, but there is no indication of a "perfect storm". On the other hand, for the national weather service the signal metrics are clearly indicative of the change in operating regime. In such instances, the challenge is to enable communication among systems at different scales. Fishing crews should regularly communicate with the NWS on timescales that allow them to make proper mitigation decisions.

Despite the challenges, the proposed framework brings a number of opportunities. First and foremost, the framework links data-collection and signal-processing methods to risk analysis, in general, and risk description in particular. The implications of this approach are significant, because such a link enables development of new systems and technologies that directly link to the risk description. For example, advances in wearable technology hold out the prospect of early warning introspection processes in healthcare. Second, the proposed framework impacts some of the key principles of system design. To ensure that early warning signs are monitored, the system designer should consider active response configurations and account for lead time and system scale effects. Third, the proposed framework provides a theoretical foundation that enables cross-pollination and integration of the research methods across the two disciplines (risk analysis and signal processing).

4.6 Summary and Conclusions

This chapter presents a general framework to develop early warning signs of surprising and unforeseen events (EWS-SUE), using system time-series data and signal-processing methods. The proposed monitoring framework is based on the notion of a change in the system's operating regime and the critical slowing-down pattern.

We show that the risk description can be reformulated in such way as to include:

- a system description based on the definition of the background knowledge using K(B,I) representations from the artificial intelligence field
- system signals and associated time-series statistics
- an abductive anomaly-detection method based on the critical slowing-down signature that compares the observed system signal to the expected signal.

We argue that such an extended formulation of the risk description provides early warning signs for surprises and unforeseen events. We use some illustrative examples to show that the universal critical slowing-down framework has its manifestation in many risk assessment instances from everyday life.

In conclusion, the presented framework provides value to both system risk analysts (the risk analysis community) and system technology developers (the sensors and signal-processing community). It gives risk analysts a framework to account for background knowledge in the context of data and early warning signs of unforeseen and surprise events. To system developers, the presented framework provides a structured approach to design technologies and processes that are capable of monitoring risks using early warning signs systems.

References

Aven, T. (2013a), A conceptual framework for linking risk and the elements of the data–information–knowledge–wisdom (DIKW) hierarchy, *Reliability Engineering & System Safety*, 111, 30–36.

Aven, T. (2013b), Practical implications of the new risk perspectives. *Reliability Engineering & System Safety*, 115, 136–145.

Aven, T. (2014), *Risk, Surprises and Black Swans: Fundamental Ideas and Concepts in Risk Assessment and Risk Management*, Routledge.

Beard, A.N. (2004), Risk assessment assumptions. *Civil Engineering and Environmental Systems*, 21(1), 19–31.

Bedard, A. (1989). Detection of avalanches using atmospheric infrasound. *Proceedings of the 57th Annual Western Snow Conference*. Fort Collins CO, USA, pp. 52–58.

Brachman, R. and Levesque, H. (2004). *Knowledge Representation and Reasoning.* Elsevier.

Carlin, B.P. and Louis, T.A. (1997). Bayes and empirical Bayes methods for data analysis. Statistics and Computing, 7(2), 153–154.

Covello, V.T. and Mumpower, J. (1985), Risk analysis and risk management: An historical perspective. *Risk Analysis*, 5, 103–120.

Crowell, V.L. (1937). The scientific method. *School Science and Mathematics*, 37(5), 525–531.

Dakos, V., Carpenter, S.R., Brock, W.A., *et al.* (2012). Methods for detecting early warnings of critical transitions in time series illustrated using simulated ecological data. *PloS One*, 7(7), e41010.

Eisenmann, R.C. (1998). *Machinery Malfunction Diagnosis and Correction: Vibration Analysis And Troubleshooting For The Process Industries.* Prentice Hall.

Ellestad, M.H. (1986). Stress testing: Principles and practice. *Journal of Occupational and Environmental Medicine*, 28(11), 1142–1144.

Flage, R. and Aven, T. (2009) Expressing and communicating uncertainty in relation to quantitative risk analysis (QRA). *Reliability and Risk Analysis: Theory and Applications*, 2(13), 9–18.

Fletcher, N.H. (1993). Autonomous vibration of simple pressure-controlled valves in gas flows. *Journal of the Acoustical Society of America*, 93(4), 2172–2180.

Funtowicz, S. and Ravetz J. (1990), *Uncertainty and Quality in Science for Policy*, Kluwer Academic Publishers.

Guckenheimer, J. and Holmes, P. (1983). *Nonlinear Oscillations, Dynamical Systems, and Bifurcations of Vector Fields* (Vol. 42). Springer Science & Business Media.

Katok, A. and Hasselblatt, B. (1997). *Introduction to the Modern Theory of Dynamical Systems* (Vol. 54). Cambridge University Press.

Linkov, I., Satterstrom, F.K., Kiker, G., *et al.* (2006). From comparative risk assessment to multi-criteria decision analysis and adaptive management: Recent developments and applications. *Environment International*, 32(8), 1072–1093.

Maglio, P., Bailey, J., and Gruhl, D. (2007). Steps toward a science of service systems. *Computer*, 40, 71–77.

Paté-Cornell, E. (2012), On "Black Swans" and "Perfect Storms": Risk analysis and management when statistics are not enough. *Risk Analysis*, 32, 1823–1833.

Peirce, C.S., Hartshorne, C., and Weiss, P. (eds). (1935). *Collected Papers of Charles Sanders Peirce* (Vol. 5). Harvard University Press.

Peria, M.S.M., Majnoni, G., Blaschke, W., and Jones, M.T. (2001). Stress testing of financial systems: an overview of issues, methodologies, and FSAP experiences. International Monetary Fund.

Scheffer, M., Carpenter, S.R., Lenton, T.M., *et al.* (2012). Anticipating critical transitions. *Science*, 338(6105), 344–348.

Scheffer, M., Bascompte, J., Brock, W.A., *et al.* (2009). Early-warning signals for critical transitions. Nature, 461(7260), 53–59.

Sornette, D., Davis, A.B., Ide, K., *et al.* (2007). Algorithm for model validation: Theory and applications. *Proceedings of the National Academy of Sciences*, 104(16), 6562–6567.

Thüring, T., Schoch, M., van Herwijnen, A., and Schweizer, J. (2015). Robust snow avalanche detection using supervised machine learning with infrasonic sensor arrays. *Cold Regions Science and Technology*, 111, 60–66.

Weick, K., Sutcliffe, K. and Obstfeld, D. (1999). Organising for high reliability: processes of collective mindfulness. *Research in Organisational Behaviour*, 21, 100.

5

Improving the Foundation and Practice of Uncertainty Analysis: Strengthening Links to Knowledge and Risk

Terje Aven

University of Stavanger, Norway

To conduct an uncertainty analysis, we need to know what we are uncertain about, who is uncertain, and how we should represent or express the uncertainties. In this chapter, we present a general framework for uncertainty analysis, building on these three dimensions. The literature on uncertainty analysis is huge, but there are still challenges related to the conceptualisation and characterisation of uncertainties. The main purpose of this chapter is to contribute to improving the foundation and practice of uncertainty analysis by highlighting these three dimensions and relating uncertainty to knowledge and risk. The framework has two distinct features:

- It makes a clear distinction between uncertainty as a concept and how uncertainty is measured or described.
- It distinguishes between the uncertainty of the analysts and that of the decision makers.

The motivation for the second point is that all judgements about uncertainty are conditioned on some knowledge, and this knowledge can be more or less strong and also erroneous. Hence decision makers need to address uncertainties and risk related to this knowledge.

5.1 Introduction

There are many types of uncertainty analysis. The basic approaches, as found in most text-books in probability and statistics, cover (Evans and Rosenthal 2010; Bean 2009):

- using frequentist probabilities and probability models to model variations in populations

Knowledge in Risk Assessment and Management, First Edition. Edited by Terje Aven and Enrico Zio.
© 2018 John Wiley & Sons Ltd. Published 2018 by John Wiley & Sons Ltd.

- using statistical tools and metrics in a frequentist probability framework, for example confidence intervals
- using subjective probability to express uncertainties about unknown quantities, as in Bayesian analysis.

To explain these items in somewhat more detail, consider the common setup used in statistics. Let X_1, X_2, ... X_n, be n observations of a random variable (quantity) X, all having a frequentist probability distribution F(x). The interpretation is that F(x) represents the variation in the observations if we could consider hypothetically or for real an infinite number of such random variables (quantities). As F(x) in general is unknown, it needs to be estimated. This is done either directly using the observations X_i or using a two-step approach by first introducing a model G of F with parameters λ (say) and then assessing these parameters in some way. This assessment of the parameters is typically conducted by establishing estimators of the parameters, and their properties can be studied using frequentist probabilities, or a Bayesian analysis can be carried out, providing subjective probability distributions for the unknown parameters, in addition to estimates of the parameters. In the frequentist case, the uncertainties of the estimators are calculated by means of measures such as variance and standard deviation. The related interpretations are of the form that, if the analysis could be repeated under similar conditions, the intervals produced would capture the underlying true parameters at some specified percentages of the times. In the Bayesian setup, it is common to say that the probability model G represents stochastic or aleatory uncertainties, whereas the uncertainties about the parameters λ represent epistemic uncertainties. With more knowledge, the epistemic uncertainties will be reduced but not the stochastic uncertainties, as they reflect variation.

This is textbook material and there is a huge body of literature on approaches and methods for uncertainty analysis within this setup. This chapter addresses situations where this setup is challenged; when the justification of frequentist probabilities and probability models is challenged. This is a common situation in practice, when we leave the world of experimentation and testing of similar units as in, for example, medical health and reliability studies of similar units. If we are to study real-life systems and activities – nuclear power plants, offshore installations, the development of new products, climate change, life in a country with people facing known and unknown types of threats – it is not straightforward to define the huge populations of similar units that are required to model the systems and activities using probability models. Yet uncertainty analyses are needed, as we face unknown quantities and unknown cause–effect relationships. Models may still be developed and used, but their accuracy is a critical issue.

An interesting challenge then is how to best conduct uncertainty analyses in such cases. The present chapter takes one step back compared to most publications on uncertainty analysis by aiming to provide a response to this challenge, linking uncertainty to knowledge and risk. The point of departure is that any judgment of uncertainty is conditional on some knowledge, and this knowledge can be poor and even erroneous. The knowledge – which is basically justified beliefs – is thus subject to risk as seen from the decisionmaker's position when they are to interpret and use these judgments. Can this type of risk be meaningfully assessed, and how should it be treated? The chapter argues that uncertainty analysis can benefit from recent developments within the risk analysis field that underline the knowledge and strength of knowledge judgments supporting the quantitative uncertainty judgements.

In the following we refer to the subjective probabilities simply as probabilities. There are also other ways of representing or expressing the uncertainties than using probability, and the question about selecting the appropriate approach is an important and interesting issue. This discussion is, however, outside the scope of this work. The present chapter aims at improving the foundation and practice of uncertainty analysis by presenting a framework for uncertainty analysis which allows for all types of uncertainty representations and measures. The framework highlights the need for clarifying what we are uncertain about, who is uncertain, and how we should represent or express the uncertainties. A main goal of the chapter is to obtain new insights into the link between the uncertainty analysis – with its different approaches and methods – and knowledge and risk as indicated above.

The present chapter reviews and summarises recent work on the topic, extending it and pointing to key challenges. It is not a broad review in the sense that it tries to include all the main contributions to the topic of recent years. The focus is on fundamental issues related to uncertainty analysis in a practical decision-making context. The subjectivity of the selection of these works, and a deliberate bias towards areas of interest for the author of this manuscript, is acknowledged.

The history of uncertainty analysis is as old as the history of probability, as any judgment about probability is a judgment of uncertainty. However, uncertainty extends beyond probability; probability is just one way of representing or expressing uncertainty. Over the last 30–40 years we have seen the development of a new research field or area – uncertainty analysis – which studies alternative ways of characterising uncertainty and how to use uncertainty analysis to improve uncertainty communication and support decision-making. One of the basic references for this development is the book by Morgan *et al.* (1990). It covers discussions about ideas and principles of uncertainty analysis and the use of such analyses in a practical decision-making context, as well as methods for assessing uncertainty. The development of this field has, to a large extent, been linked to discussions about uncertainties in relation to quantitative risk assessments (probabilistic risk assessments); see for example early contributions by Parry and Winter (1981) and Cox and Baybutt (1981), as well as more recent work by Apostolakis (1990), Helton (1994), Winkler (1996), Helton *et al*. (2004), Montgomery *et al*. (2009), Dubois (2010), NRC (2013), and Flage *et al*. (2014). The framework presented in this chapter can be seen as an input to the discussion about what the core subjects of uncertainty analysis are and how the field of uncertainty analysis is linked to the risk analysis field. The framework presented resembles existing frameworks for uncertainty analysis (de Rocquigny *et al*. 2008; Aven 2010) in some features but differs on others. The main novel aspect of this framework is the links it forges between uncertainty, knowledge, and risk.

The remainder of the chapter is organised as follows. Firstly, in Section 5.2 the framework is presented. Then an example is presented in Section 5.3, showing the use of the framework. Section 5.4 discusses the example and the framework. Finally, Section 5.5 provides some conclusions.

5.2 The Uncertainty Analysis Framework

The framework has five main pillars:

1) Some quantities of interests answering the question: what are we uncertain about?
2) Some related actors: analysts, experts, decisionmakers, other stakeholders answering the questions: who are uncertain and who have some interest in these quantities?
3) How the uncertainties are represented or expressed
4) How the uncertainties are dealt with through modelling and analysis
5) How the uncertainty characterisations are followed up and used by the relevant actors.

For all of these pillars we will discuss the links to knowledge and risk.

In brief, the main purpose of an uncertainty analysis is to represent or express uncertainty about something, to be used in some context, to gain insights – for example about risk, to improve communication and support decision-making.

5.2.1 What are we Uncertain About?

The first question to be asked is: what are we uncertain about? Think about a die to be thrown. The outcome of the next throw is unknown and we can be uncertain about it, but we can also be uncertain about the fraction of times the die will show 1,2, ..., 6, respectively in the long run if we could hypothetically throw the die over and over again; in other words, we are uncertain about the frequentist probability distribution of the die. In both cases we can identify unknown quantities: in the latter case in a constructed probability model setup. Some true, correct values are presumed to exist in both cases. We let X be a generic term expressing such a quantity. We distinguish between X being an observable quantity as in the former example and X being a model parameter in the latter example.

In the former example the outcome relates to a future event. We can also have unknown quantities related to past events, for example if we are uncertain about the result of a throw carried out last year.

The point is that we have defined a quantity X (which can be a vector), which has a presumed true underlying value, but this is unknown: it is uncertain.

If we consider an activity in the future, the consequences C of this activity are in general not known; they are uncertain. If we measure the consequences by X, we are back to the situation with unknown quantities. The degree to which X properly reflects C will also be an issue. For example, a company has defined performance measures covering production volumes and loss of lives and injuries due to accidents. However, no measure is defined in relation to loss of reputation. So we may have a situation with good scores on X but a major concern when considering reputation and the actual consequences of the activity, C.

We also talk about uncertainty in relation to phenomena, such as cause-effect relationships. Again, we can transform the problem to unknown quantities by considering a model g of the phenomenon and focusing on the model error X-g, where X is the observable quantity of interest. Consider the smoking–lung cancer example in Aven (2014). Here we let X denote the number of deaths per 100,000 persons (lung cancer mortality rate) in a specific population (women of a specific age group). An accurate model g can then be derived linking X and the intensity Y_1 (number of cigarettes per day) and duration of smoking Y_2 (years) using standard statistical analysis; see for example Flanders *et al.* (2003) and Yamaguchi *et al.* (2000). A true value of X-g exists and its uncertainty can be considered.

The framework makes a distinction between high-level quantities and low-level quantities. The high-level quantities are those of main interest for the study and the key stakeholders – and for decisionmakers in particular. The low-level quantities are more technical and mainly of interest for analysts and experts. These quantities are often parameters of models used to study the output quantities. The modelling and analysis link these two levels. We return to this idea in Section 5.2.4.

To represent quantities of interest, we use letters such as X, Y, and Z. What the quantities of interest are depends on the purpose of the analysis. Ideally, they should be requested by decisionmakers. However, what quantities to address is also a technical issue and some guidance is here provided:

- Clarify what are the high-level quantities of interest for the uncertainty analysis? Are they observable quantities or probability model parameters? Provide clear interpretations of these quantities. If such interpretations cannot be provided, remove them from the list of quantities of interest.

What is a high-level quantity or a low-level quantity (that is, not a high-level quantity) depends on the purpose of the analysis.

- If a planned uncertainty analysis relates to a low-level quantity, clarify what the purpose of the analysis is. If the quantity does not contribute to providing insights about any high-level quantity, the analysis should not be conducted.

If a planned uncertainty analysis has defined a high-level quantity of interest as the frequentist probability of a terrorist attack in a specific country in the coming year, there is a problem: such a probability cannot be meaningfully interpreted. Relevant quantities are the number of such events with different attributes or simply the occurrence of such types of event.

In a risk context, the high-level observable quantities are restricted to future events. Otherwise the uncertainty analysis can relate to any type of quantity studied in risk analysis, including unknown model parameters.

5.2.2   Who is Uncertain?

Next we need to clarify who is uncertain about X. Is it the analysts? Some experts? The decision makers or other stakeholders? Any judgment about uncertainty needs to be precise on this point to ensure proper communication and treatment of the uncertainties. An uncertainty analysis can be rather technical and, in most cases, the analysis produces judgments, made by experts and analysts, to be communicated to decisionmakers and other stakeholders. The analysis can be explicit on presenting expert judgements, but the analysis can also report analyst judgements where the experts provide input to these judgements; refer to discussions by Cooke (1991), Hoffman and Kaplan (1999) and Aven and Guikema (2011).

Decisionmakers and other stakeholders, such as political parties and non-governmental organisations with an interest in the decisions to be made, have their main interest in the high-level quantities and the critical beliefs and assumptions on which the analysts' and experts' judgements are conditional.

A distinction must be made between those people who are uncertain about the unknown quantities and have some interest in the issue raised for the uncertainty analysis, and others who have knowledge about these quantities but otherwise are not involved in or do not have any interest in the uncertainty analysis. The former category covers members of the analysis team (experts and analysts), and the decisionmakers and other stakeholders linked to the problem studied. The second category could, for example, be academics who are experts in the field of study.

The above discussion is relevant for uncertainty analysis as well as for risk analysis.

5.2.3   Representing Uncertainties: The Link to Knowledge and Risk

Firstly, let us reflect on what uncertainty actual means. Then we will address the problem of representing or expressing the uncertainties. In line with measurement theory, a distinction is made between the concept of uncertainty and how it is described or measured. Before throwing a die, one faces uncertainty, as one does not know for sure what the outcome will be; in other words, the outcome is subject to uncertainty. In general, we can define uncertainty in relation to X as not knowing the true value of X. An alternative way of expressing this is to say that having uncertainty about X is to have imperfect or incomplete information and knowledge about X (SRA 2015). If we had perfect and complete information and knowledge, there would be no uncertainty about X. Knowledge is here to be understood as justified beliefs (SRA 2015). Think about a die. My knowledge is summarised as the belief that the die is fair, which comes from looking at it and using a symmetry argument. This knowledge is not perfect or complete; it could turn out that the frequentist probability p_i (the long-run fraction) of outcome i is not 1/6, $i = 1,2,...,6$. Hence there is uncertainty about p_i. There is also uncertainty about the outcome of the next throw. We have some knowledge, but surely it is far from perfect or complete, and inadequate to determine what the outcome will be.

If X is a future observable quantity, uncertainty U about this quantity also points to the concept of risk, when considering the most general way of conceptualising this term; see SRA (2015). "Risk" essentially captures two dimensions:

- the values at stake: the future consequences of the activity considered with respect to something that humans value (such as health and lives, the environment and economic assets)
- uncertainties: what will these consequences be?

Limiting the risk concept to some specific observable quantities X, risk can thus be seen as the pair (X,U). For example, if we focus on the number of fatalities X in the operation of a system over the next 10 years, facing risk means that the activity will lead to some number of fatalities X, and today it is not known; it is uncertain (U).

The next task is then to describe or characterise the uncertainties about X. Two different ways of thinking can be adopted (Aven and Zio 2011):

- Reflect the assigner's subjective judgements about what X is or will be.
- Try to "objectively" represent the available information and knowledge.

Subjective Judgments

The common tool for the subjective judgments approach is subjective probability, as discussed by Lindley (2006) and Aven (2013). However, this tool has some limitations, as thoroughly discussed in the literature (Flage *et al.* 2014).

The main problem is that a subjective probability is in fact a probability conditional on some background knowledge (K), and this knowledge can be more or less strong, and even erroneous. Seeing the probability judgements in relation to the need of the decisionmakers, the quality of this knowledge becomes an important topic in the uncertainty assessment and management. To show this in somewhat more detail, let $P(A|K)$ denote the subjective probability of an event A given the knowledge K. Say that the analysts derive a probability of 0.1; that is, $P(A|K) = 0.1$. This probability expresses the assigner's degree of belief in event A occurring and means that he/she has the same uncertainty and degree of belief in A occurring as drawing one particular ball out of an urn of 10 balls under the standard conditions for random drawing experiments. However, the assigner can assign the same probability number for two completely different situations: If K_a and K_b correspond to these situations, we may have $P(A|K_a) = P(A|K_b) = 0.1$, but in one case the knowledge could be poor and in the other very strong. Clearly the quality of the knowledge also needs to be taken into account in some way. If only P is used to characterise the uncertainties, this characterisation is in fact a conditional judgement given the knowledge K, which we can write symbolically as $(P|K)$. However, a comprehensive uncertainty characterisation needs to also take into account the risk and uncertainties associated with K. A way to do this is described and discussed below, but first another foundational remark.

At a first glance, it may seem possible to remove the dependencies of K, by using the law of total probability as discussed by Mosleh and Bier (1996). In some simple cases this is indeed possible, but for more complicated situations involving modelling it is not, because the probabilistic analysis needs to be based on some assumptions and beliefs. In general, it is not possible or desirable to transfer all knowledge available to the probability figures. If an accurate probabilistic analysis can be carried out given a specific assumption, and this assumption is subject to large uncertainties, it may be more informative to present the conditional analysis given this assumption together with a separate analysis of the assumption, instead of establishing an unconditional integrated probability number which is influenced by a rather arbitrary probability distribution of deviations from the assumption.

Let SoK be a judgement of the strength of the knowledge K. Then the above argumentation leads to an uncertainty characterisation (P,SoK,K), covering probability P, SoK and the knowledge K on which the probability and SoK judgements are based. For examples of how the SoK judgements can be carried out, see Flage *et al.* (2014) and Aven and Flage (2017). See also Berner and Flage (2016), which compares different schemes for making such judgements, including the so-called NUSAP system (where NUSAP stands for numeral, unit, spread, assessment, and pedigree) (Funtowicz and Ravetz 1990, 1993; Kloprogge *et al.* 2005, 2011; Laes *et al.* 2011; van der Sluijs *et al.* 2005a, 2005b).

Probability meets the basic criteria commonly required for uncertainty measures (Bedford and Cooke 2001, p. 20): axioms, interpretations and measurement procedures. In its basic form, this means specifying numbers to each event of interest. However, often intervals are provided instead of specific values. The analyst may not be willing to be more precise than to express that $P(A|K) > 0.5$. Such a statement does not mean that the assessor is uncertain about P, as such an interpretation would presume the existence of an underlying true objective quantity of the probability, which is not the case for a subjective probability. There is, however, *imprecision*. The assessor is not willing to be more precise than the interval specified, given the knowledge K. Various theories exist for how to produce such intervals, including possibility theory and evidence theory; see Dubois (2010) and Aven *et al.* (2014).

The use of such intervals does not change the need for judgments about the strength of knowledge (SoK), as these intervals are also conditional on some knowledge. However, the knowledge is typically stronger than in the precise case. For a mass-produced die, a probability assignment expressing that the probability of outcome 1 occurring is between 0.1 and 0.2 has a stronger knowledge basis than a specific assignment of 1/6.

There are also other ways of expressing uncertainties, and one of the most general ones referred to in the literature is plausibility (Pl) (Halpern 2005). In a concrete situation, the analyst may state that an event B is more plausible than A; that is, $Pl(A) \le Pl(B)$. In other cases the analyst may not be prepared to order them (they are incomparable). Plausibility is:

- transitive: if $Pl(A) \le Pl(B)$ and $Pl(B) \le Pl(C)$, then $Pl(A) \le Pl(C)$
- antisymmetric: if $Pl(A) \le Pl(B)$ and $Pl(B) \le Pl(A)$, then $Pl(A) = Pl(B)$.

It is required that for two events, A and B, for which A implies B (that is, A is a subset of B in a set theory formulation), we have $Pl(A) \le Pl(B)$; that is, the plausibility of A is less than the plausibility of B.

Plausibility is a very general way of expressing uncertainty, and covers all the other methods referred to above. The problem is, however, that the measure is not very informative. Think about a situation for which an analyst states that, for a new type of activity, the plausibility of an event A occurring leading to a fatal accident is higher than for the event B. Intuitively, this statement may provide some useful information for the decisionmaker and other stakeholders, but what does the statement really say? There is no interpretation provided. In addition, the same type of statement can be used with probability: the analyst expresses that he or she considers the probability of A to be higher than B; that is, $P(A) \le P(B)$, and there is a clear interpretation of the statement using the urn standard. The analyst is not willing to be more precise than what is specified by the inequality. The statement can thus be viewed as one of imprecision but still within the probability framework. Also here, strength-of-knowledge judgments are required because the probability judgments are based on some knowledge.

The above analysis leads us to a general description or characterisation of the uncertainties. This is of the two-dimensional form (Q,K), where Q is a subjective description or characterisation of the uncertainties given some knowledge K. In the above example, Q is equal to the pair of probability and strength of knowledge judgments SoK; that is, Q = (P,SoK). Probability here can be precise or imprecise.

From this generic characterisation, specific uncertainty metrics can be derived, such as the variance, a quantile of a probability distribution as in value-at-risk (VaR), the entropy of a probability distribution, or curves expressing the probability of events leading to a loss exceeding x, for different values of x (see Bedford and Cooke 2001 and Halpern 2005). In the framework, all such metrics are supplemented with qualitative strength of knowledge judgements. It is a research challenge to develop suitable uncertainty metrics for different settings, but this is outside the scope of this work.

"Objective" Representations

In science, objectivity is considered an ideal and this ideal is often raised in relation to uncertainty analysis. The idea is to objectively transform the knowledge available to an uncertainty representation, such that it does not add or remove any information or knowledge. The aim is to replace the available knowledge K by a quantitative representation R.

However, such a representation does not exist. Any measure R is conditional on something and this something needs to be added to provide a proper characterisation of the uncertainties. To make this clear, let us return to the probability interval $P(A|K) > 0.5$ referred to in the previous section. This statement may be based on an expert expressing that it is more likely that the event A will occur or will not occur. From this statement alone, $P(A|K) > 0.5$ is all we can say. In this sense we have objectively transformed the knowledge to the uncertainty measure. However, it is still essential to add the knowledge K and a judgement of its strength to the uncertainty characterisation, as this expert may have strong or weak knowledge related to the subject matter. The knowledge is not necessarily objective, even though we are able to objectively transform it to the representation R.

The tool we are using for representing the uncertainty in the "objective" case (b) is the same as for the subjective approach (a), hence we can use Q for both. The main difference between the two approaches (a) and (b) is that for the subjective approach (a) the analysts and experts are encouraged to express, as far as possible, their subjective judgements about the unknown quantities, even if the background knowledge is somewhat weak, while in the "objective" case (b) a cautious attitude to making precise judgements is adopted when the knowledge is not strong. In practice, a combination of the approaches can be useful, as argued for by Flage *et al.* (2014). The two approaches are not in conflict; rather, they supplement each other by reflecting different strategies for expressing the uncertainties. For the subjective approach, specific probabilities may often be preferred, whereas in the "objective" case, interval probabilities could be the standard measure used. The overall and general uncertainty characterisation (P, SoK, K) can be written in both cases, but has different content depending on the strategy. As in the previous section, P here allows both precise and imprecise assignments.

Starting from the risk concept (X,U) defined in the previous section, we are led to a risk description (X,P,SoK,K), where X is the future quantity of interest related to the activity studied.

5.2.4 Dealing with Uncertainties through Modelling and Analysis

To assess the uncertainties of an unknown quantity, it is common to introduce models, as was mentioned in Section 5.2.1. Let X be the quantity of interest and g(Y) the model, where Y is a vector of model parameters. In uncertainty analysis, a lot of work is devoted to the task of expressing uncertainties about Y and propagating this uncertainty through g to obtain an uncertainty characterisation of X; see for example de Rocquigny *et al.* (2008) and Aven *et al.* (2014). Both analytical approaches and Monte Carlo methods are used for this purpose. The methods introduce computational errors, in that the method produces a value g' different from g. Hence the model error is not X-g but X-g'.

In the framework, X is the high-level quantity of interest and Y is the low-level quantity of interest. In addition, the model error Z defined by Z = X-g' is a quantity of interest. The framework allows for the use of different tools to propagate the uncertainties from low-level to high-level quantities. Examples of such tools are summarised in Aven *et al.* (2014).

Developing the model g means balancing the need for accuracy and simplification. If a lot of relevant data exist, a number of methods are available to analyse the goodness of the model – in order to validate and accredit the model – using both traditional statistical analysis and Bayesian procedures; see for example Bayarri *et al.* (2007), Jiang *et al.* (2009), Kennedy and O'Hagan (2001), Meeker and Escobar (1998), Rebba *et al.* (2006), and Xiong *et al.* (2009). However, the focus here is on situations where there is a lack of data. In these cases we are led to methods, as discussed in Bjerga *et al.* (2014), for which uncertainty characterisations of the form (P,SoK,K) provide a basis for determining whether a model is sufficiently accurate.

Another challenge relates to the identification of important factors and elements contributing to the uncertainties. The literature on this topic is huge; see for example the overview by Borgonovo and and Plischke (2015). This literature is to a large extent restricted to probability and to some extent also to probability intervals. Research is also needed to cover the knowledge dimensions represented by SoK judgements and K.

Think of an event A occurring in the case where A_1, A_2, ... or A_s, occurs (it is assumed that only one of these events can occur). Using indicator functions I, we can write the model as:

$$I(A) = I(A_1) + I(A_2) + ... + I(A_s)$$

Now suppose that there is an event A_{s+1} that this model has not included, the reason being lack of knowledge about the phenomenon addressed. This event will not be covered by the probability-based uncertainty analysis, but it will to some extent be addressed by SoK and K, for example when concluding that a model is based on poor understanding of the phenomenon studied, indicating that surprises can occur. The example illustrates the difficulties in dealing with model errors and uncertainties in cases when the knowledge is not strong and in particular the concepts of incompleteness uncertainty, surprises, and "black swans" (Bjerga *et al.* 2017; Taleb 2007; Aven 2014).

Think about a complex system, where there is strong knowledge about how its individual components work. As the system is complex it is acknowledged that, by using a simple model based on these components (such as a block diagram or a fault tree), we will not really be able to accurately predict the system performance (SRA 2015). However, alternative and better models are lacking and it is decided to use such a simple modelling approach. This means that, through the modelling, the strong knowledge on the component level is reduced to poor knowledge on the system level.

Models are useful for simplifying complex systems and activities and for obtaining insights. At the same time, it is important to acknowledge the limitations of the models, and the modelling errors and uncertainties. The next section explains how the framework takes such limitations into account.

For risk and its description (X,P,SoK,K), the discussion in this section is relevant because it concerns how to derive the probabilities and the knowledge judgements.

5.2.5 How the Uncertainty Characterisations are Followed up and Used

The analysts produce an uncertainty characterisation of the form (P,SoK,K), as discussed in the previous section. This characterisation informs the decision-makers and other stakeholders. It does not prescribe what to do, for two reasons:

- The uncertainty characterisations have limitations. For example, the knowledge K could be rather weak and even erroneous. The uncertainty characterisation is a subjective judgement made by the analysts; it does not represent the truth. There is risk related to the knowledge K in the sense that the beliefs about K can be wrong.

- Decisionmakers need to give weight to this risk and the values of other concerns of importance for their decision-making, which are not necessarily taken into account in the uncertainty assessment.

Different philosophies and policies can be defined to communicate the uncertainties, inform relevant stakeholders and use the uncertainty characterisations in decision-making. In general this framework is based on the following ideas for using the uncertainty analysis to support the decision-making:

  i) Identify and structure the problem, identify alternatives
 ii) Assess pros and cons of alternatives
iii) Assess uncertainties and risks
 iv) Use ii) and iii) to inform relevant stakeholders and decisionmakers.

These ideas are in line with the basic steps of planning theory and quality management. It is acknowledged that there is a leap from the analysis sphere to the decision-making, and that this leap cannot be replaced by any analytical method, such as for example expected utility theory or cost–benefit analysis. The point is that the analysis does not cover all aspects of interest for the decisionmakers. Aspects of unconditional risk will always be present (related to K) and it is difficult to transfer decisionmaker values and preferences to the analysis. Acknowledging the limitations of these tools, they can still provide useful information to stakeholders and decisionmakers. They should not, however, be used to prescribe what to do.

Decisionmakers are not experts on uncertainty analysis and risk assessments. Nevertheless, they need to address the unconditional uncertainties and risk as explained above, covering potential surprises related to presumed beliefs, as well as being able to balance different concerns where non-quantified uncertainties and risk are important elements. The present framework is based on the conviction that managers and decisionmakers are able to tackle this challenge. What is required is that the uncertainty and risk-analysis communities are able to present and communicate clear principles and ideas to enable proper thinking. The present chapter is intended to provide a contribution to this end.

5.3 Use of the Framework: An Example

We consider an example where the true state of a system is not known: it is either functioning as normal or in a state of "failure". A signal may be observed which gives some indication that the system is in fact in the failure state. We can think about a technical standby system, for which the state – functioning or not – is not known, and a signal may indicate that it is not functioning. An alternative interpretation is a human health situation where the human body is the system and the states refer to having or not having a disease (for example cancer). The signal is some type of physical observation that something is wrong.

Some uncertainty analyses are to be conducted. We first answer the questions:

- What are we uncertain about?
- Who is uncertain?

We also need to place these questions into the context of the reason why we are performing the analysis.

5.3.1 What are we Uncertain about? Who are Uncertain? Why Uncertainty Analysis?

The key quantity of interest here is the true state of the system. Is the system not functioning as needed or does the person have cancer? Let A denote this event: the system is in a failure state. It is, however, also possible to think about a case where the interest is not primarily A but the fraction of As, when considering a (huge) population of similar systems. This applies to both the technical system example and the disease example. Let Y denote this fraction.

Regarding "who is uncertain", we have two main actors of interest here:

- a professional analyst group performing the uncertainty analysis, with a focus on a specific A or Y
- a decisionmaker who is informed by this professional uncertainty analysis.

For this example, to simplify the discussion, we assume that we have no other stakeholders.

5.3.2 Expressing the Uncertainties. Modelling and Analysis

Next we will look into how analysts express or represent the uncertainties about A and Y. Let us first focus on Y. It represents the fraction of systems in a failure state. Hence it expresses variation in the relevant population of similar systems (say n systems): the proportion of systems in the failure state, with 1-Y expressing the proportion in the "good", non-failure state. The population studied is considered large and it is common then to approximate Y with p, representing the fraction of systems in a failure state when considering an infinite number of similar systems. This means that we have developed a probability model: Y is a binomially distributed random quantity with parameters n and p.

It is tempting to consider the case with A as a special one, with n equal to 1, so that Y is a Bernoulli random quantity where $P(Y=1)=P(A)=p$ and $P(Y=0)=1-p$. However, care must be taken in doing this, as it requires that there is a population of similar systems to the one studied in relation to A, which forms the fraction p. It needs justification. If $P(Y = 1) = P(A) = p$, it means that P is interpreted as a frequentist probability, and we should write $P_f(Y = 1) = P_f(A) = p$, and this probability is a fundamentally different concept from the subjective probability $P(A|K)$. This latter probability expresses someone's uncertainty or degree of belief that A will occur, as discussed in Section 5.2. If p is known, we may have $P(A|K) = p$, but in general $P(A|K)$ is different from p.

In this example, we seek in some way to reflect the observed signal in the modelling. In the large population case, the binomial model can easily be extended by considering a quantity V, say, which is 1 if the signal has been observed and 0 otherwise. We then need to specify the frequentist probability that the system is in the failure state given the signal and not the signal, respectively; that is, $P_f(A|V = 1)$ and $P_f(A|V = 0)$. We refer to these frequentist probabilities as p_1 and p_0, respectively.

An uncertainty analysis can then be conducted for the unknown parameters p, p_1 and p_0, of the probability model. Traditional statistical analysis can be conducted, as well as Bayesian analysis. The setup is standard and textbooks are available for this type of uncertainty analysis (see for example Evans and Rosenthal 2010 and Bean 2009).

The case when there is little information and knowledge available on how this signal is actually linked to the state of the system is of special interest for the analysis in this chapter. If the uncertainties about p_1 and p_0 are large, how should we then perform the uncertainty analysis?

The framework points to the following approach. The analyst team summarises all the information and knowledge available and expresses their degrees of belief related to p_1 and p_0 using probabilities and SoK judgements. An example is the team expressing that if one observes the signal then the frequentist probability of being in the failure state is higher than 0.1 with 90% probability. It is highlighted that the knowledge supporting this judgement is weak. The need to be specific depends on the situation and the decision being considered. The expert team may conclude that if the signal is observed the probability of being in the failure state is so high that action is required, and there is no need to explicitly express the probabilities.

If the system considered is unique, the introduction of the probability models cannot be justified. Uncertainty analysis can still be conducted. It will comprise judgements of the probability that the system is in the failure state given the signal and not the signal, respectively – $P(A|V = 1)$ and $P(A|V = 0)$ – in addition to judgements about the knowledge supporting these probabilities. Note that, in contrast to the above frequentist analysis, these probabilities are knowledge-based (subjective) probabilities, conditional on the knowledge K.

There is no point in being extremely accurate in probability characterisations when the background knowledge is poor. Depending on the situation, there could be a drive to strengthen the knowledge base to support decision-making, but time and resource constraints may require an immediate decision. It will always be possible to produce some type of probability judgement, at least in the form of intervals with SoK judgements.

5.3.3 Decision-making

Let us think about the decisionmaker as described in Section 5.3.1. The analysts provide judgements about the unknown quantities given their knowledge and they also report and make a judgement about this knowledge. The decision maker is informed by this characterisation. If, for example, the analysts find it probable that the system is in the failure state, the decision maker is led to an action about further analysis and intervention. However, if the analysts find this likelihood to be rather small, the decision maker needs to make a broader evaluation, reflecting on the knowledge on which the judgements are based and how much weight to give to the uncertainties and potential surprises relative to the judgements made by the analysts. A cautious policy could mean action and intervention for the smallest identification of something being wrong, but obviously in most cases there is a need for a balance to be made, taking into account the costs and stress involved in taking action and intervening in the event of a false alarm. Some type of policy is therefore required, balancing the desire to identify true failures and avoiding false alarms. Think about the cancer case. A *hypochondriac* would interpret any symptom as a sign of being sick, which is obviously unhealthy and not a wise strategy. The other extreme is to ignore all symptoms, the result being that the treatment could arrive too late, when the person is in fact sick.

This leads us to considerations of risk and broad evaluations of all concerns of importance for decision making. Many approaches and methods have been developed for this purpose but, as highlighted in Section 5.2, the framework underlines the importance of seeing beyond the analytical approaches. In this example, it could be useful to compute, for example, expected net present values in cases when probability models can be justified and the decision maker has an interest in a huge population of similar systems. On a national level, it is certainly interesting to study the effect of measures that could improve the ability to identify cancer early. Then cost–benefit types of analyses could be useful to guide decision makers to ensure that the available resources are effectively used. Yet, there is a need for broader evaluations, highlighting the uncertainties of relevant parameters, as well as aspects of importance for decision making that are not included in the cost–benefit analysis. For unique cases and cases with rather poor background knowledge, this type of analysis alone will not give much relevant information for the decision maker. In general, listing all the pros and cons with judgements of uncertainties and risk is the approach recommended by the framework.

No prescription of the best solution is produced, but a best solution does not exist for this type of problem. For a specific person facing a unique problem related to following up a signal, an expected-value based approach (like a cost–benefit analysis) can give some general insights, useful for decision making, but the most important information and knowledge are linked to risk and uncertainty and these are not revealed by a cost–benefit analysis. What is needed is a broad judgement of all the pros and cons, with due consideration given to risk and uncertainties.

The analysts' scope is uncertainty, but when discussing the implications of their analysis they enter the risk domain in two ways: when the quantities of interest relate to the future, and when considering possible deviations from the beliefs made or assumed in K. When facing uncertainties related to having cancer, it is all about risk, as the occurrence and severity of this state are of major interest. The judgement of uncertainty can be based on assumptions, which can turn out to be wrong. The implications could be serious; it is also about risk. The analysts may, for example, make their probability judgement without knowing that the system considered has previously experienced a weakness which could affect its resilience.

5.4 Discussion

Probability models are a fundamental pillar of uncertainty analysis. Their use is, however, problematic in many cases, in particular for analysing rare events with extreme consequences. These models allow for sophisticated probabilistic analysis and reference to concepts such as heavy and fat distribution tails. However, we seldom see this framework is justified or questioned: is it in fact suitable for studying extreme event phenomena?

Let A denote the occurrence of such an event and X the associated loss, expressed through some severity scale. If the event does not occur, X is equal to zero. A probability model would mean that frequentist probabilities have been defined for A and X, such as $P_f(A)$ and $h(x) = P_f(X > x)$ for extreme outcomes x of X. If X has a normal distribution, $h(x)$ quickly becomes small for increasing x values, whereas for a fat-tailed distribution $h(x)$ is "not so small", even for large x values. These are vague terms but sufficiently precise in this context and for the purpose of this discussion. Special forms and formulas, with parameters, are sometimes introduced, approximating or refining $h(x)$. Then standard probabilistic and statistical analysis can be conducted using these probability models as a basis. Epistemic uncertainties are expressed about unknown parameters. The setup is in fact the traditional one, with probability models reflecting stochastic (aleatory) uncertainties and probability representing or expressing epistemic uncertainties.

We find an example of this type of setup in Viscusi and Zeckhauser (2011). They write:

> Proper assessment of the magnitude of losses from a catastrophe reveals the disturbing reality that losses from disasters tend to have fat-tailed distributions (i.e., distributions where there is a nontrivial chance of extremely large losses). Such distributions look nothing like the normal distributions that are familiar, such as that used to characterize the distribution of human heights, and that play a central role in most empirical investigations in the social sciences. Even lognormal distributions, which pay greater attention to extreme outcomes, do not come close to having the fat tails found in the distributions of losses from catastrophes. Disaster losses – such as those from earthquakes, hurricanes, and floods – are much better described by a power law distribution. With a power law distribution, the greatest loss may easily be three times or even ten times as great as the second greatest loss, whereas no such variation is observed with respect to normally distributed variables such as individual height.

The perspective when making this type of analysis is an insurance company, or a big state or the world. We can think about "a man on the moon" watching what happens on Earth. Empirical distributions can be produced by describing the variation within a set of defined events. However, variation is not uncertainty. Variation can provide a basis for representing or expressing uncertainty, but the fact that something varies does not lead to a clear formulation of uncertainties. Rather, it may help us in clarifying what we are uncertain about. Is it one particular event or the fraction of events or distributions of losses when considering many possible events? And what type of events are we actually incorporating in these populations?

Further discussion on how to conceptualise and describe uncertainties will depend on the purpose of the analysis. The perspectives are completely different for an insurance company having a macro view and for the management of one specific activity, where the concern is the proper performance and uncertainty analysis of this activity.

In the former case, a probabilistic modelling approach may be justified, but not in the latter. Probabilistic models require mental constructions by considering an infinite number of similar situations or systems. Yet in both cases we need to deal with uncertainties of unknown quantities. Probability – exact or an interval – is a key tool, but always needs to be seen in relation to the background knowledge on which it is based, and its strength.

Probability is the commonly preferred tool to represent and express probability. It has a clear interpretation and its calculation is rather straightforward and well-established. The alternative quantitative approaches, such as possibility theory and evidence theory, are much more difficult to understand and use. However, with probability we also allow for imprecision intervals, for example when specifying the probability for an interval [0.1−0.01], say. The theoretical basis for these theories and the related calculations are not easily communicated and, for practical uncertainty analysis, many analysts are reluctant to use them because of this. Simplicity is important but has to be balanced against the need for quality of the information provided. It can be seen as a practical compromise to use probability together with qualitative knowledge judgements. The framework described in Section 5.2 is, however, not limited to such an approach. Probability intervals expressing imprecision also constitute a pillar of the uncertainty representations and characterisations, as such intervals are needed in many situations to properly reflect the information available. However, it is essential that these intervals are given a proper interpretation and are not hidden behind too many mathematical details. Qualitative strength of knowledge judgements are also needed for these intervals, as they represent judgements and these judgements are conditional on some knowledge.

Risk in its general form, as mentioned in Section 5.2.3, is about the future consequences C of an activity and the associated uncertainties U; that is, (C,U). Representing and expressing uncertainties U is thus a key aspect of risk characterisations. Using Q as a generic expression of a measure or description of uncertainty, we are led to a risk characterisation (X, Q, K), where X is a specification of C, and K is the background knowledge on which X and Q are based. Note the difference between C and X: C is the actual consequences of the activity if it were realised, whereas X is those specified in the risk assessment. An uncertainty analysis relates to X as well as aspects of K, for example the truth of some assumptions or beliefs. Uncertainty analysis is thus an important task within risk assessment, but it is also used outside risk assessment, as uncertainty analysis also relates to aspects not concerning the future, as is the case for risk.

5.5 Conclusions

To conduct an uncertainty analysis we need to know what we are uncertain about, who is uncertain and how we should represent or express the uncertainties. The present chapter has presented a framework which responds to these three questions, also linking uncertainty to knowledge and risk. The main conclusions can be summarised in the following points:

When performing an uncertainty analysis:

1) clarify whether the quantities of interest are probabilistic or observable quantities
2) require clear interpretations of all quantities of interest
3) justify the need to introduce probability models and other models

4) address model error and model uncertainty
5) encourage the use of probability to express degrees of beliefs for unknown quantities, add strength of knowledge judgements
6) justify use of interval probabilities reflecting imprecision, add strength of knowledge judgements
7) identify key uncertainty factors
8) clarify key assumptions and beliefs on which the uncertainty judgements are built
9) consider risk related to deviations from these assumptions and beliefs
10) encourage the decision maker to make judgements about this risk, to the degree necessary for decision making
11) acknowledge that the uncertainty analysis provides decision support, not clear guidance on what decision to make.

An uncertainty analysis represents a judgement by some people; it can be useful as these persons have some knowledge – usually rather strong – about the phenomena studied. Yet humbleness is required, as the knowledge on which their analysis is based could have limitations and even be erroneous.

Acknowledgements

This work was funded by the Norwegian Research Council as a part of the Petromaks 2 program under Grant number 228335/E30. The support is gratefully acknowledged.

References

Apostolakis, G.E. (1990) The concept of probability in safety assessments of technological systems. *Science*, 250, 1359–1364.
Aven, T. (2010) Some reflections on uncertainty analysis and management. *Reliability Engineering & System Safety*, 95, 195–201.
Aven, T. (2013) How to define and interpret a probability in a risk and safety setting. Discussion paper, with general introduction by Associate Editor, Genserik Reniers. *Safety Science*, 51, 223–231.
Aven, T. (2014) *Risk, Surprises and Black Swans*. Routledge.
Aven, T. and Flage, R. (2017) Risk assessment with broad uncertainty and knowledge characterisations: An illustrating example. In: Aven T. and Zio E. (eds) *Knowledge in Risk Assessments*. Wiley.
Aven, T. and Guikema, S. (2011) Whose uncertainty assessments (probability distributions) does a risk assessment report: the analysts' or the experts'? *Reliability Engineering & System Safety*, 96, 1257–1262.

Aven, T., Baraldi, P., Flage, R., and Zio, E. (2014) *Uncertainties in Risk Assessments*. Wiley.

Aven, T. and Zio, E. (2011) Some considerations on the treatment of uncertainties in risk assessment for practical decision-making. *Reliability Engineering & System Safety*, 96, 64–74.

Bayarri, M.J., Berger, J.O., Paulo, R., *et al.* (2007) A framework for validation of computer models. *Technometrics*, 49(2), 138–54.

Bean, M.A. (2009) *Probability: The Science of Uncertainty*. American Mathematical Society.

Bedford, T. and Cooke, R. (2001) *Probabilistic Risk Analysis*. Cambridge University Press.

Berner, C.L. and Flage, R. (2016) Comparing and integrating the NUSAP notational scheme with an uncertainty based risk perspective. *Reliability Engineering & System Safety*, 156, 185–194.

Bjerga, T., Aven, T., and Zio, E. (2014) An illustration of the use of an approach for treating model uncertainties in risk assessment. *Reliability Engineering & System Safety*, 125, 46–53.

Bjerga, T., Aven, T., and Flage, R. (2017) Completeness uncertainty: Conceptual clarification and treatment. In: Aven, T. and Zio, E. (eds) *Knowledge in Risk Assessments*. Wiley.

Borgonovo, E. and Plischke, E. (2015) Sensitivity analysis: A review of recent advances. *European Journal of Operational Research*, 248 (3), 869–887.

Cooke, R.M. (1991) *Experts in Uncertainty: Opinion and Subjective Probability in Science*. Oxford University Press.

Cox, D.C. and Baybutt, P. (1981) Methods for uncertainty analysis: A comparative study. *Risk Analysis*, 1(4), 251–258.

de Rocquigny, E., Devictor, N., and Tarantola, S. (2008) *Uncertainty in Industrial Practice. A Guide to Quantitative Uncertainty Management*. Wiley.

Dubois, D. (2010) Representation, propagation and decision issues in risk analysis under incomplete probabilistic information. *Risk Analysis*, 30, 361–368.

Evans, M.J. and Rosenthal, J.S. (2010) *Probability and Statistics: The Science of Uncertainty*, 2nd edn. W.H. Freeman and Company.

Flage, R., Aven, T., Baraldi, P., and Zio, E. (2014) Concerns, challenges and directions of development for the issue of representing uncertainty in risk assessment. *Risk Analysis*, 34(7), 1196–1207.

Flanders, W.D., Lally, C.A., Zhu, B-P, Henley, S.J. and Thun, M.J. (2003) Lung cancer mortality in relation to age, duration of smoking, and daily cigarette consumption. *Cancer Research*, 63, 6556–6562.

Funtowicz, S.O. and Ravetz, J.R. (1990) *Uncertainty and Quality in Science for Policy*. Kluwer Academic Publishers.

Funtowicz, S.O. and Ravetz, J.R. (1993) Science for the post-normal age. *Futures*, 25, 735–755.

Halpern, J.Y. (2005) *Reasoning about Uncertainty*. MIT Press.

Helton, J.C. (1994) Treatment of uncertainty in performance assessments for complex systems. *Risk Analysis*, 14, 483–511.

Helton, J.C., Johnson, J.D., and Oberkampf, W.L. (2004) An exploration of alternative approaches to the representation of uncertainty in model predictions. *Reliability Engineering & System Safety*, 85(1–3), 39–71.

Hoffman, F.O. and Kaplan, S. (1999) Beyond the domain of direct observation: how to specify a probability distribution that represents the 'state of knowledge' about uncertain inputs. *Risk Analysis*, 19, 131–134.

Jiang, X., Yang, R.J., Barbat, S., and Weerappuli, P. (2009) Bayesian probabilistic PCA approach for model validation of dynamic systems. In: *Proceedings of SAE World Congress and Exhibition*. Detroit, MI, April 2009.

Kennedy, M.C. and O'Hagan, A. (2001) Bayesian calibration of computer models. *Journal of Royal Statistical Society, Series B (Statistical Methodology)*, 63(3), 425–64.

Kloprogge, P., van der Sluijs, J., and Petersen, A. (2005) A method for the analysis of assumptions in assessments. Netherlands Environmental Assessment Agency (MNP), Bilthoven, The Netherlands.

Kloprogge, P., van der Sluijs, J.P., and Petersen, A.C. (2011) A method for the analysis of assumptions in model-based environmental assessments. *Environmental Modelling and Software*, 26, 289–301.

Laes, E., Meskens, G., and van der Sluijs, J.P. (2011) On the contribution of external cost calculations to energy system governance: The case of a potential large-scale nuclear accident. *Energy Policy*, 39, 5664–5673.

Lindley, D.V. (2006) *Understanding Uncertainty*. Wiley.

Meeker, W.O. and Escobar, L.A. (1998) *Statistical Methods or Reliability Data*. Wiley.

Montgomery, V.J., Coolen, F.P.A., and Hart, A.D.M. (2009) Bayesian probability boxes in risk assessment. *Journal of Statistical Theory and Practice*, 3(1), 69–83.

Morgan, M.G., Henrion, M., and Small, M. (1990) *Uncertainty*. Cambridge University Press.

Mosleh, A. and Bier, V.M. (1996) Uncertainty about probability: a reconciliation with the subjectivist viewpoint. *IEEE Transactions on Systems, Man, and Cybernetics. Part A Systems and Humans*, 26(3), 303–310.

NRC (2013) US Nuclear Regulatory Commission. Guidance on the treatment of uncertainties associated with PRAs in risk-informed decision making draft report for comments (NUREG-1855, rev. 1).

Parry, G. and Winter, P.W. (1981) Characterization and evaluation of uncertainty in probabilistic risk analysis. *Nuclear Safety*, 22(1), 28–42.

Rebba, R., Mahadevan, S., and Huang, S. (2006) Validation and error estimation of computational models. *Reliability Engineering & System Safety*, 91, 1390–97.

SRA (2015) Glossary. Society for Risk Analysis, www.sra.org/resources. Accessed 26 January 2017.

Taleb, N.N. (2007) *The Black Swan: The Impact of the Highly Improbable.* Penguin.

van der Sluijs, J., Craye, M., Futowicz, S., *et al.* (2005a) Combining quantitative and qualitative measures of uncertainty in model-based environmental assessment. *Risk Analysis*, 25(2), 481–492.

van der Sluijs, J., Craye, M., Funtowicz, S., *et al.* (2005b) Experiences with the NUSAP system for multidimensional uncertainty assessment in model based foresight studies. *Water Science and Technology*, 52(6), 133–144.

Viscusi, W.K. and Zeckhauser, R.J. (2011) Deterring and compensating oil-spill catastrophes: The need for strict and two-tier liability. *Vanderbilt Law Review*, 64, 1717–2011.

Winkler, R.L. (1996) Uncertainty in probabilistic risk assessment. *Reliability Engineering & System Safety*, 85, 127–132.

Xiong, Y., Chen, W., Tsui, K.L., and Apley, D.W. (2009) A better understanding of model updating strategies in validating engineering models. *Journal of Computer Methods in Applied Mechanics and Engineering*, 198(15–16), 1327–37.

Yamaguchi, N., Kobayashi, Y.M., and Utsunomiya, O. (2000) Quantitative relationship between cumulative cigarette consumption and lung cancer mortality in Japan. *International Journal of Epidemiology*, 29(6), 963–968.

6

Completeness Uncertainty: Conceptual Clarification and Treatment

Torbjørn Bjerga, Terje Aven, and Roger Flage

University of Stavanger, Norway

This chapter discusses completeness uncertainty. The interpretations of this term found in the literature are ambiguous, and its treatment appears difficult. We aim to clarify the concept and show that it can be treated essentially as model uncertainty. A simple example is used to illustrate this.

6.1 Introduction

You are to assess risk linked to the sudden flooding in a Norwegian fjord. Close to the head of the fjord, there are some mountains where rockslides are not uncommon. At the inlet of the fjord there is a hamlet of 50 people. If a big rockslide occurs, it could lead to a big wave, wiping out the hamlet. Geological examinations have been conducted and they conclude that such an event is unlikely; yet an early warning system to detect a major wave at an early stage has been installed. If this system works, it would give most people enough time to escape in the case of a tidal wave. In the assessment of this system, we can imagine that you might develop a simple event tree, as seen in Figure 6.1.

The event tree is a model of the number of fatalities, which mathematically can be written $G(X) = 2X_0X_1X_2 + 40X_0X_1(1 - X_2)$, where $X = (X_0, X_1, X_2)$ is a vector; X_0 is defined as 0 if there are no rockslides and 1 if a rockslide occurs; X_1 is an indicator quantity taking the value 1 if a tidal wave occurs and 0 otherwise, and X_2 is an indicator quantity taking the value 1 if the early warning system works and 0 otherwise.

However, the model presents only three crude scenarios of what could happen. It could, for example, matter if a rockslide occurs at night when everyone is sleeping. Another issue is cruise liners entering the fjord, giving the potential

Knowledge in Risk Assessment and Management, First Edition. Edited by Terje Aven and Enrico Zio.
© 2018 John Wiley & Sons Ltd. Published 2018 by John Wiley & Sons Ltd.

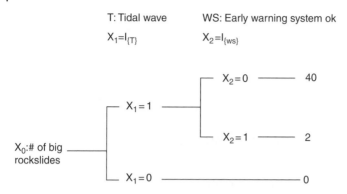

Figure 6.1 Event tree for rockslides. The numbers to the right are the assumed numbers of fatalities.

for a much higher number of fatalities. There could also be initiating events not included, such as a submarine landslide, seismic activities, or meteorites. These could all create tides similar to a rockslide. In addition, there might be events and factors that have not been thought of; that is, unknowns. What do we do about all the risk sources that are not included in the model? The question is a general one in risk analysis, not only relevant in relation to this fjord-flooding example. How should we conceptualize and treat such risk sources?

One answer is provided by the Nuclear Regulatory Commission (NRC) in the USA, through its authoritative guidelines on probabilistic risk analyses (PRAs) and its discussion of the concept of "completeness uncertainty". The NRC refers to "completeness uncertainty" as part of epistemic uncertainty (NRC 1983, 2009, 2013) and relates the concept to risk contributors not included in the PRA model. It is categorized as either being "known" or "unknown" (NRC 2013). Thus, relating this understanding to the above example, we should understand, for example, the possibilitiy of a submarine landslide or a rockslide at night as an example of known completeness uncertainty. Examples of unknown completeness uncertainties are, for obvious reasons, lacking.

From these examples, it is not clear how non-included risk contributors relate to completeness uncertainty and what the meaning of the concept of completeness uncertainty is. The closest to a precise definition and explanation found in NRC (2013, p. 2–4) is:

> Lack of completeness is not in and of itself an uncertainty, but is more of an expression of the limitations in the scope of the model. However, limitations in scope can result in uncertainty about the full spectrum of risk contributors.

The meaning of this definition is, however, difficult to understand and relate, for example, to the fjord-flooding case. What is (in)completeness linked to? The model or the scope? The example event of a rockslide at night is outside the model, but may be inside the scope. Is a model (in)complete in relation to the scope or something else? Also, what is the uncertainty about, and does the exclusion of, for example, a submarine landslide "result in uncertainty about the full spectrum of risk contributors"?

In the literature, completeness uncertainty is also referred to as:

- uncertainty as to whether all significant phenomena and relationships have been considered in the PRA (Vesely and Rasmuson 1984)
- omissions in the model due to lack of knowledge (Funtowicz and Ravetz 1990; Hellström and Jacob 2011)
- uncertainty due to the portions of risk that are not explicitly included in the PRA (Reinert and Apostolakis 2006)
- a type of model uncertainty (Reinert and Apostolakis 2006; Vesely and Rasmuson 1984; Parry 1996; see also NRC 2009)
- uncertainty about where the true risk lies (Modarres *et al.* 2009; see also NRC 2009)
- lack of completeness leads to uncertainty in the results and conclusions of the analysis (Rao *et al.* 2007).

We see from these references that there are different views on how uncertainty comes into play and what the uncertainty is about.

This chapter aims to clarify the meaning of the completeness uncertainty concept. The work is motivated by the problems pointed to above and by an overall ambition to contribute to the strengthening of the scientific basis and terminology of risk analysis. Clear and meaningful concepts are needed for risk analysis to develop as a scientific field. However, equally important as the conceptual clarity, are the implications for how to assess and manage the risk. We will argue that the lack of a clear definition of completeness uncertainty also hampers risk assessment and risk management.

In addition, it is a common perception that it is very difficult, if not impossible, to quantify and analyze completeness uncertainty (Parry 1996; Rao *et al.* 2007; Modarres *et al.* 2009; Funtowicz and Ravetz 1990; Hellström and Jacob 2011; Vesely and Rasmuson 1984; Reinert and Apostolakis 2006; NRC 1983; 2009). However, the realities are not as complicated as indicated by some of these authors, provided that a suitable conceptualization is developed. Uncertainties can always be assessed, but the assessment's basis can of course be more or less strong. We will discuss this further in Section 6.3.

According to the NUREG-1855 document, the treatment of completeness uncertainty follows different paths for known and unknown risk contributors. To meet unknown completeness uncertainty, safety margins, defense-in-depth and performance monitoring are recommended (NRC 2013). Screening processes using judgments and analysis (bounding and conservative types of analysis) on significance are used for known risk contributors. Typically, significance is decided based on probability (likelihood). If judged significant, a risk contributor can be included into an upgraded PRA model. Alternatively, if the risk contributor is judged insignificant, it may not be included (NRC 2013).

On an overall level, there seems to be broad consensus about these strategies, but we will argue that some improvements can and should be made, in particular with regard to the known risk contributors, as there is a need to see beyond probability to make judgments about significance. A probability is a judgment on the basis of some background knowledge, and the strength of this knowledge should also be taken into account when concluding if a risk contributor is significant or not. There has been considerable work recently documenting the need for such extended judgments to adequately reflect the uncertainties (Tickner and Kriebel 2006; Flage *et al.* 2014; Aven and Zio 2011; Stirling 2007; de Rocquigny *et al.* 2008).

Before presenting our analysis on how to understand the completeness uncertainty concept and discussing the implications for risk assessment and management, we provide some further details on completeness uncertainty.

6.2   Completeness Uncertainty in Detail

Contextually, the NRC introduces completeness uncertainty in relation to PRAs. PRA models are constructed as logic structures/models, such as event trees and fault trees, combined with probabilistic models reflecting variation (also known as aleatory uncertainty) in, for example, initiating events and component failures (NRC 2013). There is nevertheless (epistemic) uncertainty about the representativeness and validity of the PRA model and the predictions it makes (NRC 2013). Epistemic uncertainty is further categorized into parameter uncertainty, model uncertainty, and completeness uncertainty.

Completeness uncertainty and the challenges in understanding the concept were introduced in Section 6.1. Parameter uncertainty is uncertainty about the values of the parameters in a model, for example the X in the previous section. Model uncertainty, on the other hand, can be interpreted essentially as uncertainty about which model best represents the system (NRC 2013). We could, for example, introduce $F(X) = 45X_0X_1(1 - X_2)$ as an alternative to $G(X)$. The uncertainty is then about which model, $G(X)$ or $F(X)$, most appropriately represents the system.

One way of summarizing the NRC's thinking about model and parameter uncertainty is like this:

- *Parameter uncertainty:* uncertainty about X
- *Model uncertainty:* uncertainty about which is the better of $G(X)$ or $F(X)$.

In the literature, there are also other ways to understand model uncertainty. One way will be introduced in Section 6.3.

Completeness uncertainty relates to risk contributors not included in the PRA model, for example initiating events, hazards, modes of operation, phenomena, interactions, human and organizational factors, and component failure modes (NRC 1983, 2013; Abramson 1995; Reinert and Apostolakis 2006). It is thus a category that includes many different elements, some of which do not fit nicely into the other epistemic uncertainty categories or into the PRA model:

> Some phenomena or failure mechanisms may be omitted because their potential existence has not been recognized or no agreement exists on how a PRA should address certain effects, such as the effects on risk resulting from ageing or organizational factors. Furthermore, PRAs typically do not address them." (NRC 2013, p. 2–4)

In fact, there are many reasons why elements are in the completeness uncertainty category (based on NRC (2013), and Reinert and Apostolakis (2006)):

1) They are outside the scope.
2) They are outside the level of detail.
3) Their relative contribution is believed to be negligible.
4) Analysis methods are not developed.
5) No agreement exists on how to address them.
6) They cannot be defensibly modeled.
7) There is no tradition of including them.
8) There are limited resources.
9) They are unknown (unspecified).

Essentially, reasons 1–8 are categorized as known completeness uncertainty, while 9 is unknown completeness uncertainty. The dividing line is, however, not always clear. Sometimes, as in NRC (2009), 5 and 7 are included in the "Unknown" category. We will return to these items in Section 6.4 and discuss them further.

6.3 Understanding and Treating "Completeness Uncertainty"

If we look into the definitions reviewed in Section 6.1, we see that completeness uncertainty is tied to risk sources: events, phenomena, interactions, factors, systems, and so on that alone or in combination may lead to undesired outcomes. In our case, examples of such sources are a rockslide, tidal wave, or warning system failure. These three risk sources are associated with the model

G(X) through X. For example, X_1 is linked to a potential tidal wave and takes a value 1 in the case of a wave and 0 otherwise. The model and the X_is are constructed based on a list, kept in mind or in written form, of the identified risk sources. A list of risk sources seems a good starting point for discussing completeness uncertainty. For example, when can a list of risk sources be considered complete, and what is the uncertainty about?

6.3.1 A Complete List of Risk Sources

At first, imagine that a time jump 50 years ahead were possible. What would occur in the fjord over that timespan? It is likely that no major events would occur, but assume that a rockslide took place, giving rise to a major tidal wave, for which the warning system raised the alarm. Suppose also that there were two fatalities. No other risk sources were in play. The list of risk sources used 50 years ago, including rockslide, tidal wave and warning system reliability, corresponded well with the risk sources that actually played out. The list could be considered complete. Nevertheless, at this time, the issue is that we do not know the actual risk sources that will occur (or not occur). There are more risk sources than the three mentioned – rockslide, tidal wave, and warning system failure – that would be considered relevant today. For example, it is imaginable that a tidal wave could occur while a cruise ship is in the fjord.

Depending on who is asked, there can be differing views on what the relevant risk sources that make the list complete are. For our case, assume that a risk analyst has identified and produced a list of all risk sources known to her/him. The list contains rockslide, tidal wave, warning system failure, night scenario, precipitation, cruise liner and fishermen in the fjord. The analyst claims that the list covers all relevant risk sources (and is complete) to the best of their knowledge. Then a second risk analyst reviews the case and the list. The person agrees with the list, but in addition identifies submarine landslide as a risk source that should be included on the list. To the best of this person's knowledge, the list is not complete without inclusion of the possibility of a submarine landslide. A third risk analyst claims that the list should only contain rockslide, tidal wave, warning system failure, night scenario and cruise liner in the fjord. The other risk sources have a very low probability (≈ 0) and/or impact and can be ignored. A fourth analyst claims that the list is only complete if it also includes an "Other" category (as in Kaplan and Garrick (1981)) that includes unknown risk sources and the types of completeness uncertainty set out in Section 6.2 (items 1–9).

We can summarize potential interpretations. The list of risk sources for a future time period can be considered complete if it contains:

- B: All those known to a risk analyst, except the low probability/low impact ones
- C: All those known to a risk analyst
- D: All those known to a risk analyst and a reviewing risk analyst

Table 6.1 Lists of risk sources.

	X	B	C	D	E	A
Known	X_0	Rock slide	Rock slide	Rock slide	Rock slide	RS_1
	X_1	Tidal wave	Tidal wave	Tidal wave	Tidal wave	RS_2
	X_2	Warning system reliability	Warning system reliability	Warning system reliability	Warning system reliability	RS_3
	X_3	Night scenario	Night scenario	Night scenario	Night scenario	...
	X_4	Cruise liner	Cruise liner	Cruise liner	Cruise liner	RS_N
	X_5		Fishermen	Fishermen	Fishermen	
	X_6		Precipitation	Precipitation	Precipitation	
(Unknown) known	X_7			Submarine landslide	Submarine landslide	
Incl. unknown unknown	X_8				Other	

RS, risk source; X, input parameter in G(X); N, number of actual risk sources.

- E: All possible (known and unknown)
- A: The actual risk sources that will occur in the future. The elements of A are unknown at present.

Table 6.1 below illustrates these interpretations using the fjord case.

By comparing the lists B through E, it is evident that B is a sublist of C, which is a sublist of D, which finally is a sublist of E. Each list covers the same and additional risk sources as the previous one. Hence, with respect to possible risk sources, list B is less complete than C, which is less complete than D. However, only list E with the "Other" category is complete in the sense that all possible and actual risk sources are found on the list. Essentially, an "Other" category obliterates completeness uncertainty. Note that an "Other" category can also be introduced at the end of lists B and C.

Even though the concept of completeness uncertainty is made redundant by an "Other" category, there will always be uncertainty about whether the actual risk sources (A) would fall within the specified part of the list (or in the "Other" category). When the knowledge base is sound, as in this case, the list can be made exhaustive, and an "Out of the specified list" event is unlikely. But such a thing may occur. Assume list B, just to illustrate. At some future point, an alarm-triggering wave caused by a rockslide occurred and there was a fishing vessel trapped in the fjord. By comparing the actual risk sources with list B, there is a discrepancy. "Fishermen in the fjord" was a risk source that was not included in list B. In practice, whether or not there will be a discrepancy between the actual risk sources and the list, and what the discrepancy might consist of, is uncertain.

In addition, we can note that there must have been some actual consequences, to which the risk source "Fishermen" is linked. Otherwise, it would not be deemed relevant. If we develop the wave scenario further, we can, for example, assume that all the fishermen, say 10 of them, were killed. Now let us return to the model G(X), which has scenarios combining possible risk sources to outcomes (say, $2X_0X_1X_2$). Suppose that the input vector is $X = (X_0, X_1, X_2, X_3, X_4)$ and corresponds to list B. There will be a discrepancy between X and the actual risk sources, since there is no X_i corresponding to fishermen in the fjord. There will also be a discrepancy between what the model predicts (two fatalities) and the actual fatalities (say two villagers and ten fishermen killed). A discrepancy between a model prediction G(X) and the actual outcome Z is better known as a model error, here denoted M; that is, $M = G(X) - Z$, and the uncertainty about its magnitude is model uncertainty (Aven and Zio 2013).

6.4   Risk Sources as Model Uncertainty

To sum up, in line with Aven and Zio (2013), the uncertainty about whether there will be a discrepancy between the actual risk sources and the specified list is essentially model uncertainty and can be treated as that. Now, a model has to balance two concerns, namely accuracy and simplification. In contrast to a list, the model may not need to incorporate all specified risk sources to produce useful knowledge. Rather, too much information could easily complicate things and blur the picture. Clearly, risk sources that are presumed to be of low impact/low probability are candidates that perhaps can be excluded. However, proper analysis of model error and model uncertainties is needed to decide which X_is should be included in X and the model G, and which to place in the "Other" category, here signified by X_8. Let us look at how this can be done for the three risk sources, fishermen, precipitation and submarine landslide, in that order. We start with a model where $X = (X_0, X_1, X_2, X_3, X_4)$, corresponding to the risk sources on list B.

Say $X_i = 1$ for $i = 0,1,2$ and $X_i = 0$ for $i = 3,4$ in G(X), which corresponds to a scenario with a rockslide and an alarm-triggering tidal wave (other scenarios can be explored by conditioning on other combinations). For this scenario $G(X) = 2$ fatalities. The model error is $M = G(X) - Z = 2 - Z$. In addition, if fishermen in the fjord is the only source of uncertainty, an attempt is made to establish a boundary for Z. Say that experts are consulted, who agree that no more than 30 fishermen will ever be present at a time, spread over three boats. Because of the nature of the fishery, if there are fishermen in the fjord there are usually three boats at a time, but possibly only one or two. The distribution shown in Figure 6.2 reflects

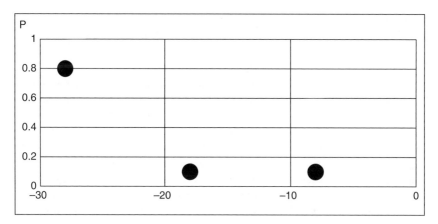

Figure 6.2 Probability distribution for the model error of $2 - Z$ fatalities if fishermen are in the fjord.

this. The probabilities, say $P(2 - Z = -8) = 0.1$, express the assessors' degree of belief in the event of a model error equal to -8 being the same as some standard event with measure 0.1 (Kaplan and Garrick 1981), say drawing at random one specific ball out of an urn containing ten balls; see for example Flage and Aven (2009), Aven (2014) and Berner and Flage (2016).

The distribution depends on assumptions, phenomenological understanding, data and so on. This is called the background knowledge, K, for the probability distribution, and the notation is P("some event"|K). For more details on what can be in K, and how it can be assessed, see for example Aven (2014) and Berner and Flage (2016). In this case, it is assumed that a major wave will kill all crew members present, which may be something of a simplified assumption but is considered to give a good idea of what would happen. Apart from that, the experts agree, and the phenomenon is well understood. The background knowledge is considered medium/strong.

However, another aspect to consider is that, due to migration of fish, there may only be one day a year when the boats are in the fjord. The chances that a fishing boat is present when a tidal wave occurs, is vanishingly small. In addition, this is a well understood phenomenon, the background knowledge is strong, and, if anything, the fishery is expected to decrease over the coming years. One can say that the unconditional probability that the model error $M = 0$, $P(M = 0|K)$, only considering fishermen in the fjord, is very high, close to 1, and the background knowledge is strong. There is perhaps no need to include this one in the model.

The arguments for including fishermen in the model are, however, many. History shows that improbable things do happen. Also, the model error is judged to possibly be quite big if the fishermen scenario occurs, and the background knowledge is found to be fairly strong. Consider also that it is not difficult to add fishermen to the model $G(X)$ as an additional parameter X_5 (which is one way of doing it). In this case, the decision is quite clear: to include X_5 and the potential related consequences in the model.

Now let us look into the two other risk sources. Take precipitation first. It rains and snows quite often in the fjord area, but is this a relevant risk source to include in the model? At first, precipitation in itself may seem harmless, but thinking it over, can it be linked to the other risk sources and undesired outcomes in some realistic way? There are some imaginable instances where that is possible. Rain, say for a long time and perhaps in combination with low temperatures, could make a rockslide more likely. It is also possible to imagine that, during an emergency, temperatures below zero Celsius could cause someone fleeing to slip on an icy surface, bump his or her head on, say, a stone, faint, and thus be unable to escape a wave. In general, precipitation could delay the escape of the entire population of the hamlet. We can also imagine that, with a changing climate, the frequency and amount of precipitation will increase over the 50-year period considered.

This risk source has a very high probability of being present, and is hence quite different from fishermen in the fjord. This is also a very well understood phenomenon and K is strong. Again, let the parameters $X_i = 1$ for $i = 0,1,2$ and $X_i = 0$ for $i = 3,4$. The model predicts two fatalities, and the model error is $M = G(X) - Z = 2 - Z$. Further, if precipitation is the only uncertainty source, the number of fatalities is not judged to deviate strongly from two. A boundary is set at three persons killed. Thus $2 - Z$ could reach -1. The probability of that is, however, judged very low, with strong background knowledge. It is concluded to not add this risk source to the model as a separate element, but rather to place it in the "Other" category, and hence it will be reflected by the parameter X_8. The model error and model uncertainty are found to be low enough for the model to be accredited without including precipitation specifically (which would correspond to the parameter X_6 in Table 6.1).

Lastly, take the submarine landslide. This is an event that is very rare, and perhaps more unlikely than a rockslide. The idea of their simultaneous occurrence is therefore difficult to justify. Rather, in the case of submarine landslide, X_0 will be 0 (making $G(X) = 0$ and $M = -Z$), otherwise the number of fatalities is judged to be similar to that of a rockslide, so that $M = -G(X)$. To assign probabilities for the model uncertainty is not found to be necessary here; rather, assessment of the strength of the background knowledge is used. The background knowledge is essentially historical observations across the coast of Norway and it is assumed that these are relevant data. However, much of the seabed surrounding the fjord is unexplored in detail. It is also known that there is a major subsea ridge further out into the Norwegian Sea, where a submarine landslide caused a massive and fatal tide roughly 8000 years ago. The strength of the background knowledge is judged as moderate. The conclusion for submarine landslides is to include this risk source in the model, given the potentially large model error and moderate model uncertainty. There is, however, a smart way to do it. Instead of adding another X_i, we can exclude X_0. Thus a wave is the initiating event/category in the model, which is sufficiently broad that whatever caused it – rockslide, submarine landslide, or other events – it is still covered.

So to summarize, the complete list is considered to be E. The list E has an exhaustive specified part (D) obtained by including presumed low-probability/low-impact risk sources, subject to peer review, plus an "Other" category. For the model G(X), the parameter becomes $X = (X_1, X_2, X_3, X_4, X_5, X_8)$. The model covers all the risk sources on the list E. Different risk source/event combinations and outcomes can be constructed in G. The model G(X), judgments about the background knowledge for the model, the complete list and model uncertainty/model error judgments for precipitation, fishermen and submarine landslides, should all be kept together and presented to a potential decision maker as one whole.

6.5 Discussion

Figure 6.3 illustrates the suggested process for how to make a list of risk sources complete, with an exhaustive known part. The two first steps essentially produce known/identified risk sources, while the third step essentially covers unknowns and minor eventualities. An aim of the first two steps is to capture as many known risk sources as practicably possible. The list is made complete to the best of the risk analyst's knowledge (in practice one could use freethinking but also well-established methods like HAZID). By exhausting the known part, the "Other" category necessarily becomes as small as practicably possible. But what is practicably reasonable? If more experts and risk analysts had been brought into our fjord case, it would perhaps have been possible to extend the known part

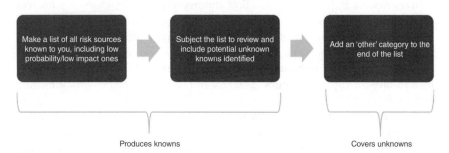

Figure 6.3 How to make a list of risk sources that maximizes knowns and covers unknowns through an "Other" category.

of the list even further. In general, research can also contribute to this end. Using more resources can reveal more risk sources, but at a financial cost. What is practicably reasonable is a management issue. It has to take into account the resources spent on identifying the additional risk sources. This is a balancing act. The level of knowledge and understanding about the situation can be important for finding a justifiable balance. When the situation was, as in the fjord scenario, a case with fairly strong knowledge, then this is a good argument that a minimum of one peer is enough. If, on the other hand, the knowledge is poor, then more resources may be needed. In a situation with poor knowledge, it can be challenging to identify risk sources, and it can be assumed that the "Other" category may very well contain many surprises. Regardless of knowledge level, the "Other" category should always be included to acknowledge the potential surprises, along with an assessment of the uncertainty/background knowledge.

In the process of making a complete list, discrimination against specified risk sources that are judged to have low probability/low consequences is not advised. This is because a probability conditions on background knowledge, as explained earlier, but it is also an argument that it is not very resource demanding to write down a list. Of course, common sense has to be used. For example, including the position of our neighboring galaxy, Andromeda, is a bit far-fetched. The same can be said about the economic situation in, say, some South American country, or when your birthday is. The point is that potential risk sources have to be linkable in some relevant way to each other, and to what is of interest, as has been shown in Section 6.3.

With a complete list, the next process is to construct a model. The model has to balance two concerns: to be as accurate as possible, and, at the same time, as simple as possible, so that useful and clear information can be obtained. We have seen in our case that the only known risk sources that can be sorted into the "Other" category with confidence are the relatively low impact ones: when M is judged to be low, and where the background knowledge is strong. In our case, this was the case for precipitation. The other two risk sources were included, regardless of probability. Following this line of thinking, the risk sources quoted in Section 6.2 – aging and organizational factors in a nuclear PRA – are characterized by poor K and hence need to be taken into the model in some way. A similar procedure, including parameters (X_is) and assessing and including their possible impact, is one way. However, these may not be as easy to include as the risk sources in our case. The result then is that the model uncertainty for the whole model is large, and this needs to be communicated and considered when using the model.

An issue with many risk sources included in a model is that they can blur the picture. However, many of them can be grouped, as we have seen. For example, since submarine landslides, rockslides, precipitation, and other happenings could lead to a wave, "Wave" is set as the initiating event in the model instead of "Rockslide"; see also Aven (2016).

We have seen that the uncertainty about risk source discrepancies essentially can be treated as model uncertainty: uncertainty about the magnitude of the model error M, where $M = G(X) - Z$. Part of the model error M can be attributed to risk/uncertainty sources that are not included in the model. Non-included risk sources were essentially what completeness uncertainty was linked to. In simple words, model uncertainty is completeness uncertainty. Many of the missing risk sources can, however, be included as input parameters X_is in a model. In some sense, the uncertainty is also about which specified risk sources, through X_is, to include in the model.

6.6 Conclusion

We conclude that "completeness uncertainty" is essentially an obsolete term, which there is no need to use in risk analysis. Lists can always be made complete by including an "Other" category. Rather, potentially non-included risk sources can be treated essentially as model uncertainty, where due consideration is given to uncertainties and the background knowledge that extends beyond common practice. A goal, though, is to minimize the "Other" category, and this can be achieved through various means, for example by using peer review. Models should include all risk sources except those that lead to a relatively insignificant model error and which have low model uncertainty. To cover low model error/uncertainties and surprises, other risk sources can be included as a separate input parameter.

Acknowledgements

The work has been partly funded by the Norwegian Research Council as a part of the Petromaks 2 program (grant number 228335/E30). The support is gratefully acknowledged.

References

Abramson, L.R. (1995) Model uncertainty from a regulatory point of view. In: Mosleh, A., Siu, N., Smidts, C. and Lui, C. (eds) *Proceedings of Workshop on Model Uncertainty: Its Characterization and Quantification*, Annapolis, Maryland, US, 1993. University of Maryland.

Aven, T. (2014) *Risk, Surprises and Black Swans: Fundamental Ideas and Concepts in Risk Assessment and Risk Management*. Routledge.

Aven, T. (2016) Ignoring scenarios in risk assessments: Understanding the issue and improving current practice. *Reliability Engineering & System Safety*, 145, 215–220.

Aven, T. and Zio, E. (2011) Some considerations on the treatment of uncertainties in risk assessment for practical decision making. *Reliability Engineering & System Safety*, 96(1), 64–74.

Aven, T. and Zio, E. (2013) Model output uncertainty in risk assessment. *International Journal of Performability Engineering*, 9(5), 475–486.

Berner, C. and Flage, R. (2016) Strengthening quantitative risk assessments by systematic treatment of uncertain assumptions. *Reliability Engineering & System Safety*, 151, 46–59.

de Rocquigny, E., Devictor, N. and Tarantola, S. (eds). (2008) *Uncertainty in Industrial Practice: A Guide to Quantitative Uncertainty Management.* John Wiley & Sons.

Flage, R. and Aven, T. (2009) Expressing and communicating uncertainty in relation to quantitative risk analysis. *Reliability & Risk Analysis: Theory & Application*, 2(13), 9–18.

Flage, R., Aven, T., Zio, E. and Baraldi, P. (2014) Concerns, challenges, and directions of development for the issue of representing uncertainty in risk assessment. *Risk Analysis*, 34(7), 1196–1207.

Funtowicz, S.O. and Ravetz, J.R. (1990) *Uncertainty and Quality in Science for Policy* (Vol. 15). Springer Science & Business Media, Kluwer Academic Publishers.

Hellström, T. and Jacob, M. (2011) *Policy Uncertainty and Risk: Conceptual Developments and Approaches.* Springer Science & Business Media, Kluwer Academic Publishers.

Kaplan, S. and Garrick, B.J. (1981) On the quantitative definition of risk. *Risk Analysis*, 1(1), 11–27.

Modarres, M., Kaminskiy, M.P. and Krivtsov, V. (2009) *Reliability Engineering and Risk Analysis: A Practical Guide*, 2nd edn. CRC Press, Taylor & Francis.

Nuclear Regulatory Commission (1983). PRA procedures guide. (NUREG/CR-2300). Washington DC; 1983.

Nuclear Regulatory Commission (2009) Guidance on the treatment of uncertainties associated with PRAs in risk-informed decision making (NUREG-1855). Washington DC; 2009.

Nuclear Regulatory Commission (2013) Guidance on the treatment of uncertainties associated with PRAs in risk-informed decision making; draft report for comments (NUREG-1855, rev. 1). Washington DC; 2013.

Parry, G.W. (1996) The characterization of uncertainty in probabilistic risk assessments of complex systems. *Reliability Engineering & System Safety*, 54(2), 119–126.

Rao, K.D., Kushwaha, H.S., Verma, A.K., and Srividya, A. (2007) Quantification of epistemic and aleatory uncertainties in level-1 probabilistic safety assessment studies. *Reliability Engineering & System Safety*, 92(7), 947–956.

Reinert, J.M. and Apostolakis, G.E. (2006) Including model uncertainty in risk-informed decision making. Annals of Nuclear Energy, 33(4), 354–369.

Stirling, A. (2007) Risk, precaution and science: towards a more constructive policy debate. *EMBO Reports*, 8(4), 309–315.

Tickner, J. and Kriebel, D. (2006) The role of science and precaution in environmental and public health policy. In: Fisher, E., Jones, J., and von Schomberg, R. (eds) *Implementing the Precautionary Principle: Perspectives and Prospect.* Edward Elgar Publishing.

Vesely, W.E. and Rasmuson, D.M. (1984) Uncertainties in nuclear probabilistic risk analyses. *Risk Analysis*, 4(4), 313–322.

7

Quality of Risk Assessment: Definition and Verification

Terje Aven[1] and Enrico Zio[2,3]

[1] *University of Stavanger, Norway*
[2] *Laboratoire Genie Industriel, CentraleSupélec, Université Paris-Saclay, France*
[3] *Department of Energy, Politecnico di Milano, Italy*

The quality of a risk assessment stands on its meeting some "scientific criteria" and on its "being useful" in a decision-making context. In this chapter we reflect on these ideas, analysing what these criteria should be and how the term "useful" should be interpreted. We bring new insights into the topic by considering two novel aspects:

- the perspectives of risk assessment that shift the focus from accurate risk estimation to the characterization of knowledge and lack of knowledge
- the recognition that decision makers need to go beyond conditional risk, as described and assessed by risk analysts and experts, to consider unconditional risk.

We then consider the quality of risk assessment within the context of these two items, addressing the questions of what it depends on, how it can be guaranteed, and how it can be checked. A main conclusion is that the current practice of risk assessment needs to be improved, in particular with respect to the way knowledge and lack of knowledge is understood and communicated.

7.1 Introduction

In risk assessment, analysts identify possible hazards/threats (such as a gas leakage or a fire), analyze their causes and consequences, and describe risk. To conduct the assessment, the analysts need to make assumptions and simplifications, collect and analyze data, and develop and use models to represent the

Knowledge in Risk Assessment and Management, First Edition. Edited by Terje Aven and Enrico Zio.
© 2018 John Wiley & Sons Ltd. Published 2018 by John Wiley & Sons Ltd.

phenomena studied. These tasks are subjective by nature, which raises the issue of how one can evaluate and ensure the quality of the assessment.

As a general term, "quality" is associated with degree of excellence, conformance to requirements, totality of characteristics which act to satisfy a need, freedom from failure, fitness for use (fitness is defined by the customer), delighting customers, the degree to which a unit meets the requirements of the customer and the (perception of the) degree to which the product or service meets the customer's expectations (expectations covering needs and requirements) (Bergman and Klefsjö 2010). But what does freedom from failure mean in a risk assessment context? And what about fitness for use or meeting the customer's expectations? If the decision maker is the customer, he or she may be very pleased with some results in a particular case, but that does not necessarily lead us to conclude that the quality of the risk assessment is good. Clearly, the decision maker cannot be used alone as the customer, to gauge the quality of a risk assessment: some quality principles and requirements must be defined in a more general sense.

In the nuclear power field, the quality of probabilistic safety assessments (PSAs) has been addressed by a number of regulatory and industry organizations. Some have argued that a good PSA should be a complete, full-scope, three-level PSA (considering the three phases of accident evolution: in the plant internal environment, within the containment vessel, and in the external environment), while others have claimed that the quality of a PSA should be measured with respect to the application and decision supported. For example, in 2001 the International Atomic Energy Agency (IAEA) released its publication TECDOC-1200 (IAEA 2001), which concerned the analysis of some limitations of PSA capability in estimating the actual reliability and risk contributions of complex and advanced systems such as nuclear power plants. Bounding analyses and sensitivity studies are suggested to estimate the possible risk significance. A distinction is also made between PSA quality and quality assurance: the former refers to the technical adequacy of the methods, level of detail, and data used to develop the PSA model; the latter refers to the approaches used to ensure that the chosen methods and data are applied and documented in an adequate and controlled manner. Emphasis is placed on the importance of having proper guidance to ensure that a PSA is of sufficiently high quality and is adequate to support risk-informed decision-making objectives. To guarantee that a PSA can meet such intended uses, it is necessary to satisfy specific characteristics and levels of detail in the analysis, so as to indirectly guarantee the adequacy and reliability of the decision informed by the PSA analysis outcomes.

In response to these recommendations and requirements, a second document was published containing a proposal for determining the quality of a PSA for application to nuclear power plants (IAEA 2006). It identifies attributes (technical features) that should be satisfied in the PSA model and analysis development to achieve the required robustness and reliability in the outcomes. A set of specific attributes and characteristics that are believed to measure the qualifications of a PSA model is defined, with respect to which assurance of quality satisfaction can be evaluated. Then, a main challenge for determining the quality of PSA is the definition of the attributes that are believed to affect the risk-informed decision making and the associated predefined quality acceptance criteria guidelines. The attributes are classified into general and special attributes, depending on their suitability to be used in all or specific PSA applications. The general attributes can be used for all typical PSA base cases, but the specific ones describe special, enhanced, and elevated capabilities supporting certain applications of PSAs.

The quality issue of risk assessment is related to that of evaluating the quality of modeling and simulation (M&S) activities (AIAA 1998; DoD 1996; Roache 1998; Software Engineering Institute 2006; West 2004). During the last few decades, modeling and simulation has dramatically impacted how engineered systems are designed and how the performance, reliability, and safety of these systems are assessed. The application of M&S to complex systems has conclusively demonstrated that there are a number of elements that are crucial to predictive capability (Oberkampf *et al.* 2007). With continually increasing resources devoted to the development of M&S capabilities and increasing reliance placed on M&S in decision making, it is necessary to develop improved methods for assessing the quality of M&S activities. A recent example of such efforts is the Predictive Capability Maturity Model (PCMM), which is a structured method for assessing the level of maturity of M&S activities. The six M&S elements used to assess maturity in this model are:

- representation and geometric fidelity
- physics and material model fidelity
- code verification
- solution verification
- model validation
- uncertainty quantification and sensitivity analysis.

For each of these elements, attributes are identified that characterize four increasing levels of maturity.

In the scientific literature, there are few works that have raised this issue from a general risk assessment and quality point of view. Two examples are Rosqvist and Tuominen (2004) and Aven and Heide (2009). Following Aven and Heide (see also Aven 2013c), two general criteria of "scientific quality" can be stated:

- The assessment is in compliance with all rules, assumptions, limitations, or constraints introduced, and the basis for all choices, judgments and so on are clear, and finally the principles, methods, and models are ordered and systematic, to ensure that any necessary critique can be raised and that it is comprehensible.

- The analysis is relevant and useful – it contributes to a development within the disciplines it concerns, and it is useful with a view to solving the "problem(s)" it concerns or with a view to further development in order to solve the "problem(s)" it concerns.

These two scientific quality requirements are based on standard requirements for scientific work (RCN 2000). However, a risk assessment needs not in general be a "fully scientific" work. Think about a oil-company risk assessment supporting decision making about the need for risk-reducing measures for an offshore operation. Should one require that the work is conducted in such a way that critique can be raised? And should we require that the assessment contributes to developments within the risk assessment discipline? For scientific studies, such requirements make sense, and risk assessment may have such an ambition in some cases, for example in a formal risk assessment comparing different medical treatments. But this is clearly not so for all risk assessments.

According to Rosqvist and Tuominen (Rosqvist 2010; Rosqvist and Tuominen 2004), quality relates to confidence in the results of the risk assessment and the recommendations derived from it. Typical questions that are raised for quality evaluations are of the type:

- Is the scope of the assessment complete?
- Are the means of analysis and the logic of inference credible?
- Is it possible that the risk characterisations lead to unjustified decisions?

By addressing these questions, the decision maker seeks evidence as to whether or not the risk assessment, the results of which they will use for informing decision making, is sound.

Related quality criteria are found in Heikkilä *et al.* (2009) and Rouhiainen and Heikkilä (2008). A set of indicators are identified as strongly influencing the performance of a risk assessment and its quality:

- definition of the object
- system definition and description, including limitations
- analysis methods, chosen according to the system and the objective of the analysis
- quality of the source and background information
- competence of the analysis leader
- availability of the required resources
- documentation
- results and the analysis process meeting the objectives of the analysis
- communication of the results.

Aven and Heide (2009) also discuss risk assessment quality in relation to the "reliability" and "validity" criteria. While reliability is concerned with the consistency of the "measuring instrument" (analysts, experts, methods, procedures), validity is concerned with the success at "measuring" what one sets out to "measure" in the analysis. More precisely, Aven and Heide (2009) make the following definitions:

- *Reliability*: the extent to which the risk assessment yields the same results when repeating the analysis (R).
- *Validity*: the degree to which the risk analysis describes the specific concepts that one is attempting to describe (V).

Depending on the objectives of the analysis, more specific and detailed interpretations (sub-criteria) of the above general definitions of reliability and validity can be formulated (Aven and Heide 2009):

Reliability:
- The degree to which the risk analysis methods produce the same results in reruns of these methods (R1)
- The degree to which the risk analysis produces identical results when conducted by different analysis teams, but using the same methods and data (R2)
- The degree to which the risk analysis produces identical results when conducted by different analysis teams with the same analysis scope and objectives, but no restrictions on methods and data (R3).

Validity:
- The degree to which the produced risk numbers are accurate compared to the underlying true risk (V1)
- The degree to which the assigned probabilities adequately describe the assessor's uncertainties of the unknown quantities considered (V2)
- The degree to which the epistemic uncertainty assessments are complete (V3)
- The degree to which the analysis addresses the right quantities (V4).

This brief review of literature work shows that the issue of the quality of risk assessment must be addressed with respect to the specific purpose of the risk assessment itself. If it is to identify potential hazards/threats, it would obviously be evaluated as not of high quality if one type of hazard, known to several experts in the company to represent a serious risk, were overlooked. In this case, the quality is judged with respect to a property of completeness of the analysis. Other situations may be more difficult to judge. Is the estimate of the probability of an event or scenario a good estimate? Is the quality related to the ability to accurately estimate some underlying true risk numbers? We need to clarify if accurate risk estimation is a goal of the risk assessment, as the issue of quality will be completely different if the aim is rather to describe the knowledge and lack of knowledge associated with potential hazards/threats and their consequences.

This chapter focuses on the risk assessment goal of describing and characterizing knowledge and lack of knowledge (for short denoted knowledge characterisations). It reflects current thinking about risk, which shows a trend towards seeing uncertainty as a key element of risk, see for example the ISO 31000 definition of risk (ISO 2009), the definition of risk by the Petroleum Safety Authority (PSA-N 2015) and the recommendation given by the new Society for Risk Analysis Glossary (SRA 2015). In line with such risk conceptualisations, more focus is placed on knowledge and lack of knowledge descriptions and characterisations, compared to more traditional probability-based perspectives. Some work has been conducted to define what quality is in relation to knowledge characterisations (see for example Aven 2013c and Hansson and Aven 2014), but the work is still at an early stage.

We seek to bring new insights to this topic by addressing the difference between risk as characterised by analysts and the risk to be considered by decision makers. The point made is that decision makers need to address unconditional risk and not only conditional risk as described by the risk analysts and experts. To illustrate, let P be the probability of an event A, as derived by an analysis team using models and expert judgments. This probability expresses judgments made by the analysts on the basis of a background knowledge K, which typically covers many assumptions. We can write this as $P = P(A|K)$. Within a traditional probability-based risk perspective, the focus is on the probabilities, but this risk description is in fact a conditional risk description; that is, "given K". And this K may conceal important aspects of risk: for example, an assumption may turn out to be wrong. The knowledge can be weak and surprises may occur relative to this knowledge. On the other hand, the decision maker must try to consider all risks for making their decisions; in other words, their judgments need to address unconditional risk and risk covered by K. The evaluation of the quality of a risk assessment must take this into account. The big question is how to bridge the gap between the conditional risk characterizations of the analysts and the judgments of the decision makers. Or, rephrased, how can we guarantee quality processes that treat this gap in a proper way. These are some of the topics we address in this chapter. We use one example to illustrate our discussions: an LNG (liquefied natural gas) plant. The example is presented in Section 7.2. Then, in Section 7.3 we formulate more precisely the challenge addressed in this chapter – the above-mentioned gap – and point to key means to improve current risk assessment practice to deal with it. The next two sections give further details on these means – reliability and validity issues in Section 7.4 and knowledge issues in Section 7.5. Section 7.6 discusses the findings and Section 7.7 provides some conclusions.

7.2 Example

An LNG plant is being planned and the operator would like to locate it not more than a few hundred metres from a residential area (Vinnem 2010). Several quantitative risk assessments (QRAs) are performed in order to demonstrate that the risk is acceptable according to some pre-defined risk acceptance criteria. In the QRAs, risk is expressed using computed probabilities and expected values. The risk metrics used include both individual risk and f–n curves, and traditional risk matrices are also used. The f–n curves show the assigned probability for accidents occurring with at least n fatalities as a function of n (Bedford and Cooke 2001). The individual risk expresses the assessed probability that an arbitrary but specific person will be killed during a specific year. It turns out that the assessments and the associated risk management approach meet with strong criticism. The neighbours and many independent experts find the risk characterisation insufficient; they argue that risk has been reported according to a risk perspective that is too narrow.

To compute the risk metrics, a number of assumptions were made:

- the event tree model
- a specific number of exposed people
- a specific fraction of fatalities in different scenarios
- the probabilities and frequencies of leakages, based on a database for offshore hydrocarbon releases
- all vessels and piping are protected by water applications, like monitors and hydrants
- that in the event of the impact of a passing vessel on an LNG tanker loading at the quay, the gas release would be ignited immediately (by sparks generated by the collision itself).

Several experts argued against this last assumption. One of them wrote:

> The implication of this assumption was that it was unnecessary to consider in the studies any spreading of the gas cloud due to wind and heating of the liquefied gas, with obvious consequences for the scenarios the public might be exposed to. Such a very critical assumption should at least have been subjected to a sensitivity study in order to illustrate how changes in the assumption would affect the results, and the robustness of the assumption discussed. None of this, however, has been provided in any of the studies" (Vinnem 2010).

7.3 Theoretical Formulation of the Challenge

The risk assessment produces a risk metric m, defined as a probability of a specific event A, which is conditional on knowledge K. We have $m = P(A|K)$. Here P is a subjective (judgmental, knowledge-based) probability. More generally, the metric could be a vector of probabilities as well as expected values.

The decision maker is in general informed by m and K. In practice, the way K is typically described varies, from a list of assumptions with the results of an associated sensitivity analysis, to basically no coverage of the content and significance (strength) of K. To ensure that the basic requirements for the quality of a risk assessment are satisfied, the following conditions are needed:

- The background knowledge K is revealed and discussed.
- The risk metric's dependence on K is analyzed (e.g. using sensitivity and uncertainty analyses) and discussed.

Current risk assessment practice acknowledges the importance of these two conditions, and their role in ensuring a high quality assessment, when considered together with the quality requirements for the risk assessment process, the latter covering questions such as:

- Is the purpose of the assessment clearly defined?
- Is the object of the analysis well defined?
- Does the analysis group have the necessary competence?
- Are the methods used for the analysis scientifically recognized and widely accepted?
- And so on.

Transparent information about such quality issues provides the decision maker with an understanding of the degree of the risk metric's dependence on K and brings attention to aspects of importance for the quality of the assessment work carried out. However, a gap still remains between the information provided by the risk analyst and the decision maker's need for decision support. This chapter argues that current practice can be improved by acknowledging this gap and addressing it in a rational, scientific approach. More specifically, we see a potential for improvement by implementing systematic procedures to deal with these points in a transparent way.

To this end, it is necessary to make a clear distinction between the risk metric m used by the analyst and the unconditional risk that the decision maker has to handle, understood as the occurrence of events with consequences for something that humans value, and the associated uncertainties. The gap between the analyst risk metric m and the decision maker's unconditional risk needs to be addressed by considering and evaluating:

i) The reliability and validity of the risk description.
ii) The strength of the knowledge K (SoK) that the risk metric m is based on.
iii) The potential for surprises relative to the knowledge K.

These points are considered in current practice only to a limited degree. Their evaluation should be conducted by the risk analyst, to allow the decision maker understand what the risk assessment considers and represents, what its results do and do not express, what insights have guided the analyst's assessment, and what open issues remain that need to be taken into account when making the decision. These evaluations should clarify what key assumptions represent for the risk message produced by the metric m, how solid and robust this is, and should indicate if judgments about these assumptions could be questioned. Informed of this, the decision maker may have their own assessment of the effects of deviations from these assumptions on the risk. The risk assessment process should support such reasoning by decision makers, rather than giving the impression that the risk assessment tells the "truth" about the risk.

Of course, the decision maker's risk understanding is also subjective and conditional on some knowledge, but their focus on unconditional risk ensures that more weight is placed on scrutinising the concealed risk contributors in the background knowledge than is the case in a more traditional approach.

In the following sections, we will look further into the issues in the list above, using the LNG example of Section 7.2 as an illustration.

7.4 Reliability and Validity Issues

With regards to the item (i) of the list in the previous Section 7.3, we first consider the validity and then reliability.

7.4.1 Validity Criteria

The validity criterion is the degree to which the risk assessment describes the specific concepts that one is attempting to describe, and the three sub-criteria V2–V4 – see Section 7.1 – are relevant.

It is not straightforward to verify that the validity requirement V2 is met: that the assigned probabilities adequately describe the assessor's uncertainties and the unknown quantities considered. There is an ongoing research and discussion in the scientific literature addressing this issue (Flage *et al.* 2014). It is outside the scope of this chapter to give a full account of this research and discussion, but we will point to some important principles and procedures (Aven 2011; Cooke 1991; Lindley *et al.* 1979):

- Coherent uncertainty assessments are achieved by using the rules of probability, including Bayes' theorem for updating of assessments in the light of new information.
- Comparisons are made with relevant observed relative frequencies if available. For example, if history shows that out of a population of 1000 units, two have failed, we can compare our probability to the rate 2/1000.
- Training in probability assignment is required, to make assessors aware of heuristics (such as the availability heuristic; Tversky and Kahneman 1974) as well as other problems of quantifying probabilities such as superficiality and imprecision (which relate to the assessor's possible lack of feeling for

numerical values). Heuristics also need to be attended to when professional analysts and experts assign probabilities, but this is mainly a problem when lay people assign probabilities.

- Models, including probability models, should be used to simplify the assignment process.
- Procedures for incorporating expert judgments should be used.
- Accountability: the basis for all probability assignments must be identified.

In addition, motivational aspects will always be an important part of evaluating probabilities and thus the usefulness of analyses that include expert judgements. In general, we should be aware of the existence of incentives that in some cases could significantly affect the assignments. However, we will conclude that motivational aspects are not a problem when professionals perform the risk assessment. On the contrary, in general, professional analysts would not, by intention, perform a biased assessment, influenced by motivational factors. Their jobs would not last long if their reputation were questioned. However, their approach to the assessment and the methods used could be strongly in favour of one specific party. For example, when performing a standard risk analysis of a process plant, such as the LNG plant discussed in Section 7.2, one may argue that important uncertainty factors are camouflaged, and hence V3 is not met: see the discussion below. Do the analysts do anything about this? Do they report on this? Probably not, as it is not in the interest of the client (the plant operator). Thus indirectly, motivational aspects are an important issue when assessing the results of risk assessments.

These principles and procedures provide a basis for establishing a standard for the probability assignments, the aim being to extract and summarize knowledge about the unknown quantities (parameters), using models, observed data and expert opinions. It seems reasonable to say that the requirement V2 is met, provided that this standard is followed.

Next, we address V3. It is a challenge to express the epistemic uncertainties about all the unknown quantities and parameters. In practice, a common approach is to specify some marginal distributions on some selected quantities and parameters, so that the uncertainty distributions on the output probabilities just reflect some aspects of the uncertainty. This makes it difficult to interpret the produced uncertainties. This problem is relevant for the LNG example, where the assessment is based on complex models with hundreds of parameters. A way of dealing with the issue is to focus on the observable quantities, for example the number of fatalities, and let the epistemic uncertainties be based on both (subjective/judgmental/knowledge-based) probability and strength of knowledge (SoK) judgments. The idea of the SoK judgments is to reveal risk and uncertainties covered by the background knowledge K that the probabilities are based on. For the LNG example, let us consider the assumption that in the event of impact of a passing vessel on an LNG tanker loading at the quay, the gas release would be ignited immediately, presumably by sparks generated by the collision itself. This assumption could be wrong. Uncertainties in the risk results are not fully revealed if uncertainties about this assumption are not assessed. See more detailed discussion of this issue in Section 7.5.

Next we address the criterion V4: the degree to which the analysis addresses the right quantities. If probabilistic parameters are introduced, we need to question whether these are really the quantities of interest. The goal is to express the risk of an activity but does the average performance of a thought-constructed population of similar situations express meaningful representations of the system or activity being studied? As discussed, it may be more informative to focus on the observable quantities such as the number of fatalities. To meet criterion V4, it is essential to have clear interpretations of the quantities addressed. If we define models with parameters, interpretations are needed. Only then can we make a judgment about whether the quantities are relevant for describing risk. For the LNG case, this criterion V4 can be seen to be met if we are able to provide such interpretations, and this is clearly the case if we focus on observables as discussed above. If instead the point of departure is some underlying frequentist probabilities that we should assess, it is not so straightforward to provide meaningful interpretations. Are we interested in the average performance, and not the performance of the specific activity analyzed? If we focus on the frequentist probability, we presume that this average is representative for the specific unit studied.

7.4.2 Reliability Criteria

Now let us look at the reliability criterion R: the extent to which the risk analysis yields the same results when repeating the analysis. One may expect that, following the standard for probability assignments (that is, meeting V2) would ensure that the reliability requirement R is met. However, the background knowledge that the assignments are based on need not be exactly the same from analysis to analysis. Hence, we would experience differences in the probability assignments. However, the differences are not likely to be large if V2 is met. This observation applies to both R1 and R2. The criterion R3 (the degree to which the risk analysis produces identical (similar) results when conducted by different analysis teams with the same analysis scope and objectives, but no restrictions on methods and data) would in general not be met, as the background information would be different from analysis to analysis, and often the difference could be very large due to different levels of competence, research schools, tools available and so on. This issue is relevant to the LNG case in particular, as the assessments are based on many subjective judgments and assumptions (see the benchmarking exercise in Lauridsen *et al.* (2002)), which illustrates this problem of lack of reliability (R3)).

We may question the appropriateness of the reliability criteria in this case. Obviously, we would require the results not to depend on the person running the computer calculations and so on, but it should not be an objective to strive for identical results from different analysis teams. According to V2, the uncertainties are assessed using subjective probabilities. The background information for these assignments could be different from one analysis team to another, and often this difference could be very large, as mentioned in the previous paragraph. Reflecting these differences may be considered an important aim of the analysis. To some extent, this aspect is reflected in the strength of knowledge judgments.

7.5 Knowledge Issues

We take the position that the current descriptions of risk and the related frameworks for its assessment need to be extended for a proper characterization of the knowledge upon which the descriptions are built, and any lack of knowledge that limits them. This should enable characterization of the gap between the conditional risk resulting from the assessment and the unconditional risk that the decision makers need to consider for managing risk properly. In this view, the probability metric used within a classical description of uncertainty does not provide information about the quality of the assessment: the quality and strength of the knowledge that supports the assumptions made for the assessment itself. This information could conceal important aspects affecting the consequent predictive capability of the risk assessment.

By characterizing the strength of knowledge that supports the assumptions underpinning the risk metrics, the decision maker is made aware of the gap with the unconditional risk and the fact that surprises may occur relative to what is captured in the assessment based on the analyst's knowledge, enabling them to be more or less cautious in their decisions.

Uncertainty intervals are used as an extension of the standard risk description to account for the many different situations that could occur in a risk setting like that of the LNG plant risk assessment example described in Section 7.2. For example, different situations related to the leakage position, the weather conditions, or the number of persons potentially exposed, would lead to different consequences with different probabilities of occurrence.

The uncertainty intervals clearly reflect variations due to the many situations that could occur, but they also are conditional on the analyst's knowledge and the intervals themselves do not express the strength of such knowledge. Information about this strength would obviously inform the decision maker that uses the results of the risk assessment to inform their decisions. The questions are, then:

- What does it mean that the knowledge is strong or poor?
- How do we assess this?
- How do we communicate it to the decision makers?

Aven (2013a, 2014) presents two methods for describing the strength of knowledge that supports the risk assessment.

The first one is a direct grading of the strength of knowledge, in line with the scoring proposed in Flage and Aven (2009), which looks at the knowledge, data and expertise related to the risk setting of interest. This approach relates to the Predictive Capability Maturity Model (PCMM), mentioned in Section 7.1, for assessing the level of maturity of M&S activities, but has a different focus, in that it addresses specifically the knowledge supporting the probabilities assigned.

The second one is based on an analysis of the main assumptions on which the risk assessment is constructed, using the "assumption deviation risk" concept. For instance, in the case of the LNG plant risk assessment, six main assumptions have been identified (see Section 7.2 above). Then, for each assumption one assesses the deviations from the conditions/states defined and assigns a risk score, using score categories such as high, medium or low, for each deviation. These reflect:

- the magnitude of the deviation
- the probability of this magnitude occuring
- the effect of the change on the consequences C
- the strength of knowledge supporting these judgments.

This "assumption deviation risk" score, which is to be seen as a measure of the criticality or importance of the assumption, captures the basic components of the risk description of the extended risk perspectives:

- the deviation from the assumptions made, with associated consequences
- a measure of uncertainty of this deviation and consequences
- the knowledge that the deviation is based on.

With these evaluations, we can draw conclusions about the overall strength of the knowledge that supports the probabilistic analysis. For example, if we have a low number of assumptions with high criticality/risk score, we would classify the strength of knowledge as high. If, however, there are many assumptions with high criticality/risk scores, we would conclude that the strength of knowledge is poor. And we may use an intermediate category or categories to reflect situations in-between these two extremes.

In Aven (2013a), the strength of knowledge assessment for the example of Section 7.2 led to an evaluation of weak/medium, due to many of the six main assumptions being given rather high risk/criticality scores. This additional information on the strength of knowledge is an essential addition to the numerical results produced for decision makers and stakeholders. This risk/criticality scoring can also be used as a guideline for where to place the focus to improve the risk assessment: the assumptions with high score should be examined to see if they can be dealt with in some way, so that they can be moved to a lower risk/criticality category.

The strength of knowledge, then, becomes an additional dimension of the risk assessed, informing the decision maker of the quality of the risk assessment and the level of confidence that can be placed in its results.

Another aspect to be included in the extended risk perspective is the identification of possible surprises relative to the knowledge that is used in the assessment to produce the (conditional) risk results (the surprises – "Black swans" – of type II; Aven 2013b). Different methods can be used to reveal such events; see Aven (2014) and the following discussion.

Again, the output of a risk assessment is conditional on the models chosen, assumptions taken and judgments made by the analyst and other experts, based on their background knowledge K. This must be transparent in the analysis and made clear to the decision makers, who eventually must handle the unconditional risk. In fact, a conditional risk description, given K may not capture important aspects of risk. The knowledge can be weak and surprises may occur relative to this knowledge. The question is, then, how to qualify the risk assessment, which entails finding a way to say something about the gap between the conditional risk characterizations of the analysts and the decision maker's need to address all risk aspects, the unconditional risk. This entails addressing the uncertainties linked to the models and their parameters, the potential scenarios and hazards identified, so that the decision maker can be made aware and take her or his decision confidently with respect to what is known and what is not known.

The quality of a risk assessment (meeting some "scientific criteria" and "being useful" in a decision making context) can, then, be improved if the knowledge K is improved, reducing the gap between conditional risk (from the analysis) and the unconditional risk that the decision maker needs to address. It is in this direction that a number of efforts have recently focused on new approaches for understanding, identifying, and discovering potential accident scenarios, particularly in complex risk contexts involving heterogeneous elements (physical, human, software, organizational), very large spatial scales and long time horizons (like the modern cyber-physical systems and critical infrastructure), for which probabilities are difficult to define. More "knowledgeable" assumptions and models of potential accidents allow for a better understanding of the risk situation and thus can help in reducing surprises.

In this vein, the Functional Resonance Accident Model (FRAM) provides a way to examine individual system functions and determine their interrelationships at system level (Hollnagel 2004, 2012). FRAM models the functions of a complex socio-technical system that contribute to its successful operation. Knowledge of how some functions are coupled for successful operation and how variability may affect them can reveal how surprising scenarios may occur. FRAM makes no assumptions about how the system under investigation is structured or organized, nor about possible causes and cause–effect relations. Instead of searching for failures and malfunctions, FRAM looks at how functions become coupled and how variability may "resonate" into surprising outcomes. The accident is not seen as arising from a linear combination of causal links but rather as due to the inability to anticipate, timely recognise, and react to anomalous and critical situations that arise due to problems in system functions surprisingly combining in resonance, developing into a dynamic accident. The identification of the system functions and their coupling for successful system operation, the study of possible variabilities and the potential for resonance, and of the (damping) protective and resilience barriers installed in the system can give a better understanding of how accidents may develop and of the risk context, thus strengthening K.

Another method is the Anticipatory Failure Determination (AFD) method, based on I-TRIZ, a form of the theory of inventive problem solving, which enables the identification of failure scenarios to be viewed as a creative process carried out systematically, exhaustively, and with diligence (Zlotin *et al.* 1999). Traditional failure analysis addresses the questions:

- "How did this failure happen?"
- "How can this failure happen?"

AFD and TRIZ go one step further and pose the question:

- "If I wanted to create this particular failure, how could I do it?"

The technique continues by deliberately "inventing" failure events and scenarios, to reveal situations that would not emerge in traditional causal-based reasoning.

Exploring and treating variations in the system functions that contribute to successful operation is also at the core of the System-Theoretic Accident Model and Process (STAMP) and the control theory view of safety, in which accidents are seen as being due to loss of control, resulting from deviations/variations from nominal behaviour due to a lack of appropriate constraints (control actions) on system design, or from inadequate enforcement of constraints (control actions) in system operation (Belmonte *et al.* 2011; Cowlagi and Saleh 2013; Ishimatsu *et al.* 2014; Leveson 2004, 2011; Liu *et al.* 2013; Rosa *et al.* 2015; Song 2012). Concepts of observability and controllability seem to offer a promising way to understand predictability and unpredictability, with respect to "common-cause variations" (predictable in view of historical experience and knowledge) and "special-cause variations" (unpredictable, because beyond experience and knowledge). See Bergman (2008) and Deming (2000).

Finally, the computational models used in risk assessment can be used in the exploration of the scenario space using advanced simulation techniques. In this case, the aim of simulation is neither completeness nor accuracy of probability estimation, as in traditional risk analysis. Instead, it is to enable the generation of "surprising" scenarios (because not foreseen and of significant consequences) that may provide useful insights about what could happen in the system (Turati *et al.* 2015, 2016, 2017). Methods of "adjoint" simulation of reverse stress testing may be of particular interest for generating deductive (anticipatory, backwards) scenarios, where we start from a future imagined, large-consequence state of the system and find the scenario (of stress, of deviation) that must develop for this state to occur. Interpretation of these scenarios by system thinking, to reveal the holes and interconnections, is critical if one is to identify surprising events. In contrast, using for example an event tree to reveal scenarios has strong limitations, as the analysis is based on linear inductive thinking about the chain of events resulting from an accident initiator (Kaplan *et al.* 1999).

7.6 Discussion

The issue of risk assessment and management lies in the gap between the conditional risk provided as the output of a risk assessment, the result of a process of assumptions, modeling choices, and analyst and expert judgments, based on their knowledge, and the unconditional risk that the decision maker must manage.

Confidence can be built on the quality of the assessment, which comes from further knowledge of the risk context for its better characterization, thus reducing the gap between conditional and unconditional. Methods are being developed for exploring system functionalities in order to capture the effects of variations that may lead to accidents. FRAM, STAMP, and AFD are systemic methods of analysis that allow generation of new insights about system behavior and accident causality and variability. Advanced simulation methods can also contribute to improvements in knowledge, revealing surprising and unforeseen scenarios.

However, a model is exactly that: a model, and not the system or context it represents. There will always be limitations in how well the model matches the system behavior. Assumptions have to be made about resolution, system boundaries, and so on. Also in FRAM, for example, many assumptions about reasonable variability need to be made and STAMP contains many assumptions, for example about how a system is organized (Leveson 2015).

For quality of risk assessment, one needs to improve knowledge by reducing uncertainty through improved system understanding and modeling, but also by better characterization of uncertainty itself. The accuracy of the model is important, but this accuracy cannot be judged without taking into account the uncertainty about how well the model with scenarios/hazards matches the system. FRAM, STAMP, AFD and scenario exploration by simulation essentially improve knowledge of the system and, therefore, its modelling. But there will still be uncertainties and potential for surprises that are not addressed, and this fact needs to be communicated to the decision maker. Along with the more accurate model there has to be a statement about uncertainties, to enable its accuracy, and therefore the quality of the risk assessment, to be judged. One way of doing this has been presented in papers by Aven and Zio (2013) and Bjerga *et al.* (2014). In these papers, the difference between the true variation pattern F (which in theory can be known with time) and the model G(X) (X being a vector of parameters), is called the model error; that is the model error is F – G(X), and the uncertainty about the magnitude of the model error is called the "model uncertainty". Based on a model uncertainty analysis, a model can be accredited or remodeled, or at the very least the analysis produces a statement about the uncertainties that can be presented to the decision maker, who is thus made aware of the quality of the risk assessment in terms of its prediction capability. Different models can also be compared on the basis of the model uncertainty analysis.

Models of this type provide input to epistemic uncertainty characterizations, typically using subjective (judgmental, knowledge-based) probability. Formally, we may write such statements as $P(A|K)$, where A is the event of interest, which is then linked to G in a direct or indirect way. The model uncertainty is an aspect of the "quality" of the background knowledge K. To make a full assessment of this quality, we need to consider a set of aspects, as discussed by Aven (2014) and Flage and Aven (2009):

- the degree to which assumptions made represent strong simplifications
- the availability of relevant data
- the degree of agreement/consensus among experts
- the degree of understanding of the phenomena involved
- the existence of accurate models.

Assumptions are of particular importance and separate assessments could be conducted. An approach is presented in Aven 2013a using the assumption–deviation risk concept. Assumptions for example about variability or interactions need to be stated, and then evaluated as to what deviations can occur, how likely the deviations are, the potential consequences, and the strength of the background knowledge. Other approaches are also available to address assumptions, such as Assumption-Based Planning (Dewar 2002; Leveson 2015).

It is also relevant to address potential surprises relative to the knowledge/beliefs held. If the surprises carry extreme consequences, they are called black swans (Aven 2013b; Taleb 2007). These can be addressed using, for example, "red teams", and monitoring of signals and warnings (Aven 2014; Paté-Cornell 2012). A red team in a risk analysis would consist of an "external" analysis group, whose job is to challenge the models, assumptions and judgments made by the risk assessment analyst group. A list of potential black swans can then be handed to the decision maker.

In the end, the quality of the risk assessment is essentially about knowledge and uncertainty, which condition the risk description, thus defining the gap from the unconditional risk to be handled by the decision maker, who needs to be made aware of it for conscious and confident management. The risk characterization obtained from a risk assessment must include the standard elements of risk, such as the events and scenarios and their consequences and probabilities, but also uncertainty intervals and indications related to the conditional risk in terms of strength of knowledge evaluations and considerations of surprises with respect to the model and knowledge considered. This extended risk quality information provides insights that decision makers and other stakeholders can consider in their decision making. The results are conditional on the analysts and experts, and the impact of this conditioning needs to be analysed and accounted for.

7.7 Conclusions

In this chapter, we have raised and discussed the issue of the quality of a risk assessment. Why? Because we are convinced that in many practical situations, this is fundamental for a proper use of the risk assessment to inform decision making. Our conviction comes from the fact that we believe that risk assessment should help frame the knowledge of, and the lack thereof, of the phenomena and processes involved in the assessment. The example used in the paper is enlightening. The risk assessment conducted in the LNG was a traditional one, which aimed to show that the plant was safe by reference to pre-defined risk acceptance criteria. This practice is problematic because the risk is not adequately described by the probabilities and the issue of being safe should not be judged on the basis of the computed numbers alone. A risk assessment conducted in this way fails to meet basic quality requirements. Instead, we advocate a risk assessment approach that aims at knowledge characterisations and where the framing of the assessment is built on an acknowledgment that there is a gap between the conditional risk picture produced by the risk analyst and the decision maker's need to address the unconditional risk. The quality of the risk assessment is very much dependent on how one is able to deal with this gap. In the LNG case, this gap was not even acknowledged by key actors. In this chapter we discussed the importance of this gap and highlighted issues that should be focused to bridge it.

If we think of a hypothetical case where the LNG case was analysed in line with the suggested approach, the decision makers would be faced with a decision basis that did not provide a clear conclusion about the plant being safe or not, but rather provided insights that would enable them to draw conclusions themselves. This shift in perspective raises challenges, as many decision makers would expect clear recommendations from the risk assessments, and in the LNG case such a way of using a risk assessment would have been demanding for the politicians that had to make a decision. However, in our view, this is the only meaningful use of risk assessment in such a case, and it would place the ball in the right court, as the managers' and politicians' main task is to balance different concerns and make judgments in view of risks and uncertainties. The risk analysts have one main role, namely to properly inform the decision makers. They should not make the decisions for them.

Acknowledgements

The work has been partly funded by the Norwegian Research Council, as a part of the Petromaks 2 program (grant number 228335/E30). The support is gratefully acknowledged.

References

AIAA (1998). AIAA guide for the verification and validation of computational fluid dynamics simuations (G-077–1998). AIAA.

Aven, T. (2011). On some recent definitions and analysis frameworks for risk, vulnerability, and resilience. *Risk Analysis*, 31(4), 515–522.

Aven, T. (2013a). A conceptual foundation for assessing and managing risk, surprises and black swans. Paper presented at the Network Safety Conference, Toulouse, FR.

Aven, T. (2013b). On the meaning of a black swan in a risk context. *Safety Science*, 57, 44–51.

Aven, T. (2013c). Practical implications of the new risk perspectives. *Reliability Engineering & System Safety*, 115, 136–145.

Aven, T. (2014). *Risk, Surprises and Black Swans: Fundamental Ideas and Concepts in Risk Assessment and Risk Management*. Routledge.

Aven, T. and Heide, B.R. (2009). Reliability and validity of risk analysis. *Reliability Engineering & System Safety*, 94(11), 1862–1868.

Aven, T. and Zio, E. (2013). Model output uncertainty in risk assessment. *International Journal of Performability Engineering*, 9(5), 475–486.

Bedford, T. and Cooke, R.M. (2001). Probability density decomposition for conditionally dependent random variables modeled by vines. *Annals of Mathematics and Artificial intelligence*, 32(1–4), 245–268.

Belmonte, F., Schön, W., Heurley, L., and Capel, R. (2011). Interdisciplinary safety analysis of complex socio-technological systems based on the functional resonance accident model: An application to railway trafficsupervision. *Reliability Engineering & System Safety*, 96(2), 237–249.

Bergman, B. (2008). Conceptualistic pragmatism: a framework for Bayesian analysis? *IIE Transactions*, 41(1), 86–93.

Bergman, B. and Klefsjö, B. (2010). *Quality from Customer Needs to Customer Satisfaction*. Studentlitteratur.

Bjerga, T., Aven, T., and Zio, E. (2014). An illustration of the use of an approach for treating model uncertainties in risk assessment. *Reliability Engineering & System Safety*, 125, 46–53.

Cooke, R.M. (1991*). Experts in Uncertainty: Opinion and Subjective Probability in Science*. Oxford University Press.

Cowlagi, R.V. and Saleh, J.H. (2013). Coordinability and consistency in accident causation and prevention: formal system theoretic concepts for safety in multilevel systems. *Risk Analysis*, 33(3), 420–433.

Deming, W.E. (2000). *The New Economics: For Industry, Government, Education*. MIT Press.

Dewar, J.A. (2002). *Assumption-based Planning: A tool for Reducing Avoidable Surprises*. Cambridge University Press.

DoD (1996) Department of Defense instruction 5000.61: DoD modeling and simulation (M&S) verification, validation, and accreditation (VV&A).

Flage, R. and Aven, T. (2009). Expressing and communicating uncertainty in relation to quantitative risk analysis. *Reliability & Risk Analysis: Theory & Application*, 2(13), 9–18.

Flage, R., Aven, T., Zio, E. and Baraldi, P. (2014). Concerns, challenges, and directions of development for the issue of representing uncertainty in risk assessment. *Risk Analysis*, 34(7), 1196–1207.

Hansson, S.O. and Aven, T. (2014). Is risk analysis scientific? *Risk Analysis*, 34(7), 1173–1183.

Heikkilä, A.-M., Murtonen, M., Nissilä, M. and Rouhiainen, V. (2009). Quality of risk assessment and its implementation. In: *Scientific Activities in Safety & Security*, VTT Technical Research Centre, Espoo, Finland, pp. 66–67.

Hollnagel, E. (2004). *Barriers and Accident Prevention*. Ashgate.

Hollnagel, E. (2012). *FRAM, the functional Resonance Analysis Method: Modelling Complex Socio-technical Systems*: Ashgate Publishing, Ltd.

IAEA. (2001). IAEA-TECDOC-1200 Applications of probabilistic safety assessment (PSA) for nuclear power plants. International Atomic Energy Agency.

IAEA. (2006). IAEA-TECDOC-1511 Determining the quality of probabilistic safety assessment (PSA) for applications in nuclear power plants. International Atomic Energy Agency.

Ishimatsu, T., Leveson, N.G., Thomas, J.P., *et al.* (2014). Hazard analysis of complex spacecraft using systems-theoretic process analysis. *Journal of Spacecraft and Rockets*, 51(2), 509–522.

ISO (2009) 31000 Risk management-principles and guidelines. International Standards Organization.

Kaplan, S., Visnepolschi, S., Zlotin, B. and Zusman, A. (1999). *New Tools for Failure and Risk Analysis: Anticipatory Failure Determination*. Ideation International Inc.

Lauridsen, K., Kozine, I., Markert, F., *et al.* (2002). Assessment of uncertainties in risk analysis of chemical establishments. The ASSURANCE project. Final summary report (8755030637).

Leveson, N. (2004). A new accident model for engineering safer systems. *Safety Science*, 42(4), 237–270.

Leveson, N. (2011). *Engineering a Safer World: Systems Thinking applied to Safety*. MIT Press.

Leveson, N. (2015). A systems approach to risk management through leading safety indicators. *Reliability Engineering & System Safety*, 136, 17–34.

Lindley, D.V., Tversky, A., and Brown, R.V. (1979). On the reconciliation of probability assessments. *Journal of the Royal Statistical Society. Series A (General)*, 142(2), 146–180.

Liu, Y.-Y., Slotine, J.-J., and Barabasi, A.-L. (2013). Observability of complex systems. *Proceedings of the National Academy of Sciences*, 110(7), 2460–2465.

Oberkampf, W.L., Pilch, M., and Trucano, T.G. (2007). *Predictive capability maturity model for computational modeling and simulation*. Retrieved from http://prod.sandia.gov/techlib/access-control.cgi/2007/075948.pdf.

Paté-Cornell, E. (2012). On "Black Swans" and "Perfect Storms": risk analysis and management when statistics are not enough. *Risk Analysis*, 32(11), 1823–1833.

PSA-N (2015) Definition of risk. Petroleum Safety Authority Norway. http://www. ptil.no/framework/category408.html#_Toc438219158. Accessed 31 July 2017.

RCN. (2000). *Quality in Norwegian Research: An overview of terms. methods and means*. [In Swedish] Norwegian Research Council, Oslo.

Roache, P.J. (1998). *Verification and Validation in Computational Science And Engineering*. Hermosa.

Rosa, L.V., Haddad, A.N., and de Carvalho, P.V.R. (2015). Assessing risk in sustainable construction using the Functional Resonance Analysis Method (FRAM). *Cognition, Technology & Work*, 17(4), 559–573.

Rosqvist, T. (2010). On the validation of risk analysis: A commentary. *Reliability Engineering & System Safety*, 95(11), 1261–1265.

Rosqvist, T. and Tuominen, R. (2004). Qualification of formal safety assessment: an exploratory study. *Safety Science*, 42(2), 99–120.

Rouhiainen, V. and Heikkilä, A.-M. (2008). Ensuring the quality of safety analyses in industry. Paper presented at the PSAM 9 International Conference on Probabilistic Safety Assessment and Management.

Software Engineering Institute. (2006). Capability maturity model integration. Retrieved from http://www.sei.cmu.edu/cmmi/.

Song, Y. (2012). *Applying System-theoretic Accident Model and Processes (STAMP) to Hazard Analysis*. MSc dissertation, McMaster University. https:// macsphere.mcmaster.ca/bitstream/11375/11867/1/fulltext.pdf. Assessed 1 August 2017.

SRA (2015). SRA glossary. Society of Risk Analysis. Retrieved from http://www. sra.org/sites/default/files/pdf/SRA-glossary-approved22june2015-x.pdf.

Taleb, N.N. (2007). *The Black Swan: The impact of the Highly Improbable*. Random House.

Turati, P., Pedroni, N., and Zio, E. (2015). An entropy-driven method for exploring extreme and unexpected accident scenario in the risk assessment of dynamic engineered systems. Paper presented at the Proceedings of the 25th ESREL, Safety and Reliability of Complex Engineered Systems, Zurich, Swiss.

Turati, P., Pedroni, N., and Zio, E. (2016). An adaptive simulation framework for the exploration of extreme and unexpected events in dynamic engineered systems. *Risk Analysis*, 37(1), 147–159.

Turati, P., Pedroni, N., and Zio, E. (2017). Simulation-based exploration of high-dimensional system models for critical regions identification. *Reliability Engineering & System Safety*, 165, 317–330.

Tversky, A. and Kahneman, D. (1974). Judgment under uncertainty: Heuristics and biases. *Science*, 185(4157), 1124–1131.

Vinnem, J.E. (2010). Risk analysis and risk acceptance criteria in the planning processes of hazardous facilities: A case of an LNG plant in an urban area. *Reliability Engineering & System Safety*, 95(6), 662–670.

West, M. (2004). *Real Process Improvement using the CMMI*. CRC Press.

Zlotin, B., Zusman, A., Kaplan, L., *et al.* (1999). TRIZ beyond technology: The theory and practice of applying TRIZ to nontechnical areas. https://pdfs. semanticscholar.org/c7d7/653f22df8c3e448b261e2a45a54c2b137cb6.pdf. Accessed 31 July 2017.

8

Knowledge-driven System Simulation for Scenario Analysis in Risk Assessment

Pietro Turati[1,2], Nicola Pedroni[1,3], and Enrico Zio[1,4]

[1] *Laboratoire Genie Industriel, CentraleSupélec, Université Paris-Saclay, France*
[2] *Eleven Strategy and Management, Paris, France*
[3] *Department of Energy, Politecnico di Torino, Italy*
[4] *Department of Energy, Politecnico di Milano, Italy*

List of Acronyms

AEMO	Australian Energy Market Operator
AK-MCS	adaptive kriging–Monte Carlo simulation
ANN	artificial neural network
AR	acceptance ratio
BIS	Bank of International Settlement
Cdf	cumulative density function
CR	critical region
CSN	Consejo de Seguridad Nuclear (Nuclear Safety Council)
DD	damage domain
DE	differential evolution
DET	dynamic event tree
DEX	deep exploration
DOE	design of experiment
ET	event tree
ENS	energy not served
ES	end-state
GOC	gas provided in overloaded conditions
GSC	gas provided in safe conditions
I/O	input/output
INL	Idaho National Laboratories
ISA	integrated safety assessment
kNN	k-near neighbours
LAR	least angle regression

Knowledge in Risk Assessment and Management, First Edition. Edited by Terje Aven and Enrico Zio.
© 2018 John Wiley & Sons Ltd. Published 2018 by John Wiley & Sons Ltd.

LHS	Latin hypercube sampling
LOF	local outlier factor
LOO	leave-one-out
MC	Monte Carlo
MCMC	Markov Chain Monte Carlo
M–H	Metropolis-Hastings
MM	meta-model
MS	main source
MVL	multiple-valued logic
NFE	number of simulations need for the first complete exploration
NPP	nuclear power plant
NSE	number of simulations need for the second complete exploration
NSS	not supplied set
PCE	polynomial chaos expansion
PCP	parallel coordinates plot
QMC	quasi Monte Carlo
RSM	response surface method
SAMG	severe accident management guidelines
SLOCA	seal loss of coolant accident
SoS	system of systems
SPLOM	Scatter plot matrix
SVM	support vector machine
UCR	unexplored critical region
UECR	unexplored extreme critical region

8.1   Introduction

In recent years, discussions have arisen on the fundamental concept of "risk" and other foundational issues related to its assessment (Aven 2012a, 2012b, 2016b; Cox 2015). From a general perspective, it is understood that the outcomes of risk assessment are conditioned on the knowledge and information available about the system and/or process under analysis (Aven 2016a; Aven and Zio 2014; Zio 2016b). This leads to the inevitable existence of a residual risk to be dealt with, related to the unknowns in the system and/or in the process characteristics and behaviors.

It is important to be aware of the incomplete knowledge conditioning the assessment outcomes, somewhat along the lines of thought of the former United State Secretary of Defense, Donald Rumsfeld, who said the following at the press briefing on 12 February 2002, addressing the absence of evidence linking the government of Iraq with the supply of weapons of mass destruction to terrorist groups (Aven 2013):

There are known knowns: things we know we know. We also know there are known unknowns: that is to say, we know there are some things we do not know. But there are also unknown unknowns: the one we don't know we don't know.

Correspondingly, different events can been classified according to the degree of knowledge available for the risk assessment (Flage and Aven 2015):

1) Unknown-unknown
2) Unknown-known
3) Known-unknown
4) Known-known

Category 1 identifies those events that were unknown to everyone, at the time of the risk assessment, Category 2 indicates those events unknown to the risk analysts performing the assessment, but known to someone else, Category 3 identifies situations of awareness where the background knowledge is weak but there are indications or justified beliefs that a new, unknown type of event (new in the context of the activity) could occur in the futurea and Category 4 indicates events that are known to the analysts performing the risk assessment, and for which evidence exists.

According to Flage and Aven (2015), events and scenarios in Categories 1, 2, and 4, and with negligible probabilities of occurrence, are "black swans" in the sense of (Taleb 2007). Category 3 represents emerging risks, defined as new risks or familiar risks that become apparent in new or unfamiliar conditions (IGRC 2015). Note that the concepts of "new" and "unfamiliar" are clearly dependent on the background knowledge available.

As an example, consider the South Australia power network, which underwent a massive blackout, a cascading failure that was triggered by a heavy storm on the 28 September 2016. Around 1.7 million people remained without power for 3 h and some days were required to restore completely the energy supply. According to the preliminary report of the Australian Energy Market Operator (AEMO), the heavy storm was a "non-credible event": either an unknown-known or a known-known with a negligible associated probability (AEMO 2016).

From the above qualitative discussion, we can see that risk assessment amounts to a systematic and structured effort to present the knowledge and information available on events, processes, and scenarios that affect specific decisions for the management of risk. Risk assessment can be seen as a tool for organizing the knowledge that analysts have on the system of interest (Flage and Aven 2015).

When the unknowns and uncertainties in the assessment are many and the object of the assessment is a complex system, identifying and characterizing scenarios and conditions leading to critical situations becomes non-trivial: a large set of scenarios and conditions is possible, and only few, rare ones are of interest because they lead to critical situations.

In this chapter, we investigate the possibility of using system simulations for scenario analysis, to increase knowledge about the response of a system to different conditions, with the aim of identifying possible unexpected or emergent critical states of the system. Indeed, verified and validated numerical models (or "simulators") offer an opportunity to increase knowledge regarding the system under analysis. In a simulation-based scenario analysis, the analyst can run a number of simulations with different initial configurations of the system and operational parameters, and identify a posteriori those leading to critical system states. These states form the so called "critical regions" (CRs) or "damage domains" (DDs) (Montero-Mayorga *et al.* 2014). The identified CRs can correspond to the prior knowledge of the analyst – the analyst is already aware that those configurations lead to critical outputs – or they can be "surprising" and the analyst is not aware of the potential consequences and is "surprised" by them.

In the remainder of the chapter, we address the following issues with respect to the contribution of system simulation to risk assessment: challenges in simulation-based CR exploration (Section 8.2); existing methods (Section 8.3); two approaches proposed by the authors to drive scenario exploration for CR identification (Section 8.4). Finally, in Section 8.5, some conclusions are drawn and future perspectives are discussed.

8.2 Problem Statement

Simulation models of system behavior can be complex because they are:

- high-dimensional, that is, with a large number of inputs and/or outputs
- nonlinear, due to the complexity of the relationships among the system elements
- dynamic, because the system evolves in time
- computationally demanding, as a consequence of the above characteristics and of the numerical methods employed.

The high dimensionality in the inputs implies that the conditions and scenarios to explore, and the corresponding system end-states that must be check for the identification of the CRs, increase exponentially with the space dimensions (Zio 2014). Also, it is a challenge for effective visualization for interpretation of the results, calling for specially designed representation tools. Similar issues also arise for the high dimensionality of the output space, where clustering techniques can be employed to identify groups of outputs having similar behavior, for their characterization as critical (Di Maio *et al.* 2011; Mandelli *et al.* 2013a, 2013b).

Nonlinearities in the model usually make it difficult to predict the output associated with a specific input configuration, particularly in the inverse problem of interest: of discovering the set of inputs leading the system to a specific (critical) output. In practice, when the computational model is a black box (because of an empirical nature or because too complicated), the only feasible way to solve the problem is to run simulations and post-process the results to retrieve the information of interest from the generated data.

The analysis of dynamic systems calls for methods capable of dealing with (deterministic or stochastic) changes occurring during the time horizon of the analysis (by simulations), for example sequences of events occurring (possibly stochastically, say component failures, or deterministically, say due to control actions) at different times that affect the operation of the system.

Under the conditions depicted above, typically encountered in practice, computational cost becomes an issue for simulation-based system response analysis for risk assessment. The high computational cost of a single simulation prevents the analyst from running and exploring a large number of configurations, as necessary to gain knowledge about the system CRs. Then, there is a need for methods capable of extracting information on the system, resorting to a limited number of well-designed simulations. To achieve this goal, the methods should be capable of automatically revealing, during the simulation, which configurations are most promising for exploration of the system CRs.

8.3 State of the Art

In the context of risk assessment, the combination of event trees (ETs) – diagrams representing the sequential logic of the system response to accident initiating events – and mathematical models of the system dynamics has been advocated as a way to determine the end-states (ESs) that can be reached by the system in accident scenarios and to derive the corresponding causality relations among the events occurring in the scenarios (Aldemir 2013; Li *et al.* 2011; Siu 1994; Zio 2014). Studies of dynamic event trees (DETs) (Cepin and Mavko 2002; Cojazzi 1996; Hakobyan *et al.* 2008; Hsueh and Mosleh 1996; Kloos and Peschke 2006; Labeau *et al.* 2000) have highlighted that the ESs reached by a system as a result of an accident scenario do not depend only on the order of occurrence of the events in the sequence of the accident scenario, but also on the exact time at which these events occur and on their magnitude (Aldemir 2013; Di Maio *et al.* 2015a, 2015c; Garrett and Apostolakis 1999; Li *et al.* 2011; Smidts and Devooght 1992). However, exploring all dynamic sequences amounts to moving in a system state space of theoretically infinite dimension (because of the continuous time and magnitude variables). To address this issue, the majority of the methods available in the literature proceed after a discretization of the time and magnitude dimensions to reduce the state-space size and/or the pruning of branches associated with sequences having low probability of occurrence. However, these techniques may miss "rare" sequences that are of interest because they lead to CR outcomes (Hakobyan *et al.* 2008; Rutt *et al.* 2006).

To tackle these issues, some authors have introduced an adaptive simulation framework to drive the exploration of scenarios (that is, ET branches) towards those having more uncertain outcomes (Hu *et al.* 2004; Turati *et al.* 2015). In simple terms, the event times and magnitudes worthy of exploration are those that can generate scenarios with outcomes different from those already identified. If sequences with different times of occurrence and magnitudes of the same events lead to exactly the same scenario outcome, thoroughly exploring them does not add any additional information to the system CRs. On the other hand, if the same scenario can lead to several outcomes for different occurrence times and magnitudes of its events, it is worth running many simulations to discover the relations between the occurrence time and magnitude of the events and the scenario outcomes.

As mentioned earlier, a fundamental issue in risk assessment is the identification of the so-called CRs or DDs: the input configurations that lead the system to safety-critical outcomes. In mathematical terms, given a deterministic input/output (I/O) model $Y = f(X)$, where the inputs X are uncertain and where the outputs Y are realizations of simulations, the objective is to identify the set of inputs satisfying specific conditions for the output: those having output values above given safety-critical thresholds $\chi = \{x \, s.t. \, y \geq Y_{thres}\}$, which correspond to critical system state and therefore belong to a CR. To search for these conditions, one approach is Design Of Experiments (DOE) (Fang *et al.* 2005; Kuhnt and Steinberg 2010; Santner *et al.* 2003), in which a set of input configurations is selected with a given logic to probe the input state space, the corresponding outputs are computed by simulation, and those leading to safety-critical outputs are identified. Then, these available I/O data are post-processed, say by means of expert analysis or machine learning, to get insights into the CRs such as: the causality relations between inputs and outputs, safety-oriented characteristics, the shapes and number of the CRs, and so on. For example, the Spanish Nuclear Safety Council has developed an Integrated Safety Assessment methodology that has been recently used to verify whether the current Severe Accident Management Guidelines are properly defined for a "seal loss of coolant accident" (Queral *et al.* 2016). The authors exploited expert knowledge to limit the input state space to within a specific domain. The reduced domain was probed by means of several simulations, the results of which allowed a repartition of the state space according to the different types of consequences for the nuclear plant during the accident (such as core uncovering, fuel melting, vessel failure). Substantial expert knowledge was involved in the post-processing to give a physical interpretation of the events characterizing the accident scenario and of the impact of time on the occurrence of a failure and recovery from it. Despite the large number of simulations performed, only a single accident scenario was analyzed due to the high computational cost. Di Maio *et al.* (2016), in collaboration with the US Idaho National Laboratories, made use of a surrogate model to reproduce the limit surface that separates the CRs from the safety regions during a station blackout in a boiling water reactor. This was simulated using the nuclear safety code RELAP5-3D (RELAP5-3D 2005). Then, the identified CRs were projected onto the subspace of the controllable variables and the safest operational conditions were identified as those furthest from the CR limit surface by means of a K–D tree algorithm (Bentley 1975).

The identification of CRs leads to the identification of "prime implicants", as an extension of the concept of minimal cut sets in the ET analysis. Prime implicants are defined as the minimal sets of process parameter values and component failure states that are sufficient to cause a failure of the dynamic system. Di Maio *et al.* (2015a, 2015b) proposed two different frameworks for prime implicant identification upon discretization of the input space by means of multiple-valued logic. In the first paper, the authors employed a differential evolution algorithm for the identification of the prime implicants, whereas in the second paper they resorted to a visual interactive method that allowed retrieval of the values of the main features characterizing the prime implicant sequences.

In parallel to the use of simulation for CR identification, but with a slightly different objective, techniques for the falsification of temporal properties have been proposed (Dreossi *et al.* 2015; Fainekos *et al.* 2012; Nghiem *et al.* 2010). Dynamic systems are designed to satisfy certain specifications. For example, if the liquid level of a tank is controlled by automatic valves to stay between two threshold values, falsification looks for trajectories that lead the system out of the design specifications, "falsifying" the expected system behavior. Whereas falsification techniques aim at showing that at least one trajectory that does not satisfy the design specifications exists, CR identification methods aim at discovering and characterizing *all* trajectories that do not satisfy the design specifications.

Furthermore, systems are nowadays more and more interconnected ("Systems of Systems"; SoS) and new behavior can emerge unexpectedly (emergent behavior) (Zio 2016a, 2016b). A method called ARGUS has been proposed for discovering emergent behavior in dynamic SoS (Kernstine 2012). In particular, an iterative adaptive DOE is combined with parallel computing. The method takes the advantages of the available computing technologies (cloud computing and clusters), keeping the efficiency and flexibility of an adaptive DOE. The adaptive algorithm is used to select at each iteration a batch of candidate configurations to explore, while a cluster of processors is employed to run the simulations in parallel. However, since the method has been specifically designed for the exploration of a stochastic model, it loses its advantages when applied to a deterministic one. In addition, ARGUS makes use of polynomial harmonics to estimate the mean of the response function, an approach which has been shown to be inefficient in high dimensionality situations.

Nuclear and financial industries have recently increased their attention to extreme yet possible scenarios (EBA 2016; European Commission 2013). For example, the European Commission, in response to the 2011 Fukushima nuclear accident, has requested to all state members to perform specific stress tests to assess the resilience of their nuclear power plants to several types of extreme events: earthquakes, floodings, terrorist attacks, and aircraft collisions. Similarly, the Bank for International Settlements requires financial institutions to perform stress tests for assessing their robustness against extreme financial scenarios (Sorge 2004). Stress tests allow analysts to collect information regarding system response. However, the response is evaluated only with respect to extreme scenarios, so stress tests do not allow them to discover whether, in the normal range of input values and scenarios, critical events can emerge.

When the computational cost becomes a constraint for the analysis, meta-models (or, equivalently, surrogate models) can represent a possible solution (Gorissen *et al.* 2010). Meta-models usually involve a set of input/output observations obtained from the real model to train a "surrogate" capable of reproducing the behavior of the real model at a lower computational cost. Once the meta-model has been validated (say, by means of its out-of-sample prediction accuracy), it can be used to replace the real model and to simulate the behavior of the system. Many types of meta-model are available, each one with characteristics that suit specific conditions. Among the large number of methods available in the literature (Simpson *et al.* 2001; Wang and Shan 2007), we recall here just some that have been used in the context of risk assessment:

- Polynomial Chaos Expansion (PCE), which resorts to a particular basis of the probability space to represent the real-model input/output relation (see Appendix 8.A for details) (Sudret 2008).
- Response Surface Method (RSM), where usually a low-order set of polynomials is used to fit the data observations available and the corresponding polynomial coefficients can be estimated by linear regression (Myers *et al.* 2016); nonetheless, the intrinsic linearity of the method makes it unsuitable for nonlinear models.
- Artificial Neural Networks (ANNs) and all their associated evolutions, which resort to a large set of models (neurons) connected by means of nonlinear transformations (network) for reproducing any model behavior, including nonlinear (Cheng and Titterington 1994; Haykin 2004); nevertheless, ANNs usually require a large number of input/output observations for their training.
- Support Vector Machines (SVM), which are capable of reproducing nonlinear behaviors by mapping the inputs in a larger feature space; in practice, the

meta-model is linear between the mapped features and the output, but can be nonlinear between the input and the output (Clarke *et al.* 2004).

- Kriging, which makes use of a Gaussian process to exactly interpolate the available input/output observations, allowing there to be at the same time an estimate and an associated confidence interval for the response function for any input configuration (Clarke *et al.* 2004; Kleijnen 2009; Rasmussen and Williams 2006). Kriging is especially indicated for reproducing nonlinear models that present humps and regional behavior (see Appendix 8.A for details).

Many researchers have been developing toolboxes and software to support sequential DOE, meta-models, iterative sampling, simulation, and so on:

- DAKOTA (Eldred *et al.* 2014) from the Sandia National Laboratories
- UQLab (Marelli and Sudret 2014) from the ETH of Zurich
- OpenCOSSAN (Patelli *et al.* 2014) from the Institute for Risk and Uncertainty of the University of Liverpool
- SUMO (Gorissen *et al.* 2010) from the Surrogate Modeling Lab of Ghent
- SCAIS (Queral *et al.* 2016) from the Spanish Nuclear Safety Council (CSN)
- RAVEN from the INL (Alfonsi *et al.* 2016)
- OpenTURNS from a collaboration of academic institutions and industrial companies such as EDF, Airbus and Phimeca (Baudin *et al.* 2016).

These tools are continuously updated and have open-source versions in Matlab (UQLab, OpenCossan, SUMO) or in developer C++/Python source code (DAKOTA, SCAIS, RAVEN, OpenTURNS). Commercial versions with associated interfaces are available for all of them, except for SUMO, RAVEN, and OpenTURNS.

It must be pointed out that these software packages are not specifically designed to address the research issues here, concerning the exploration of scenarios. Rather, they are designed to render the state of the art of many statistical analysis methods accessible to industry and practitioners. In any case, they remain a practical starting point for reducing programming time and speeding up the design process of new methods for model exploration and knowledge retrieval.

To sum up, the issue of knowledge retrieval by simulation for scenario exploration in risk assessment of safety-critical systems has been considered in two main approaches:

- *massive simulation*, which exploits parallel and cloud computing advancements for increasing the number of simulations
- *adaptive simulation*, which makes use of machine learning algorithms to extract information from the available simulations and to use it to "drive" the simulations towards the states of interest for the analysis, thus limiting the number of computationally expensive calls to the simulation model.

Meta-modeling can be used in both approaches to further reduce the computational cost. In what follows, two recently proposed adaptive strategies are presented, showing the efficiency and the added value that this kind of analysis can bring to the analyst.

8.4 Proposed Approaches

Two exploration strategies proposed by the authors for increasing knowledge in a risk assessment context are presented in this section. Both the theory behind the methods and some simple but representative applications are given.

The first strategy has been designed to explore accident scenarios that could occur within a given dynamic system. In particular, it allows probing of the time dimension and assessment of the impact that time has on the progression of accident scenarios (Section 8.4.1). The second strategy aims at identifying the CRs: those configurations of inputs and parameters values that lead a given system to a critical output. The strategy has been developed with the main objective of dealing with high-dimensional systems described by computationally-demanding models. For this reason, particular attention has been devoted limiting the number of calls to the numerical model used to precisely characterize the CRs (Section 8.4.2).

8.4.1 Exploration of Extreme and Unexpected Events in Dynamic Engineered Systems

8.4.1.1 Method

Accident scenario analysis requires identification, list and analysis of all possible failure scenarios that can occur in the system under analysis. DETs have been used to identify (dynamic) accident scenarios and characterize their consequences. A large effort is required to consider the time dimension and its impact on the accident consequences. To keep the analysis feasible, methods have been introduced to either a priori discretize the time dimension and/or to prune some branches in the accident evolution. However, excluding branches having low probability of occurrence without considering the associated consequences and time discretization can miss possible "rare" critical accident sequences (Di Maio *et al.* 2015a; Garrett and Apostolakis 1999; Li *et al.* 2011).

Before introducing the main characteristics of the method, some definitions should be given. We define a scenario as an ordered sequence of events in the life evolution of the dynamic system – within its mission time T_{Miss} - which may involve a particular group of components, safety functions or actions (say mechanical failures, activation of safety systems, and human decisions). For example, scenario S_1 could be defined by event A (failure of a component) at time T_A, followed by event B (failure of the safety system) at time $T_A < T_B < T_{Miss}$; scenario S_2 could be defined by the opposite order of the events B and A, with $T_B < T_A < T_{Miss}$. Since the events in the sequences may occur with the *same* order but at *different* times, an *infinite* number of sequences exist for a *single given* scenario, potentially leading to different outputs (system states), as demonstrated by Di Maio *et al.* (2015a, 2015c).

In accident progression analysis, which is the case in this section, the system output Y usually represents the worst condition reached by the system during the simulation (Queral *et al.* 2016). In what follows, we define the end-state (ES), a categorical variable synthetically representing the state of the system on the basis of its outputs. This is the case in many applications. For example, in a nuclear power plant loss-of-coolant accident the output can be classified according to the different ESs reached by the reactor: core uncovering, embrittlement condition, fuel melting, fuel relocation, vessel failure, and so on. These have consequences of different severity (Ibáñez *et al.* 2016).

The idea underlying the proposed strategy is that not all scenarios need to be explored in the same level of detail. Consider two scenarios: one representing normal operation conditions, where no failure occurs, and one characterized by a component failure at time T_F and a corresponding repair at time T_R. Obviously, there is no interest in running many simulations exploring the normal condition scenario, since we already know its corresponding ES. In the component failure scenario, meanwhile, we are interested in exploring the impact on the ES of failures occurring at different times. Indeed, we can expect that if the repair is performed just after the failure, the impact of the component failure will be lower than if it is performed later in the scenario.

For an efficient exploration of the scenarios, an adaptive simulation framework has been proposed by the authors (see Figure 8.1) (Turati *et al.* 2016a). The framework is based on three main steps:

- *preliminary exploration* (Section 8.4.1.1.1): a global exploration of the whole space of the dynamic system scenarios;
- *interactive decision making* (Section 8.4.1.1.2): after the preliminary exploration, the analyst can decide to either improve their global view of the state space by increasing the number of simulations in the *preliminary exploration* (step 1), or focus the attention on a specific event of interest (step 3)

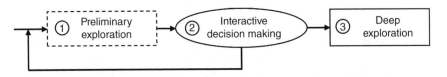

Figure 8.1 Sketch of the adaptive exploration framework.

- *deep exploration* (Section 8.4.1.1.3): a thorough exploration of a particular event; for example, the objective can be that of retrieving the possible evolutions within a specific scenario S_j that can potentially reach a given ES ES_i, indicated hereafter as the pair $\{S_j, ES_i\}$.

For generating time sequences within a scenario of interest, we resort to a joint uniform distribution over each scenario support (the region of variability of the times of occurrence of the ordered events in the scenario) in order to thoroughly explore the scenario and discover the whole set of possible ESs that each scenario can reach. To this end, Markov chain Monte Carlo (MCMC) Gibbs sampling is employed (Robert and Casella 2004).

8.4.1.1.1 Preliminary Exploration

Hereafter, we assume that preliminary exploration is run under the constraint of limited computational resources; that is, of a fixed number of simulations to run. This step aims at enhancing the global knowledge regarding system dynamic behavior during accident scenarios. The exploration consists of two steps:

- selection of the scenario to explore according to a driving function
- simulation of a time sequence within the selected scenario.

The driving function should be flexible enough to take into account different analyst objectives and backgrounds. For example, the analyst could be interested in exploring and collecting information regarding the scenarios leading to a specific set of ES ES^*, say the most critical ones. In this light, the choice of the scenario during the preliminary exploration is made by selecting the scenario S^* which maximizes the driving function $I_{\gamma,\beta}(S_j, ES^*)$:

$$S^* = \underset{j \in S}{\operatorname{argmax}}\, I_{\gamma,\beta}(S_j, ES^*), \tag{8.1}$$

where $I_{\gamma,\beta}(S_j, ES^*)$ is defined as:

$$I_{\gamma,\beta}(S_j, ES^*) = I_{\gamma,\beta}(N_j^{ES}, n_j, I_{ES^*}) = \begin{cases} \dfrac{(N_j^{ES})^{\gamma}}{n_j}, I_{ES^*} = 0 \\ \dfrac{(N_j^{ES})^{\gamma}}{n_j} \cdot \beta, I_{ES^*} = 1 \end{cases}, \tag{8.2}$$

where N_j^{ES} is the number of ESs that scenario S_j can reach (if this information is not available, then it represents the number of ESs that have already been visited within the scenario and it is updated whenever a new ES is discovered by a new simulation run), n_j is the number of simulations that have already been run within S_j, I_{ES^*} is a Boolean variable, which equals 1 if the simulations of scenario S_j can reach at least one of the ESs in ES^* and 0 otherwise, $\gamma \in (-\infty, +\infty)$ and $\beta \in (1, +\infty)$ are two design parameters which reflect the preference of the analyst: γ represents analyst preference concerning scenario variability and β represents analyst preference concerning an ES set ES^*. If $\gamma < 0$, the driving function more frequently chooses those scenarios that can reach a small number of ESs; if $\gamma = 0$, no preference is given to any scenario on the basis of its variability; otherwise, if $\gamma > 0$, the driving function is more likely to select those scenarios that can reach a large number of ESs. Meanwhile, the higher the β value, the more frequently the algorithm selects those scenarios that can reach an ES belonging to ES^*. It is worth noting that if $\beta = 1$, no preference is given to any ES.

For the sake of clarity, two examples are reported here, to separately show the impact of the two preference parameters. Consider a simple dynamic system where only four scenarios S_1, ..., S_4 can occur and where each scenario can reach a different number of ESs, $N_1^{ES} = 1, N_2^{ES} = 2,..., N_4^{ES} = 4$. Finally, let us assume that all reachable ESs in the same scenario have the same probability of occurring and that the analyst has no preference regarding the ES to explore; that is, $\beta = 1$. Table 8.1 reports the average of 1000 explorations, performed with 100 simulations each, that have been distributed among the different scenarios according to three different values of the parameter γ: $\gamma = -1$ (left), $\gamma = 0$ (middle) and $\gamma = 1$ (right). Column "Tot" represents the total number of simulations run within the respective scenario.

The choice of parameter $\gamma = 1$ is particularly suitable because, in this case, the exploration algorithm distributes the simulations among all the scenarios in order to guarantee that each scenario S_j "gathers" a number of simulations proportional to the number N_j^{ES} of ESs that each scenario can "generate".

Assuming now, instead, that the analyst is interested in the most variable scenarios – that is, $\gamma = 1$ – and the most critical ESs; say, $ES^* = \{ES_3; ES_4\}$. Table 8.2 reports the effects of different choices of parameter $\beta = \{1; 2; 4\}$ on the final distribution of the simulation runs among the scenarios. If $\beta = 1$, the algorithm turns to the preliminary guided exploration described above (left); otherwise, if $\beta > 1$, the scenarios that can reach the set ES^* are favored in the selection step (middle, right).

Table 8.1 Results when the analyst has no preference regarding the ES to explore.

	ES_1	ES_2	ES_3	ES_4	Tot	ES_1	ES_2	ES_3	ES_4	Tot	ES_1	ES_2	ES_3	ES_4	Tot
S_1	47.9	0.0	0.0	0.0	**47.9**	25.0	0.0	0.0	0.0	**25.0**	10.0	0.0	0.0	0.0	**10.0**
S_2	12.0	11.9	0.0	0.0	**23.9**	12.4	12.6	0.0	0.0	**25.0**	10.0	9.9	0.0	0.0	**20.0**
S_3	5.3	5.3	5.3	0.0	**15.9**	8.4	8.3	8.3	0.0	**25.0**	10.0	10.0	10.0	0.0	**30.0**
S_4	3.0	3.1	3.0	3.1	**12.2**	6.2	6.2	6.3	6.3	**25.0**	10.0	10.0	9.9	10.1	**40.0**

Table 8.2 Results when the analyst is interested in the most variable scenario.

	ES_1	ES_2	ES_3	ES_4	Tot	ES_1	ES_2	ES_3	ES_4	Tot	ES_1	ES_2	ES_3	ES_4	Tot
S_1	10.0	0.0	0.0	0.0	**10.0**	7.0	0.0	0.0	0.0	**7.0**	3.1	0.0	0.0	0.0	**3.1**
S_2	10.0	9.9	0.0	0.0	**20.0**	7.0	6.0	0.0	0.0	**12.9**	3.0	2.9	0.0	0.0	**5.9**
S_3	10.0	10.0	10.0	0.0	**30.0**	12.5	11.7	11.7	0.0	**36.0**	12.6	12.3	12.5	0.0	**37.4**
S_4	10.0	10.0	9.9	10.1	**40.0**	12.7	11.8	11.8	11.7	**48.1**	13.4	13.4	13.4	13.3	**53.5**

For the preliminary exploration, we have proposed only one function based on two parameters, which can reflect the analyst interest about scenario variability and a set of known ESs; however, a variety of functions could be used at this stage to drive the selection of scenarios according to other desirable criteria.

8.4.1.1.2   *Interactive Decision Making*

Every time a preliminary exploration is performed, matrices, such those reported in Table 8.1 and Table 8.2, become available. Hence, based on the events visited (that is, on the pairs scenario-ES (S_j, ES_i)) and on the number of simulations that have been run to visit them, the analyst can decide either to increase the number of simulations according to the criteria adopted in the preliminary exploration phase or to perform a deeper and more refined exploration of specific events of interest. According to their preference, the analyst has to iteratively choose the maximum allowable number of simulations that can be run according to the *preliminary* or *deep* exploration, respectively. In many cases, the dimension of the system (state space) and the variability of its behavior (in practice, the number of ESs a scenario can reach and the corresponding probabilities), are not known a priori; on the contrary, the computational cost needed for a system simulation can be known (say in terms of average time per simulation). So the computational effort can be considered as a constraint that the analyst needs to take into account in accordance with their preferences among the different exploration criteria. In this respect, it must be noticed that the proposed method does not guarantee that the whole event space is probed: inevitably, if the computational capacity available (in practice, the total number of simulations that can be run) is small compared to the size of the system state space, only a limited number of ESs can be explored for each scenario.

8.4.1.1.3   *Deep Exploration*

The objective of the deep exploration is to identify, as precisely as possible, which system evolutions (which transition times) can lead to a given event of interest. For the sake of clarity, we assume that an event of interest is defined as the pair (Scenario, ES) = (S_j, ES^*); nonetheless, with no loss of generality ES^* can also represent a set of ESs. Given the structure of the mathematical model, the guiding idea of deep exploration is to generate time sequences "around" those that have already reached the event (S_j, ES^*). In order to achieve this goal, we resort to a MCMC method, which allows us to generate a set of random samples from any desired (namely, *target*) probability distribution p (Robert and Casella 2004). In detail, we utilize a Metropolis–Hastings (M–H) algorithm (Chib and Greenberg 1995) to sample component transition times uniformly on the support SES^* of the event of interest (S_j, ES^*); in other words, to sample uniformly among the transition times that lead to the event of interest. The M–H algorithm consists of two steps:

- proposal of a new candidate T^* (in this case, a vector of transition times) in accordance with a *proposal* distribution q
- acceptance or rejection of the proposed time vector.

The interested reader is referred to Appendix 8.A for more details on the algorithm.

It must be underlined that the acceptance ratio (AR) between the proposed samples and the accepted ones plays a fundamental role. High acceptance ratios (AR > 0.9) are a symptom of a proposal q with too small variability; that is, most of the proposed T^* are too close to the original ones and thus the algorithm is too slow in probing the support SES^*; on the contrary, small acceptance ratios (AR < 0.2) are a symptom of a proposal q with too high variability: most of the proposed T^* are likely to fall out of the support of interest SES^*. In this respect, adaptive MCMC methods exploiting an adaptive proposal distribution have been presented in the literature and can be employed at this stage to "optimally" fill the support SES^* of interest (Andrieu and Thoms 2008; Roberts and Rosenthal 2009).

Regarding the approach used to choose the number of simulations to run for performing the deep exploration, two criteria are proposed:

- a fixed number of simulations (as in the Preliminary Exploration subsection above)
- level of filling of the support of the event of interest.

For the second criterion, the idea is to keep on generating new simulation outcomes until SES^* is filled by a number of points (configurations) that "sufficiently" cover the entire outcome variability. In detail, after the preliminary exploration, a set of occurrence time vectors $EX_V(SES^*) = \{T_1, \ldots, T_V\}$ that lead to the event of interest (S_j, ES^*) is available. As a measure of the (time) space filling, the maximum of the minimum distances among these time vectors is considered: then, a time filling index $D_V(EX_V(SES^*))$ after the preliminary exploration is computed as:

$$D_V(EX_V(SES^*)) = \max_{i \in EX_V(SES^*)} \min_{j \neq i} d(T_i, T_j) \tag{8.3}$$

Table 8.3 Sketch of the algorithm describing the deep exploration stopping criterion.

---

1) For $i = 1, \ldots, V$ evaluate the minimum distances from the vector T_i and save them in the vector d_V:

$$d_V(i) = \min_{j \neq i} d(T_i, T_j).$$

According to this notation $D_V(EX_V(SES^*)) = \max d_V$.

2) Given a new time vector T_n, update the d_{n-1} vector for $i = 1, \ldots, n-1$:

$$d_n(i) = \min(d_{n-1}(i), d(T_i, T_n)),$$

3) Add the nth component to d_{n-1} resorting to the distance already available from the previous step:

$$d_n(n) = \min_{j \neq n} d(T_n, T_j).$$

4) Evaluate the filling index:

$$D_n(EX_n(SES^*)) = \max d_n.$$

5) Check if the stopping criteria are satisfied:

$$\frac{D_n(EX_n(SES^*))}{D_V(EX_V(SES^*))} < \delta \text{ or } n > n_{max}$$

If not, return to step 2.

---

where $d(\cdot, \cdot)$ represents a suitable distance between two vectors. Herein, for example, we consider the Euclidean one. Whenever a new time vector T_n is accepted during the exploration, it is added to the set of time vectors that lead to the event of interest – $EX_n(SES^*) = \{EX_{n-1}(SES^*); T_n\}$ – and the filling index $D_n(EX_n(SES^*))$ is consequently updated. The deep exploration ends when the ratio between the current filling index and the preliminary one falls below a fixed threshold $\delta \in [0, 1]$; that is, when the "density" of time vectors in the support SES^* of interest is $\sim (1/\delta)^l$ times higher than the preliminary one, l being the size of the time vector T_n. Thus, the space-filling capability of the algorithm is strictly related to the dimension of the vectors involved: in practice, the higher the dimension, the larger the number of random vectors needed to reduce the filling index. In this light, a maximum allowable number n_{max} of samples is also set, in order to limit in any event the maximum computational effort. Then, the stopping criterion becomes:

$$\frac{D_n(EX_n(SES^*))}{D_V(EX_V(SES^*))} \left\langle \delta \text{ or } n \right\rangle n_{max}. \tag{8.4}$$

The corresponding algorithm is summarized in Table 8.3.

8.4.1.2 Gas Transmission Subnetwork

This case study is of a gas transmission subnetwork, comprising two pipes in parallel and another one in series. The input of each pipe is controlled by a

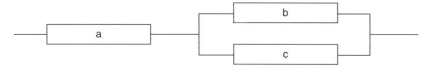

Figure 8.2 Block diagram of the gas transmission subnetwork.

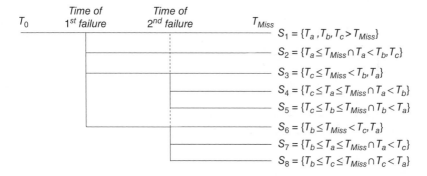

$S_1 = \{T_a, T_b, T_c > T_{Miss}\}$

$S_2 = \{T_a \leq T_{Miss} \cap T_a < T_b, T_c\}$

$S_3 = \{T_c \leq T_{Miss} < T_b, T_a\}$

$S_4 = \{T_c \leq T_a \leq T_{Miss} \cap T_a < T_b\}$

$S_5 = \{T_c \leq T_b \leq T_{Miss} \cap T_b < T_a\}$

$S_6 = \{T_b \leq T_{Miss} < T_c, T_a\}$

$S_7 = \{T_b \leq T_a \leq T_{Miss} \cap T_a < T_c\}$

$S_8 = \{T_b \leq T_c \leq T_{Miss} \cap T_c < T_a\}$

Figure 8.3 Event tree representation of the eight scenarios that can occur. T_a, T_b, T_c are the times of failures of components a, b, c, respectively, and T_{Miss} is the mission time.

valve. The block diagram is shown in Figure 8.2, where each pair valve-pipe is considered as a single block.

Each pipe can transmit gas with a maximum flow rate of $[\phi_a, \phi_b, \phi_c] = [8, 5, 5] \times 10^4$ m^3/day, for pipes a, b, c, respectively. A control system adjusts the opening of the valves in order to guarantee equilibrium between the input and output flows. Figure 8.3 shows the ET containing all the scenarios that can occur in the system. If one of the pipes in parallel breaks, the control system immediately closes the corresponding valve and increases the flow rate of the remaining pipe to the maximum, in order to compensate for the diminished flow. No repair strategies are considered. The system presents eight possible scenarios with different operating conditions:

- *safe*: all pipes are functioning correctly
- *overloaded*: one of the pipes in parallel is closed
- *broken*: no gas is provided by the system.

The ESs for each scenario have been defined and classified on the basis of two output variables Y_1, Y_2:

- the amount of gas provided in safe conditions (GSC = Y_1), when all the components are functioning correctly
- the amount of gas provided in overloaded conditions (GOC = Y_2), when one of the two pipes in parallel is down and the remaining one is working at its maximum flow rate.

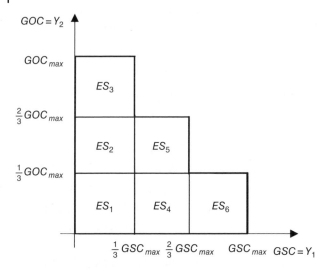

Figure 8.4 Classification of ESs according to the output variables GSC and GOC.

GSC_{max} and GOC_{max} indicate the maximum quantities of gas that can be provided within the mission time $T_{Miss} = 900d$, in safe and overloaded conditions, respectively; that is, $GSC_{max} = \phi_a \cdot T_{Miss}$ and $GOC_{max} = \max(\phi_b, \phi_c) \cdot T_{Miss}$. The outputs are then divided into six ESs according to the criteria reported in Figure 8.4. For example, $ES_4 = \left\{ \frac{1}{3}GSC_{max} < GSC \leq \frac{2}{3}GSC_{max} \cap 0 \leq GOC \leq \frac{1}{3}GOC_{max} \right\}$, which means that the system has operated for a medium period of time in *safe* conditions $\left(\frac{1}{3}GSC_{max} < GSC \leq \frac{2}{3}GSC_{max} \right)$ and, then, once it goes in *overloaded* conditions, it breaks down $\left(0 \leq GOC \leq \frac{1}{3}GOC_{max} \right)$.

It should be noticed that not all the ESs can be reached by all scenarios. Table 8.4 (left-hand matrix) indicates those ESs that can be reached by a given scenario (indicated by 1) and those that cannot (indicated by 0): each column in the table represents an ES and each row represents a scenario. This information is usually not available a priori and, in general, its retrieval represents one of the objectives of the state space exploration. However, it is used here to analyze the performance of the proposed method. In Table 8.4 (middle and right), two additional matrices show the reachable ESs for two sets of different gas flow rates, $[\phi_a, \phi_b, \phi_c] = [8, 3.7, 5] \times 10^4 \ \text{m}^3/\text{day}$ and $[\phi_a, \phi_b, \phi_c] = [8, 2.2, 6] \times 10^4 \ \text{m}^3/\text{day}$, respectively. These values have been chosen in order to analyze the performance of the method for different parameter values, which imply that the number of reachable ESs varies.

Table 8.4 End-states that the system can reach for each scenario for different sets of flow rate parameter values.

	$[\phi_a,\phi_b,\phi_c]$																	
	$[8,5,5] \times 10^4$						$[8,3.7,5] \times 10^4$ m^3/day						$[8,2.2,6] \times 10^4$ m^3/day					
	ES_1	ES_2	ES_3	ES_4	ES_5	ES_6	ES_1	ES_2	ES_3	ES_4	ES_5	ES_6	ES_1	ES_2	ES_3	ES_4	ES_5	ES_6
S_1	0	0	0	0	0	1	0	0	0	0	0	1	0	0	0	0	0	1
S_2	1	0	0	1	0	1	1	0	0	1	0	1	1	0	0	1	0	1
S_3	0	0	1	0	1	1	0	1	1	1	1	1	0	1	0	1	1	1
S_4	1	1	1	1	1	1	1	1	1	1	1	1	1	1	0	1	0	1
S_5	1	1	1	1	1	1	1	1	1	1	1	1	1	1	0	1	0	1
S_6	0	0	1	0	1	1	0	0	1	0	1	1	0	0	1	0	1	1
S_7	1	1	1	1	1	1	1	1	1	1	1	1	1	1	1	1	1	1
S_8	1	1	1	1	1	1	1	1	1	1	1	1	1	1	1	1	1	1

8.4.1.2.1 Preliminary Exploration

To evaluate the performance of the *preliminary exploration*, two indices are introduced:

- the number of simulations needed for the first complete exploration (NFE): the number of simulations that should be run to visit at least once all the reachable ESs for all the scenarios
- the number of simulations needed for the second complete exploration (NSE): the number of simulations that should be run to visit all the reachable ESs for all the scenarios at least twice.

NFE gives information about the number of simulations needed to explore all the events defined by the pairs (Scenario, ES)$= (S, ES)$, when the matrices shown in Table 8.4 (the ESs) are not known yet. In contrast, NSE gives information about how the simulations are efficiently distributed among the different scenarios once the matrices in Table 8.4 (the ESs) start to become known as a result of the preliminary exploration. We analyzed two different situations: in the former, the analyst has a very poor background knowledge regarding the system, while in the latter they already know the system and are interested in collecting information regarding the scenarios that can reach a specific ES. For this reason, in the first case $\beta = 0$ and $\gamma = 1$, whereas in the second case, $\beta > 1$.

Considering the case with low prior knowledge, the results of the preliminary explorations are compared to those of:

- a crude Monte Carlo simulation method (MC), that randomly selects the scenario and then simulates the proper transition times according to the same uniform sampling criterion proposed in Section 8.4.1.1
- an entropy-driven exploration (Turati *et al.* 2015), which follows a procedure similar to the preliminary exploration, but with an entropy-driven function instead of $I_{\gamma,\beta}(\cdot)$.

For all the gas flow rates reported in Table 8.4, the preliminary exploration has been performed 1000 times and the corresponding empirical cumulative density functions (cdfs) of NFE (left) and NSE (right) are computed. Preliminary exploration achieves better, or at least comparable, performance than the entropy-driven exploration in all flow configurations tested. This is depicted in Figures 8.5–8.6, where the cdfs associated to the preliminary exploration (light-dashed line) are "shifted" to the left with respect to those associated to the entropy-driven exploration (dark-dotted line). On the other side, both the preliminary and the entropy-driven explorations largely outperform the MC one (light line) regarding both NFE and NSE. In particular, the difference is even larger in NSE; that is, when the exploration algorithm is already aware of all the events (S, ES) that can occur. The results of flow configuration $[\phi_a,\phi_b,\phi_c]=[8,3.7,5]\times10^4$ m^3/day are not depicted, due to the similarity with those in Figure 8.5. Finally, it should be noted that in one case the MC exploration is more effective than the other techniques (Figure 8.6, NFE). This is because the rarest event (S, ES) occurs in a scenario that can reach a few different end-states. However, while the entropy-driven method is stuck, the *preliminary* exploration allows changing of parameter γ in order to increase the exploration effectiveness.

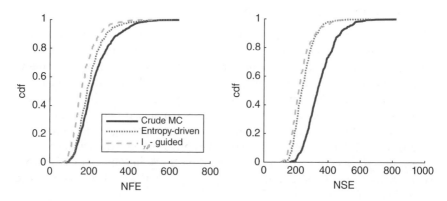

Figure 8.5 Empirical cdfs of the NFE (left) and of the NSE (right) for crude MC (light line), for an entropy-driven method (dark dotted line) and for the preliminary guided exploration with $\gamma=1$ (light dashed line) and with flow rate parameters $[\Phi_A,\Phi_B,\Phi_C]=[8,5,5]\times10^4$ m^3/day.

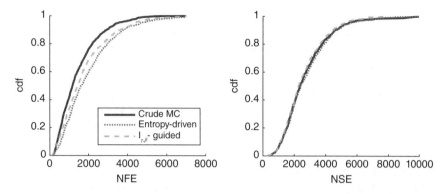

Figure 8.6 Empirical cdfs of the NFE (left) and of the NSE (right) for crude MC (light line), for an entropy-driven method (dark dotted line) and for the preliminary guided exploration with $\gamma=1$ (light dashed line) with flow rate parameters $[\Phi_A, \Phi_B, \Phi_C] = [8, 2.2, 6] \times 10^4$ m^3/day.

Considering now the case where the analyst has some prior knowledge, we consider the flow rate configuration $[\phi_a, \phi_b, \phi_c] = [8, 2.2, 6] \times 10^4$ m^3/day and we suppose that the analyst is interested in scenarios leading to ES_3. To assess the impact of parameter β on the performance of the preliminary exploration, the average percentage increment of simulation falling into the scenarios of interest with respect to those falling in the same scenarios when no preferences are given (that is, $\beta = 1$), is computed for different values of $\beta = (2, 4, 8)$ and for different numbers of simulation runs $N_{\text{simul}} = [250; 500; 1000; 2000; 4000]$. 1000 experiments were done for each combination of β and N_{simul}. Since similar behaviors are observed for all scenarios leading to the ES of interest, only the boxplots associated with scenario S_7 are depicted in Figure 8.7. The larger the

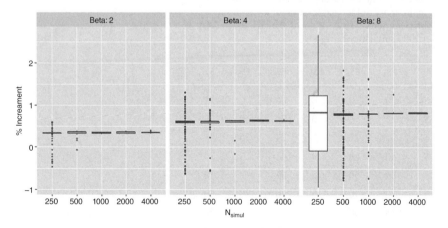

Figure 8.7 Boxplots of the percentage increment of simulations in a given scenario of interest S_7, for parameter $\beta = \{2; 4; 8\}$ and for different numbers of simulations.

β value, the larger the percentage increment, for example around (35, 60, 80)% for $\beta = \{2; 4; 8\}$, respectively. However, it must be noted that, if β is too large with respect to N_{simul} (say, $\beta = 8$ and $N_{simul} < 1000$), there is high uncertainty in the performance. Indeed, if β is too large, the algorithm focuses its exploration effort (its simulation runs) on the first scenario that reaches the ES of interest, "preventing" the algorithm from discovering other scenarios that can lead to the ES of interest. In particular, the larger the number of scenarios that can reach the ES of interest, the larger the sensitivity to the number of simulations, given β.

8.4.1.2.2   Deep Exploration
After a preliminary guided exploration of the system defined by parameters $[\phi_a, \phi_b, \phi_c] = [8, 3.6, 5] \times 10^4$ m^3/day, large variability in the outcomes is observed within scenario S_5, as highlighted in Table 8.5. Thus, it is interesting to retrieve the event time sequences that lead to two chosen ESs: ES_1, which represents the worst final condition, and ES_3, which has been visited only a few times during the preliminary exploration.

The space-filling parameter is set to 0.2, with the maximum number of simulations to run set to 5000. Multivariate Gaussian distributions have been used as proposal probability density functions within the M–H algorithm. The covariance matrix associated to ES_1 has been estimated from the vectors of transient times obtained from the preliminary exploration. In contrast, since only two vectors are available for ES_3, a diagonal covariance matrix with standard deviation equal to the Euclidean distance between the two vectors is considered. The chosen standard deviation provides an idea of the dimension of the support to explore. Figure 8.8 reports the transition time vectors of the

Table 8.5 Matrix reporting the ESs visited by a preliminary guided exploration of the system with parameters $[\phi_a, \phi_b, \phi_c] = [8, 3.6, 5] \times 10^4$ m^3/day, for 1000 simulations.

	ES_1	ES_2	ES_3	ES_4	ES_5	ES_6
S_1	0	0	0	0	0	29
S_2	21	0	0	38	0	28
S_3	0	27	10	24	36	47
S_4	46	29	0	41	5	23
S_5	39	50	2	57	7	18
S_6	0	0	23	0	28	36
S_7	38	36	22	36	14	26
S_8	34	39	24	41	12	22

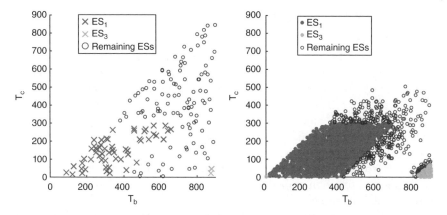

Figure 8.8 Preliminary guided exploration of S_5 (left) and deep exploration of ES_1 and ES_3 in the same scenario (right).

scenario of interest S_5 after the preliminary exploration (on the left) and after the deep exploration (on the right). Results confirm that the deep exploration is capable of increasing the number of simulations around the time sequences that reach the ES of interest. The results increase knowledge regarding the time sequences that lead to the event of interest. For example, in order to obtain ES_3, pipe c should break within the initial 100 days whereas pipe b should work at least for 800 days after the failure of the first one.

8.4.1.3 Discussion

Discovering and understanding the possible outcomes of an accident progression, leaving out as little as possible of the unexpected, adds significant value to a risk assessment. The proposed adaptive simulation framework guides the exploration of the accident scenarios towards those that show the highest variability in their outcomes, thus increasing the possibility of discovering a priori unexpected situations. The method allows for inclusion of the analyst's prior knowledge regarding the accident scenarios and their preferences about which specific outcomes to look for, making the method very flexible. In addition, new driving functions can be designed for meeting specific objectives during the exploration, such as guiding the simulations towards the most risky scenarios.

Some weak points still remain in the proposed framework:

- It is assumed that the analyst is already aware of the accident scenarios that the system can undergo, which is not always the case in large systems involving a large number of components; nevertheless, some methods have been developed to automatically generate possible risk scenarios (Li *et al.* 2011).
- The proposed framework, in its present formulation, is not designed for parallel computing. However, by selecting and simulating batches of time sequences, it is possible to benefit from parallel computational resources.

8.4.2   Critical Region Identification

8.4.2.1   Method

With reference to Section 8.3, let us assume that a mathematical model $Y = f(X)$ of the system behavior is available, whose input $X \in D_X \subset \mathbb{R}^M$, represents a given system operational configuration and whose output $Y \in D_Y \subset \mathbb{R}$ reflects the condition/state of the system. We define the conditions where $Y \geq Y_{thres}$ as "critical" and the corresponding configurations of inputs as the CR: that is, $CR = \{x \in D_X \subset \mathbb{R}^M : y = f(x) \geq Y_{thres}\}$. From a mathematical perspective, we are looking for the solution of the inverse problem $x = f^{-1}(y)$, with $y \geq Y_{thres}$. However, this is not viable in the majority of engineering systems where $f(x)$ is a function embedded in numerical code that is complex, a black-box, and not invertible.

A solution is, then, to resort to a DOE for exploring the I/O relation by means of numerical simulations, then retrieving information concerning the CRs through post-processing (Levy and Steinberg 2010; Santner *et al.* 2003). However, this approach is hard to pursue when models have the characteristics mentioned in Section 8.2.

In what follows, a self-adaptive algorithm for exploring the numerical model and retrieving information regarding the CRs is presented. Eventual probabilistic distributions associated with X are not considered, since the focus is, instead, on its range of values (that is, on its domain), in order to explore all possible configurations during the CR research. Hence, hereafter, without loss of generality, we assume that all inputs are standardized, say as $X \in D_X = [0,1]^M$ (Rosenblatt 1952). Likewise, a standardization can be applied to the output Y. This helps in designing a general, problem-independent algorithm and in removing effects related to the different orders of magnitudes possibly existing among inputs.

The driving idea of the proposed framework is to iteratively:

- run a (possibly small) number of model simulations
- retrieve knowledge from the available simulations
- guide the selection of new configurations towards the regions of interest (Turati *et al.* 2016b).

The framework is characterized by four principal steps (see Figure 8.9). In short, the first step – dimensionality reduction by PCE-based sensitivity analysis –aims at identifying the inputs that most affect the output of the model, so that the exploration can be limited to the corresponding (reduced) subspace (Sudret 2008). The second step aims at training a computationally cheap-to-run meta-model that accurately reproduces the response of the real model in the reduced space, with particular attention to its ability to discriminate between the CRs and normal conditions. An example is a kriging meta-model (Kleijnen 2009). The third step resorts to the meta-model to deeply explore the

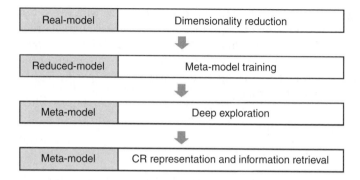

Figure 8.9 Flow diagram of the exploration framework.

reduced state space by means of MCMC, with the objective of visiting and, consequently, discovering those configurations of inputs leading to critical outputs (Andrieu and Thoms 2008). Finally, the last step uses clustering (say, k-means; Jain 2010) and graphical representation techniques such as parallel coordinates plot PCP (Inselberg 2009), for retrieving information and describing the CRs found.

8.4.2.1.1 Dimensionality Reduction

In general terms, dimensionality reduction includes a number of strategies for identifying a lower-dimensional subspace of variables where it is possible to build a reduced and simplified, yet representative and understandable, model of the system behavior (Fodor 2002; Liu and Motoda 2012). From the point of view of the exploration, reducing the dimensionality of the state space that must be explored allows for the definition of a more effective DOE. Two main strategies have been proposed in the literature:

- feature selection, which aims at selecting a subset of the available variables and parameters input to the model (Guyon and Elisseeff 2003)
- feature extraction, which aims at identifying a subset of "new" features created by means of transformations of the initial ones (Guyon and Elisseeff 2006).

Nevertheless, dimensionality reduction methods usually rely on a large set of input/output data examples that are not usually available when the system model is computationally expensive.

As an alternative, sensitivity analysis methods can be employed to achieve the same final objective as feature selection. These rank the inputs according to their influence on the output of the model (Borgonovo and Plischke 2016; Saltelli 2008; Sudret 2008). To this end, global order sensitivity indices are more appropriate than local sensitivity indices, because they provide a measure of how the inputs globally affect the output of the model; that is, with respect to different configurations of the inputs. Specifically, we resort to the total order sensitivity index S_T (Homma and Saltelli 1996; Sobol 2001), which is a variance-based global sensitivity measure, assessing the expected fraction of the total variance of the output Y that is due to the variation of a specific input i and to its interactions with the others:

$$S_{Ti} = \frac{E_{X_{-i}}\left[V_{X_i}\left(Y \mid X_{-i}\right)\right]}{V(Y)}, \tag{8.5}$$

where X_i represents the ith component of the input vector X, X_{-i} represents the rest of the components of the vector X, and $S_T \in [0,1]$. A large value of S_{Ti} indicates that the ith input heavily affects Y and thus should be kept in what is hereafter called the "reduced-model". In contast, a very low value of S_{Ti} indicates that the ith input does not affect Y and thus it can be discarded or set to a constant value. Usually, a threshold $S_{thres} = 1 / M$ is adopted to discriminate the important inputs (Saltelli 2008).

Although S_T usually requires a large number of MC or quasi-Monte-Carlo (QMC) simulations to be accurately computed (Saltelli 2008), PCE has been shown to achieve the same accuracy with a much lower number of simulations (Sudret 2008) (see Appendix 8.A for details). For this reason, PCE is here employed to identify those inputs that must be kept in the reduced model. All the analyses involving both the PCE approximation and the corresponding computation of the sensitivity indices are conducted using the UQLab Toolbox for Matlab (Marelli and Sudret 2014).

8.4.2.1.2 *Meta-modeling*

The main objective of a meta-model is to reproduce the behavior of the real system model (typically computationally expensive) with a less expensive computational model. The meta-model is trained by resorting to a typically limited number of I/O observations from the real reduced model; on this basis, it should be capable of predicting the output values associated with input configurations that have not been explored yet. Since the real model is assumed to be deterministic (simulations of the same input configuration lead to the same output), it is desirable that the meta-model also predicts the exact output values corresponding to those of the training configurations (known with absolute certainty). In this respect, among the numerous methods available in the literature (Jin *et al.* 2001; Shan and Wang 2010), we resort to kriging (Kleijnen 2009; Matheron 1963); that is, Gaussian process modeling (see Appendix 8.A for details). Kriging is capable of modeling local behaviors of the response function and of diversifying the levels of accuracy of the same model within different regions.

For example, in this case, the meta-model should be accurate in discriminating whether a configuration belongs to CR or not. For this reason, the meta-model should be more refined in the proximity of the CRs, whereas it can be rough in the rest of the space. To achieve this goal, sequential adaptive training strategies have been developed recently (Bect *et al.* 2012; Echard *et al.* 2011; Picheny *et al.* 2010). Instead of resorting to a static DOE to select the input/output configurations, new configurations are iteratively added to the training set to minimize a proper cost function. The adaptive kriging–Monte Carlo simulation (AK-MCS; Echard *et al.* 2011) is used here.

In the AK-MCS, an initial kriging model is trained with a small set of I/O observations, say sampled according to the Latin hypercube sampling (LHS) scheme. Then the algorithm proceeds iteratively according to the following steps:

i) randomly sample a large set of input configurations $\mathcal{X} = (x^{(1)}, \ldots, x^{(N_{MCS})})$, e.g., by means of LHS
ii) evaluate the associated responses using the kriging meta-model $\hat{\mathcal{Y}} = (\hat{y}_1, \ldots, \hat{y}_{N_{MCS}})$
iii) check if a convergence criterion has been reached: if so, the meta-model is sufficiently accurate; otherwise
iv) select, according to a predefined learning function/criterion, the best candidate subset $\mathcal{X}* \subset \mathcal{X}$ to add to the current DOE and evaluate the corresponding real model output $\mathcal{Y}*$
v) retrain a new kriging meta-model by adding the $\{\mathcal{X}*, \mathcal{Y}*\}$ to the training set and go back to step (i).

As the learning function – step (iv) above – we consider the so-called U-function, which is based on the concept of misclassification (Echard *et al.* 2011):

$$U(x) = \frac{\left| Y_{thres} - \mu_{\hat{Y}}(x) \right|}{\sigma_{\hat{Y}}(x)}. \tag{8.6}$$

In practice, $U(x)$ represents the distance in terms of standard deviations of the meta-model prediction from the limit state Y_{thres}. The smaller the value, the closer the prediction is to the limit state and thus the higher the interest in adding the corresponding I/O observation to the training set, because it reduces the prediction uncertainty regarding configurations "close" to the limit surface (in a probabilistic sense). Theoretically, the best DOE is obtained by adding only one best candidate configuration at each iteration. However, this increases the computational cost related to the training of the meta-model, which can be significant when a large number of I/O configurations are used and/or when many parameters have to be estimated due to the high dimensionality.

To overcome this problem, a larger number of I/O configurations can be added to the training set at the same time. Due to the correlation function, prediction points that are close share similar prediction values and misclassification probabilities, so it is likely that in the best candidate set there are configurations with similar input values. However, evaluating the real model with respect to similar configurations increases the computational cost without adding the desired amount of knowledge to the meta-model. To this end, clustering techniques are employed here to select, from the best candidate set, the most representative configurations before evaluating the corresponding real model output (Schöbi *et al.* 2016). An alternative method for optimally adding multiple observations to the training set has been recently proposed by Chevalier *et al.* (2014).

As a stopping criterion – step (iii) above –, we resort to the leave-one-out estimate of the correction factor $\hat{\alpha}_{\text{corr LOO}}$ (Dubourg *et al.* 2013):

$$\hat{\alpha}_{corr\ LOO} = \frac{1}{N_{Krig}} \sum_{n=1}^{N_{Krig}} \frac{\mathbb{1}_{f\left(x^{(n)}\right) \geq Y_{thres}}\left(x^{(n)}\right)}{P\left(\hat{Y}_{DOE\backslash x^{(n)}}\left(x^{(n)}\right) \geq Y_{thres}\right)}, \tag{8.7}$$

where $\hat{Y}_{\text{DOE}\backslash x^{(n)}}\left(x^{(n)}\right)$ is the prediction of the output associated to the inputs $x^{(n)}$, obtained with a kriging model having as training set all the I/O observations except $(x^{(n)}, y_n)$. This verifies that the probabilistic discriminating function (the prediction) converges towards the real discriminating function (the real limit surface). In practice, a value of $\hat{\alpha}_{corr\ LOO}$ close to 1 indicates a satisfactory approximation of the real model, whereas very small or very large values indicate an inaccurate approximation. It must be noticed that, since the estimation is based on a leave-one-out cross-validation, a minimum number of initial I/O observations, (say, 30; Dubourg *et al.* 2013), has to be provided to guarantee accurate estimates. On the other hand, a maximum number of iterations can be set, in order to limit the number of calls to the real model.

For building the meta-model, we resort to the UQLab Toolbox for Matlab (Marelli and Sudret 2014). The sequential training algorithm was developed by the authors.

8.4.2.1.3 Deep Exploration

During the deep exploration phase, the aim is to exploit the meta-model, to thoroughly explore the system space, and in particular to discover possible unexpected CRs. An algorithm based on the MCMC M–H algorithm has been designed. Although we refer the reader to the corresponding paper (Turati *et al.* 2016b), we list here the main ideas. The iterative algorithm, at each step, firstly identifies the number of CRs already discovered using clustering techniques. Then, several Markov chains are distributed among the CRs in order to guarantee that each CR has been explored with the same meticulousness. In practice, the CRs with a low density of simulation runs within them are more likely to be underexplored than those having a higher density, so more Markov chains will be assigned to the underexplored regions. For each configuration visited by the Markov chains, the corresponding meta-model is evaluated and, if it leads to a critical output, it is added to the CRs. The algorithm continues until the number of CRs identified remains equal for a given number of iterations (that is, until no more new CRs are identified) or alternatively until a certain density of simulations is reach for all the CRs. In any case a maximum number of simulations can be set for controlling the maximum computational effort.

8.4.2.1.4 Critical Region Representation and Information Retrieval
The outcome of the deep exploration is typically a large dataset containing a large set of points belonging to several CRs. However, when the state space dimensionality is higher than 3–4 dimensions, high-dimensional data visualization techniques are necessary to retrieve useful insights. The interested reader is referred to Liu, S. *et al.* (2015) for an extended review of the state of the art. In what follows, we make use of two of the most known techniques: scatterplot matrix (Hartigan 1975) and the PCP (Inselberg 2009), which help in retrieving complementary information about the CRs, such as their shapes and the corresponding input values in a unique, "readable", graphical representation.

8.4.2.1.5 Exploration Assessment
Assuming that the real limit function representing the configurations in the CRs is available, the objective of the assessment phase is to measure how satisfactorily the exploration method has identified the configurations leading to critical conditions. For illustrative purposes, the left-hand part of Figure 8.10 shows the output of an accurate exploration of a two-dimensional space, where the real CR (shadowed) is sufficiently covered by the configurations selected by

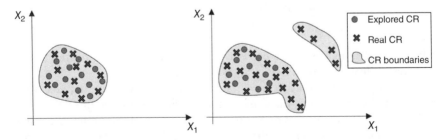

Figure 8.10 Representation of an accurate CR exploration (left) and of an incomplete CR exploration (right).

the explorative method (circles). In contrast, the right-hand part shows an incomplete exploration, where a part of a CR is identified, but not entirely covered, and another CR is not even explored.

Quantitative metrics are here introduced to assess the quality of the exploration: in particular, the population of critical configurations visited by the proposed methodology $\mathcal{X}_{exp}^{CR}$ (circles) is compared to a uniformly distributed population of samples belonging to the real CRs $\mathcal{X}_{real}^{CR}$ (crosses), according to a distance-based criterion.

A one-vs-all version of the local outlier factor (LOF) is used to this end. Each configuration in the real CRs is compared to the whole population of critical configurations obtained by the exploration method. For the sake of completeness, LOF is a density-based outlier detection method capable of measuring how isolated a sample is from the rest of a given population of interest (Breunig *et al.* 2000). In our case, the more isolated a real CR configuration is from the explored ones, the higher the probability that it belongs to an unexplored CR.

The definition of the LOF relies on the concept of reachability distance between points x and o:

$$d_{reach}\left(x, o\right) = \max\left(d_{kNN}\left(o\right), d\left(x, o\right)\right), \tag{8.8}$$

where $d(\cdot,\cdot)$ is a generic distance and $d_{kNN}(o)$ is the distance of the kth near neighbor (kNN) of o. In this paper, the Euclidean distance is employed, but the Manhattan or even lower-order L^p distances can be preferable in high dimensionality situations (Aggarwal *et al.* 2001). Then, the local reachability distance, which measures how close the configuration x is to its $kNNs$, can be defined as:

$$lrd_k\left(x\right) = \frac{k}{\displaystyle\sum_{o \in kNN(x)} d_{reach}\left(x, o\right)}. \tag{8.9}$$

In this light, the LOF of a configuration x is defined as:

$$LOF(x) = \frac{1}{k} \sum_{o \in kNN(x)} \frac{lrd_k\left(o\right)}{lrd_k\left(x\right)}, \tag{8.10}$$

where the parameter k has to be set by the analyst (and is not related to the number of clusters K identified in Section 8.4.2.1.4).

In general, a value of $LOF(x) \approx 1$ indicates that the configuration x is well represented by the rest of the configurations, whereas a value of $LOF(x) \gg 1$ indicates that the configuration x is isolated. In order to have a reference value for detecting a critical configuration as unexplored, the LOF is evaluated for all critical configurations $x \in \mathcal{X}_{exp}^{CR}$ (namely, LOF_{exp}). Likewise, LOF_{real} represents the random variables corresponding to the one-vs-all evaluations of the configurations $x \in \mathcal{X}_{real}^{CR}$. A configuration $x \in \mathcal{X}_{real}^{CR}$ is considered "unexplored", if $LOF(x) > \overline{LOF}_{exp}$, where:

$$\overline{LOF}_{exp} = \max_{x \in \mathcal{X}_{exp}^{CR}} LOF(x) \tag{8.11}$$

is the LOF corresponding to the most isolated configuration explored.

The following distance-based statistics have been considered to synthesize the overall performance of the exploration method:

Expected LOF

$$\mu_{LOF}^{real} = E[LOF_{real}] \tag{8.12}$$

A value of $\mu_{LOF}^{real} \gg 1$ indicates that some CRs are probably unexplored.

Unexplored critical region

$$UCR = \frac{\#\left(LOF_{real} > \overline{LOF}_{exp}\right)}{\#\mathcal{X}_{real}^{CR}} \tag{8.13}$$

which is the ratio between the number of real critical configurations identified as unexplored and the cardinality of $\mathcal{X}_{real}^{CR}$. In practice, it represents the "fraction" of CRs that have not been explored by the method.

Unexplored extreme critical region

$$UECR_{\gamma\%} = UCR_{\gamma\%} \mid \mathcal{X}_{real}^{ECR} = \frac{\#\left(LOF_{real} > \overline{LOF}_{exp} \mid \mathcal{X}_{real}^{ECR}\right)}{\#\mathcal{X}_{real}^{ECR}} \tag{8.14}$$

where $\mathcal{X}_{real}^{ECR} \subset \mathcal{X}_{real}^{CR}$ is the subset of the CRs leading to the most "extreme" outputs. In particular, $\gamma \in [0,100]\%$ is the quantile used to characterize the extreme outputs: letting $\gamma = 0.9$, a critical configuration is considered "extreme" if its output is larger than the output of 90% of the population. This metric allows the analyst to understand whether the method has discovered the CRs leading to the most critical outputs.

Conditional Expected LOF

$$\mu_{LOF|UCR} = E\left[\frac{LOF_{real}}{\overline{LOF}_{exp}} \mid LOF_{real} > \overline{LOF}_{exp}\right] \tag{8.15}$$

which indicates how isolated, on average, the unexplored critical configurations are with respect to the most isolated critical configuration explored. In practice, values of $\alpha_{LOF|UCR} \gg 1$ indicate the presence of critical configurations that are very isolated from the explored CRs, thus providing a warning to the analyst of the presence of CRs disconnected from those already identified.

8.4.2.2 Power Distribution Network

A power distribution network is analyzed in order to discover its associated CRs (Mena *et al.* 2014). The network, represented in Figure 8.11, comprises ten feeders, transporting energy from a unique main source (MS) to eight demand nodes (consumers) characterized by different daily load profiles.

The load profiles L_j assume different shapes according to the corresponding type of consumers associated. These include residential consumers and offices, whose per unit (p.u.) daily spot load profiles are reported in Figure 8.12. In detail, the daily load L_j of a demanding node is given by:

$$L_j(t) = r_j R(t) + o_j O(t) \qquad (8.16)$$

where $R(t)$ and $O(t)$ are the p.u. daily loads, whereas r_j and o_j are the corresponding average loads for the residential consumer and office, respectively

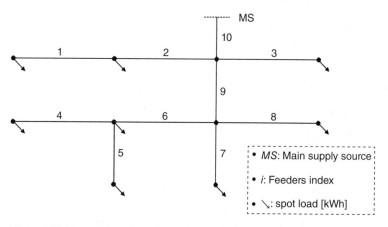

Figure 8.11 Power network configuration.

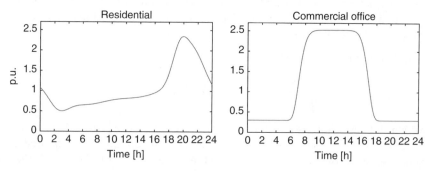

Figure 8.12 Power load profiles for a residential consumer (left) and for a commercial office (right).

Table 8.6 Average load values for the 10 nodes of the network in kW.

Node	1	2	3	4	5	6	7	8	9	10
r	0	0	0	1	1	5	5	5	0	0
o	5	5	100	0	0	0	0	0	0	0

(Jardini *et al.* 2000). The values of the average loads used in this paper are reported in Table 8.6. Uncertainty and seasonality effects on the average loads can be easily embedded into the model. Nevertheless, since the focus of the study is on the exploration of the daily profiles to verify the impact of feeder failures, they are not taken into account in the analysis.

We assume that each feeder can independently fail only once within a 24-h period, at a random time $T_i \in [0, 24)$ and with associated magnitude of the failure F_i. When the *i*th feeder fails, no power can flow through it for a time proportional to the magnitude of the failure: for example, $F_i = 0.5$ means that the feeder is out of service for half an hour. In this view, $X = [T_1, \ldots, T_{10}, F_1, \ldots, F_{10}]$ is the M-dimensional vector of the inputs to the model and represents a given failure configuration.

The electrical energy not served (ENS) to the consumers is considered as the output of the model and it is defined in this case as:

$$ENS(X) = \int_0^{24} \sum_{i=1}^{10} 1_{NSS(t)}(i) \cdot L_i(t) dt, \tag{8.17}$$

where $NSS(t)$ indicates the not supplied set at time t (the set of nodes that are not served at time t) and 1 is the indicator function, which takes value 1 if $i \in NSS(t)$ and 0 otherwise. Moreover, ENS is used to discriminate the critical conditions: a value of $ENS(X) \geq ENS_{thres}$ implies that the failure configuration X is critical; otherwise X is considered as "normal". The value of ENS_{thres} is set equal to 500 kWh, in order to focus attention on critical events.

8.4.2.2.1 *Dimensionality Reduction*
For the dimensionality reduction step, we resort to PCE, where the maximum degree of the polynomials is fixed to 5 in order to reduce the computational cost and focus attention on the main trend of the model. The coefficients of the PCE are estimated by least angle regression on the basis of a DOE of 500 samples obtained with a QMC Sobol' sequence (Sobol *et al.* 2011). Figure 8.13 shows that there is a huge difference between the total order indices S_T of the inputs: those for feeders 3 and 10 (T_3, T_{10}, F_3, F_{10}) take values larger than 0.2, whereas the others take values lower than 0.05. This is in accordance with the

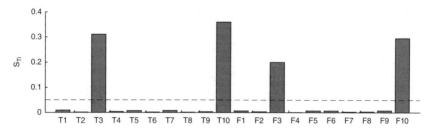

Figure 8.13 Sobol′ total order indices for the 20 inputs.

fact that feeders 3 and 10 are the only two that can affect the energy supplied to the most demanding consumer (user 3). In this light, the dimensionality of the reduced-model is set to 4 with $X^* = (T_3, T_{10}, F_3, F_{10})$, and the rest of the inputs are set to randomly fixed values, since they are expected to have no effect on the output.

8.4.2.2.2 *Meta-model*

For training the meta-model, we resort to ordinary kriging: the trend is assumed to be unknown but constant, which allows the Gaussian process to completely adapt to the training data. An ellipsoidal anisotropic correlation function is used to take into account possible different behaviors of the response function with respect to different inputs: in particular, we resort to the 3/2 Matérn one (Abramowitz and Stegun 1964; Rasmussen and Williams 2006):

$$h(x,x';\theta) = \sqrt{\sum_{m \in M'} \left(\frac{x_m - x'_m}{\theta_m} \right)^2}$$

$$R\left(h, v = \frac{3}{2} \right) = (1 + h\sqrt{3}) \cdot e^{-h\sqrt{3}} \tag{8.18}$$

where v is the shape parameter and θ the scale one.

Given the dimensionality of the reduced-model, 100 configurations sampled with a Sobol′ QMC and the corresponding ENS are used for initializing the meta-model. Then, through the iterative AK-MCS introduced in Section 8.4.2.1.2, 10000 configurations are sampled by means of LHS and a maximum of 50 candidate configurations are evaluated and added to the DOE $\{\mathcal{X}_{krig}, \mathcal{Y}_{krig}\}$ at each step. Only configurations having a value of the U-function lower than 4 are eligible as candidates. Actually, $U(x) > 4$ indicates that the corresponding configuration is, in a probabilistic view, very distant from the critical threshold. A maximum number of 1000 I/O observations for training the meta-model is set in order to limit the maximum computational effort. Figure 8.14 shows the projection on the two-dimensional subspace $[T_3, T_{10}]$ of

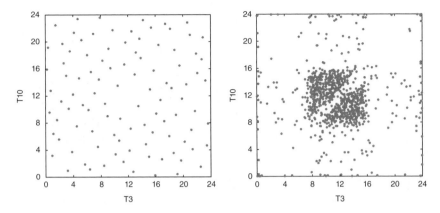

Figure 8.14 Projection of the DOE used for training the meta-model. The Figure on the left shows the initial 100 Sobol' QMC samples, whereas on the right those added by the AK-MCS are shown.

the configurations used to train the meta-model: on the left, we report the initial 100 samples used for the initialization, and on the right, those added iteratively by the AK-MCS. It is worth noticing how the adaptive DOE distributes the observations differently in the different portions of the input domain (that is, with a significantly higher density in the CRs).

8.4.2.2.3 Deep Exploration

From the kriging DOE, 169 configurations are identified as critical. In order to deeply explore the CRs, five iterations of the method proposed in Section 8.4.2.1.3 are run with five Markov chains and a maximum number of samples equal to 5000. Figure 8.15 shows the projections on the two-dimensional subspace $[T_3, T_{10}]$ of the configurations belonging to the CRs. The left-hand panel reports the configurations available from the meta-model DOE, while that on the right contains those obtained as a result of the deep exploration (~3000 configurations). It noteworthy that the deep exploration allows better highlighting of the boundaries of the CRs and, is thus better at retrieving their shapes and characteristics. This is even more apparent in high-dimensional spaces. Only one projection of the CR configurations is reported for brevity; nevertheless, a detailed analysis is given in the following sections.

8.4.2.2.4 Representation and Information Retrieval

A sequence of k-means clusterings with different cluster cardinality (from $K=1$ to 10) is applied to the critical configurations for identifying the representative number of separate CRs. Several cluster validity indices (such as Hubert statistic, Dunn, Silhouette, Davies and Bouldin, Calinski and Harabasz indices) have been computed to this end. However, since this analysis goes beyond the

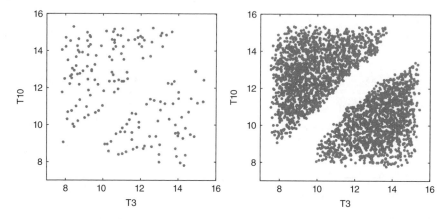

Figure 8.15 Two-dimensional projections of the observations belonging to the CRs: those available from the DOE of the meta-model (left) and those obtained with the deep exploration step (right).

present scope, the reader is referred to the publications by Arbelaitz *et al.* 2013 and Charrad *et al.* 2014 for details of the definition and interpretation of the indices used. Two clusters have been identified and the corresponding PCP is reported in Figure 8.16. For the sake of clarity, the envelopes of the parallel coordinates representing the two clusters (the ranges of values characterizing the clusters) are shown in Figure 8.17. By observing these ranges, it is also possible to have an idea of the dimension of the CRs. In this case, for example, they occupy respectively around (30%, 30%, 20%, 20%) of the entire range of the four important inputs T_3, T_{10}, F_3 and F_{10}, which corresponds to ~0.36% of the entire input domain. The CRs are characterized by failures occurring during the

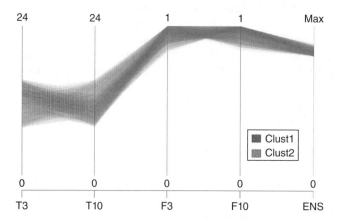

Figure 8.16 Parallel coordinates plot of the two CRs identified.

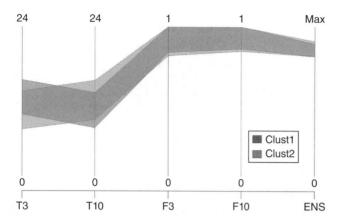

Figure 8.17 Envelopes of the PCP representing the input ranges.

central hours of the day (between 8:00 and 15:00) and with a failure magnitude above 0.8; that is, the feeders are out of order for at least 48 min each. In addition, it is worth noticing that the two clusters show different behaviors on the two axes corresponding to the failure times, T_3 and T_{10}.

For this reason, the corresponding scatterplot matrix is given in Figure 8.18, where the "envelopes" identified on the PCP are represented in the panels above the diagonal by means of shadowed rectangles. It can be observed that the two clusters are recognizable and well separated on the subspace defined by $[T_3, T_{10}]$: cluster 1 is characterized by an initial failure of feeder 10 followed by a failure of feeder 3 with a delay of at least 1 h, whereas cluster 2 is characterized by the inverse sequence, still with a delay of at least 1 h between failures. Indeed, if both failures happen at the same time, the ENS associated with node 3 is the same as if only one of the two failures had happened, because both feeders are put under repair at the same time and thus the total time with no energy supplied to user 3 is "just" 1 h.

Concerning the subspace defined by $[F_3, F_{10}]$, it must be noticed that there is no difference between the two clusters. However, the triangular shape of the region shows that the sum of the two failure magnitudes must be at least equal to 1.80, i.e., the consumer at node 3 is not served for at least 1h:48m. Finally, although the two-dimensional projections of the convex hulls slightly overestimate the regions of the associated CRs, they provide a synthetic representation, which can be useful as first approximation of the CRs.

8.4.2.2.5 *Performance Assessment*
In order to have a representative picture of the real CRs, a large number of configurations involving all 20 inputs of the model have been sampled by means of LHS and the corresponding output has been evaluated. Moreover,

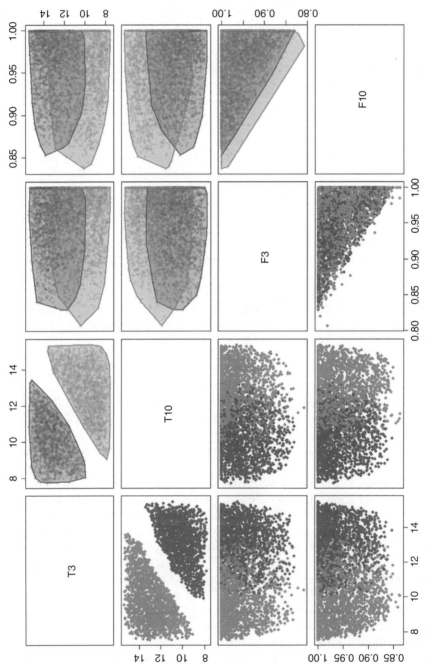

Figure 8.18 Scatterplot matrix of the two CRs discovered by the exploration algorithm. Above the diagonal, the two-dimensional convex hull of the identified clusters is depicted.

the outputs of the reduced-model involving the projections of the 20 inputs on the 4-dimensional space defined by $[T_3, T_{10}, F_3, F_{10}]$ have been evaluated as representative of the ideal "target", meta-model representation. The number of calls to the expensive model and/or to the cheap one (i.e., the meta-model) is given in Table 8.7 for each exploration strategy.

Among the large number of configurations sampled, those leading to critical values of ENS are selected and the corresponding LOF evaluated to verify to what extent the CRs discovered by the meta-model are similar to those found by the reduced and real-models (see Section 8.4.2.1.5). The values of the associated statistics are given in Table 8.8. The CRs of the meta-model are used as the reference set, so only the corresponding expected value of the LOF can be evaluated. By looking at the results obtained for the reduced model, it should be observed that all the statistics assume low values: the average value of LOF is very close to that of the meta-model; the percentage of CRs that remains unexplored is only 3%, and the associated conditional value is still very low at 1.08, which means that the unexplored CRs are very close to the boundaries of the CRs identified by the meta-model. In this light, it can be stated that the meta-model exploration has accurately explored and discovered the CRs associated with the reduced-model.

On the other hand, with respect to the real model, the average LOF takes a large value compared to the meta-model, suggesting that a portion of the CRs remain unexplored. This is confirmed by the percentage of unexplored CRs. However, it must be noticed that the percentage of unexplored extreme CRs is very low, so the meta-model exploration has been able to

Table 8.7 Number of calls made to the computationally cheap and/or expensive model for the different exploration strategies.

Computational cost	Meta-model	Reduced model	Real model
Cheap	~200000	0	0
Expensive	1500	100000	100000

Table 8.8 Local Outlier Factor (LOF)-based statistics for the different exploration strategies.

Metric	Meta-model	Reduced model	Real model
μ_{LOF}	1.02	1.03	2.66
UCR	—	3%	72%
$UECR_{90\%}$	—	0%	7%
$\mu_{LOF|UCR}$	—	1.08	2.20

identify the configurations leading to the most critical outputs. Finally, the conditional expected value $\mu_{LOF|UCR}$ takes a value that is not very large, suggesting that the unexplored portion of CRs is likely to be close to the boundaries.

In order to visualize the results, we use a scatterplot matrix where the CRs identified by the meta-model exploration are depicted by light circles and the configuration belonging to the CRs associated with the real model are depicted by crosses and squares according to their values of LOF. In particular, in accordance with Section 8.4.2.1.5, those configurations having $LOF \leq \overline{LOF}_{exp}$ (see Equation 8.11) are defined as identified CRs (crosses), whereas those having $\overline{LOF}_{exp} < LOF$ are defined as undiscovered CRs (squares). It must be noticed that there is not a significant difference between the meta-model (MM)-based and the real model-based exploration in the subspace characterized by the failure times $[T_3, T_{10}]$. On the contrary, there is a significant difference in the failure magnitude subspace $[F_3, F_{10}]$: according to the real model, it is enough that the sum of the magnitudes is larger than $\sim$1.60. This means that the real model can reach a critical condition even if the consumer at node 3 is not served for at least 1h:36m. Indeed, the rest of the ENS needed to reach the critical threshold can come from the failures of the feeders discarded during the dimensionality reduction step. Finally, by looking at the last column of Figure 8.19, it can be seen that the largest values of ENS – the most critical ones – are correctly discovered by our methodology (crosses).

A sort of sensitivity analysis for the model parameters has also been conducted to verify the performance of the proposed methodology when the impacts of the discarded inputs is very low; that is, when the reduced model is likely to represent the real model. To this end, all the loads except that of node 3 have been reduced of a factor 10 (the corresponding values are reported in Table 8.9). In order to ensure the presence of a CR despite the loading reduction, the threshold ENS_{thres} has been set equal to 475 kWh, 5% lower than the initial one. All the analyses have been run with the same settings and with the same number of calls to the model as in the initial case.

Table 8.10 reports the result of the statistics associated to the LOF for the reduced and the real model-based exploration. The average value of the LOF is for all types of exploration very close to 1, indicating that it is likely that all CRs have been discovered. This is confirmed by the percentage of unexplored CRs, which is null for both models. The value of $\mu_{LOF|UCR}$ is not reported, since no configuration has been identified as unexplored.

Figure 8.20 shows that all critical configurations discovered by means of the real model based exploration (dark crosses) lay inside or at the boundaries of the CRs discovered by the proposed methodology (light circles). These results demonstrate how the proposed methodology is capable of identifying the CRs using a limited number of calls to the real model: in this case, two orders of magnitude lower than with exploration based on the real model.

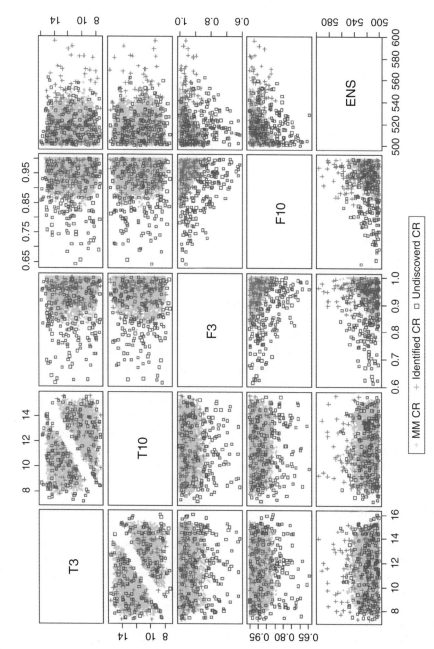

Figure 8.19 Scatterplot matrix of the CRs discovered by the meta-model exploration (MM; light circles). The CRs of the real model are depicted with different symbols whether identified (cross) or not (square).

MM CR   + Identified CR   □ Undiscoverd CR

Table 8.9 Average load values (kW) for the ten nodes of the network.

Node	1	2	3	4	5	6	7	8	9	10
r	0	0	0	0.1	0.1	0.5	0.5	0.5	0	0
o	0.5	0.5	100	0	0	0	0	0	0	0

Table 8.10 Local Outlier Factor (LOF)-based statistics for the different exploration strategies.

Metric	Meta-model	Reduced model	Real model
μ_{LOF}	1,02	1,01	1,07
UCR	—	0	0
$UECR_{90\%}$	—	0	0

8.4.2.3 Discussion

In Section 8.4.2 a new strategy was proposed to identify and characterize CRs by simulations of models that are: computationally expensive, high-dimensional, and complex.

The main advantage of the proposed method is the capability to explore and retrieve information with a limited number of simulations. Furthermore, the method is general and modular: it can be applied to a variety of problems and cases. For example, if the numerical model is not high-dimensional (or computationally expensive), the dimensionality reduction step (or the meta-model one) can be avoided.

Finally, since the proposed method relies on the capability of the meta-model to accurately reproducing the behavior of the real model, the performance of the method is in a way conditioned by that of the kriging. In particular, kriging performance tends to decrease with the dimensionality of the important input space: the dimensionality of the reduced-model input space.

8.5 Conclusions

In this chapter, the possibility of gaining knowledge for system risk assessment by scenario simulations has been discussed and investigated. The trivial idea is to explore how the system behaves by running simulations and retrieving, a posteriori, the information of interest, specifically with respect to those unexpected or unusual critical configurations forming the so-called CRs. Such exploration becomes obviously challenging, when the simulation model is high-dimensional, complex, a black box, and computationally expensive.

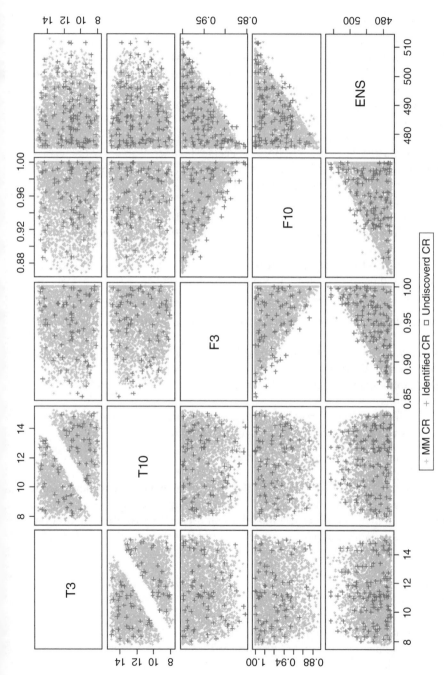

Figure 8.20 Scatterplot of the CRs discovered by the meta-model exploration (light circles). The CRs of the real model are depicted with different symbols, whether identified (cross) or not (square).

Specific methods are then needed to obtain the information of interest with a limited number of calls to the (computationally expensive) model. Two main strategies have been considered in the literature to this end. One resorts to parallel computing to reduce the time required to achieve a satisfactory level of detail during the exploration. The other one resorts to iterative adaptive strategies, which exploit the knowledge available from the results of the simulations already run, to select the best configuration for a new "informative" simulation (which should, in principle, add more information on the states of the system that are of interest for the analysis).

Two methods have been presented in the chapter. One explores the uncertainty associated with different possible accident scenarios in order to increase the knowledge about the impact that time has on the evolution of scenarios of interest. The method identifies those scenarios characterized by a large variability in their output and, consequently, concentrates the simulation runs on them. At the same time, the method can embed the prior knowledge of the analyst. This allows attention and the majority of the computational effort to be focused on the exploration of a limited number of accident scenarios.

The other method aims at identifying and characterizing the configurations of inputs and parameters leading a system to abnormal conditions, namely the CRs. The proposed framework makes use of:

- dimensionality reduction techniques, to limit the dimensionality of the input space
- meta-modeling to reproduce the real model and reduce the computational cost for a model run
- an adaptive exploration algorithm to identify and thoroughly probe the critical regions
- clustering and high-dimensional data visualization techniques to retrieve and visualize the knowledge enclosed in the simulations run.

The framework is modular and flexible, making it easy to adapt to different types of applications.

Finally, it must be emphasized that the knowledge that can be retrieved from the simulations is conditioned on the knowledge available in the model: the more detailed and accurate the model, the more challenging the exploration, but also the more complete and informative the information that can be retrieved.

References

Abramowitz, M. and Stegun, I.A. (1964). *Handbook of Mathematical Functions: with Formulas, Graphs, and Mathematical Tables* (Vol. 55). Courier Corporation.

AEMO. (2016). Third preliminary report –black system event in South Australia on 28 September 2016. Retrieved from https://www.aemo.com.au/-/media/Files/Electricity/NEM/Security_and_Reliability/Reports/Integrated-Third-Report-SA-Black-System-28-September-2016.pdf

Aggarwal, C.C., Hinneburg, A. and Keim, D.A. (2001). *On the Surprising Behavior of Distance Metrics in High Dimensional Space*. Springer.

Aldemir, T. (2013). A survey of dynamic methodologies for probabilistic safety assessment of nuclear power plants. *Annals of Nuclear Energy*, 52, 113–124.

Alfonsi, A., Rabiti, C., Mandelli, D., *et al.* (2016). *RAVEN Theory Manual*. Technical report INL/EXT-16-38178, Revision 1, Idaho National Laboratory, Idaho Falls.

Andrieu, C. and Thoms, J. (2008). A tutorial on adaptive MCMC. *Statistics and Computing*, 18(4), 343–373. doi:DOI 10.1007/s11222–008–9110-y

Arbelaitz, O., Gurrutxaga, I., Muguerza, J., Pérez, J.M., and Perona, I. (2013). An extensive comparative study of cluster validity indices. *Pattern Recognition*, 46(1), 243–256.

Aven, T. (2012a). Foundational issues in risk assessment and risk management. *Risk Analysis*, 32(10), 1647–1656.

Aven, T. (2012b). On the critique of Beck's view on risk and risk analysis. *Safety Science*, 50(4), 1043–1048.

Aven, T. (2013). On the meaning of a black swan in a risk context. *Safety Science*, 57, 44–51.

Aven, T. (2016a). Ignoring scenarios in risk assessments: Understanding the issue and improving current practice. *Reliability Engineering & System Safety*, 145, 215–220.

Aven, T. (2016b). Risk assessment and risk management: Review of recent advances on their foundation. *European Journal of Operational Research*, 253(1), 1–13.

Aven, T. and Zio, E. (2014). Foundational issues in risk assessment and risk management. *Risk Analysis*, 34(7), 1164–1172

Baudin, M., Dutfoy, A., Iooss, B., and Popelin, A.-L. (2016). OpenTURNS: An industrial software for uncertainty quantification in simulation. In: R. Ghanem, D. Higdon and H. Owhadi (eds), *Handbook of Uncertainty Quantification*. Springer International Publishing.

Bect, J., Ginsbourger, D., Li, L., Picheny, V., and Vazquez, E. (2012). Sequential design of computer experiments for the estimation of a probability of failure. *Statistics and Computing*, 22(3), 773–793.

Bentley, J.L. (1975). Multidimensional binary search trees used for associative searching. *Communications of the ACM*, 18(9), 509–517.

Blatman, G. and Sudret, B. (2011). Adaptive sparse polynomial chaos expansion based on least angle regression. *Journal of Computational Physics*, 230(6), 2345–2367.

Borgonovo, E. and Plischke, E. (2016). Sensitivity analysis: A review of recent advances. *European Journal of Operational Research*, 248(3), 869–887.

Breunig, M.M., Kriegel, H.-P., Ng, R.T., and Sander, J. (2000). LOF: identifying density-based local outliers. Paper presented at the ACM Sigmod Record.

Burnaev, E., Panin, I., and Sudret, B. (2016). Effective design for Sobol indices estimation based on polynomial chaos expansions conformal and probabilistic prediction with applications. In: *Proceedings of the 5th International Symposium on Conformal and Probabilistic Prediction with Applications*; Madrid, Spain — April 20–22, 2016; Vol. 9653, pp. 165–184. Springer International Publishing.

Cepin, M. and Mavko, B. (2002). A dynamic fault tree. *Reliability Engineering & System Safety*, 75(1), 83–91.

Charrad, M., Ghazzali, N., Boiteau, V., and Niknafs, A. (2014). NbClust: An R package for determining the relevant number of clusters in a data set. *Journal of Statistical Software*, 61(6), 36.

Cheng, B. and Titterington, D.M. (1994). Neural networks: A review from a statistical perspective. *Statistical Science*, 9(1), 2–30.

Chevalier, C., Bect, J., Ginsbourger, D., Vazquez, E., Picheny, V., and Richet, Y. (2014). fast parallel kriging-based stepwise uncertainty reduction with application to the identification of an excursion set. *Technometrics*, 56(4), 455–465.

Chib, S. and Greenberg, E. (1995). Understanding the Metropolis-Hastings algorithm. *American Statistician*, 49(4), 327–335.

Clarke, S.M., Griebsch, J.H., and Simpson, T.W. (2004). Analysis of support vector regression for approximation of complex engineering analyses. *Journal of Mechanical Design*, 127(6), 1077–1087.

Cojazzi, G. (1996). The DYLAM approach for the dynamic reliability analysis of systems. *Reliability Engineering & System Safety*, 52(3), 279–296.

Cox, A.L.J. (2015). Special (virtual) issue of *Foundations of Risk Analysis*.

Di Maio, F., Secchi, P., Vantini, S., and Zio, E. (2011). Fuzzy C-means clustering of signal functional principal components for post-processing dynamic scenarios of a nuclear power plant digital instrumentation and control system. *IEEE Transactions on Reliability*, 60(2), 415–425.

Di Maio, F., Baronchelli, S., and Zio, E. (2015a). A computational framework for prime implicants identification in noncoherent dynamic systems. *Risk Analysis*, 35(1), 142–156.

Di Maio, F., Baronchelli, S., and Zio, E. (2015b). A visual interactive method for prime implicants identification. *IEEE Transactions on Reliability*, 64(2), 539–549.

Di Maio, F., Vagnoli, M., and Zio, E. (2015c). Risk-based clustering for near misses identification in integrated deterministic and probabilistic safety analysis. *Science and Technology of Nuclear Installations*, 501, 693891.

Di Maio, F., Bandini, A., Zio, E., Alfonsi, A., and Rabiti, C. (2016). An approach based on support vector machines and a K-D tree search algorithm for identification of the failure domain and safest operating conditions in nuclear systems. *Progress in Nuclear Energy*, 88, 297–309.

Dreossi, T., Dang, T., Donzé, A., Kapinski, J., Jin, X., and Deshmukh, J.V. (2015). Efficient guiding strategies for testing of temporal properties of hybrid systems. In K. Havelund, G. Holzmann and R. Joshi (eds), *NASA Formal Methods: 7th International Symposium*, NFM 2015, Pasadena, CA, USA, April 27–29, 2015. Springer International Publishing.

Dubourg, V., Sudret, B., and Deheeger, F. (2013). Metamodel-based importance sampling for structural reliability analysis. *Probabilistic Engineering Mechanics*, 33, 47–57.

EBA (2016) 2016 EU-wide stress test – Methodological notes. Retrieved from http://www.eba.europa.eu/-/eba-launches-2016-eu-wide-stress-test-exercise.

Echard, B., Gayton, N., and Lemaire, M. (2011). AK-MCS: An active learning reliability method combining kriging and Monte Carlo simulation. *Structural Safety*, 33(2), 145–154.

Eldred, M.S., Hough, P.D., Hu, K.T., *et al.* (2014). Dakota, a multilevel parallel object-oriented framework for design optimization, parameter estimation, uncertainty quantification, and sensitivity analysis: Version 6.0 user's manual.

European Commission (2013). Technical summary on the implementation of comprehensive risk and safety assessments of nuclear power plants in the European Union (SWD287). Retrieved from http://eur-lex.europa.eu/legal-content/EN/TXT/PDF/?uri=CELEX:52012SC0287R(01)&from=EN.

Fainekos, G.E., Sankaranarayanan, S., Ueda, K., and Yazarel, H. (2012). Verification of automotive control applications using S-TaLiRo. Paper presented at the Proceedings of the American Control Conference.

Fang, K.-T., Li, R., and Sudjianto, A. (2005). *Design and Modeling for Computer Experiments*. CRC Press.

Flage, R. and Aven, T. (2015). Emerging risk – Conceptual definition and a relation to black swan type of events. *Reliability Engineering & System Safety*, 144, 61–67.

Fodor, I.K. (2002). A survey of dimension reduction techniques. Center for Applied Scientific Computing, Lawrence Livermore National Laboratory, 9, 1–18.

Garrett, C. and Apostolakis, G. (1999). Context in the risk assessment of digital systems. *Risk Analysis*, 19(1), 23–32.

Ghanem, R.G. and Spanos, P.D. (1991). *Stochastic Finite Elements: A Spectral Approach*. Springer.

Gorissen, D., Couckuyt, I., Demeester, P., Dhaene, T., and Crombecq, K. (2010). A surrogate modeling and adaptive sampling toolbox for computer based design. *Journal of Machine Learning Research*, 11(Jul), 2051–2055.

Guyon, I. and Elisseeff, A. (2003). An introduction to variable and feature selection. *Journal of Machine Learning Research*, 3, 1157–1182.

Guyon, I. and Elisseeff, A. (2006). An introduction to feature extraction. In: I. Guyon, M. Nikravesh, S. Gunn and L.A. Zadeh (eds), *Feature Extraction: Foundations and Applications*. Springer.

Hakobyan, A., Aldemir, T., Denning, R., *et al.* (2008). Dynamic generation of accident progression event trees. *Nuclear Engineering and Design*, 238(12), 3457–3467.

Hartigan, J.A. (1975). Printer graphics for clustering. *Journal of Statistical Computation and Simulation*, 4(3), 187–213.

Hastings, W.K. (1970). Monte Carlo sampling methods using Markov chains and their applications. *Biometrika*, 57(1), 97–109.

Haykin, S. (2004). *Neural Networks: A Comprehensive Foundation*, 2nd edn. Prentice Hall.

Homma, T. and Saltelli, A. (1996). Importance measures in global sensitivity analysis of nonlinear models. *Reliability Engineering & System Safety*, 52(1), 1–17.

Hsueh, K.S. and Mosleh, A. (1996). The development and application of the accident dynamic simulator for dynamic probabilistic risk assessment of nuclear power plants. *Reliability Engineering & System Safety*, 52(3), 297–314.

Hu, Y., Groen, F., and Mosleh, A. (2004). An entropy-based exploration strategy in dynamic PRA. Paper presented at the Probabilistic Safety Assessment and Management.

Ibáñez, L., Hortal, J., Queral, C., *et al.* (2016). Application of the integrated safety assessment methodology to safety margins. Dynamic event trees, damage domains and risk assessment. *Reliability Engineering & System Safety*, 147, 170–193.

IRGC (2015). Guidelines for emerging risk governance. Technical Report. International Risk Governance Council, Lausanne, Switzerland. Available at: https://www.irgc.org/wp-content/uploads/2015/03/IRGC-Emerging-Risk-WEB-31Mar.pdf.

Inselberg, A. (2009). *Parallel Coordinates*. Springer.

Jain, A.K. (2010). Data clustering: 50 years beyond K-means. *Pattern Recognition Letters*, 31(8), 651–666.

Jardini, J.A., Tahan, C., Gouvea, M., Ahn, S.U. and Figueiredo, F. (2000). Daily load profiles for residential, commercial and industrial low voltage consumers. *IEEE Transactions on Power Delivery*, 15(1), 375–380.

Jin, R., Chen, W. and Simpson, T.W. (2001). Comparative studies of metamodelling techniques under multiple modelling criteria. *Structural and Multidisciplinary Optimization*, 23(1), 1–13.

Kernstine, K.H. (2012). Design space exploration of stochastic system-of-systems simulations using adaptive sequential experiments. PhD thesis, Georgia Institute of Technology.

Kleijnen, J.P.C. (2009). Kriging metamodeling in simulation: A review. *European Journal of Operational Research*, 192(3), 707–716.

Kloos, M. and Peschke, J. (2006). MCDET: A probabilistic dynamics method combining Monte Carlo simulation with the discrete dynamic event tree approach. *Nuclear Science and Engineering*, 153(2), 137–156.

Kuhnt, S. and Steinberg, D.M. (2010). Design and analysis of computer experiments. *Advances in Statistical Analysis*, 94(4), 307–309.

Labeau, P.E., Smidts, C., and Swaminathan, S. (2000). Dynamic reliability: towards an integrated platform for probabilistic risk assessment. *Reliability Engineering & System Safety*, 68(3), 219–254.

Le Matre, O.P., Reagan, M.T., Najm, H.N., Ghanem, R.G., and Knio, O.M. (2002). A stochastic projection method for fluid flow. II. Random process. *Journal of Computational Physics*, 181(1), 9–44.

Levy, S. and Steinberg, D.M. (2010). Computer experiments: a review. *Advances in Statistical Analysis*, 94(4), 311–324.

Li, J.H., Kang, R., Mosleh, A., and Pan, X. (2011). Simulation-based automatic generation of risk scenarios. *Journal of Systems Engineering and Electronics*, 22(3), 437–444.

Liu, H. and Motoda, H. (2012). *Feature Selection for Knowledge Discovery and Data Mining* (Vol. 454): Springer Science & Business Media.

Liu, S., Maljovec, D., Wang, B., Bremer, P.-T., and Pascucci, V. (2015). Visualizing high-dimensional data: Advances in the past decade. Paper presented at the Proc. Eurographics Conf. Visualization.

Mandelli, D., Smith, C., Rabiti, C., *et al.* (2013a). Dynamic PRA: An overview of new algorithms to generate, analyze and visualize data. Paper presented at the Transactions of the American Nuclear Society.

Mandelli, D., Yilmaz, A., Aldemir, T., Metzroth, K. and Denning, R. (2013b). Scenario clustering and dynamic probabilistic risk assessment. *Reliability Engineering & System Safety*, 115, 146–160.

Marelli, S. and Sudret, B. (2014). UQLab: a framework for uncertainty quantification in MATLAB. Paper presented at the International Conference on Vulnerability, Risk Analysis and Management (ICVRAM2014), Liverpool (United Kingdom).

Matheron, G. (1963). Principles of geostatistics. *Economic Geology*, 58(8), 1246–1266.

McKay, M.D., Beckman, R.J., and Conover, W.J. (1979). Comparison of three methods for selecting values of input variables in the analysis of output from a computer code. *Technometrics*, 21(2), 239–245.

Mena, R., Hennebel, M., Li, Y.-F., Ruiz, C., and Zio, E. (2014). A risk-based simulation and multi-objective optimization framework for the integration of distributed renewable generation and storage. *Renewable and Sustainable Energy Reviews*, 37, 778–793.

Montero-Mayorga, J., Queral, C., and Gonzalez-Cadelo, J. (2014). Effects of delayed RCP trip during SBLOCA in PWR. *Annals of Nuclear Energy*, 63, 107–125.

Myers, R.H., Montgomery, D.C. and Anderson-Cook, C.M. (2016). *Response Surface Methodology: Process and Product Optimization using Designed Experiments*. John Wiley & Sons.

Nghiem, T., Sankaranarayanan, S., Fainekos, G., *et al.* (2010). Monte-carlo techniques for falsification of temporal properties of non-linear hybrid systems. Paper presented at the Proceedings of the 13th ACM international conference on hybrid systems: computation and control, Stockholm, Sweden.

Patelli, E., Broggi, M., Angelis, M.D. and Beer, M. (2014). OpenCossan: An efficient open tool for dealing with epistemic and aleatory uncertainties. Paper presented at the Vulnerability, Uncertainty, and Risk: Quantification, Mitigation, and Management.

Picheny, V., Ginsbourger, D., Roustant, O., Haftka, R.T., and Kim, N.-H. (2010). Adaptive designs of experiments for accurate approximation of a target region. *Journal of Mechanical Design*, 132(7), 071008–071008.

Queral, C., Mena-Rosell, L., Jimenez, G., Sanchez-Perea, M., Gomez-Magan, J., and Hortal, J. (2016). Verification of SAMGs in SBO sequences with Seal LOCA. *Multiple damage domains. Annals of Nuclear Energy*, 98, 90–111.

Rasmussen, C.E. and Williams, C.K.I. (2006). *Gaussian Processes for Machine Learning*. MIT Press.

RELAP5-3D. (2005). RELAP5-3D. Idaho National Laboratory.

Robert, C.P. and Casella, G. (2004). *Monte Carlo Statistical Methods*, 2nd edn. Springer.

Roberts, G.O. and Rosenthal, J.S. (2009). Examples of adaptive MCMC. *Journal of Computational and Graphical Statistics*, 18(2), 349–367.

Rosenblatt, M. (1952). Remarks on a multivariate transformation. *The Annals of Mathematical Statistics*, 23(3), 470–472.

Rutt, B., Catalyurek, U., Hakobyan, A., *et al.* (2006). Distributed dynamic event tree generation for reliability and risk assessment. In: *Challenges of Large Applications in Distributed Environments, Proceedings*, IEEE, pp. 61–70.

Saltelli, A. (2008). *Global Sensitivity Analysis: The Primer*. John Wiley.

Santner, T.J., Williams, B.J., and Notz, W. (2003). *The Design and Analysis of Computer Experiments*. Springer.

Schöbi, R., Sudret, B., and Marelli, S. (2016). Rare event estimation using polynomial-chaos kriging. *ASCE-ASME Journal of Risk and Uncertainty in Engineering Systems, Part A: Civil Engineering*, 3(2), D4016002.

Shan, S. and Wang, G.G. (2010). Survey of modeling and optimization strategies to solve high-dimensional design problems with computationally-expensive black-box functions. *Structural and Multidisciplinary Optimization*, 41(2), 219–241.

Simpson, T.W., Poplinski, J.D., Koch, N.P., and Allen, J.K. (2001). Metamodels for computer-based engineering design: Survey and recommendations. *Engineering with Computers*, 17(2), 129–150.

Siu, N. (1994). Risk assessment for dynamic-systems – an overview. *Reliability Engineering & System Safety*, 43(1), 43–73.

Smidts, C. and Devooght, J. (1992). Probabilistic reactor dynamics. 2. A Monte-Carlo study of a fast-reactor transient. *Nuclear Science and Engineering*, 111(3), 241–256.

Sobol. (2001). Global sensitivity indices for nonlinear mathematical models and their Monte Carlo estimates. *Mathematics and Computers in Simulation*, 55(1–3), 271–280.

Sobol, A,D., Kreinin, A., and Kucherenko, S. (2011). Construction and comparison of high-dimensional Sobol' generators. *Wilmott*, 2011(56), 64–79.

Soize, C. and Ghanem, R. (2004). Physical systems with random uncertainties: chaos representations with arbitrary probability measure. *SIAM Journal on Scientific Computing*, 26(2), 395–410.

Sorge, M. (2004). Stress-testing financial systems: an overview of current methodologies. Retrieved from SSRN: http://ssrn.com/abstract=759585 or https://dx.doi.org/10.2139/ssrn.759585

Sudret, B. (2008). Global sensitivity analysis using polynomial chaos expansions. *Reliability Engineering & System Safety*, 93(7), 964–979.

Taleb, N.N. (2007). *The Black Swan: The Impact of the Highly Improbable.* Random house.

Turati, P., Pedroni, N., and Zio, E. (2015). An entropy-driven method for exploring extreme and unexpected accident scenario in the risk assessment of dynamic engineered systems. Paper presented at the Proceedings of the 25th ESREL, Safety and Reliability of Complex Engineered Systems, Zurich, Swiss.

Turati, P., Pedroni, N., and Zio, E. (2016a). An adaptive simulation framework for the exploration of extreme and unexpected events in dynamic engineered systems. *Risk Analysis*, 37(1), 147–159.

Turati, P., Pedroni, N. and Zio, E. (2016b). Simulation-based exploration of high-dimensional system models for critical regions identification. *Reliability Engineering & System Safety*, 165, 317–330.

Wang, G.G. and Shan, S. (2007). Review of metamodeling techniques in support of engineering design optimization. *Journal of Mechanical Design*, 129(4), 370–380.

Zio, E. (2014). Integrated deterministic and probabilistic safety assessment: Concepts, challenges, research directions. *Nuclear Engineering and Design*, 280, 413–419.

Zio, E. (2016a). Challenges in the vulnerability and risk analysis of critical infrastructures. *Reliability Engineering & System Safety*, 152, 137–150.

Zio, E. (2016b). Some challenges and opportunities in reliability engineering. *IEEE Transactions on Reliability*, 65(4), 1769–1782.

Appendix 8.A

8.A.1 Metropolis-Hastings Method

Metropolis-Hastings (M–H) is a well-known Markov chain Monte Carlo (MCMC) method for sampling from unconventional probability distributions. The general idea of a MCMC method is to generate a Markov chain having the *target* distribution p as its stationary distribution (Robert and Casella, 2004).

For generating the Markov Chain, the M–H algorithm iteratively samples a candidate T^* from a *proposal distribution q*, and then there is an *accept-reject* of the proposed sample according to an acceptance criterion (Hastings, 1970).

For the *proposal* step, easy-to-sample distributions are usually considered. For example, in Section 8.4.1 we use to a multivariate Gaussian distribution $q(T^*|T_n) \sim N(T_n, \Sigma)$, having as mean value the last accepted sample T_n and as covariance matrix Σ, whose coefficient can be estimated using a set of samples available from the *target* distribution, or can be set a priori by the analyst. Once sampled, the candidate T^* can be accepted ($T_{n+1} = T^*$) or rejected ($T_{n+1} = T_n$) with a probability $\alpha(T_n, T^*) = \min(r(T_n, T^*), 1)$, where r is defined as follows:

$$r\left(T_n, T^*\right) = \begin{cases} \dfrac{p(T^*) \cdot q(T_n|T^*)}{p(T_n) \cdot q(T^*|T_n)}, \ p(T_n) \cdot q(T^*|T_n) > 0 \\ 1, otherwise, \end{cases} \tag{8.19}$$

p being the *target* distribution from which we want to sample. If the *proposal* distribution is symmetric – that is, $q(T_n|T^*) = q(T^*|T_n)$ – then (8.19) can be rewritten as:

$$r(T_n, T^*) = \begin{cases} \dfrac{p(T^*)}{p(T_n)}, \ p(T_n) > 0 \\ 1, otherwise. \end{cases} \tag{8.20}$$

Finally, if the target distribution is uniform on the support Ω_I of the event of interest, then the probability $\alpha(T_n, T^*)$ can be written as:

$$\alpha(T_n, T^*) = \begin{cases} 1, T^* \in \Omega_I \\ 0, otherwise. \end{cases} \tag{8.21}$$

In order to reach the stationary distribution with a small number of samples, a critical indicator is the acceptance ratio (AR) between the proposed candidate and the accepted ones: if AR is too high (AR > 0.9), it is likely that the proposed candidate is very close to the previous one, meaning that the Markov chain is too slow in spanning the space of interest. On the contrary, if AR is small

(AR < 0.2), the proposal distribution is sampling candidates that are too distant from the accepted ones and thus in regions where the target distribution is very low or even outside the target domain Ω_I, meaning that distribution is approximated with several repetitions of the same samples.

8.A.2 Polynomial Chaos Expansion Based Sensitivity Analysis

Consider a function $Y = f(X)$, where X represents a vector of random inputs and Y is the associated output. It is possible to decompose the function by means of the polynomial chaos expansion (PCE) representation (Ghanem and Spanos, 1991):

$$Y = f\left(X_1, \ldots, X_M\right) = \sum_{\alpha \in \mathbb{N}^M} y_\alpha \psi_\alpha\left(X_1, \ldots, X_M\right), \tag{8.22}$$

where y_α is the coefficient associated to the multivariate Hilbertian basis $\psi_\alpha(\cdot)$, orthonormal with respect to the multivariate distribution characterizing the inputs (usually the uniform or the normal distribution are considered). In order to be valid, the Hilbertian space should be chosen such that it contains the response function Y (Soize and Ghanem, 2004). If the input multivariate distribution is uniform, then $\psi_\alpha(\cdot)$ is a multivariate Legendre polynomial, where the multi-index $\alpha = (\alpha_1, \ldots, \alpha_M)$ indicates the order of the polynomials associated with each component of the vector X. For example, if $\alpha = (3, 1, 0, 2)$, then the associated Legendre polynomial is characterized by a third-order polynomial for X_1, a first-order polynomial for X_2, a zero-order polynomial for X_3 and a second-order polynomial for X_4. The polynomial chaos expansion, in order to keep reasonable the numerical cost, can be truncated to a maximum polynomial order p, providing an approximation of the real response function:

$$Y = f\left(X_1, \ldots, X_M\right) \approx \sum_{\alpha \in A^{M,p}} y_\alpha \psi_\alpha\left(X_1, \ldots, X_M\right), \tag{8.23}$$

where $A^{M,p} \subset \mathbb{N}^M$ is the multi-index subset corresponding to polynomials having maximum order equal to p – that is, $A^{M,p} = \{\alpha \in \mathbb{N}^M \ s.t. |\alpha| < p\}$ – with corresponding cardinality $\# A^{M,p} = \binom{M+p}{p}$.

The great advantage of the PCE is that, once the approximation (8.23) has been computed, the total order sensitivity indices can be trivially approximated as:

$$S_{Ti} \approx \tilde{S}_{Ti} = \frac{\sum_{u \in U^i} y_u^2}{\sum_{\alpha \in A^{M,p}} y_\alpha^2}, \tag{8.24}$$

where $U^i = \{\boldsymbol{u} \in A^{M,p} \, s.t. u_i \neq 0\}$ is the subset of all the multi-indices corresponding to multivariate Legendre polynomials with non-zero degree associated with the ith component; that is, the subset of multi-indices representing polynomials that include the ith component (Sudret, 2008). The approximated total order sensitivity indices $\tilde{S}_{Ti}$ converges to the real ones with the degree of the polynomial truncation p. In practice, the computational cost required for estimating S_T depends only on the computational cost needed to approximate the output function with the PCE.

The estimation of the PCE coefficients can be conducted both via projection and regression. Even though the projection technique is more rigorous, it requires knowing explicitly the definition of the function f (Le Matre *et al.* 2002), which is typically not the case when dealing with black box functions or complex numerical codes. For this reason, we resort to a regression method, in particular least angle regression, coupled with an adaptive sparse PCE representation (Blatman and Sudret, 2011), which is devised to automatically detect the significant PCE coefficients, limiting at the same time the computational cost for the PC approximation. The sparse representation of the coefficient matrix, indeed, allows retaining in memory only those coefficients having a non-negligible value, which is typically the case in many real applications. In order to train the regression model, a number N_{PCE} of input configurations is usually sampled according to Latin hypercube sampling or other quasi Monte Carlo techniques (McKay *et al.* 1979; Sobol *et al.*, 2011). Consequently, the corresponding real model outputs are evaluated and used to fit the regression model. Recently, an optimal DOE for the estimation of the PC coefficients has been proposed to further reduce the number of calls to the possibly computationally expensive model (Burnaev *et al.* 2016).

Finally, it must be pointed out that PCE is a meta-modeling technique capable of well representing the global behavior of the response function. Nonetheless, when the response function presents local behavior such as spikes or step changes, although a good fit can be theoretically achieved by increasing the polynomial order of the PCE, the corresponding computational cost to estimate the parameters can become burdensome.

8.A.3 Kriging

Kriging is a stochastic interpolation algorithm, which assumes that the model output $Y = f(X)$ is the realization of a Gaussian process indexed by $X \in D_X \subset \mathbb{R}^M$ where, in our case, D_X is the domain of validity of the meta-model and M is the dimensionality of input state space (Kleijnen, 2009; Matheron, 1963). In practice, kriging is a linear regression model in which the residuals are correlated by means of a Gaussian process, instead of being independent:

$$Y = f(X) = N\left(h(X)^T \beta, \sigma^2 Z(X)\right), \tag{8.25}$$

where $h(X)^T\beta$ represents the mean value, also known as the trend, which is a general linear regression model (for example, $h(X)$ can involve polynomial terms and it reflects the prior knowledge about the model), σ^2 is the variance of the Gaussian process, and $Z(X)$ is a zero-mean, unit-variance stationary Gaussian process whose underlying correlation function is represented by $R(x, x'; \theta)$. The correlation function typically depends on the distance d of the two vectors x, x': the closer they are, the higher their correlation. Due to the Gaussian process hypothesis, every set of realizations of the model output can be described by a Gaussian vector:

$$\begin{bmatrix} \hat{Y}(x) \\ y \end{bmatrix} \sim N_{N_{Krig}+1}\left(\begin{bmatrix} h(x)^T \beta \\ H\beta \end{bmatrix}; \sigma^2 \begin{bmatrix} 1 & r^T(x) \\ r(x) & R \end{bmatrix}\right). \tag{8.26}$$

Assuming that $y = (y_1, \ldots, y_{N_{Krig}})$ is an experimental design with associated information matrix H and correlation matrix R (that is, $R_{ij} = R(x^{(i)}, x^{(j)}, \theta), i, j = 1, \ldots, N_{Krig}$), then the prediction of the output $\hat{Y}$ for a given configuration x is given by:

$$\hat{Y}(x) \mid y, \sigma^2, \theta \sim N\left(\mu_{\hat{Y}}; \sigma_{\hat{Y}}^2\right), \tag{8.27}$$

where

$$\mu_{\hat{Y}}(x) = h(x)^T \beta + r(x)^T R^{-1}(y - H\beta), \tag{8.28}$$

$$\sigma_{\hat{Y}}^2(x) = \sigma^2\left(1 - r(x)^T R^{-1} r(x)^T\right) \\ + \left(h(x)^T - r(x)^T R^{-1} H\right)\left(H^T R^{-1} H\right)^{-1}\left(h(x)^T - r(x)^T R^{-1} H\right)^T \tag{8.29}$$

with the regression coefficients estimated by $\beta = (H^T R^{-1} H)^{-1} H^T R^{-1} y$.

One of the main advantages of this formulation is that a confidence interval can be associated with each prediction $\hat{Y}(x)$. This can be used for assessing the accuracy and precision of the meta-model: the smaller the confidence interval, the more precise the model prediction for the corresponding configuration.

Part II

Risk Assessment and Decision Making

9

A Decision Support Method for Prioritizing Investments Subject to Uncertainties

Shital Thekdi[1] and Terje Aven[2]

[1] University of Richmond, USA
[2] University of Stavanger, Norway

This chapter presents a decision support prioritization method that incorporates uncertainty through strength of knowledge (SoK) and target sensitivity assessments. Current thinking for assessing these uncertainties and their importance in the decision-making process is based on a probabilistic perspective and decision analysis, including evidence combined with multi-criteria scenario analysis. This thinking needs to be further developed to reflect the SoK supporting the probabilistic analysis. The chapter presents a new method for prioritizing investments with consideration of the most influential uncertainties from the decision-making point of view, thereby allowing for systematic SoK considerations. The illustrated multi-criteria priority setting approach concurrently evaluates future uncertainties with utilization of target sensitivity decision support. The method is demonstrated on an emergency management system that is vulnerable to future economic, environmental, and political factors.

9.1 Introduction

Investment decision-making and prioritization tools commonly consider the role of uncertainty within the modeling process. The uncertainties relate to, for example, potential extreme events or emerging conditions, such as accidents, natural disasters, climate change, and economic cycles. They are often poorly understood. For instance, consider the case of investment decision making for energy infrastructure. Investment decisions may be contingent upon future economic performance, climate change scenarios, availability of natural

Knowledge in Risk Assessment and Management, First Edition. Edited by Terje Aven and Enrico Zio.
© 2018 John Wiley & Sons Ltd. Published 2018 by John Wiley & Sons Ltd.

resources, political environments, and many other uncertain future conditions. The common analysis and modeling approaches to address the uncertainties are based on a probabilistic reasoning, using stochastic modeling and decision analytical tools such as Bayesian networking, Monte Carlo simulations, decision-tree analysis, and multi-criteria decision making. The probabilities are of two types: frequentist probabilities representing variation and used as basis for probability models, and subjective probabilities expressing the assigner's degree of belief. These tools make use of both type of probabilities but our main focus is the latter category as they express the analysts' uncertainties about the future states and the unknown quantities. The present work is based on the conviction that to properly analyze these uncertainties we need to see beyond the subjective probabilities. The argument for this stand is documented elsewhere (see for example Aven and Zio 2011), but the key point is the following: a subjective probability is conditional on a background knowledge K, and this knowledge can be more or less strong. This fact leads to considerations of the strength of this knowledge, reflecting aspects like justification of assumptions made, amount of reliable and relevant data/information, agreement among experts, and understanding of the phenomena involved. The set of probabilities and judgments of the SoK together constitute a broader way of expressing the uncertainties than just probability assignments.

Often, analysts produce a conditional performance–uncertainty description, but the decision maker needs to also take into account the "risk" associated with K (Aven 2015). This could cover risk linked to deviations from assumptions and lack of awareness of potential events (unknown unknowns and unknown knowns). The decision maker needs also to be informed about the "risk" related to K and to make their own judgments about it. How to do this is, however, not straightforward.

The purpose of this chapter is to meet this challenge for the problem setting described above. More specifically, this chapter will develop a method to identify the most influential uncertainties for risk mitigation in investments and policies using assessment of uncertainties with probability and SoK judgments. We will integrate the uncertainty concepts with multicriteria decision support for prioritization of investments. We will use an emergency management system as an example to illustrate the analysis, but the approach is general and can be applied to all types of risk management applications, such as corporate risk, industrial safety, project planning, emergency management, and infrastructure management.

This chapter builds on literature describing enhanced approaches and models related to sensitivity and uncertainty in this type of analysis. A variety of methods can be used to model uncertainty, including the use of scenario analysis (Durbach 2014), imprecision (Guillaume *et al.* 2014), sensitivity (Liesiö and Punkka 2014; Baucells and Borgonovo 2013), credibility ratings based on evidence (NASA 2008), and others (Cox 2012). Some incorporate imprecision in probability values within optimization methods (for example Goerigk and Schöbel 2011 and Aven and Hiriart 2013). Others avoid the need to assign probabilities to uncertain events by instead focusing on priorities that are robust to scenarios (for example Thekdi and Lambert 2014). However, current literature in this area has not investigated investment decision-making in relation to the issue raised above concerning the risk related the background knowledge K.

This chapter also expands on literature describing the prioritization of investments under conditions of risk and uncertainty. Multicriteria and risk methods are well established and used for applications such as water supply (Pinto *et al.* 2015; Scholten 2015), law enforcement (Camacho-Collados *et al.* 2015), selection of medical devices (Ivlev 2015), and emergency management (Wilson *et al.* 2014). Often, the methods rely on weighting the relative importance of criteria and using value functions (Morton 2015; Podinovski 2013, Simon *et al.* 2015; Siskos and Tsotsolas 2015). Particularly challenging applications also consider the meeting of performance targets and multiple stakeholders (Bordley and LiCalizi 2000; Grushka-Cockayne *et al.* 2008; Wallenius *et al.* 2008). This chapter expands on the usage of multicriteria methods by providing prioritization decision-support for performance target sensitivity while considering SoK in evaluations.

The chapter is organized as follows. In Section 9.2 we present a general setup of the analysis and modeling concepts. Section 9.3 uses the setup to present the method to solve the problem described above. Section 9.4 illustrates the method with a case study applied to emergency management investments. In Section 9.5 we discuss the implications of the method presented in this chapter. Section 9.6 provides conclusions and opportunities for future work.

9.2 Set-up

The conceptual set up for the analysis is described in this section. Table 9.1 provides an overview of the framework described in detail below.

We consider a decision-making situation related to a set of potential risk mitigation investments and policies, $M = (M_1, M_2, ..., M_k)$, for example M_1 representing investment in increased safety control, while M_2 represents a policy directed towards economic development.

A set of criteria $C = (C_1, C_2, ..., C_r)$ are used to represent the performance objectives for the potential investments and policies, reflecting elements such as economic indicators (GDP, unemployment rate, and so on), safety (crash rates, crime rates, and so on), and social indicators (quality of life measurements, graduation rates, and so on).

The actual consequences of the investments and policies are denoted by $V = (V_1, V_2, ..., V_r)$ and represent measurements of the criteria C. We define

Table 9.1 Summary of method inputs and outputs, including decision support findings derived from results.

Inputs		Outputs	
M	Set of k risk mitigation investments	DS1:	Which investments result in best consequences for each criterion
C	Set of r criteria for potential investments	DS2:	Which investments provide a consistently high consequence across criteria
		DS3:	Which investments are consistently ranked below others (dominated)
V	Set of r measurements of criteria C	DS4:	Which investments vary in priority the most across criteria
		DS5:	Which criteria matter the most to priorities
		DS4:	Which investments vary in priority the most across criteria
		DS5:	Which criteria matter the most to priorities
F(V)	Probability distribution for V, based on background knowledge		
SoK	Strength of knowledge judgment for F(V)		
S	Set of strength of knowledge scores for each of k risk mitigation investments		

DS, decision support.

$V_i = 0$ if the investment and policy has no effect on the criterion i. The larger the values of V_i, the more positive effect the investment and policy has on C_i.

At the point of analysis, V is unknown. To assess V and the uncertainties about what values it will take, a relevant measure of uncertainty must be used. As indicated in Section 9.1, we will here use the set probability and SoK judgments. Here, probability is a knowledge-based (subjective, judgmental) probability, interpreted by reference to a standard: if for example a probability of 0.1 is assigned, the assessor compares the uncertainty – the degree of belief – with drawing a particular ball out of an urn of ten balls under a standard random drawing (Lindley 2006; Aven 2014). More generally, we may use interval probabilities: for an interval say [0.1, 0.2], the assessor expresses that the degree of belief of the event occurring is greater than the urn chance of 0.1 (as interpreted above), and less than or equal to an urn chance of 0.2. The assessor is not willing, given their background knowledge, to assign more precise numbers.

If V_i is a quantity on the real line, with cumulative distribution $F(v)$ defined by $F(v) = P(V \leq v \mid K)$, where K is the background knowledge that the probability is based on, the interval probability distribution for V_i can be expressed by [FL (v), FU(v)], such that FL (v) $\leq F(v) \leq$ FU(v).

Next, a scoring system to reflect judgments of the strength of the knowledge (SoK) is needed. We adopt the commonly used approach described by Flage and Aven (2009) and Aven (2014): the knowledge is weak if one or more of these conditions are true:

W1. The assumptions made represent strong simplifications.
W2. Data/information are non-existent or highly unreliable/irrelevant.
W3. There is strong disagreement among experts.
W4. The phenomena involved are poorly understood, models are non-existent, or known/believed to give poor predictions.

If, on the other hand, all (whenever they are relevant) of the following conditions are met, the knowledge is considered strong:

S1. The assumptions made are seen as very reasonable.
S2. Large amount of reliable and relevant data/information are available.
S3. There is broad agreement among experts.
S4. The phenomena involved are well understood; the models used are known to give predictions with the required accuracy.

Cases in between are classified as having a medium SoK.

A simplified version of these criteria is obtained by using the same scoring system as for strong knowledge but giving medium and weak scores if some number of conditions is not met. For example, a medium score is given if one or two of the conditions (S1)–(S4) are not met and a weak score when three or four of the conditions are not met.

We then define a scoring system to reflect the SoK for each of the maintenance investments. This can be conducted in different ways. An example of a quantitative approach is outlined in the following.

Let $Sok_{i,j}$ be a quantitative metric representing the SoK for each criterion i and maintenance investment j, $i = 1,2,\ldots,$ r and $j = 1,2, \ldots k$. The quantitative metric can be chosen as appropriate for the given application, for example, $SOK_{i,j} = 6$ when SoK is *high*, $SOK_{i,j} = 3$ when SoK is *medium*, and $SOK_{i,j} = 1$ when SoK is *low*. Then an integrated score for the j-th investment can be defined as a function of the $SoK_{i,j}$, $j = 1,2,\ldots k$.

A variety of policies can be used to represent the scoring function. For example, a simplified metric such as the following can be used where the S_j is obtained by summing the individual SoK values across the criteria, as follows:

$$Score_j = S_j = \sum_{i=1}^{r} SoK_{i,j}$$

Another policy is to use the minimum SoK across criteria, as follows:

$$Score_j = S_j = \min_{i \in r} SoK_{i,j}$$

Experts or decision makers can then transform these scorings to categories of high, medium, or low for each maintenance investment. See Section 9.3. Alternatively, a qualitative direct assessment approach can be used to determine whether high, medium, or low levels of SoK exist for each maintenance investment, by evaluating the SOK for all the criteria.

9.3 Method

9.3.1 Overview of the Method

The overall method recommended is illustrated in Figure 9.1. First, we introduce the key concepts as defined by the set-up of Section 9.2: the potential risk mitigation investments, $M = (M_1, M_2, ..., M_k)$, the set of relevant criteria $C = (C_1, C_2, ..., C_r)$ and the consequences of the investments, $V = (V_1, V_2, ..., V_r)$. To assess the uncertainties related to V we use probability P (or probability

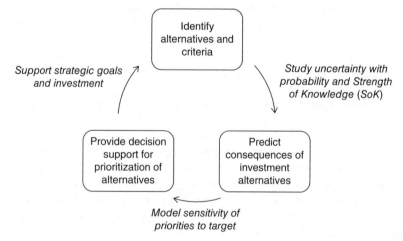

Figure 9.1 Illustration of overall methodology for prioritizing investments subject to uncertainties using strength of knowledge and target sensitivity analysis.

intervals) and associated SoK, and from this analysis we derive predictions of V. Then, we provide decision support by modeling the sensitivity of investment priorities to target levels defined by the relevant criteria. Finally, we promote iteration of the process for more refined priority-setting based on additional information and adapted requirements. The various elements of the method are explained in more detail in the coming sections.

9.3.2 Identify Alternatives and Criteria

It is assumed that there is initially a set of investment alternatives that have no initial rank and for which there is no initial preference. For example, consider the situation of a highway investment for which there are two (k = 2) alternative policies. Policy M_1 represents implementation of some safety policies across the highway network, while policy M_2 represents implementation of some economic growth policies on selected segments of the highway network.

To determine the consequences of each investment alternative, relevant criteria need to be specified. For example for the highway investment case considered above, the criterion C_1 could represent the crash rate on the highway network, while criteria C_2 represents the percentage economic growth for the region impacted by the highway policies. As the most relevant criteria may not have been specified during the initial planning stage analysis, additional criteria may be added during the iteration phase.

9.3.3 Predict Consequences of Investment Alternatives

The consequences of the investments $V = (V_1, V_2, ..., V_r)$ represent measurements of the criteria C. Here it is assumed that V_i will assume integer values such that a value of zero implies the investment meets a target value defined for criterion i, increasing positive values have an increasing positive effect on the criterion relative to the target, while negative values have a detrimental effect on the criterion relative to the target. Because the future consequences are unknown, probabilities and SoK values are applied to this assignment. Table 9.2 provides an example of probability values that could be applied to the potential consequences of investments for specified criteria. For example, investment policy M_1, involving investment in safety across the highway network, results in positive consequence for the crash-rate, associated with criterion C_1. However, this same policy results in either only meeting or falling short of targets for economic growth, associated with criterion C_2. As crash rates have been well studied, the consequence of both investment policies on criterion C_1 is associated with a high SoK, based on expert judgement. However, the impact of investment policies on the economic growth rate C_2 is less understood, and is therefore associated with medium and low SoKs for investment policies M_1 and M_2 respectively.

Table 9.2 Example of prediction for consequence of investments for specified criteria.

Investment policy M_1 (high SoK)			Investment policy M_2 (high SoK)		
V_1	V_1 definition	Probability	V_1	V_1 definition	Probability
2	Significantly above	0.6	2	Significantly above	0.0
1	Above	0.2	1	Above	0.0
0	Meet	0.2	0	Meet	0.5
−1	Below	0.0	−1	Below	0.5
−2	Significantly below	0.0	−2	Significantly below	0.0
Investment policy M_1 (medium SoK)			Investment policy M_2 (low SoK)		
V_2	V_2 Definition	Probability	V_2	V_2 Definition	Probability
2	Significantly above	0.0	2	Significantly above	0.4
1	Above	0.0	1	Above	0.3
0	Meet	0.5	0	Meet	0.1
−1	Below	0.5	−1	Below	0.1
−2	Significantly below	0.0	−2	Significantly below	0.1

9.3.4 Provide Decision Support for Prioritization of Alternatives

As firms may have flexibility in meeting some relevant criteria, this step allows decision makers to determine the sensitivity of priorities to criteria targets. We do so by comparing the prediction of each investment consequence against all criteria. Here, we avoid aggregating across criteria to avoid weighting the relative importance of particular criteria. Figure 9.2 provides an example decision-support chart for prediction of the investment consequences (V_1) for the crash-rate criterion. Investment policy M_1 is predicted to have positive consequences, as determined by the 90th percentile v_1 ($P(V_1 \leq v_1) = 0.90$), the median v_1 ($P(V_1 \leq v_1) = 0.50$), and the 10th percentile v_1 $P(V_1 \leq v_1) = 0.10$). The SoK is judged to be high for the crash-rate criterion. Investment policy M_2 is predicted to have a negative consequence, also with a high SoK.

We then conduct an SoK judgment for each of the k maintenance investments as described in Section 9.2. First we consider the SoK for each criterion, then we make the overall judgment for each investment.

Using the findings above, the following decision-support topics are addressed:

- DS1: Which investments provide a consistently high consequence across criteria?
- DS2: Which investments are consistently ranked below others (dominated)?

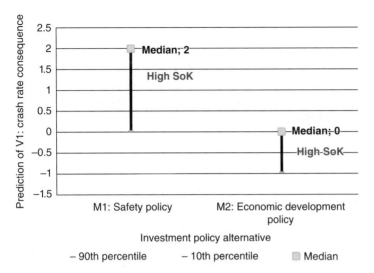

Figure 9.2 Example of decision-support chart for prediction of maintenance investment consequence (V1) for crash-rate criteria. The gray boxes represent the median while the horizontal lines represent the 90th and 10th percentiles.

- DS3: Which investments vary in priority the most across criteria?
- DS4: Which investments result in best consequences for each criterion?
- DS5: Which criteria matter the most to priorities?

Figure 9.2 is used to determine how priorities change as targets change. For example, if the target for the crash-rate criterion (V_1) is set to a value of 0, it can be inferred that investment M_1 will likely meet this target (with 10th percentile outcome), while investment M_2 will be unlikely to meet this target (with 90th percentile outcome). As both potential investments were assigned a high SoK, they can be directly compared. For some decision makers, investment M_1 is clearly preferred based on the single criterion V_1.

However, consider a situation in which investment M_1 is now associated with a low SoK, while all other parameters of the problem remain constant. Although investment M_1 is higher ranked than investment M_2, there is less certainty about its performance. This is critical information for decision makers, requiring further study of the implications for future investment performance. As a result, there may be need to be further study of the implications of investment M_1. Conversely, if the decision makers are content with lowering the target for this criterion, it would also be acceptable to assume investment M_2 meets the requirements with high SoK.

Decision makers should also consider the sensitivity of investments to targets. For example, investment M_1 has a relatively larger distance (compared to M_2) between the 10th and 90th percentiles for crash-rate criterion (V_1)

performance. This implies a higher range in the performance of this investment. This type of range may not be preferable for some applications.

In addition, consider each investment's priority across many criteria. An investment that is robust, or with high priority across all criteria, may also be preferred by decision makers. Conversely, if an investment is of low priority across all criteria, it can be eliminated from a list of preferred alternatives.

The next section of this chapter will provide an application of the method described above.

9.4 Example

9.4.1 Overview of the Example

Principles of the target sensitivity analysis approach presented in the previous section can be applied for decision-making across domains such as transport infrastructure, energy, supply chain planning, and others. Consider the case of the Homeland Security Grant Program in the USA. In 2014, $1,043,346,000 was available for funding allocation. The grant allocations are targeted to support national preparedness by meeting core capability goals. Core capability goals are categorized as prevention, protection, mitigation, response, and recovery. The core capability goals include topics such as cybersecurity, threat and hazard identification, critical transportation, infrastructure systems, environmental response/health and safety, mass care services, and others (FEMA 2015b). The resulting grant activity supports tasks such as preventing acts of terrorism, protecting citizens, mitigating loss of life and property by lessening the impact of disasters, responding quickly to incidents, and recovering from incidents (FEMA 2015a).

Although a single grant allocation is not responsible for meeting all core capability goals, ideally allocation will meet some of the goals. The risk-based methodology defined by the Department of Homeland Security considers three elements:

- the threat, or likelihood of an attack
- the vulnerability, or likelihood an attack is successful
- the consequence, or effect of an event. (FEMA 2014).

Grant allocation decisions may be based on the risk evaluation and other factors of the proposed project such as efficacy, viability, necessity, and long-term needs.

Planning and evaluation of a proposed project requires alignment of project goals with general criteria for grant-funding. Preliminary feasibility planning for potential investments that will eventually be proposed for grant funding involve assurance about the ability of the investment to meet desired targets. As targets are defined across several criteria, multi-criteria decision support is necessary. However, as some of the proposed investments have never been implemented before and have not been studies, there are varying levels of uncertainty related to the ability of investments to meet targets. An analysis of this possibility is given below.

9.4.2   Identify Alternatives and Criteria

Potential investments and relevant criteria were determined using a private database of grant funding awards for emergency management activities. The organization is considering three (k = 3) potential risk mitigation investments. It is initially assumed that there is a set of investment alternatives that have no rank or preference. Investment M_1 involves creating a local geospatial data system to be used for emergency planning, investment M_2 consists of increased engagement and participation of the whole community in emergency communication, and investment M_3 consists of conducting and planning workshops aimed at community preparedness. The set of three (r = 3) relevant criteria are determined. These are core capability categories that may be achieved by the potential investments. Criterion C_1 consists meeting prevention goals for the locality, criterion C_2 consists of mitigation of incidents, and criterion C_3 is the response to incidents.

9.4.3   Predict Consequences of Investment Alternatives

Next, there is a need to predict the consequences of investments for each of the three relevant criteria. Documentation for the proposed projects along with expert managerial evidence are necessary to classify both the consequences and associated SoKs. Suppose the project leaders define uncertainties related to V as shown in Table 9.3. Investment policy M_1, involving the procurement of a GIS system, involves high SoK due to the decision-maker familiarity with the product. This GIS system expected to meet target or achieve above target for all considered criteria. Investment policy M_2, involving increased community engagement, involves low and medium SoK due to the organization's limited experience with this practice. This practice may be at or above target for prevention and mitigation, but may perform at or below target for response. Investment policy M_3, involving workshops with emergency management professionals, also involves low and medium SoK due to the organization's limited experience with this practice. The workshops are expected to perform at or above target for all criteria.

9.4.4   Provide Decision Support for Prioritization of Alternatives

The ideal choice of investment policy requires concurrent discussion of the ability to achieve desired outcomes across criteria and associated SoKs in the prediction of outcomes. Again, the following score system is adopted: $SOK_i = 6$ when SoK is high, $SOK_i = 3$ when SoK is medium, and $SOK_i = 1$ when SoK is low.

Table 9.3 Prediction of performance to target using probability represented by probability density function f, and associated SoK.

Investment	Criterion C_1 (prevention)	Criterion C_2 (mitigation)	Criterion C_3 (response)
M_1 (GIS system)	$f(v_1) = \begin{cases} 0, v_1 \in \{-2,-1\}\} \\ 1/3, v_1 \in \{0,1,2\} \end{cases}$ High SoK	$f(v_2) = \begin{cases} 0, v_2 \in \{-2,-1\} \\ 1/2, v_2 \in \{0,1\} \\ 0, v_2 \in \{2\} \end{cases}$ High SoK	$f(v_3) = \begin{cases} 0, v_3 \in \{-2,-1\} \\ 1/2, v_3 \in \{0,1\} \\ 0, v_3 \in \{2\} \end{cases}$ High SoK
M_2 (Engagement)	$f(v_1) = \begin{cases} 0, v_1 \in \{-2\} \\ 1/4, v_1 \in \{-1,0,1,2\} \end{cases}$ Low SoK	$f(v_2) = \begin{cases} 0, v_2 \in \{-2,-1\} \\ 1/3, v_2 \in \{0,1,2\} \end{cases}$ Low SoK	$f(v_3) = \begin{cases} 1/3, v_3 \in \{-2,-1,0\} \\ 0, v_3 \in \{1,2\} \end{cases}$ Medium SoK
M_3 (Workshops)	$f(v_1) = \begin{cases} 1/3, v_1 \in \{-2,-1,0\} \\ 0, v_1 \in \{1,2\} \end{cases}$ Low SoK	$f(v_2) = \begin{cases} 0, v_2 \in \{-2,-1\} \\ 1/4, v_2 \in \{0,1\} \\ 1/2, v_2 \in \{2\} \end{cases}$ Medium SoK	$f(v_3) = \begin{cases} 0, v_3 \in \{-2,-1\} \\ 1/3, v_3 \in \{0,1,2\} \end{cases}$ Medium SoK

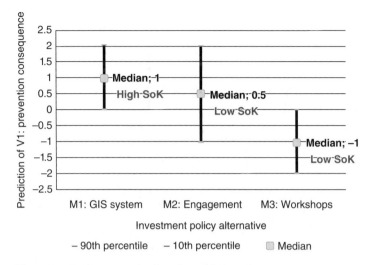

Figure 9.3 Decision-support chart for prediction of maintenance investment consequence (V1) for prevention criterion. The gray boxes represent the median while the horizontal lines represent the 90th and 10th percentiles.

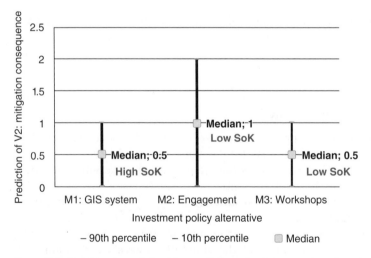

Figure 9.4 Decision-support chart for prediction of maintenance investment consequence (V_2) for mitigation criterion. The gray boxes represent the median while the horizontal lines represent the 90th and 10th percentiles.

Figure 9.3 shows the decision-support chart for prediction of the investment consequence (V_1) for the prevention criterion. Figure 9.4 shows the decision-support chart for prediction of an investment consequence (V_2) for the mitigation criterion. Figure 9.5 provides the decision-support chart for prediction of an investment consequence (V_3) for the response criterion.

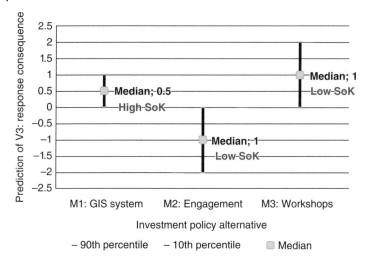

Figure 9.5 Decision-support chart for prediction of maintenance investment consequence (V_3) for response criterion. The gray boxes represent the median while the horizontal lines represent the 90th and 10th percentiles.

Discussion of the implications of these decision-support charts is given in Section 9.5.

9.5 Discussion

9.5.1 Discussion of Case Study

Based on the decision-support charts given in Section 9.4, several conclusions can be drawn. Table 9.4 summarizes the main findings. Investment M_1: GIS system has the best consequences for the prevention criterion, Investment M_2: Engagement is best for the mitigation criterion, and Investment M_3: Workshops is best for the response criterion. Investment M_1: GIS System has a consistently high consequence across criteria, thereby suggesting a robustness in performance. None of the potential investments were consistently ranked below others, so none of the alternatives were clearly dominant. Investment M_3: Workshops showed the most variability in performance across the criteria.

The decision-support results of this exercise provide several benefits for a decision maker reviewing these results. If the decision maker values investment alternatives that are robust across all relevant criteria, the result from decision support question 1 would be most useful. Any dominated alternatives from decision support question 2 would not be considered further. If further studies will be conducted to understand the performance of investments, the

Table 9.4 Key decision support findings from example.

Decision-support question	Investments
DS1: Which investments provide a consistently high consequence across criteria	M_1: GIS system
DS2: Which investments are consistently ranked below others (dominated)	None
DS3: Which investments vary most in priority across criteria	M_3: Workshops
DS4: Which investments result in best consequences for each criterion	M_1: GIS system for prevention criterion M_2: Engagement for mitigation criterion M_3: Workshops for response criterion
DS5: Which criterion matters the most to priorities	(V_2) Mitigation criterion.

result from decision support question 3 would be involved. If the decision maker highly values a single criterion, the results from the decision support question 4 would be sufficient.

In addition, it is clear that some uncertainties matter more than others. For example, knowledge of the investment M_2: Engagement was associated with a low SoK and also the largest distance between the 90th and 10th percentiles for all studied criteria. Thus, decision makers should consider how uncertainties associated with this investment might be reduced through additional study. Using the additional information generated, the process of this chapter should be repeated.

Decision makers may seek to revise current alternatives to better meet targets. For example, the scope for investment M_3: Workshops could be broadened to address risk mitigation topics, thereby potentially increasing the ability for the investment to meet targets related to the maintenance investment consequence (V_1) for the prevention criterion. Conversely, the decision makers may wish to revise some targets to align with philosophies or insights gained from this exercise. For example, the core principles of the agency may prioritize mitigation or response, with little emphasis on prevention activities.

9.5.2 Discussion of Methodology

The case study has highlighted several benefits for decision making. First, the SoK judgements within the multicriteria analysis allow decision makers to address the subjectivity of probabilities that are conditional on varying levels of background knowledge. The knowledge is used to justify assumptions based on information from experts and data. The resulting conditional performance–uncertainty description allows decision makers to understand how well potential investments meet criteria while concurrently recognizing that these prioritizations are based on varying levels of knowledge.

More specifically, the methodology supports decision making without prescribing particular outcomes. For example, the conclusion from decision support question 1 allows for the identification of investments that perform well against most criteria, while recognizing that knowledge may be weak for some options. In contrast, the conclusion from decision support question 2 allows for the identification of investments that may clearly be least preferred. The use of multiple decision-support questions suggests that no one question is given preference over another. It is the decision maker's responsibility to use individual judgement and the information gained from the decision-support questions to make conclusions.

Once decision makers have fully assessed the decision-support results, it is important to further refine the conclusions. It may be necessary to use the result from decision support question 5 to reframe, remove, or add criteria to the model. In addition, it may be necessary to use the results from all the decision-support questions to revise the alternative investments to further include options that are more appropriate for the accepted decision criteria.

9.6   Conclusions

This chapter has presented an approach to prioritization of potential investments with consideration of the most influential uncertainties relevant to decision makers. The multi-criterion approach addresses deficiencies in previous decision-support tools by concurrently addressing varying SoKs.

The approach aids decision makers by identifying the most influential uncertainties for risk mitigation investments and policies. As with any decision-support tool, the goal is to post relevant questions (as shown in decision-support questions 1–4) and to allow the values of decision makers to dictate the most appropriate strategy.

The results can be incorporated into broader decision-support strategies for complex problems. The results can guide detailed investigations and planning of high-priority investments. The results can guide efforts to reduce uncertainty for various criteria and investments across a firm. The process allows for reiteration of the methods with non-dominated alternatives combined with newly formed alternatives. Finally, the results can aid in the identification of opportunities to revise investment alternatives to better meet targeted performance levels.

References

Aven, T. (2014) *Risk, Surprises and Black Swans: Fundamental Ideas and Concepts in Risk Assessment and Risk Management.* Routledge.

Aven, T. (2015) Implications of black swans to the foundations and practice of risk assessment and management. *Reliability Engineering & System Safety,* 134, 83–91.

Aven, T. and Hiriart, Y. (2013) Robust optimization in relation to a basic safety investment model with imprecise probabilities. *Safety Science,* 55, 188–194.

Aven, T. and Zio, E. (2011). Some considerations on the treatment of uncertainties in risk assessment for practical decision making. *Reliability Engineering & System Safety,* 96(1), 64–74.

Baucells, M. and Borgonovo, E. (2013) Invariant probabilistic sensitivity analysis. *Management Science,* 59(11), 2536–2549.

Bordley, R. and LiCalzi, M. (2000) Decision analysis using targets instead of utility functions. *Decisions in Economics and Finance,* 23(1), 53–74.

Camacho-Collados, M., Liberatore, F., and Angulo, J.M. (2015) A multi-criteria police districting problem for the efficient and effective design of patrol sector. *European Journal of Operational Research,* 246(2), 674–684.

Cox, L.A.T. (2012) Confronting deep uncertainties in risk analysis. *Risk Analysis,* 32(10), 1607–1629.

Durbach, I.N. (2014) Outranking under uncertainty using scenarios. *European Journal of Operational Research,* 232(1), 98–108.

FEMA (2014) Fiscal year (FY) 2014 Homeland Security Grant Program (HSGP) frequently asked questions (FAQs). Federal Emergency Management Agency. http://www.fema.gov/media-library-data/1395150571234-0b433243a3e4c6cd0 a5346e807a591c0/FY_2014_HSGP_FAQs_Final.pdf.

FEMA (2015a) Homeland security grant program. Federal Emergency Management Agency. https://www.fema.gov/ homeland-security-grant-program

FEMA (2015b) Core capabilities. Federal Emergency Management Agency. https://www.fema.gov/core-capabilities

Flage, R. and Aven, T. (2009). Expressing and communicating uncertainty in relation to quantitative risk analysis. *Reliability & Risk Analysis: Theory & Application,* 2(13), 9–18.

Goerigk, M. and Schöbel, A. (2011) A scenario-based approach for robust linear optimization. In: *Theory and Practice of Algorithms in (Computer) Systems.* Springer.

Guillaume, R., Houé, R., and Grabot, B. (2014) Robust competence assessment for job assignment. *European Journal of Operational Research,* 238(2), 630–644.

Grushka-Cockayne, Y., Reyck, B.D., and Degraeve, Z. (2008) An integrated decision-making approach for improving European air traffic management. *Management Science,* 54(8), 1395–1409.

Ivlev, I., Vacek, J., and Kneppo, P. (2015) Multi-criteria decision analysis for supporting the selection of medical devices under uncertainty. *European Journal of Operational Research*, 247(1), 216–228.

Liesiö, J. and Punkka, A. (2014) Baseline value specification and sensitivity analysis in multiattribute project portfolio selection. *European Journal of Operational Research*, 237(3), 946–956.

Lindley, D. V. (2006). *Understanding Uncertainty*. John Wiley & Sons.

Morton, A. (2015) Measurement issues in the evaluation of projects in a project portfolio. *European Journal of Operational Research*, 245(3), 789–796.

NASA (2008) NASA-STD-7009. Standard for models and simulations. NASA, Washington.

Pinto, F.S., Figueira, J.R., and Marques, R.C. (2015) A multi-objective approach with soft constraints for water supply and wastewater coverage improvements. *European Journal of Operational Research*, 246(2), 609–618.

Podinovski, V.V. (2014) Decision making under uncertainty with unknown utility function and rank-ordered probabilities. *European Journal of Operational Research*, 239(2), 537–541.

Scholten, L., Schuwirth, N., Reichert, P., and Lienert, J. (2015) Tackling uncertainty in multi-criteria decision analysis – An application to water supply infrastructure planning. *European Journal of Operational Research*, 242(1), 243–260.

Simon, J., Kirkwood, C.W., and Keller, L.R. (2013) Decision analysis with geographically varying outcomes: Preference models and illustrative applications. *Operations Research*, 62(1), 182–194.

Siskos, E. and Tsotsolas, N. (2015) Elicitation of criteria importance weights through the Simos method: A robustness concern. *European Journal of Operational Research*, 246(2), 543–553.

Thekdi, S.A. and Lambert, J.H. (2014) Quantification of scenarios and stakeholders influencing priorities for risk mitigation in infrastructure systems. *Journal of Management in Engineering*, 30(1), 32–40.

Wallenius, J., Dyer, J.S., Fishburn, P.C., *et al.* (2008) Multiple criteria decision making, multiattribute utility theory: recent accomplishments and what lies ahead. *Management Science*, 54(7), 1336–1349.

Wilson, D.T., Hawe, G.I., Coates, G., and Crouch, R.S. (2013) A multi-objective combinatorial model of casualty processing in major incident response. *European Journal of Operational Research*, 230(3), 643–655.

10

Risk Analysis under Structural Uncertainty

Sven Ove Hansson

KTH, Sweden

Standard decision theory is devoted to problems in which we have a choice among well-defined and already-evaluated alternatives. We are assumed to know what we are going to decide, what options we can choose among, and what their potential consequences are. Real-life decisions often have to be made when much of that information is missing. This applies not least to many safety management decisions. When the decision procedure starts, it is often unsettled or unknown exactly what issues are going to be decided upon, whether a single decision is going to be made about all of them or if the decision will be subdivided and in that case how, when the decision(s) should be made, what options are open to the decision maker(s), what the criteria are for a successful decision, and so on. In summary, the structure of the decision is undefined from the beginning and has to be constructed as part of the decision-making process. In this chapter, the structuring of decisions is systematized by dividing it into ten major components. Conceptual tools are introduced that can be used for the analysis and management of each of these components. Careful investigation of the consequences of different ways of structuring decisions can provide decision makers with the knowledge needed to ensure the efficiency and transparency of the decision process.

10.1 Introduction

The importance of how decisions are delimited and structured was pointed out by Nicolas de Condorcet (1743–1794) in his account of the stages of public decision making. It was included in his preparatory text for the French constitution of 1793. There, he divided decision making into three phases. In the first of these, one "discusses the principles that will serve as the basis for decision in

Knowledge in Risk Assessment and Management, First Edition. Edited by Terje Aven and Enrico Zio.
© 2018 John Wiley & Sons Ltd. Published 2018 by John Wiley & Sons Ltd.

a general issue; one examines the various aspects of this issue and the consequences of different ways to make the decision". At this stage, the opinions are personal, and no attempts are made to form a majority. After this follows a second discussion in which "the question is clarified, opinions approach and combine with each other to a small number of more general opinions". The third stage consists of the actual choice of one of these alternatives. (Condorcet, [1793] 1847, pp. 342–343) This is, of course, the part of the process that modern decision theory and its applied variants focus on. The first two stages are largely concerned with determining the *structure* of the decision: the issue(s) to be settled, whether there will be one single decision point or several subdecisions, what options will be available, and so on.

I have recently proposed that we call the process of settling these issues the *structuring* of a decision. (Hansson 2017). This process precedes and prepares for the well-structured decision problems that are the usual topics of decision theory. The following are ten major components of decision structuring. (Hansson 2017)

1) **Scope** The scope of a decision is its decision matter; that is, the totality of issues that will be covered by it. The scope is often limited by background decisions that are (rightly or not) assumed to be unalterable. The scope can be changed by the addition or removal of issues during the decision process.

2) **Subdivision** Decisions on complex issues are often divided into several smaller parts. For instance, as a student you can make a single decision on how much you are going to study each of the remaining days before an exam. Alternatively, you can decide on each occasion when you have the opportunity to study whether you will do so and in that case for how long.

3) **Agency** It is not always clear from the beginning of the process who will make the decision(s). For instance, a public decision process can start with the presumption that the government will make the decision, but end up with a decision by parliament, or the other way around.

4) **Timing** In most formal approaches to decision making, either the time for decision making is assumed to have been settled beforehand, or else it is entirely abstracted from. In practice, decision makers often adjust the timescale, for instance by advancing or postponing a decision or making a preliminary decision for later reconsideration.

5) **Options** The identification of the options available to be chosen is usually an important component of the early phases of decision making. In some decisions, this part of the process develops into an innovative activity in which new options are created.

6) **Control ascriptions** The degree of control that agents are assumed to have over their own future actions can have a large impact on decision processes and their outcomes. For instance, if you decide to go to the gym three times

a week, will you actually do so? Under the assumption that you are in control of the execution of this decision, we can assume a deterministic relationship between the decision and your future gym habits. If we instead assume that you are not in full control of your future actions when you make this decision, then it may be more appropriate to assign probabilities to different levels of future compliance with the decision.

7) **Framing** It makes a difference if you say that a glass is half full or half empty, even though the two phrases have the same meaning. Several studies have shown that our decisions are influenced by how the options are described. The choice how to describe a given decision and its options is called the "framing" of the decision.

8) **Horizon** What types of potential consequences should we take into account when evaluating decision outcomes? How far into the future should we go, and whose interests should be taken into account? For instance, how much should a government's decision be influenced by effects in other countries? And when decisions are made by a company, to what extent should effects outside of the company be taken into account; for instance, effects on the general public, customers, or competitors?

9) **Criteria** When the horizon of the decision has been determined, it remains to decide how the various aspects included in the horizon should be evaluated. Even if it has been settled that a certain potential effect should be taken into account, it remains to be determined how large its influence should be in relation to other factors that will also be included in the assessment.

10) **Restructuring** The structuring of a decision will mainly take place in what risk analysts have called the "pre-assessment" phase of decision making (Ikeda 1986, p. 397; Barnthouse and Stahl 2002, p. 2; Renn 2005); that is, a first preliminary identification and assessment of the issues to be dealt with. However, reasons to reconsider the structuring can come up in later stages of the process. Any of the nine factors mentioned above can be subject to revision. Decision processes differ in the degree to which such restructuring is facilitated or impeded.

Some comments about the terminology may be useful. First, the distinction between *scope* and *horizon* is a specification of the rather ambiguous use of these terms in the decision sciences. As the terms are used here, the scope of a decision is the set of issues that is decided upon, whereas the horizon is the set of aspects that are "seen" or taken into account when options and potential outcomes are evaluated. This way of using the two words has support in the general usage of the words. According to the *Oxford English Dictionary*, by scope can be meant "[t]he sphere or area over which any activity operates or is effective" or the "[r]oom for exercise, opportunity or liberty to act". The same source gives as a meaning of horizon: "that which bounds one's mental vision or perception; limit or range of one's knowledge, experience, or interest".

The term *agency* was chosen for lack of a better word. By agency is often meant the "[a]bility or capacity to act or exert power" (OED). Here the word is used to refer to the capacity to make decisions. Perhaps a neologism with that meaning would be a useful addition to the language, but here the word "agency" will be used to cover it. Following the convention in the decision sciences, the term *framing* will be used for the way in which a decision is described. I will return to the meaning of this term in Section 10.2.7.

In current practice, many decisions on risk are structured in questionable ways. Sometimes the chosen structure is inefficient, for instance since some of the available options have not been included. Sometimes the structure is controversial, or biased in one way or the other. Risk analysis should therefore include a careful analysis of the structuring of the risk-related decision problems under its purview. It is the purpose of the present contribution to provide some basic tools and concepts for such an analysis.

10.2 The Ten Components of Structuring

The above list of ten components can be used as a starting point for the analysis of decision structures.

10.2.1 Scope

After a serious accident in a refinery, management has a brief meeting with safety personnel and representatives of the workforce. Everyone agrees that "everything" must be done to prevent such accidents from happening again, and the safety division receives the task of preparing a decision with that purpose. The next day the safety division has a staff meeting. "What is our mandate?" they ask themselves. "Of course we can propose changes in the technology that was involved in the accident. But can we propose technological improvements that would reduce the risk of other types of accidents? We can propose improved routines that would have prevented this accident, but can we propose a new management structure, worker co-determination in safety-related issues, or perhaps even a reduced rate of return for the next few years to make room for some safety investments?"

When we determine the scope of a decision, we draw a line between, on the one hand, the *decision matter* – the totality of issues to be decided – and, on the other hand, the *background conditions* – that is, all the rest. The background conditions often include *background decisions*: decisions that will be treated as already settled and not up for reconsideration. In our example, the safety division needs to know if the plant's management structure is part of the decision matter or has to be treated as a background condition. A couple of examples can illustrate the importance for risk analysis of identifying background decisions.

> Work in a particular underground mine is unusually dangerous due to a high risk of rock falls. When workers complain, they are told that they have themselves decided to take this job, in full knowledge of its dangers, and that they can reduce the risk by being careful and observant. (Hansson 2013, p. 118)

The risk of rock falls depends largely on decisions that have been made about the technology, the organization, and the work processes. It is generally agreed in the health and safety profession that these decisions should not be treated as background decisions. Instead, they should be a focus in discussions on workplace accidents. (However, there have been attempts to move the focus to the decisions and actions of individual workers, as part of efforts to relieve employers of responsibility for the working conditions that they offer their employees; see Machan 1987 and, for a rebuttal, Spurgin 2006.)

> The worldwide yearly death toll from road traffic is more than 1.2 million, and between 20 and 50 million sustain non-fatal injuries (WHO 2013). According to conventional accident analyses, the direct causes of traffic accidents are usually factors pertaining to the behaviour of the driver, such as speeding and drunk or reckless driving. In public discussions, the focus is largely on the decisions by individual drivers, such as decisions to speed or to drive while drunk.

However, there are important background decisions about motor vehicles that should arguably be brought into the foreground. For instance, most motor vehicles lack alcohol interlocks, and they can therefore be driven by an inebriated driver. They also lack automatic speed limiters, and they can therefore be driven at dangerous and illegal speeds. Both of these are cheap and life-saving technologies that car manufacturers have decided not to install and regulators have decided not to require. There are also other measures that can reduce traffic fatalities, for example collision-proof fences between opposing lanes of traffic. A risk analysis that focuses exclusively on the decisions by individual drivers would miss out on the most efficacious means of saving lives in traffic.

The choice of scope is largely a policy issue, but risk analysts can help make sure that it is dealt with in a reasoned and transparent way. In particular, scope delimitations that prevent efficient risk reductions should be brought to light and carefully scrutinized.

10.2.2 Subdivision

> *"We should have a safety budget at the company level. Each plant can then apply for money for safety investments. In this way, we make sure that the money spent on safety is used as efficiently as possible."*

> *"No, that would be the wrong way to do it. Safety investments should be integrated with other investments, not treated as optional add-ons. The management of each plant should be fully responsible for all aspects of safety in that plant."*

> *"But then the plants with economic difficulties will invest less in safety than the others. How can you defend that?"*

When the decision matter is large, it may be advantageous or perhaps even necessary to divide it into manageable parts. Subdivisions can be made in different ways. For instance, decision making on national traffic policies can be subdivided according to the mode of transportation, with separate decisions for railroads, highways, aviation, and maritime traffic. Alternatively, traffic decisions can be subdivided according to geographic criteria, with decisions organized according to regions and routes.

The subdivision of risk decisions can have a large impact on decision outcomes. This is perhaps best illustrated with the debates on how much we should be willing to pay for reductions in fatality risks. Our willingness to pay for safety, measured as the marginal cost of saving a life, differs widely between policy areas (Ramsberg and Sjöberg 1997). Some cost–benefit analysts are dissatisfied with this. They claim that decisions on risk acceptance should be co-ordinated so that willingness to pay is equalized across all policy areas. Viscusi (2000, p. 855) is representative of this view, proposing that we should "spend up to the same marginal cost-per-life-saved amount for different agencies". There is an obvious and quite persuasive argument in favour of this approach: for any given amount of money spent on saving lives, it will maximize the number of lives saved.

But there are also arguments *against* such a large-scale co-ordination of risk and safety decisions. We may have legitimate reasons to assign different priorities to the prevention of different cases of death. In many cultures, the death of children is perceived as particularly tragic, and higher costs are accepted for accident prevention if children's lives are at stake. We are also willing to pay much more to prevent deaths from crimes, in particular terror crimes, than from most other causes. This may not be irrational, considering the effects that crimes and terror have on the lives of people who are not themselves victims.

In addition, any serious attempt to apply a uniform cost per life saved will be hampered by the fact that risk decisions are intricately interwoven with other decisions in all areas of society. It is difficult to see how we could co-ordinate the risk aspects of all decisions while retaining an uncoordinated and decentralized decision structure for the other components of these decisions. Attempts to create large unified decision agendas have been called "super-synopticism" (Hornstein 1993, p. 387). It is well known that large-scale optimization tends to become inefficient due to problems with the collection and processing of such massive amounts of information.

There is no simple recipe for how to subdivide a decision. Often, different considerations point in different directions, and the choice of a subdivision will then have to depend on how we weigh these considerations against each other. The following list of considerations, or types of arguments, can be used as a checklist.

1) Information processing arguments
   - *Information access arguments*: Decisions should be made by people who have access to the information needed for making them.
   - *Complexity arguments:* The demands on information collection and processing should be kept within the bounds of practicality. This usually speaks in favour of subdividing large decisions into more manageable parts.
2) Procedural arguments
   - *Organizational arguments*: The decision structure should be congruous with the organizational structure.
   - *Competence arguments.* If is often preferable to assign each part of the decision matter to people who understand that part thoroughly.
   - *Influence arguments.* It is desirable and often indispensable to include those who are affected by a decision in the decision procedure. When different groups of people are affected by different parts of the decision matter, influence arguments speak in favour of subdividing the decision accordingly.
   - *Majority-seeking and consensus-seeking arguments.* It is usually desirable to make decisions with the largest majorities possible. In many cases, agreements can be reached more easily if several issues are combined into a larger combination that allows for give and take on all sides. In other cases a partial consensus can be achieved by subdividing the decision so that its uncontroversial parts can be decided in wide agreement.
3) *Outcome-related arguments*
   - These refer to desirable properties of the decision outcome. Even if a decision is controversial, there may be some desirable features of an outcome that can be generally agreed upon, and the decision can then be subdivided in a way that furthers the achievement of these features. For instance, budgetary balance is more easily obtained if a budget is adopted in one single decision than if separate decisions are made on each of its components.

10.2.3 Agency

"I can report that the workers in Hall B all accept the higher noise levels that will result from the introduction of new power presses next year. I've talked to each of them individually, and they all consented."

"Did you tell them that the noise levels would have been about ten decibels lower if we had bought the other type of presses with multiple anti-vibration dampers?"

"No. The CEO has ruled out that option, so I didn't consider it appropriate to mention it."

As noted above, the term "agency" is used here for lack of a better word to denote the property of being a decision maker. It is usually not the role of risk analysts to appoint decision makers. However, risk analysts can point out potential problems in such appointments.

Generally speaking, there are two major ways in which a person can qualify to participate in a decision: *expertise* and *concernment*. (The latter word refers to the property of being influenced or concerned by the decision, or having a stake in it.) Some of the considerations mentioned in the previous section refer to the usefulness of subdividing a decision matter in ways that facilitate the involvement of people who satisfy one of these two criteria. The structuring of a decision should include explicit deliberations on whether some of the required expertise is missing and whether people who are concerned by the decision have been left out of the process.

In risk-related decisions, the representation of risk-exposed people is of course crucial. The form of their participation is a large issue that cannot be treated here (Hansson and Oughton 2013). However, it is important to distinguish between consent and participation. By "consent" is meant that a person agrees to something proposed by someone else. That a person consents to a decision does not necessarily imply that she participated in the decision process as a whole, in which alternative options were discussed and compared.

The notion of (informed) consent has its origin in medical ethics, but it is increasingly applied in a wider context. Unfortunately, the limitations of its use in the original context have often been forgotten when it is used elsewhere (Hansson 2006). In clinical medicine, informed consent serves to ensure that no medical procedure is performed on the patient unless she is informed about its pros and cons and has approved of it (Faden and Beauchamp 1986). According to the standard view in medical ethics, consent is a necessary but insufficient condition for the legitimacy of an intervention. It is unethical to administer a treatment that is known to do more harm than good to the patient's health, however much the patient consents (WMA 2013).

Against this background, two important warnings must be raised against the use of consent to justify risk exposures. First, the fact that a person has consented to a risk does not necessarily absolve those who expose her to that risk from responsibility (Hansson 2013, pp. 116–121). Secondly, consent to a risk exposure is very different from full participation in the decision process. Participation in decision making cannot be replaced by the process of "drawing forth" the consent of affected groups that some discussants seem to consider sufficient (Simmons, 1987, p. 6). It should be an important task for risk analysts to find out beforehand who may have a legitimate claim to participation in the decision-making process.

10.2.4 Timing

"We don't know for sure that the proposed underground depositories for nuclear waste will prevent leakage for the very long period that the waste is harmful. Nuclear waste disposal should be deferred until we know for sure that we have a safe method."

"Are you aware of the risks involved in the temporary storage facilities where all the nuclear waste is being kept now? Although the proposed solution for long-term storage may not be perfect, it is many orders of magnitude safer than the temporary storage. Can you really take responsibility for delaying the decision, so that the waste will be above ground in temporary storage for many more years to come?"

The point in time at which we make a decision can have large impacts on the outcome. The nuclear waste example illustrates that the problem a decision is aimed at solving can aggravate while we are waiting for a decision. This is a common situation in risk and safety, and also in environmental issues. The same example illustrates that the state of knowledge can change during the time a decision is delayed. New knowledge can be gained, and old knowledge can become outdated. Furthermore, new options can become available, and previous options can be lost ("missed windows of opportunity"). In decisions requiring negotiations or the formation of coalitions, the passage of time can either increase or decrease the willingness of others to enter the necessary agreements.

The *timing* of a decision is the point(s) in time when the decision, or its different parts, are made. A *temporal strategy* for a decision is a plan for its timing. Many decisions are made without a temporal strategy; their timing is improvised rather than chosen. Arguably, more decisions should have temporal strategies.

We can distinguish between four major temporal strategies. The first of these is *closure*, which means that a definite decision is taken more or less immediately. This means that the decision will take effect as soon as possible, which is usually an advantage. On the other hand, closure has the disadvantage that that no opportunity is given to investigate the problem more closely, or learn from experience, before a definite decision is taken.

The second temporal strategy is *postponement;* that is, deferring the decision to a later point in time. Postponements come in many variants. We can subdivide them according to two important, crossing distinctions. One of these is that between active and passive postponement. *Active postponement* is characterized by preparations for the postponed decision, for instance information gathering, investigations, and efforts to develop better options. In *passive postponement*, no such preparations are made. This is the strategy of "wait and see".

The other distinction is that between *scheduled* and *unscheduled postponements.* A scheduled postponement includes a point in time at which the decision has to be made. An unscheduled postponement has no such fixed date, which means that a new initiative must be taken at some later point in time in order to resume the decision-making process. Since the two distinctions cross, they give rise to four types of postponements: active scheduled, active unscheduled, passive scheduled, and passive unscheduled postponements. If the postponed decision is important, the active scheduled variant is usually the most appropriate one.

The third temporal strategy is *semi-closure.* This means that one of the available options is selected (and carried out), but at the same time preparations are made for later reassessment and reconsideration. Semi-closure requires, of course, that the original, preliminary decision is reversible. Just like postponements, semi-closures can be either scheduled or unscheduled, depending on whether a date has been set for a later decision that will replace the first, provisional one. An interesting form of scheduled semi-closure is a moratorium, during which a new technology is not used. When the moratorium ends, a decision is made on whether the technology should henceforth be permitted and which if any conditions should in that case be imposed on its use (Hansson 2016b). Unscheduled semi-closure is represented by various forms of adaptive management of natural resources, in which management decisions are explicitly provisional but will only be changed if specific initiatives are made to do so (Hirsch Hadorn 2016).

The fourth temporal strategy is *sequential decisions*, by which is meant that different parts of a decision are scheduled to take place at different points in time, typically in order to accommodate differences between these parts, for instance in terms of urgency and the need to acquire more information.

A first version of this typology of temporal strategies, containing only the first three of the four major classes, was introduced in Hansson (1996). The fourth class, sequential decisions, was added by Hirsch-Hadorn (2016). The distinction between scheduled and unscheduled postponements and semi-closures is a new addition.

The choice of a temporal strategy will typically depend on several considerations that have to be weighed against each other. The following list of questions can be used as a checklist of such considerations:

- *Do all the available alternatives have serious drawbacks?* If so, then that speaks against closure.
- *Would a search for new alternatives be costly?* If so, then that speaks in favour of closure.
- *Are there large decision-relevant uncertainties, and good chances to reduce these uncertainties?* If so, then that speaks against closure.
- *Are there differences between the parts of the decision, so that some of them are subject to more uncertainty than the others?* If so, then that speaks in favour of a sequential decision.
- *Does the problem to be solved aggravate with time?* If so, then that speaks against postponement.
- *Is the best among the reversible alternatives significantly worse than the best among all the alternatives?* If so, then that speaks against semi-closure.
- *Is there a considerable risk that the decision maker's capacity for and inclination to responsible and well-informed decision making will deteriorate?* If so, then that speaks against postponement and sequential decision making.

10.2.5   Options

> *"There are two ways to reduce exposure to solvents in the parts cleaning shop. We can either introduce local exhaust ventilation or provide the workers with respirators. Respirators are much cheaper, but they may impede work performance. I would like you to assess both alternatives, in terms of both effectiveness and costs."*
>
> *"Fine, I will do so. But would you allow me to investigate other alternatives as well, such as using less harmful solvents or perhaps an entirely different cleaning process?"*

In risk analysis as well as other branches of the decision sciences, it is commonly assumed that the set of available options is settled and well defined. In practice, this is often not the case. There are at least two important reasons why risk analysts should make their own inventories of potential options, and be careful not to assume that the originally given list of options is complete.

The first reason is that risk-related decisions are often structured in ways that *exclude some options for reasons that are unrelated to risk reduction.* This can of course be legitimate. A risk-reducing option may be too expensive, or have other disadvantages that justify its exclusion from serious consideration. However, such exclusions should have a tenable justification, and be transparently presented. The definition of the so-called "substitution principle" provides an interesting example of this. This is a principle in chemicals control that has been defined as "the considered transition from a chemical of particular concern to safer chemicals or non-chemical alternatives" (Auer 2006). Several authors have emphasized that the substitution can consist either in the use of less hazardous chemicals or in the use of some safer process that does not require chemicals (Oosterhuis 2006; Hansson et al 2011). However, in a policy statement by the European Chemical Industry Council (CEFIC) the principle is defined as follows:

> Substitution is the replacement of one substance by another with the aim of achieving a lower level of risk. (CEFIC 2005, p. 1)

According to this definition, the outcome of applying the substitution principle will always include the use of some chemical. The purpose of this attempt to restrict the set of options in substitution decisions is too obvious to be pointed out. It is difficult to believe that CEFIC would have chosen to "define away" safe uses of chemicals as means to solve problems in unsafe, non-chemical work processes.

More generally speaking, it is fairly common that the best solution to a safety problem requires a rather thorough-going change of the work process. Consider, for instance, a process industry that makes use of an explosive reactant, which is bought from an external supplier. Various measures can be taken to reduce the risk or the magnitude of an explosion, such as explosion-proof storage facilities and the elimination of ignition sources. However, it is usually much better to change the process so that the substance is not needed at all or, if that is not possible, to produce the substance locally in small quantities and transfer it continuously to the reaction. Safety professionals have often encountered resistance when trying to introduce such far-reaching changes on the list of options to be considered (Kletz 2004; Hansson 2010). Smaller modifications in the form of add-on safety devices tend to be accepted less reluctantly. It is an obvious task for risk analysts to ensure that options involving considerable changes in technologies and work processes are seriously considered.

The other major reason why risk analysts should look for additions to the given list of options is that the best solution to a safety problem may very well not have been invented yet. By pointing out problems to be solved, risk analysts can create a demand for new and innovative solutions. There is considerable evidence that "environmental and health and safety regulation – if appropriately designed, implemented, and complemented by economic incentives – can lead to radical technological developments that can significantly reduce exposure to toxic chemicals in the natural and working environments, and in consumer products" (Ashford and Hall 2011, p. 277). There are strong reasons to believe that market demand can have the same type of effect even if it is not supported by regulation.

10.2.6   Control Ascriptions

"I just found out that you have ordered a new production line to be installed within two years. But you don't seem to have included the rather extensive equipment that is needed to minimize exposure to toxic chemicals in the new process."

"Don't worry. I'm as concerned as you with workers' health, but that part of the investment will be made about eighteen months from now."

"Of course I don't doubt your good intentions. But are you sure that you will fulfil them eighteen months from now, irrespective of what happens with our financial situation?"

It is commonly assumed in decision analysis that the decision maker is in full control over her own actions. There is, so to say, no distance between the decision and the action that implements it. If you decide to do something, then you will also do it. This assumption comes out particularly clearly when a decision requires implementation at some later point(s) in time. The traditional approach assumes that we can always make a decision that will bind our future actions; in other words that we are in full control of how we will act under various future circumstances.

But we have all had experiences showing that life is not that simple. We have asked ourselves questions like:

- Can I open the box of chocolates and take just one single piece?
- If I join my friend at the pub, will I return home sufficiently early and sober to finish the work that I promised to deliver early tomorrow morning?
- Since I have decided to go to the gym twice a week from now on, should I buy a 12 months gym membership? Or should I pay for each visit, which is more expensive if I carry through my plans but much less expensive if I fail to do so?

In all these examples, the decision seems to depend crucially on whether you consider yourself to be in control of your future decisions.

One way to deal with such situations is to treat the degree of control as an empirical issue. It should be possible, at least in principle, to find out how probable it is that one will change one's mind or succumb to weakness of will. In some cases, this empirical approach appears to be quite adequate. For instance, there are some types of temptation that we can almost always resist and others that are nearly sure to conquer us. But there are also cases in which the strength of our determination can make a big difference. For instance, the chances that I will go to the gym the whole year will increase if I make a serious effort to make myself as strongly determined as possible to do so. Buying a 12-month membership can be part of my efforts to convince myself that

I will follow through on my plans. This is not a matter of just finding out some facts about oneself. It is a matter of making up one's mind in earnest and then persevering.

In this example neither of the two simplified approaches captures the complexities of the situation. Whether I will follow through on my intentions is to some extent an empirical issue that I can treat in the same way as corresponding empirical issues about other people. But at the same time it is to some extent something that I can control by sheer willpower, which I certainly cannot do with other people's decisions. This is a highly convoluted situation from the viewpoint of decision theory. On the one hand, I can treat my own future decisions as events that are entirely separate from the decisions I make now, in the same way that I would treat decisions by other people. On the other hand, I can treat my own future decisions as something that I can simply settle now, thus making no difference at all between myself now and myself in the future. In other words, we have tools to deal with the two extreme cases of no control and complete control over one's future decisions. However, we lack adequate tools for intermediate situations with imperfect control. This is unfortunate since such intermediate situations are anything but rare.

There is a strong tradition in the safety professions to opt for the no-control endpoint; that is, to assume that decision makers cannot be sure to follow through on risk-avoiding decisions. That is why we prefer machines that cannot chop off fingers to an operator's determination never to put her hands close to the dangerous parts. This approach is borne out by experience. Although there may be exceptions, it is usually a good strategy for risk analysts to stick to the no-control endpoint of the control scale.

10.2.7 Framing

> *"I don't like the way you describe our development plans for the new area. You say that 'in spite of the environmental measures it is expected that five unique insect species will become extinct'. I don't like that phrase at all."*

> *"What's wrong? Isn't it true?"*

> *"Of course it's true, but I do not like the way you are putting it."*

> *"What do you want me to write instead?"*

> *"Well, you can for instance write that due to the extensive environmental measures that we take, 98% of the about 250 unique insect species in the area are expected to survive."*

The term "frame" was used in the social sciences by Gregory Bateson already in the 1950s, and it was taken up by Ervin Goffman in the 1970s. Both used the word in a very wide sense, to cover all sorts of concepts and ideas that individuals use to interpret the world and their own experiences of it (Denzin and Keller 1981). In the early 1980s, Tversky and Kahneman (1981) introduced "framing" into the decision sciences. They also gave the discussion of framing an entirely new, much more restricted focus, namely on the effects of redescribing a decision without actually changing it. There is now an impressive collection of empirical evidence showing that human decision makers are much influenced by such redescriptions. The most famous example is the so-called Asian disease problem. This is a hypothetical decision problem in which a choice has to be made between two ways to deal with an outbreak of a serious disease. The potential outcomes can be expressed either in positive or negative terms (the number of people saved by some measure or the number of people killed by the disease). Although the positive and the negative descriptions refer to exactly the same risk, experimental subjects tend to treat them differently in decision making (Tversky and Kahneman 1981). This experiment is the paradigm example of a framing effect. It has been repeated many times and with numerous variations of the set-up.

Kühberger (1998) distinguishes between a "strict" and a "loose" sense of framing. The strict sense refers to "a semantic manipulation of prospects whereby the exact same situation is simply redescribed", as in the Asian disease example. The loose sense of the word "refers to framing as an internal event that can be induced not only by semantic manipulations but may result also from other contextual features of a situation and from individual factors, provided that problems are equivalent from the perspective of economic theory" (p. 28). Current discussions on framing are dominated by the approach initiated by Tversky and Kahneman, and therefore the strict sense of framing is much more common than the loose one. However, it should be pointed out that the term also has a third sense that is even looser than Kühberger's "loose sense". This "even looser" sense includes cases in which the different framings of a decision problem are not even equivalent in terms of economic theory. They may, for instance, differ substantially in the decision horizon and in the criteria used to evaluate the decision outcome (Buijs 2009).

As indicated already in Section 10.1, I will follow common practice in the decision sciences and use the term "framing" in the restricted sense that it acquired after the pioneering work of Tversky and Kahneman; that is, in essence, the "strict" sense according to Kühberger. It could be argued that the term is misleading since the word "frame" hints at the surrounding context of a decision rather than how it is described. However, this usage is now well established. Attempts to change an established but confusing terminology often create more confusion than they eliminate.

Research and discussions on framing effects (in the strict sense) have largely been fuelled by controversies on whether it is irrational to decide differently depending on how the decision is framed. Kenneth Arrow (1982) has proposed a precise statement of the contested issue in these discussions, in the form of a requirement that the decision maker's behaviour should satisfy a postulate of *extensionality*. This means that her decision should be the same for different but logically equivalent descriptions of a decision problem.

Several authors have pointed out that extensionality is quite a strong a criterion. Two descriptions of a decision can be logically equivalent but still differ in the information they convey. For instance, a statement that "95% of those who receive the vaccine are fully protected" may give the impression that the vaccine has satisfactory coverage. A statement that "5% of those who receive the vaccine are not fully protected" may give the opposite impression. In this and many other cases, a choice among logically equivalent formulations can provide information about what is considered to be an acceptable or unacceptable outcome. Although standard decision theory has no use for such information, there are decision rules that take it into account. Two prominent examples are decision rules employing sufficientarian and regret-avoiding criteria. According to sufficientarianism, what matters most is that the outcome is sufficiently good (that it is acceptable). Improvements above that minimal level are given low priority. Regret-avoiding rules put the focus on the difference between the value of the outcome one obtains and the value of what one could at best have obtained if one had made another choice. A rational decision maker who employs a rule belonging to either of these categories should therefore be expected to violate extensionality.

But on the other hand, if two descriptions of a decision are not only logically equivalent but also convey the same information, then it is much more plausible to claim that a rational decision maker should react to them in the same way (Sher and McKenzie 2006). Till Grüne-Yanoff (2016) has proposed the term *invariance* for this weakened version of extensionality. It is more plausible than extensionality, but unfortunately it is also more difficult to define precisely. It is usually much easier to find out whether two descriptions are logically equivalent than to determine exactly what they suggest non-logically.

Stakeholders with a vested interest often search for framings (in both a strict and a looser sense) that support their message. For instance, industries seeking acceptance of potentially harmful activities or products search for framings that facilitate the public's acceptance, whereas environmental activists favour framings that have the opposite effect. Risk professionals are often commissioned to search for framings that serve certain purposes. Such endeavours are potentially manipulative, and may therefore be questionable from the viewpoint of professional ethics. A much less controversial approach is to present alternative framings to decision makers (including the public) so that they can make their own decisions in full awareness of the framing effects (Grüne-Yanoff and Hertwig 2016). In this way, knowledge about framing effects can be used to empower the public, rather than as a means to nudge them to move in a direction chosen by someone else.

10.2.8 Horizon

> *A proposal has been put forward to reduce carbon dioxide emissions in a member country in the European Union. A careful analysis shows that its implementation would have negative economic consequences for the country due to the expected creation of competitive disadvantages in relation to other European countries that do not reduce their emissions. For the country's government, this is a valid argument against taking the measure in question. However, for the European Commission it is not, because it has outweighing benefits in other European countries (Hansson 2007, p. 168).*

The decision horizon is the total set of considerations that we take into account when evaluating decision options and decision outcomes. Obviously, we cannot include everything. We must keep down the workload of decision makers to a reasonable level. Since the decision horizon can be limited in many ways, there are quite a few variables that have to be settled in order to specify it. Three important such variables are those that give rise to plausibility-based, temporal, and responsibility-based limits:

Plausibility-based limits Ideally, we should take all potential consequences of each decision option into account. In practice, we only include those that we consider to be reasonably plausible. Lack of attention to (allegedly) implausible potential events has sometimes had dire consequences. For instance, it was most unfortunate, to say the least, that the designers of the Fukushima Daiichi nuclear plant did not include rare, very large tsunamis in their decision horizon. But admittedly, it is often difficult to draw the limit between the potential events that need to be included in the analysis and those that can be excluded. In principle, all decision options can have severe consequences that we cannot foresee. Any new medicine may have serious side effects of an entirely new type. Any new industrial product may be used by consumers in dangerous ways not foreseen by the design team. We do not usually pay much attention to such possibilities, but sometimes opponents of a technology bring them into the discussion. On the one hand, we need to take some rather implausible potential events into account, but on the other hand, we cannot include them all. Which of them we choose to include can be no less important for the outcome of a risk analysis than the detailed investigation of those that we choose to include in the final analysis. See Hansson (2016a) on how this choice can be systematized.

Temporal limits There are both good and bad arguments for limiting the reach into the future of a risk analysis. Lack of care for what happens in the distant future is a bad reason. Lack of information about what can happen beyond a certain point in time can be a good reason. However, the various consequences that we wish to take into account often differ in how far we can follow them into the future. What we do now will probably have social consequences hundreds of years into the future, but in many cases we cannot meaningfully assess these consequences, and we may therefore have to leave them out. In contrast, many environmental consequences can be assessed on a rather long timescale, due to the greater predictability of many natural phenomena. This can be a reason to apply different time limits to the different aspects of a decision.

Responsibility limits Decision makers tend to restrict their concern to those aspects of the decision that they are – or can be made – responsible for. The limits of legal responsibility can usually be determined with some precision, but those of ethical responsibility tend to be much less clear. For instance, a company is responsible for the working conditions of its own employees, but to what extent is it responsible for the working conditions of its subcontractors and their employees? Companies are also held responsible when local residents are negatively affected by their activities. But how far does this go? Can a company be held responsible for the effects of its activities on competitors and their employees? Similar questions can be asked about the responsibilities of governments. A government is supposed to focus on what is good for the country, but it is considered responsible for the effects abroad of the country's environmental emissions. Attempts have been made to hold countries in the rich world responsible for the effects of their economic and trade policies in developing countries, but usually with limited success. Obviously, a national perspective on decision making is legitimate, and so are global, regional, and local perspectives. How much governments should worry about the effects of their decisions in other countries, or how much companies should take effects outside of the company into account, are essentially moral issues. It is not the task of risk analysts to dictate one or other answer to such questions, but risk analysts can help ensure that these delimitations are made in a transparent and well-reasoned way.

10.2.9 Criteria of Evaluation

"The experiment on healthy human subjects that you propose will expose them to unacceptable risks. According to your own estimate, there is a 50% probability that the drug will give rise to a serious autoimmune reaction."

"Yes, but if it doesn't, then we are almost sure that this will be an efficient drug against several forms of childhood cancer. How can you take responsibility for stopping a drug trial that has such a large chance of providing us with an efficient remedy against these diseases?"

"And how can you take responsibility for potentially sacrificing these human subjects? You are treating them as means for the benefit of others, not as ends in themselves."

The decision horizon specifies the aspects of the decision options and outcomes that will be taken into account when they are evaluated. But that is not enough. We also need to have criteria for that evaluation. Two of the major issues that have to be settled in that context can be described as the problem of many values and the problem of many people.

10.2.9.1 The Problem of Many Values

Most risk-related decisions involve several types of value that cannot easily be measured against each other. One and the same decision may have impacts on risks of death, various diseases, different kinds of environmental degradation, monetary losses, and so on. When evaluating the options, we have to combine these values or weigh them against each other. In a cost–benefit analysis, this is done by translating all other values into monetary values. This means, for instance, that a monetary value is assigned to the loss of a human life. Such "life values" are standard in cost–benefit analyses, but they have also been heavily criticized. Intuitively, the idea of assigning a value in dollars or euros to a human life is revolting. However, life values can be defended as a technical means to ensure that our life-saving activities save as many lives as possible.

Importantly, the incommensurability between life and money is only one of the many incommensurabilities that we have to deal with, with or without a cost–benefit analysis. Death, disease, and environmental damage are not easily compared to each other. There is no definite answer to the question how many cases of juvenile diabetes correspond to one death, or what amount of human suffering or death corresponds to the extinction of an antelope species. Yet such "impossible" comparisons are part and parcel of social decision making, not least in risk management. The basic difficulty will remain even if we remove money from the analysis (Hansson 2007).

There is no simple solution to the problem of many values. Rational people may differ in the relative values they assign, for instance, to human health, economic prosperity, and preservation of the environment. The task of risk analysis is not to promote one particular assignment of relative values, but to clarify what impact the choice between such assignments can have on risk management decisions.

10.2.9.2 The Problem of Many People

Risk analysis often involves the interests of many people who are affected negatively or positively to different degrees. The standard way to deal with this problem is based on utilitarian moral philosophy. In classical utilitarianism, the value of an option is equal to the sum of its values to all concerned individuals. It makes no difference how these values are distributed among people; only the sum matters. This approach is based on the collectivist weighing principle, according to which an option is acceptable to the extent that the sum of all individual costs that it gives rise to is outweighed by the sum of all individual benefits to which it gives rise. However, this is not the only way in which costs can be weighed against benefits. Another possibility is to perform the weighing individually for each affected person, and require a positive balance for each of them. According to the individualist weighing principle, an option is acceptable to the extent that the costs affecting each individual are outweighed by benefits for that same individual. Individualist weighing has a strong tradition in both medicine and research ethics (Hansson 2004). If an experiment on human beings gives rise to serious risks for the experimental subjects, then this cannot (according to a broad consensus in research ethics) be outweighed by advantages to other people, such as future patients who are expected to benefit from the research. Disadvantages to one person cannot in this context be outweighed by advantages to other people.

The conflict over so-called NIMBY (not in my backyard) attitudes has a lot to do with the difference between collectivist and individualist weighing. Local inhabitants who oppose the construction of a potentially hazardous plant tend to see the issue from the perspective of an individualist weighing: "The disadvantages for me are not outweighed by any advantages that I receive." Risk managers who promote the new plant see it from the perspective of a collectivist weighing: "The total advantages of this plant outweigh its disadvantages." The basic issue here is under what circumstances a person is morally required to accept a disadvantage that is imposed on her in order to obtain advantages for others (Hansson 2013). This is a value-laden issue that risk analysis cannot solve. However, risk analysts can contribute to its clarification by performing analyses based on both types of weighing, so that decision makers have access to them both in their deliberations.

10.2.10   Restructuring

"I believe we made a big mistake when we delegated all decisions on chemical safety to local management. It seemed to be a good idea since they know the exposure conditions. But the recent accident reports show that some of them are unable to combine that information with toxicity data and make a sensible risk assessment. So what should we do now?"

"Perhaps we should just rescind the delegation and let the central safety division take over again?"

"But we have already tried that solution, and it had its own problems. Perhaps we can find some way to make them combine their competences?"

The way in which we structure a decision will always depend on our priorities and our state of knowledge at the time of structuring. When we learn more, we often see reasons to structure the problem differently. Perhaps the decision matter has to be extended to issues that we did not include from the beginning. Perhaps we have found additional options, consequences, or criteria of evaluation that we want to include. Perhaps we have developed entirely new ways of thinking about the decision problem and its relations to other issues we need to solve. But once a structuring of a decision has been established, we run the risk of losing sight of alternative structurings. To avoid this from happening, we need to make sure that risk decisions are regularly reconsidered and that these reconsiderations include a systematic discussion of their structuring.

10.3 Discussion

"Has Nadia submitted a paper to the safety conference?"

"I don't know. I guess you can found out on the website, or else you can ask her."

"Will you come to conference yourself?"

"I don't know. I have not made up my mind yet."

The dialogue illustrates that "not knowing" can mean two things. In the first case it refers to lack of information, which can be remedied by finding out the facts of the matter. In the second case it refers to undecidedness, and it can be resolved by making up one's mind. The term "uncertainty" has the same ambiguity. It can refer both to what we have not found out and to what we have not (yet) decided. The responder in our example is presumably uncertain both about whether Nadia has submitted a paper and about her/his own participation in the conference.

Risk analysis has rightly focused on factual knowledge and on what we can do when we lack it. But there are also important issues in risk analysis that have to be settled by decision-making rather than fact-finding. Most of the structuring issues discussed above are of this nature. It is important to recognize that risk analysis is based not only on facts but also on the structuring chosen for risk decisions. Such choices are usually not very transparent, and they sometimes only involve doing as we have always done, or following the instructions or expectations of decision makers. But their impact on decision making is so large that they need to be carefully discussed, and made in an open and transparent way.

Figure 10.1 provides a simplified picture of the major ways to deal with lack of knowledge in the risk decision process. The process it depicts is in fact quite complex, not least due to the difficulties of determining the ambit of a decision-maker's control, as discussed in Section 10.2.6.

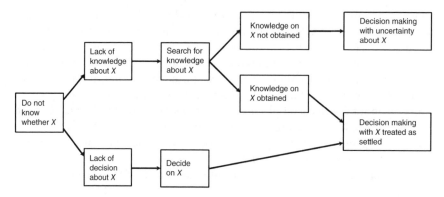

Figure 10.1 A schematic of how lack of knowledge (uncertainty) can be dealt with in risk analysis.

10.4 Conclusion

This outline has shown that the structuring of decision problems can have a decisive impact on decision outcomes. Therefore, an exploration of alternative structurings should be a self-evident component of risk analysis. Structuring can be investigated in precise ways, and performing such investigations is a suitable task for risk analysts. To accept, without due reflection, the ways in which risk decisions have conventionally been structured should not be an option.

References

Arrow, K.J. (1982) Risk perception in psychology and economics, *Economic Inquiry*, 20, 1–9.

Ashford, N.A. and Hall. R.P. (2011) The importance of regulation-induced innovation for sustainable development. *Sustainability*, 3, 270–292.

Auer, C. (2006) US experience in applying "informed substitution" as a component in risk reduction and alternatives analyses. Transcript of an oral presentation given at the Chemicals, Health, and the Environment Conference Ottawa, Ontario, Canada, October 2006. BASTA, 2010. BASTAonline AB, http://www.bastaonline.se/english/bastaonline.4. 3d9ff17111f6fef70e9800039672.html. Accessed 2010–11–03.

Barnthouse, L.W. and Stahl, R.G. Jr. (2002) Quantifying natural resource injuries and ecological service reductions: challenges and opportunities. *Environmental Management*, 30, 1–12.

Buijs, A.E. (2009) Public support for river restoration. A mixed-method study into local residents' support for and framing of river management and ecological restoration in the Dutch floodplains, *Journal of Environmental Management*, 90, 2680–2689.

CEFIC (2005) CEFIC paper on substitution and authorisation under REACH, pp. 1–3.

Condorcet, N. de ([1793] 1847) Plan de Constitution, presenté a la convention nationale les 15 et 16 Février 1793, *Oeuvres*, vol. 12, pp. 333–415.

Denzin, N.K. and Keller, C.M. (1981) Frame analysis reconsidered, *Contemporary Sociology*, 10, 52–60.

Faden, R. and Beauchamp T. (1986) *A History and Theory of Informed Consent*. New York: Oxford University Press.

Grüne-Yanoff, T. (2016) Framing. In: S.O. Hansson and G. Hirsch Hadorn (eds), *The Argumentative Turn in Policy Analysis*. Springer.

Grüne-Yanoff, T. and Hertwig, R. (2016) Nudge versus boost: How coherent are policy and theory?, *Minds and Machines*, 26, 149–183.

Hansson, S.O. (1996) Decision-making under great uncertainty. *Philosophy of the Social Sciences*, 26, 369–386.

Hansson, S.O. (2004) Weighing risks and benefits. *Topoi*, 23, 145–52.

Hansson, S.O. (2006) Informed consent out of context. *Journal of Business Ethics*, 63, 149–154.

Hansson, S.O. (2007) Philosophical problems in cost–benefit analysis. *Economics and Philosophy*, 23, 163–183.

Hansson, S.O. (2010), Promoting inherent safety. *Process Safety and Environmental Protection*, 88, 168–172.

Hansson, S.O. (2013) *The Ethics of Risk. Ethical Analysis in an Uncertain World*. Palgrave Macmillan.

Hansson, S.O. (2016a) Evaluating the uncertainties. In: S.O. Hansson and G. Hirsch Hadorn (eds), *The Argumentative Turn in Policy Analysis*. Springer.

Hansson, S.O. (2016b) How to be cautious but open to learning: Time to update biotechnology and GMO legislation. *Risk Analysis*, 36(8), 1513–1517.

Hansson, S.O. (2017) Scope, options and horizons – key issues in decision structuring. *Ethical Theory and Moral Practice* (in press).

Hansson, S.O. and Oughton, D. (2013) Public participation – potential and pitfalls. In: D. Oughton and S.O. Hansson (eds), *Social and Ethical Aspects of Radiation Risk Management*. Elsevier Science.

Hansson, S.O., Molander, L., and Rudén, C. (2011) The substitution principle. *Regulatory Toxicology and Pharmacology*, 59, 454–460.

Hirsch Hadorn, G. (2016) Temporal strategies for decision making. In: S.O. Hansson and G. Hirsch Hadorn (eds), *The Argumentative Turn in Policy Analysis*. Springer.

Hornstein, D.T. (1993) Lessons from Federal pesticide regulation on the paradigms and politics of environmental law reform. *Yale Journal on Regulation*, 10, 369–446.

Ikeda, S. (1986) Managing technological and environmental risks in Japan. *Risk Analysis*, 6, 389–401.

Kletz, T.A. (2004) Inherently safer design: the growth of an idea. *Process Safety Progress*, 15, 5–8.

Kühberger, A. (1998) The influence of framing on risky decisions: A meta-analysis. *Organizational Behavior and Human Decision Processes*, 75, 23–55.

Machan, T.R. (1987) Human rights, workers' rights, and the "right" to occupational safety. In: G. Ezorsky (ed.), *Moral Rights in the Workplace*. State University of New York Press.

Oosterhuis, F. (2006) Substitution of hazardous substances. A case study in the framework of the project 'Assessing innovation dynamics induced by environmental policy'. Institute for Environmental Studies, Vrije Universiteit, Amsterdam 2006. http://dare.ubvu.vu.nl/bitstream/handle/1871/48351/198998. pdf?sequence=1.

Ramsberg, J. and Sjöberg, L. (1997) The cost-effectiveness of life saving interventions in Sweden. *Risk Analysis*, 17, 467–478.

Renn, O. (2005) *Risk governance towards an integrative approach. White paper No. 1*. International Risk Governance Council.

Sher, S. and McKenzie, C.R.M. (2006) Information leakage from logically equivalent frames. *Cognition*, 101, 467–494.

Simmons, J. (1987) Consent and fairness in planning land use. *Business and Professional Ethics Journal*, 6(2), 5–20.

Spurgin, E.W. (2006) Occupational safety and paternalism: Machan revisited, *Journal of Business Ethics*, 63, 155–173.

Tversky, A. and Kahneman, D. (1981) The framing of decisions and the psychology of choice. *Science*, 211(4481), 453–458.

Viscusi, W.K. (2000) Risk equity. *Journal of Legal Studies* 29, 843–871.

World Health Organization (2013) WHO global status report on road safety 2013: Supporting a decade of action. World Health Organization.

World Medical Association (2013) WMA Declaration of Helsinki – Ethical principles for medical research involving human subjects. https://www.wma. net/policies-post/wma-declaration-of-helsinki-ethical-principles-for-medical-research-involving-human-subjects/.

Part III

Applications

11

A Practical Approach to Risk Assessments from Design to Operation of Offshore Oil and Gas Installations

Vegard L. Tuft, Beate R. Wagnild, and Olga M. Slyngstad

Safetec Nordic AS, Trondheim, Norway

A quantitative risk analysis (QRA) is a powerful decision-support tool, used in many industries exposed to major accident risk. QRAs, for example, form part of the design of oil and gas installations on the Norwegian continental shelf. These QRAs are often large and comprehensive and are sometimes criticized for providing results too late, being too costly, and not adequately addressing uncertainty and possible deviations in input parameters. One particular challenge faced by risk analysts is to provide dimensioning accident loads in the very early design phase, with limited knowledge of what the final design will look like. Unless there are significant changes in design from the early design phase, the final as-built, dimensioning accidental loads should be similar to the first, early-stage results. It is, in this respect, imperative that the risk analysts inform decision makers about how deviations from the expected design may affect the risk results.

In order to provide a basis for decision making at the right time, we present a practical approach to performing and presenting input to the design. This type of work normally comprises a long list of assumptions and other premises, and hence it is important to see the results of risk assessments in view of the premises made; in other words, to understand how the premises affect the results. Examples are given of how to establish the dimensioning fire and explosion loads early in the design phase, as well as how to evaluate the uncertainty in the input parameters. Information is conveyed in a manner that is suitable as input to decision making, with an emphasis on the knowledge dimension. Early-stage results form a basis for further evaluations and updates throughout design phases, in a cost-efficient and flexible approach. The approach may result in a QRA at the end, or alternatively result in a series of smaller studies. The outcome of the approach depends on government

Knowledge in Risk Assessment and Management, First Edition. Edited by Terje Aven and Enrico Zio.
© 2018 John Wiley & Sons Ltd. Published 2018 by John Wiley & Sons Ltd.

regulations and the decision maker's needs. The approach also facilitates the use of important results from the design phase in barrier management during the operational phase of the installation.

11.1 Introduction

A quantitative risk analysis (QRA) is a powerful decision-support tool, used in many industries exposed to major accident risk; see for example Zio (2007) and Vose (2008). The QRA is often a large and comprehensive analysis used to provide input to the design, document whether the risk level is acceptable, and identify cost-effective risk-reducing measures. One example is the QRA in the design phase of offshore oil and gas installations on the Norwegian continental shelf (NCS). Ideally, the results and contents of the QRA should also be used actively to control major accident risk in the operational phase of the installation.

However, the role of the QRA as a decision-support tool in the oil and gas industry has lately been challenged. One challenge is that information resulting from the QRA may not be readily available to the people involved in the day-to-day decision-making. There are several reasons for this. The risk analysis may be time consuming to perform, and quantitative risk results may not be available when the decision needs to be made. Overall results may be too "high-level", not reflecting the level of detail required, or results may be presented in a strongly theoretical and method-intensive manner. Many authors have also highlighted the need for increased attention to uncertainty and addressing the strength of knowledge on which results are based; see for example Flage *et al.* (2014). This is particularly important when the risk analyst provides results early in the design phases, when there is limited knowledge of the design. It is imperative that the risk analyst produces a thought-through assessment of potential pitfalls in design and variations in the risk results.

Furthermore, QRAs of oil and gas installations are often criticized for being too costly, especially at times where the oil price is low. The cost of performing a comprehensive QRA is measured against its usefulness. Even more important, modifications to design due to changes in risk during the late, detailed-engineering or even as-built phases can be much costlier than incorporating measures early in the design phase, for example during specification of the concept. Hence, if the design does not change significantly during the design phases, neither should the QRA results. As mentioned above: potential pitfalls and variations should be assessed early.

This chapter describes a practical approach to performing and presenting input to designs, based on the interaction that typically takes place between risk analysts and engineers during the analysis. The approach addresses the issues mentioned above:

- Results from the early stage assessments must be calibrated against as-built models of similar installations.
- The effect of variations in design parameters must be investigated.
- There must be flexibility when it comes to cost of the study itself and time to delivery of results.
- Information must be conveyed in a manner that is suitable as input to informed decision-making.

Examples of how to provide early input to the design are presented using a case related to fire and explosion loads. The input is established before traditional, quantitative risk results are ready. Therefore, at this stage, there are no results to compare against traditional, quantitative risk acceptance criteria like the 1E-4 criterion. The 1E-4 criterion has been established in the Norwegian Facilities Regulations (PSA 2015) as the maximum acceptable annual frequency of impairment of the main safety functions.

The presented approach is cost-efficient and flexible for three reasons:

- Desired input to engineering can be established at an early stage
- It addresses uncertainty and deviations in the input parameters
- The level of complexity may be increased if required.

Early stage results form a basis for further evaluations and updates throughout the design phases. These updates may not be time-consuming to perform and may minimize the need for complete, costly QRA updates. The approach may result in a QRA at the end, or alternatively result in a series of smaller studies. The outcome of the process depends on government regulations and the decision makers' needs.

Many authors have highlighted the importance of seeing the results in view of the assumptions made and understanding how the assumptions affect the risk assessments, for example Beard (2004), Pate-Cornell (1999) and Aven (2012). Investigating uncertainty and the effect of deviations is an inherent part of the approach, and this chapter shows several examples on how results can be presented. However, as the studies grow in complexity and level of detail, more overall presentations of parameters and their effect on results may be required. When the studies comprise a large number of assumptions and other premises, it is a challenge to provide an easy-to-understand overview of these premises. This chapter describes a method denoted a "map of premises" (MoP) that:

1) provides an overview of premises in a risk analysis/assessment,
2) provides an overview of relevant premises for a given decision,
3) assesses uncertainty and the knowledge behind relevant premises,
4) and presents the results from that assessment at a manageable level of detail in order to support the decision making process.

A "map of premises" is illustrated by using results from the QRA of the example case.

The next sections of this chapter describes the example case (Section 11.2), how a traditional QRA may be executed and what results a typical QRA delivers (Section 11.3). This chapter then describes the alternative, practical approach (Section 11.4) and how results can be extended from the design phase to barrier management for follow-up of risk in the operational phase (Section 11.5). Section 11.5 also describes a stepwise approach to establishing an MoP. Advantages and disadvantages are discussed in Section 11.6.

11.2 Example Case

Offshore oil and gas installations vary in form, size, shape and complexity. The example case used throughout this chapter is a combined living quarters, wellhead, and production platform. It is shown in Figure 11.1. It represents a common design on the NCS as well as in other parts of the world. The installation consists of five main areas: the living quarters, the utility module, the wellhead area, the main process area and the gas compression module. The process area comprises a basic process system with first and second stage separators, a test separator, oil export pumps, one gas export riser top, and

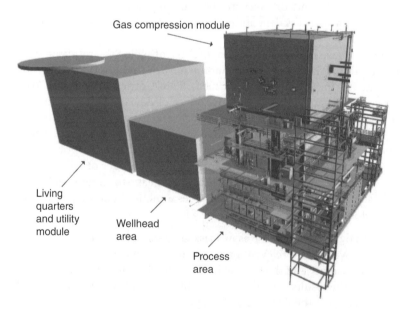

Figure 11.1 Simplified example of topside of an offshore oil and gas platform.

one oil export riser top. Production and gas injection manifolds as well as wellheads are located in the wellhead area, whereas a three-stage gas compression system is located in the gas compression module on top of the process area. Drilling and well operations are performed by a jack-up rig that is not included in the illustration.

11.3 The Traditional Approach

The QRA of an oil and gas installation is a comprehensive study. It models all events that may cause fatalities on the installation, such as helicopter accidents, ship collisions, fires and explosions due to process system leaks and blowouts, fires and explosions due to utility system leaks and so on. This is necessary to provide a complete risk picture of the installation. A QRA is conducted during several phases of an installation's lifetime, from concept, through front-end and detailed engineering, as-built, and further into the operations phase. Beginning with relatively high-level information in the early design phase, the QRA evolves to give more refined and detailed information on risk throughout the engineering and as-built phases, reflecting the increasing level of detail available.

A common perception of the QRA process is shown schematically in Figure 11.2. The bottom part of the figure shows that a QRA is performed for several phases during engineering. The topmost part of the figure details the QRA process in one of the phases. The QRA often begins with a kick-off, followed by a comprehensive analysis phase, draft report delivery, receipt of comments from the decision makers and finally, update of the analysis to a final report. As illustrated in Figure 11.2, results from the analysis phase are not necessarily aligned with the decision milestones of the engineering project. In addition, the total risk analysis may include studies with a level of detail higher than needed in the current engineering phase, or that are not needed at all. The process, as shown in Figure 11.2 is extensive and covers all potential, initiating, and accidental events. This is important when establishing the overall, quantitative risk picture for an installation in operation, but many of these hazards are not relevant during design. Regulations and standards also play an important role in installation design in addition to risk results.

The main purpose of a QRA in the design phase is typically to establish dimensioning accidental loads; these are the minimum loads the design must be able to withstand. Examples are the fire durations and explosion overpressures that the walls, structure and equipment must be able to withstand. This is used as input to choosing the design accidental load: the accidental load the installation is designed to withstand. Figures 11.3 and 11.4 show the output of a QRA for the example case: probability distributions for fire durations and

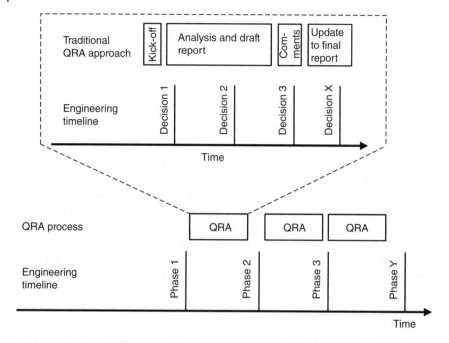

Figure 11.2 Timeline of a traditional QRA compared to the timeline of an engineering project going through various phases, from concept to detailed engineering and as-built. A QRA is performed in each phase and several engineering decisions are made in each phase.

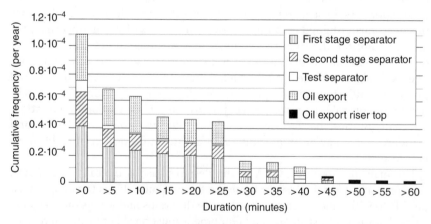

Figure 11.3 A "frequency-duration graph" for the process area in the example case: the cumulative frequency of pool fires lasting more than X minutes.

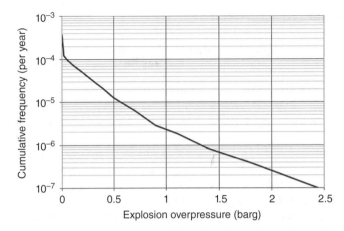

Figure 11.4 A "pressure-frequency graph" for the process area in the example case: the cumulative frequency for explosions with an overpressure higher than X barg.

explosion pressures, respectively. The different columns in Figure 11.3 indicate the annual frequency of fires lasting more than 0 min, more than 5 min and so on; that is, the cumulative frequency of fires lasting X minutes or more. Typically, one graph is established for pool fires and one graph is established for gas fires.

Figure 11.4 is an example of how explosion loads are presented. A so-called "pressure-frequency" graph shows the annual frequency of explosions producing an overpressure of X barg or higher towards a specific explosion barrier.

A fire duration or explosion overpressure corresponding to an annual frequency of 1E-4, 5E-5, or any other value below 1E-4, can be chosen as the design accidental load. If 5E-5 is chosen as basis for design, structural elements and walls must be able to withstand 15 min of pool fire and 0.2 barg explosion overpressure according to Figures 11.3 and 11.4, respectively.

These results are the outcome of a detailed risk analysis. As all details are not available in the early design phase, the frequency analysis can be based on generic data: industry averages and the knowledge available at the time of the study. Relevant questions to ask are, for instance:

- If changes are done to the design during the engineering project, how will this affect the fire duration or explosion pressures the installation must withstand?
- What if the equipment is changed, or the number of wind walls or amount of ventilation in an area is changed?
- What if the type and number of flanges are changed?

11.4   The Alternative Approach

A practical approach to design input was described by Tuft *et al.* (2016) and is illustrated in Figure 11.5. The approach comprises the following main steps:

1) Perform layout review and hazard identification to target main issues with the current design proposal and screening of analyses to perform. Determination of preliminary accidental loads based on experience from similar designs.
2) Perform simplified analyses of essential issues as selected in Step 1, for example fire duration and explosion overpressure studies. Establish a base case and perform associated sensitivity studies.
3) Undertake detailed analyses if required, including for example supplementary fire simulations, gas dispersion simulations, structural response analyses, or probabilistic fire and explosion analyses.
4) Complete a QRA, if required. The scope of the QRA should take findings from Steps 1–3 into consideration, study in more detail the topics where issues have been identified and focus on the areas where the QRA or more specialized studies can provide input to the decision makers.

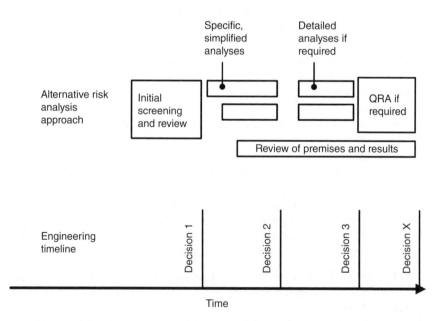

Figure 11.5 Suggested practical approach with timeline and scope of risk analysis process adapted to the engineering project.

The ultimate goal is to align the risk analysis process with the engineering project. This chapter describes the important start-up of this process: Steps 1 and 2 above. The process shown in Figure 11.5 also includes a continuous review of the important premises and results from Step 2. Premises and results must be presented in a manner that simplifies evaluation of future changes to design. This review of relevant premises and results can be continued into the operational phase, as a part of barrier management in operation. The aim is that decision makers can evaluate whether the design or operation is within the boundaries established in the early design phase. As the studies become more detailed and complex, an overall presentation of parameters as well as their sensitivity and effect on results must be established. This chapter also presents a way of establishing an overview of parameters in QRAs.

11.4.1 Step 1: Layout Review

When the purpose of the risk analysis is to provide input to a design, the risk analysis must be initiated at an early stage when it is possible to influence the design. Early in the project phase, where only the main equipment and a rough layout is available, the basis of the analysis is usually a hazard identification and layout review. This phase includes early assessments of the design to identify critical issues, for example:

- which fire scenarios may expose escape routes
- which fire scenarios may expose evacuation means
- areas with large inventories that can produce large gas clouds and/or sustain long lasting fires
- areas with limited ventilation where small gas clouds can result in high explosion pressures.

Topics that influence the fire and explosion accidental loads and should be discussed are, for example, ventilation (amount of weather cladding, grating and so on), placement of equipment, equipment density, composition of oil/gas and operating conditions, potential volume of inventories, dimensions of the modules and so on. It is then possible to compare the expected installation design to earlier projects, similar installations and so on, using as-built results for comparison. In this evaluation, it is critical that several of the participants have long experience with engineering and design against the relevant accidental loads and have the capability to understand the complex nature of these loads.

Another purpose of Step 1 is to identify which analyses must be performed in Step 2; that is, where more knowledge is needed, for example if the design deviates too much from the available as-built models or to verify the first estimate.

11.4.2   Step 2: Simplified Analyses

In this section, a simplified approach to fire and explosion analyses is described. The former is based on relatively simple-to-perform leak-duration calculations whereas the latter is based on simulations in a 3D computer model of the installation. It is possible to proceed to Step 2 even if the engineering crew has not yet established a computer model of the installation. If there is an existing installation with a similar design and if an as-built model of that installation is available, Step 2 can be performed on that model. It is especially important to assess the possibility of deviations from the chosen model and the effect of those deviations.

11.4.2.1   Fire Accidental Loads

The simplified input to fire accidental loads consists of estimating potential leak and fire durations, with the following steps:

- Establish a base case. Based on current knowledge of the main process equipment, choose one or two types of representative equipment, for example separators with a long duration and many potential leak points. This is typically equipment that will contribute significantly to the traditional frequency-based estimation of accidental fire loads, for example as shown in Figure 11.3. A gas compression stage should also be chosen as representative equipment if relevant. Estimate a set of values for inventory, operating temperatures and pressures, and so on, as input to the leak-duration model.
- Assume that detection, isolation and blowdown is successful. The reason for this is that scenarios in which these three safety systems do not function as intended, do not contribute significantly to the traditional frequency-based estimation of accidental fire loads.
- Calculate the leak duration: the time from the leak starting until the leak has reached a specific cut-off rate (for example 2 kg/s as input to specification of passive fire protection of equipment; another cut-off may be more relevant when assessing exposure of firewalls and load-bearing structures). This is the base-case duration.
- Keeping every input parameter constant except one, estimate a realistic interval in which this one parameter may vary and calculate the corresponding variation in leak duration. This is in practice a uniform probability distribution of the given input parameter. Repeat this procedure for all relevant input parameters. Plot the results in a diagram, as shown in Figure 11.6. Horizontal lines in Figure 11.6 indicate the base-case leak duration for two different leak hole sizes. Squares and circles show how leak duration varies when one parameter is varied while the other parameters remain fixed at the base-case value.
- Calculate leak duration for a large number of realistic combinations of input parameter values, without restricting some parameters to the base-case value. Show results in pivot tables, histograms, scatter plots, and so on, and

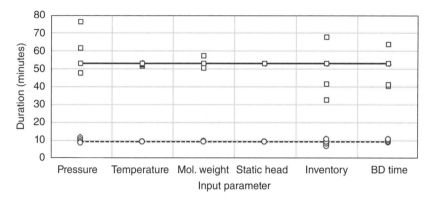

Figure 11.6 Illustration of a sensitivity study, showing how different input parameters impact leak duration when one parameter is varied while the other parameters remain fixed at the base case value. Horizontal lines indicate the leak duration of the base case for medium (topmost line) and large (dashed line) leaks. Square markers represent duration calculations for a medium leak hole size. Circles represent duration calculations for a large leak hole size.

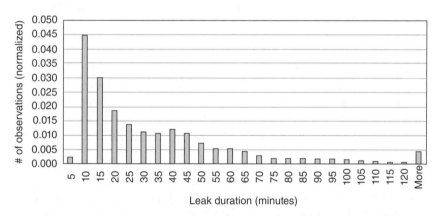

Figure 11.7 Histogram showing potential leak durations for 230 000 combinations of input parameter values and leak hole sizes, without restricting some parameter values to the base-case value.

identify combinations of input parameters that produce longer durations than the base case. A scatter plot with horizontal and vertical axes representing the parameter value and corresponding leak duration, respectively, is an easy way to illustrate the effect of an input parameter. An example histogram is shown in Figure 11.7 and a scatter plot is shown in Figure 11.8.

• Assess the effect of bunding, grating, and so on, on the fire size and duration.

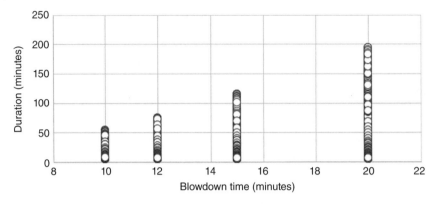

Figure 11.8 Scatter plot showing potential leak durations when the blowdown time varies.

Figure 11.6 shows potential durations of oil leaks from the first stage separa-tor in our example case. Two typical leak hole sizes (medium and large) are included in the calculations. Cut-off is set to 2 kg/s. According to Figure 11.6 there are some realistic input parameter values resulting in longer leak dura-tions than the base case, especially for medium-sized leaks.

In order to identify unfavourable combinations of parameters, leak duration was calculated for 230 000 combinations of realistic input parameter values and leak hole sizes, and the result is shown in Figure 11.7. The figure is a histo-gram of leak duration calculations, showing that approximately 85% of the leaks have a duration shorter than 60 min. There are also combinations of parameters resulting in durations up to 200 min. Note that the histogram does not take into consideration the probability of each leak occurring, nor the igni-tion probability of each leak.

Figure 11.8 is a scatter plot showing how the leak duration in Figure 11.7 varies as the blowdown time varies. By limiting the blowdown time to 15 min, leak durations can be limited to 120 min. Figure 11.9 shows how the leak dura-tion varies as the amount of oil in the separator varies, when the blowdown time is limited to 15 min. By also limiting the volume of oil in the separator to, for example, 55 m^3, the maximum leak duration can be reduced to 100 min.

In our example case the procedure can be repeated for all the process equip-ment in order to investigate how the chosen leak scenario compares to other leak scenarios and whether it is representative, conservative, and so on.

The accidental fire load is a combination of thermal radiation and fire dura-tion. It is common to apply thermal radiation levels specified in NORSOK S-001 (SN 2008) if the design does not dictate otherwise. In the example case, there is a combination of a plated deck and grating in the process area. There is no bunding that will affect the spread of the pool significantly, and the leak duration is considered representative for the fire duration. However, the drain

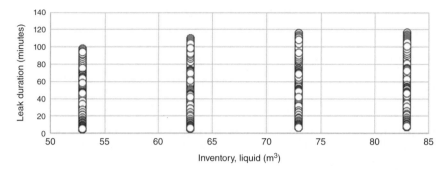

Figure 11.9 Scatter plot showing potential leak durations when the inventory varies and when limiting blowdown time to 15 min.

system is not credited, and grating will affect the pool size and which parts of the module that are exposed to the fire. The next step (Step 3) is typically to specify dimensioning fire scenarios, perform fire simulations, and specify in more detail heat loads towards structural elements and equipment.

11.4.2.2 Explosion Accidental Loads

The complex nature of an explosion makes it difficult to easily come up with design accidental loads without any analysis as a basis. The explosion risk depends on several parameters, such as:

- release scenario (duration of a leak and amount of gas released)
- gas composition
- confinement (enclosure and ventilation conditions)
- gas accumulation within module (dispersion of gas)
- ignition location
- congestion/equipment density
- layout configuration/geometry.

A base case for explosion simulations is established based on the available geometry model. Geometry and the equipment density are important factors that affect the explosion risk significantly. A critical task is to apply artificial congestion to represent realistic equipment densities, based on experience from similar as-built geometries. To ensure that the explosion risk is not underestimated, wind walls should be included to a large extent in the model.

When the geometry model has been established the following steps may be conducted:

- Run explosion simulations. A gas cloud may accumulate anywhere within an area, and the gas cloud size is dependent upon the release scenario and ventilation conditions. A large number of different gas cloud sizes should be reviewed in order to establish a trend. Ignition may also take place at any

Cloud	Ignition point					
size (%)	1	2	3	4	5	6
5	0.00	0.06	0.00	0.08	0.06	0.04
15	0.06	0.16	0.08	0.29	0.17	0.14
30	0.14	0.21	0.12	0.26	0.43	0.26

Figure 11.10 Matrix showing maximum explosion overpressure for different combinations of ignition locations (gas cloud locations) and cloud sizes (size given as a volume percentage of the module) for the base case.

location in an area as, for instance, electrical equipment can be a potential ignition source. Areas with rotating equipment, like pumps and compressors, represent additional potential ignition sources. The ignition may take place in different locations in the gas cloud, either at the edge/corner or within the gas cloud itself, depending on what type of ignition source ignites the gas. Based on the above considerations, a set of cloud sizes and ignition points are established, applying center and edge/corner ignition for all gas clouds, based on recommendations in, for instance, NORSOK Z-013 (SN 2010) or other relevant standards. As a large number of ignition locations along with both center and edge/corner ignition is applied, it is considered that the explosion risk in the area is sufficiently covered.

- Establish an explosion overpressure matrix that shows maximum explosion overpressure towards a specific barrier. An example is shown in Figure 11.10. This matrix shows what explosion loads can be expected for different cloud sizes and ignition points and indicates if there are any particularly problematic cloud sizes or ignition locations.
- Establish representative explosion loads. Discuss the realistic explosion loads that the barriers (wall, deck, or equipment) can withstand, and indicate this, for example, with colour coding in the matrix in Figure 11.10. A white background in the figure indicates explosion pressures the engineers know that the structure can withstand, whereas white text on a dark grey background (see Figure 11.12) indicates pressures the structure cannot withstand. A medium grey background means pressure levels the structure may or may not withstand.
- Present additional results (optional). Create a histogram, as shown in Figure 11.11, or a cumulative distribution of explosion overpressures. Many simulations are expected to produce high explosion pressures and the results are not weighted with respect to their probability of occurring. Thus a balanced, not overly conservative presentation is required. One way of doing this is to let the histogram distinguish between, for example, three different cloud sizes, as shown in Figure 11.11.

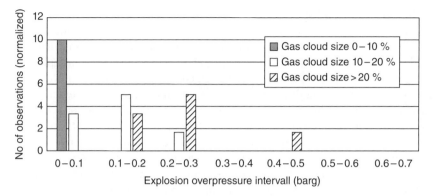

Figure 11.11 Number of simulations producing an explosion overpressure within a given pressure interval. The histogram distinguishes between different gas cloud sizes (0–10, 10–30, and 30–100 volume % of the module).

Cloud size (%)	Ignition point					
	1	2	3	4	5	6
5	0.00	0.07	0.01	0.10	0.08	0.06
15	0.06	0.16	0.10	0.33	0.24	0.17
30	0.15	0.22	0.12	0.33	0.64	0.32

Figure 11.12 Matrix showing maximum explosion overpressure for different combinations of ignition locations (gas cloud locations) and cloud sizes (size given as a volume % of the module) for sensitivity with increased congestion.

- Run supporting gas dispersion simulations (optional): The discussion in the steps above can be supported by a limited number of gas dispersion simulations to indicate what gas clouds could potentially be generated in the area. If a coarse assessment of structural capacity is available, this will then give an indication of what typical maximum gas cloud sizes are acceptable without any need for increasing the structural design/capacity.
- Run explosion simulations with different equipment densities: As the equipment density (congestion) is one of the most critical input parameters, identical simulations should be performed for additional equipment density arrangements, for example one set with increased density and one set with reduced density. The results will indicate the criticality of ensuring a representative equipment density. Figure 11.12 shows the simulations in Figure 11.10 repeated with increased equipment density.

Figure 11.10 shows the base case results for the process area. Explosion pressures are in general low compared to the ability of the structure to resist an explosion. However, Figure 11.10 shows that gas cloud ignition in locations 4 and 5 in particular may produce relatively high explosion pressures. Equipment density in the area is based on typical values from similar offshore installations on the Norwegian continental shelf. Figure 11.12 shows the change in explosion pressures when equipment density (artificial congestion) is increased. Now, gas clouds reaching and igniting in location 5 produce explosion pressures the structure cannot withstand, if the gas cloud is large enough. This could be due to unfavourable positioning of equipment close to the ignition point, and more sensitivities of the main equipment layout should therefore be performed.

Potential explosion overpressures can be identified in a short period of time, and the sensitivity of the design to differences in equipment density is investigated as part of the approach. The results may indicate a need for further review of the design and improvement of the layout arrangement. Identification of critical areas or unfavourable layout arrangements are also important results from the analysis.

It is important to notice that the results from this study may be easily "upgraded" to a probabilistic analysis in Step 3, including a frequency assessment as well as ventilation and dispersion simulations. The explosion results will indicate what dispersion simulations should be prioritized if a limited number of gas dispersion simulations is to be performed.

11.5   Input to Evaluation in Design, Operation and Barrier Management

11.5.1   Continuous Evaluation

The calculations in the simplified approach rely on a set of input parameters. As the effect of changes in these parameters has been investigated as an inherent part of the approach, some changes in design can be evaluated continuously throughout the design phases and also during operations, based on the early-stage results. This requires that the study is presented in a way that simplifies further evaluation and updates. An overview of input parameters, other premises, assessments and calculation results must be presented in an easy-to-follow manner. The same system as presented for barrier management later in this chapter can be used for this purpose. Parameters and corresponding accidental loads presented in pivot tables, scatter plots, and so on, provide the updated load if a parameter is changed within the already investigated interval.

11.5.2   Assessing and Communicating Uncertainty in Complex Analyses

The overview of input parameters and calculations presented in Figures 11.6–11.12 are easy to follow when there is a limited number of parameters. When there are more complex analyses or even a full QRA, a top-level overview is required. The general idea is that it should be possible to "drill down" from the top-level overview to the details provided by the analysis.

A "map" of premises (MoP) was presented by Tuft *et al.* (2015) as an example of a top-level overview covering the basis of QRAs. The steps for establishing a map are described below. The word "premises" here includes methodology, historical data, and other bases for the risk analysis, as well as the assumptions. In summary, the steps described below are performed for each premise to assess uncertainty in the results. Steps A and B imply that the method is tailored towards assessing a specific decision or result rather than assessing the overall uncertainty in the QRA results. A map is here applied to the dimensioning accidental fire load presented in Figure 11.3.

A) Organize premises and assess relevance. Which premises influence the result and conclusion? For example, what premises are relevant for calculating annual frequency of fires and fire duration?

B) Assess and present the effect deviations in assumed values and premises have on results (sensitivity). To what extent do the relevant premises influence fire duration and/or frequency of fires?

C) Assess and present strength of knowledge (SoK). To what extent are deviations from assumptions and premises possible, and is more knowledge of the parameter in question required?

A typical QRA covers a long list of scenarios modelled by event trees and may comprise hundreds of premises. An event tree represents the possible sequence of events, from accident to possible outcome. In case of hydrocarbon leaks, the event trees start with the leak occurring, and cover how the leak may develop, and the possible consequences of that leak. We need a system to group and summarize all relevant premises used in the event tree and present the results in an easy-to-follow manner. In the method described here, the premises are divided into groups that represent the nodes in the event tree. Figure 11.13 shows a simplified schematic that summarizes which nodes are included in a typical event tree and presents them roughly in the order they may appear.

The circles (nodes) in Figure 11.13 are:

- HC leak: the annual frequency of the initiating leak
- gas detection: the probability of detecting a hydrocarbon leak
- ignition: the probability of immediate or delayed ignition

Chain of events

Figure 11.13 Schematic representing the chain of event for hydrocarbon leaks. See main text for definitions.

- fire detection: the probability of detecting a fire
- isolation: the probability of isolation valves closing
- blowdown: the probability of successful blowdown
- deluge: the probability of releasing deluge
- escalation: the probability of a fire or explosion escalating to other equipment containing hydrocarbons and becoming a bigger event than the initial fire/explosion
- consequence: the probability of impairing main safety functions and/or personnel.

In addition, a node "Plf." must be introduced into the diagram to represent premises in the design or operation of the platform that are not completely covered by the nodes in the event tree.

Step A of the method is to establish what premises are associated with which node (that is, with which circle in the diagram in Figure 11.13). Table 11.1 is a list of premises that are related to each node, although Table 11.1 shows only a selection of all premises of a QRA, for the sake of simplicity. Normally, all premises should be included. Several premises may also be relevant in several parts of the chain of events. The items "deluge" and "consequence" are considered irrelevant in this context as the effect of deluge and fire water is not to be credited when establishing dimensioning accidental loads and because criteria for impairment of personnel and equipment are irrelevant when assessing the duration of the fire. Escalation to other hydrocarbon-containing equipment is not part of this duration assessment.

It is common to divide premises further into three categories, making it easier to find relevant premises:

- analytical (premises related to the methodology used in the QRA)
- operational (related to daily operation and condition of the platform)
- design.

There may be other suitable categories as well. The categorization should be included in the final overview, shown in Figure 11.14.

A method for assessing sensitivity – how the results or conclusions change when premises change – is required. We adopt the method presented by Flage and Aven (2009) and demonstrated by Aven and Pedersen (2014), although here adapted to the specific example case. It is beyond the scope of this chapter to present the details of the method. Instead the interested reader is referred to the abovementioned papers.

The sensitivity is categorized into "low", "medium", and "high" according to certain criteria. The criteria will vary from analysis to analysis and depend on the decision to be made and what are considered realistic changes in assumptions and premises. For illustration purposes, the sensitivity criterion is here defined as the change in dimensioning fire duration for a 10%

Table 11.1 A selection of premises from the QRA.

ID	Associated nodes	Premise name	Premise
P1	Consequence	Location and amount of grating	Grating close to firewall on mezzanine level in process area
P2	Plf./escalation	Sectioning of process equipment	(List of emergency shutdown valves)
P3	HC leak/escalation	Condition of hydrocarbon segment (corrosion etc.)	New equipment, no corrosion
P4	HC leak	Amount and type of equipment in the area	(Description of equipment in the area, number of valves, flanges etc.)
P5	HC leak	Probability of leak per type of equipment	According to the UK Health and Safety Executive database
P6	Plf./gas detection/ ignition/escalation/ consequence	Inventory of process equipment	73 m^3 in first-stage separator, ...
P7	HC leak/gas detection/Ignition	Operation conditions (pressure, temperature) of process equipment	50 bar, 80°C in first-stage separator, ...
P8	HC leak	Categorization of leaks according to leak rate	Small leaks: 0.1–2 kg/s, medium leaks: 2–10 kg/s, large leaks: >10 kg/s
P9	Ignition	Probability of immediate ignition	0.01 for large leaks, ...
P10	Fire detection	Reliability of fire detection	0.98
P11	Fire detection	Response time of fire detectors	5 s
P12	Fire detection	Vulnerability of fire detection	If one detector fails due to the fire itself, other detectors are still in operation.
P13	Isolation	Reliability of emergency shutdown valves and logic	0.99
P14	Isolation	Vulnerability of emergency shutdown valves	Can resist a jet fire for 30 min, ...
P15	Isolation	Time to close shutdown valves	2 s per inch
P16	Blowdown	Reliability of blowdown valves and logic	0.99

(Continued)

Table 11.1 (Continued)

ID	Associated nodes	Premise name	Premise
P17	Plf./blowdown	Capacity of blowdown system	According to API 512
P18	Blowdown	Vulnerability	Can resist a jet fire for 30 min, ...
P19	Blowdown	Time to open blowdown valves	2 s per inch
P20	Deluge	Reliability of deluge system	0.99
P21	Deluge	Vulnerability of deluge system	Can resist a jet fire for 30 min, ...
P22	Deluge/escalation/ consequence	Capacity of deluge system	10 (l/min)/m²
P23	Escalation	Fire resistance of equipment containing hydro carbons	350 kW/m² for 15 min
P24	Consequence	Criteria for death of personnel	25 kW/m² due to fire causes immediate fatality,...
P25	Consequence	Criteria for impairment of load bearing structure etc.	Jet fire exposing load bearing structure for more than 30 min, ...

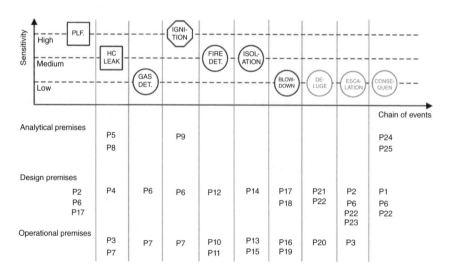

Figure 11.14 Example map of premises for dimensioning accidental fire load.

change in the assumed value. Low sensitivity is less than 5 min change, medium sensitivity is 5–15 min change, whereas high sensitivity is more than 15 min change. All relevant premises are evaluated against this criterion, either through a qualitative assessment or through a quantitative sensitivity analysis. However, some premises are not quantitative by nature, for example whether process equipment is segmented into two smaller segments or one large one. In this case a "realistic" change in the premise is considered instead of the 10% change.

Premise P2, related to the node "Plf.", is an example of a premise where the latter criterion applies. In the example case, a realistic change in segmentation is that one segment could be split into two segments. This could have a large impact on segment volumes and thus fire durations; that is, high sensitivity. When the sectioning has been established by P2, P6 (inventory) is the assumed amount of hydrocarbons in the segments, which can vary since, for example, different manufacturers of separators may have different sized separators. P6 is a premise where the quantitative criterion applies. In the example case, a 10% change will have a medium impact on the fire duration, i.e. medium sensitivity. The overall sensitivity of the node "Plf." is set to "high" due to at least one related premise having high sensitivity.

A 10% increase in process leak frequency (node "HC leak"), related either to the condition of process equipment (P3), the amount of process equipment in the area (P4), and the probability of leak per type of equipment (P5), can lead to a 5–15 min increase in dimensioning fire duration, which falls into the category of medium sensitivity. The other premises are considered to have low sensitivity. Since at least one premise has medium sensitivity, the overall sensitivity of "HC leak" is defined as medium. If none of the premises associated with a node has high sensitivity, but at least one premise has medium sensitivity, the overall sensitivity of the node is "medium".

A part of assessing uncertainty in the result is to evaluate the background knowledge of assumed values and judgements and to consider the possibility of deviations in the premises. This is also referred to as a strength of knowledge (SoK) assessment in the analysis. The method of assessing SoK presented by Flage and Aven (2009) and demonstrated by Aven and Pedersen (2014) is adopted. Again, it is beyond the scope of this chapter to describe the details of this method. Here, one concept of its use is illustrated, and the interested reader is referred to the above-mentioned papers or Aven (2014) for more details and discussions, as well as to Chapter 1 of this book.

The SoK can be categorized as weak, medium, or strong according to certain criteria. Flage and Aven (2009) defines the knowledge as weak if one or more of these conditions is true:

- The assumptions made represent strong simplifications.
- Data/information are/is nonexistent or highly unreliable/irrelevant.

- There is strong disagreement among experts.
- The phenomena involved are poorly understood, models are nonexistent or known/believed to give poor predictions.

If all of the following conditions are met (whenever they are relevant), the knowledge is considered strong:

- The assumptions made are seen as very reasonable.
- Large amounts of reliable and relevant data/information are available.
- There is broad agreement among experts.
- The phenomena involved are well understood; the models used are known to give predictions with the required accuracy.

Cases in between are classified as having a medium strength of knowledge.

Again the criteria may depend on the decision to be made and vary from analysis to analysis. In this example case, it is also practical to introduce another criterion: as uncertainty often is related to whether a certain type of equipment or system is to be installed or whether a certain activity is to be performed, strong SoK is defined as "it has been decided to install the system/equipment or to perform the activity". Medium SoK is defined as "it has been decided to install the equipment or perform the activity, but the exact design or configuration has not been decided upon and minor changes may occur". Weak SoK is then "It has not yet been decided to install the equipment or perform the activity", or "it has been decided to install the equipment or perform the activity, but there may be significant changes to its configuration or the extent of the activity". The knowledge associated with each premise is then assessed according to these criteria.

During platform design, in the example case, the final design of the process system has not been decided upon as there are two alternative configurations under consideration, with different volumes and amounts of equipment. It is assessed that some major changes to the design may occur and that the SoK is weak according to the criterion above. This is related to premises P2 and P4. When at least one premise associated with a node has weak SoK, the overall SoK of that node is also defined as weak. If none of the premises associated with a node has weak SoK, but at least one premise is medium SoK, the overall SoK of the node is "medium". Otherwise SoK of the node is strong. Thus, "Plf." and "HC leak" are both set to "weak".

The total assessment of sensitivity and knowledge can be summarized in a map of premises, as shown in Figure 11.14. This identifies which node and category the different premises belong to, as well as the overall sensitivity and knowledge of each node. The y-axis indicates the sensitivity of the node. Weak, medium, and strong SoK are indicated by square, chamfered rectangular, and round nodes, respectively. Sensitivity and SoK of each premise could also be indicated by, for example, text colour or underlining in the map. This map must of course be supplemented by a description of the assessments.

In order to decide the design accidental load, measures should be taken to deal with nodes with weak and medium SoK that also have a large influence on results (high sensitivity), for example "HC leak". Design accidental load specifications should have ample margins but without being overly conservative.

The map provides an overview of which premises are related to which nodes in the chain of events. Thus, the decision maker can go into more detail on a critical part in the chain of events, see what premises are relevant, and see whether those premises may influence other parts in the chain of events. An alternative approach is to let each node represent a barrier function instead of nodes in an event tree, using the map as a tool in barrier management. This is discussed next.

11.5.3 Barrier Management

Barrier management is the processes of monitoring, verifying, and evaluating the performance of barriers that prevent or mitigate major accident risks on an installation. The process ensures that evaluations regarding barrier degradation are conducted continuously and that modifications and improvements are initiated if needed.

The term "barrier" is commonly defined as any "technical, operational and organizational elements which are intended individually or collectively to reduce possibility for a specific error, hazard or accident to occur, or which limit its harm/disadvantages". This is the definition given by the Petroleum Safety Authority in Norway (PSA 2013).

A QRA is frequently used as input in the barrier management process to identify which major accident hazards can occur in each area on an installation, and to a certain extent to identify which barriers are available. PSA states that "the industry must ensure that relationships between risk assessments and barrier management are made clear" (PSA 2013). A required step in this process is to identify the necessary barrier functions and elements, but also to link the risk assessments to these functions and elements.

A barrier grid is a graphical overview of different major accident hazards that can occur in an area, including the sequence of events and barrier functions that prevent and mitigate the hazards. The topmost part of Figure 11.15 shows an example of a barrier grid for hydrocarbon leaks. The grid illustrates dependencies between barrier functions (boxes with white background) and possible scenarios if a barrier function fails to fulfil its function (grey boxes). It is beyond the scope of this chapter to discuss the details of barrier functions, grids, and management. Reference is made to, for example, Blix *et al.* (2015), the PSA (PSA 2013), and other introductions to the topic.

The grid is an alternative way of presenting a sequence of events and differs slightly from the QRA event trees. Table 11.2 shows the relationship between

Table 11.2 The relation between barrier functions and the chain of events from the QRA.

Barrier function	Part of chain of events (event tree) in QRA								
	HC leak	Gas detection	Ignition	Fire detection	Isolation	Blowdown	Deluge	Escalation	Consequence
Prevent leak	X								
Limit size of leak		X		X	X	X			
Prevent ignition			X						
Prevent escalation				X	X	X	X	X	
Prevent fatalities during escape and evacuation									X

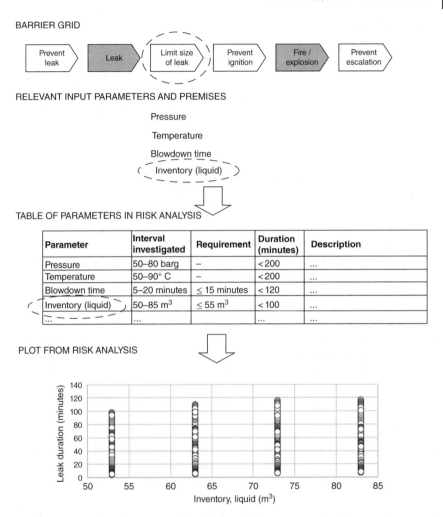

Figure 11.15 Illustration of how information is conveyed from top-level barrier grid to low-level calculations via an overview of parameters.

barrier functions and the QRA way of analysing the chain of events for hydro-carbon leaks.

Figure 11.15 illustrates how parameters in the fire analysis can be listed below their relevant barrier functions. This is a mapping of risk-related parameters to barrier management. The parameters can be linked to a table of input parameters to the risk analysis, and also to a plot showing the effect of changes in this parameter. Input parameters to the leak durations belong to the "Limit size of leak" barrier function.

11.6 Discussion

The underlying principle of the simplified analyses is that premises and the effect of deviations from those premises are discussed and communicated early in the design process. Changes in premises can thereafter be evaluated throughout the various stages of the design process, based on these early results, instead of by updating a full QRA.

The suggested approach:

- can be applied today as it does not require extensive development of new methods, but relies on methods from current QRAs
- indicates the potential fire durations and explosion pressures early in the design phase
- is independent of frequency, meaning that if more potential leak points are introduced, the fire specification is still valid; the specification is not based on a fire occurring at a given frequency but is based on an informed decision on which potential fire durations the installation shall be able to withstand: a worst case scenario or any other choice of dimensioning scenario
- is based on fewer premises than a traditional probabilistic assessment of accidental loads
- gives an understanding on the criticality of input parameters like blowdown time and equipment density
- can be easily expanded to cover the fire scenarios where isolation and blow-down fail
- indicates typical maximum gas cloud size that can give explosion loads above design
- indicates unfavourable ignition locations
- indicates how quickly the gas detection system should respond; if small gas clouds give explosion loads close to expected capacity, a quick and reliable detection system is required to ensure that a hydrocarbon release is detected quickly
- indicates if there is a need for smaller inventories in process equipment, as small inventories will produce small gas clouds
- identifies unfavourable layout arrangements.
- can easily be used as part of a probabilistic analysis later in the project phase when the detailed input to such an analysis is available.

A larger amount of process equipment can be included in the leak duration analysis to improve the basis for decision making. This does not require much extra computation time. However, the amount of information to digest can be very large for large installations. This requires that the information is presented in an easy-to-follow manner.

The main concern with the presented approach for explosion analyses is the reduced understanding of gas accumulation in the area. As the simplified method is not based on gas dispersion simulations, the gas build-up potential and information on typical stagnation zones are not identified. As a result, gas dispersion simulations should be performed to support the explosion pressure calculations. A probabilistic analysis can give a good understanding of the complex nature of an explosion, taking into account how an initial release develops and the pressure build-up upon ignition.

Unlike the traditional QRA, the simplified approach does not focus on the total risk picture. No probabilities or frequencies are determined in the early phase. There may be a chance of choosing a dimensioning accidental load which in a QRA would have a low calculated probability. Instead, the choice of dimensioning load is scenario based. Figure 11.3 shows that the dimensioning fire duration found from a probability-based approach is 15–35 min, depending on whether 5E-5 or 1E-5 is chosen as dimensioning fire frequency. The calculations in the simplified approach show that medium-sized leaks may have longer fire durations, which is not accounted for by choosing 35 min as the specification for passive fire protection. On the other hand, these leaks have a smaller ignition probability than the large leaks in the QRA. It is important that the party that performs the risk analysis has a good understanding of the different risk contributors and the impact of different accident scenarios.

The QRA often presents risk results as a fatal accident rate or a single frequency for impairment of a main safety function. This may lead the reader to believe that the results are based on stronger knowledge than they are in reality. By presenting the results not as a single answer, but as a sample space where the outcome varies with the possible choices in installation design, the reader is no longer led to believe that there is a high degree of certainty in the answer. However, it is still equally important to describe the level of uncertainty and the impact of the assumptions made in the analyses.

A map of premises (MoP) was presented as a way of organizing premises in QRAs. Although possible, it is not considered practicable to establish a map of premises for every result in the QRA or every decision to be made. One solution for overcoming this challenge is to automate the process of assessing sensitivity, implementing a routine that adjusts an input parameter to a certain value and recalculates the risk result automatically, where possible. An alternative approach is to establish a simplified, general map for the installation that shows the SoKs of all premises but does not show the sensitivities. A selection of results based on nodes with weak or medium SoKs can then be subject to a complete map of premises, as described in this chapter.

All premises from the analysis should be assessed and included in the MoP, even premises that are considered "obvious", and normally not considered important, or those that are left out or missing from a typical list of premises for other reasons. Finding these premises may require a review of methods and tools used in the QRA, as well as a review of design and operational premises.

As a consequence, the map may grow larger and become less easy to follow, but that can be handled by the way the map is presented.

The map can also be used for qualitative risk analyses, scenario assessments, and so on. Finding proper criteria for sensitivity and SoK may in some cases be challenging, whether the analysis is quantitative or qualitative, and will depend on the decision to be made and the type of analysis.

There may be a tighter integration between the risk analysis and barrier management in operation by defining barrier functions at an early design phase. In this way, the relevance of the premises and assessments in the risk analysis towards barrier management is secured from the beginning by adapting the way results are presented. Including operational premises from the risk analysis in barrier grids allows for barrier management evaluations and implementations of measures when these premises are not met. For instance, one could include the premise that an area has a specified ventilation level. If containers are stored such that ventilation is blocked, or if equipment, scaffolding, or weather walls are added, the ventilation in an area may not be as good as assumed in the risk analysis. Decreased ventilation may influence several barrier functions in a sequence of events, for example "Prevent ignition" (due to changed gas dispersion) and "Prevent escalation" (due to increase in explosion pressures). Barrier elements within these barrier functions, for example blast walls, may not be able to cope with the explosion pressure if the design premises are exceeded. In such instances, an operator must evaluate whether or not to introduce compensating measures or decide not to do certain activities (for example hot work).

11.7 Conclusions

QRAs of oil and gas installations are often criticized for being too costly, especially at times when the oil price is low. The cost of performing a comprehensive QRA is measured against its usefulness. Even more important, modifications to design due to changes in risk results in late detailed engineering or even as-built phases can be much costlier than incorporating measures early in the design phase, for example during specification of the concept. It is imperative that the risk analyst produces a sound assessment of potential pitfalls in design and variations in the risk results.

This chapter presents a practical approach to providing input to design, exemplified by fire and explosion accidental loads. The aim of this approach is to have the essential input ready at the various project decision milestones and to increase the level of detail in the analyses as required through the engineering project.

The simplified fire and explosion studies are specialized and relatively small studies that can be performed in a short time. Sensitivity studies provide knowledge of which parameters affect fire durations and explosion overpressures. These early stage results are the basis for assessing design changes and are inputs to barrier management in the operational phase.

The presented approach focuses on the physical effect of adjusting design parameters. The probability of a scenario or accidental load occurring is not quantified. This is a challenge, as the traditional approach and associated decision making is often based on the "1E-4 criterion". This criterion is established in Norwegian government regulations, such as the Facilities Regulations (PSA 2015). New definitions of risk acceptance criteria and acceptable accidental loads must be established if simplified studies are not to result in a traditional QRA.

This chapter also describes a method for providing an overview of the premises in a QRA, including the limitations of the premises and potential effects on the results. The method has been applied to a case on dimensioning accidental fire loads. This chapter shows how premises, relevance, sensitivity, and strength of knowledge can be summarized in a schematic denoted a "map of premises". This map is closely related to the event trees implemented in the QRA. The overall aim of this method is to improve the way the QRA communicates results and their premises.

Acknowledgements

Several people have indirectly or directly contributed to the work summarized in this chapter, and their contributions are greatly acknowledged: Trine Holde, Arve Olaf Torgauten, Therese Moen van Roosmalen, Zhongxi Chao, Torleif Veen, Jan Dahlsveen and Ranveig Niemi from Safetec Nordic, Norway; Malene Sandøy and Henning Myrheim from ConocoPhillips, Norway; and Terje Aven from the University of Stavanger. The work has been partly funded by ConocoPhillips and by the Norwegian Research Council, as a part of the Petromaks 2 program (grant number 228335/E30). The support is gratefully acknowledged.

References

Aven, T. (2012) The risk concept – historical and recent development trends. *Reliability Engineering & System Safety*, 99, 33–44.

Aven, T. (2014) *Risk, Surprises and Black Swans: Fundamental Ideas and Concepts in Risk Assessment and Risk Management.* Routledge.

Aven, T. and Pedersen, L.M. (2014) On how to understand and present the uncertainties in production assurance analyses, with a case study related to a subsea production system. *Reliability Engineering & System Safety*, 124, 165–170.

Beard, A.N. (2004) Risk assessment assumptions. *Civil Engineering and Environmental Systems*, 21(1), 19–31.

Blix, E., Nyheim, O.M., Roosmalen, T.M., *et al.* (2015) Barriers – from safety studies to safety management. In: Proc. of the 25th European Safety and Reliability Conference (ESREL), Zurich, 7–10 October 2015. Leiden: Balkema.

Flage, R. and Aven, T. (2009) Expressing and communicating un-certainty in relation to quantitative risk analysis. *Reliability and Risk Analysis: Theory and Applications*, 2(13), 9–18.

Flage, R., Aven, T., Baraldi, P. and Zio, E. (2014) Concerns, challenges and directions of development for the issue of representing uncertainty in risk assessment. *Risk Analysis*, 34(7), 1196–1207.

Pate-Cornell, E. (1999) Conditional uncertainty analysis and implications for decision making: the case of WIPP. *Risk Analysis*, 19(5), 995–1002.

Petroleum Safety Authority Norway (PSA) (2013) Principles for barrier management in the petroleum industry. Available from www.ptil.no.

Petroleum Safety Authority Norway (PSA) (2015) The Facilities Regulations. Available from www.ptil.no.

Standards Norway (SN) (2008) NORSOK S-001 - Technical Safety. Available from www.standard.no.

Standards Norway (SN) (2010) NORSOK Z-013 - Risk and emergency preparedness assessment. Available from www.standard.no.

Tuft, V.L., Wagnild, B.R., Pedersen, L.M., Sandøy, M., Aven. T. (2015) Uncertainty and strength of knowledge in QRAs. In: Proc. of the 25th European Safety and Reliability Conference (ESREL), Zurich, 7–10 October 2015. Balkema.

Tuft, V.L., Wiggen, O.M., Torgauten, A.O., *et al.* (2016) Risk assessments as input to decision making during design of oil and gas installations. In: Proc. of the 26th European Safety and Reliability Conference (ESREL), Glasgow, 25–29 September 2016. Balkema.

Vose, D. (2008) *Risk Analysis: A Quantitative Guide* (3rd edn). Wiley.

Zio, E. (2007) An Introduction to the Basics of Reliability and *Risk Analysis*. Singapore: World Scientific Publishing.

12

A Semi-quantitative Approach for Assessment of Risk Trends in the Norwegian Oil and Gas Industry

Eirik Bjorheim Abrahamsen[1], Jon Tømmerås Selvik[1], Bjørnar Heide[2], and Jan Erik Vinnem[3]

[1] *University of Stavanger, Norway*
[2] *Petroleum Safety Authority Norway, Norway*
[3] *Norwegian University of Science and Technology, Norway*

The current method used by the Norwegian Petroleum Safety Authority to express the level of risk and to detect trends in risks in the Norwegian petroleum industry is reviewed and discussed. The method provides risk insights and is important for decision making. However, when used for such a purpose, the method is not considered sufficiently informative. The main analytical problem is that knowledge and robustness issues in the conclusions, such as the amount of relevant information available, are not systematically described and dealt with. To contribute to the ability to make decisions that are more informed on risk levels and trends, the incorporation of specific robustness and knowledge assessments is suggested. A more consistent and transparent approach is then achieved. A relevant example is included to illustrate the main points.

12.1 Introduction

In 1999 the Norwegian petroleum regulatory authorities (now the PSA – Petroleum Safety Authority Norway) initiated a significant project: the RNNP project. "RNNP" is a Norwegian abbreviation for "trends in risk level in the petroleum activity". An objective was to contribute to the establishment of a realistic and jointly agreed picture of trends in HSE (Health, Safety and Environment) work, to support the efforts made by the authorities and the industry to improve the HSE levels in offshore oil and gas operations, as described in Vinnem *et al.* (2006). The project was later expanded to cover

Knowledge in Risk Assessment and Management, First Edition. Edited by Terje Aven and Enrico Zio.
© 2018 John Wiley & Sons Ltd. Published 2018 by John Wiley & Sons Ltd.

onshore oil and gas operations regulated by the PSA, as described in Heide *et al.* (2007). The RNNP project is still running, and the PSA issues annual reports from the project (see for example PSA, 2016; 2014).

The project addressed the challenge of directly measuring the risk of future accident events. When observing the Norwegian oil and gas industry for a limited period, the number of accidental events is likely to be low and thus far too low to be able to draw conclusions about status and trends. As a response to this challenge, Vinnem *et al.* (2006) argue that it is useful to observe indicators, unplanned incidents, and safety barrier performance tests, and to put these alongside our knowledge of the physical phenomena that occur (for example, spills or leaks, gas dispersion, ignition, and fire) and general knowledge about the oil and gas industry. Based on these ideas, a framework for monitoring risk trends was developed.

It was further argued that there were different ways to express the relevant risk levels by using indicators. Hence, to achieve the relevant information, a "triangulation framework" was applied, as it was argued that such a framework could produce valuable information about risk levels and trends. The "triangulation framework'" suggested by Vinnem *et al.* (2006) consists of three features:

- triangulation of scientific methods
- triangulation within the indicators
- triangulation of the stakeholders' views.

The triangulation of scientific methods is achieved by applying a combination of methods from several disciplines – statistics, social sciences, and risk analysis – and using these to provide a broad risk illustration. By using all these complementary scientific methods, more trustworthy results can be achieved than by relying on a single discipline's method alone. The framework makes it possible to draw from a range of qualitative and quantitative information sources: personnel interviews, surveys, audits, inspections, investigations, risk analyses, and data from recorded incidents and barrier performance tests.

With regard to the set of indicators, each indicator is triangulated in order to obtain a more complete risk-level overview. For instance, indicators can be both summarised and viewed separately over different incidents, installations, or company categories. Furthermore, they can be normalised over exposure, production, activity levels and categories, and weighted based on various risk importance measures from risk analyses.

Additionally, experts with strong safety and industry knowledge should evaluate the data, to ensure that the results are not misinterpreted. As part of this process, all the stakeholder parties are invited to share their opinions and perspectives. We refer to this as the "triangulation of the stakeholders' views".

The RNNP project also developed a quantitative method to aid in detecting trends (Kvaløy and Aven, 2005), contingent on having relevant and reliable data from a preceding period that could be used to describe the future period of interest: for example, a one- or five-year period. In the method, a 90% prediction interval is calculated for a future period, based on the average level in the preceding period for each of the indicators. For more information about the indicators, see Vinnem *et al.* (2006) and Heide *et al.* (2007).

If an observed value in the next period for an indicator falls within the prediction interval, the result indicates that no statistical trend has been detected for this specific indicator. Otherwise, if the observed value is higher than the calculated prediction interval, a negative statistical trend has been detected and vice versa: if the observed value is lower, this indicates a positive statistical trend.

The result from the quantitative trend detection method suggested in Kvaløy and Aven (2005) gives an important input for the triangulation of the stakeholders' views. Thus, it is of importance that potential limitations in the quantitative trend detection method and analysis are properly described and dealt with. It is from this starting point that we will discuss the appropriateness of applying this method to inform decision making and risk management in general.

We show that the quantitative trend detection method neither reflects upon the assumptions and premises on which the trend detection method is conditioned (background information), nor the degree to which the conclusion is robust with respect to the underlying population data.

For a more informative approach, an assessment of both the background knowledge and robustness should be included. One way of achieving this is to apply a simple 3×3 matrix, visualising strength-of-knowledge on one axis and robustness on the other.

The suggested approach is described in the following sections. In Section 12.2, a short review of the current trend detection method is given, while Section 12.3 describes some challenges related to this method. The recommended approach for assessing risk trends in the Norwegian oil and gas industry is provided in Section 12.4. This approach is in the following referred to as a "semi-quantitative" approach. Then, in Section 12.5, an example is presented to illustrate the practical implications of the proposed approach. Finally, in Section 12.6, we draw some conclusions.

12.2 Review of Trend Detection Method

In this section, an example is used to illustrate the technique adopted in the RNNP project to detect trends. We should mention that there are also other important aspects of this project beyond the trend detection method, but these are not reviewed here. For more information about the project, we refer to PSA (2016, 2014) and Vinnem *et al.* (2006).

In the example, we will focus on one specific technical safety barrier element: a pressure safety valve (PSV). A data set from safety barrier tests is used in the

Table 12.1 Number of onshore PSV tests and failures registered in the period 2009–2013.

Year (i)	2009	2010	2011	2012	2013
Number of PSV tests: n_i	733	572	680	759	702
Number of failures registered: x_i	8	5	4	9	7

example, as safety barrier data have been more difficult to interpret in the RNNP project than the incident data. The number of PSV failures and the corresponding number of tests for these valves in the period 2009–2013, for one of the land-based plants, are shown in Table 12.1. Due to the large differences between onshore plants, it is considered more useful to analyse the performance data per plant than to sum the data for all plants. Based on these data, one may decide how large the deviation would have to be in 2014 to detect a trend: a statistically significant change.

Following the suggested trend detection method, a main indicator is the failure fraction, FF. This indicator is calculated as the ratio between the number of failures, x, and the corresponding number of tests performed (see also Selvik and Abrahamsen, 2015):

$$FF = x/n \qquad (12.1)$$

One first predicts the fraction of failures in 2014 simply by using the mean of the observations in the period 2009–2013, given that these data are assessed as relevant for the prediction of a similar situation in the following year. To assess uncertainties of the fraction of PSV failures during the next year, a binomial distribution for Y failures during n tests is used, with the proportion of failures, q, as described in Kvaløy and Aven (2005), Røed and Aven (2009), and Heide *et al.* (2007). Although the tests are not independent, the binomial distribution is considered a suitable description of our uncertainty, as long as the number of previous tests is at least twice as large as n (see Røed and Aven, 2009).

A 90% prediction interval for q in 2014 is thus [0.0043, 0.014], based on an estimated 700 tests in 2014. For more details about prediction intervals, see Vinnem *et al.* (2006) and Kvaløy and Aven (2005).

The prediction interval is used to conclude upon the 2014 trend. No trend is detected with reference to the quantitative trend detection method if the observed failure fraction in 2014 is within the calculated prediction interval. A positive trend is detected if the indicator value for 2014 is lower than the calculated prediction interval. If the indicator value is higher, then a negative trend is detected.

For the sake of the discussions in the next sections, we assume that 9 failures in 700 tests are found in 2014.

12.3 Discussion of the Current Trend Detection Method

The current method for expressing the risk level and detecting trends in risks in the Norwegian oil and gas industry, as described in Section 12.2, is intuitively appealing. As already mentioned in Section 12.1, however, there are some limitations or methodological challenges that could influence the results. In addition to those already mentioned, PSA (2014) argues in the 2013 annual report for the RNNP project (see also PSA, 2016) that

- typical industry requirements for barrier test performance are often not fulfilled
- a more thorough test regime is necessary in order to demonstrate fulfilment of the barrier performance requirements in the regulations, especially for onshore plants.

We focus on the methodological challenges, which are described in Sections 12.3.1 and 12.3.2.

12.3.1 Methodological Challenges: Background Knowledge

The background knowledge aspect is not systematically taken into consideration in the current approach for detecting trends in risks for the Norwegian oil and gas industry. The lack of this dimension means, for example, that probability (as a measure of uncertainty or degree of belief), is unable to reflect both the strength of the knowledge on which the probabilities are based, and the fact that the assumptions within the probabilistic analysis could conceal important aspects of uncertainties.

It is not sufficient to study only parts of the uncertainty picture, as surprises may occur relative to the knowledge of the analysts or experts conducting the assessment, as also argued in Aven (2014, p. 100).

In particular, the assessment of background knowledge (the strength-of-knowledge) should reflect the amount of data that has been available for the calculation of the prediction interval. Such information is not communicated through the results produced in the current approach, as attention is only given to the average failure fraction, FF, in the preceding period.

Another aspect of importance is the relevance of data. In some situations, a great deal of relevant data are available, while in others the available data are less relevant. As stated in Section 12.1, the current method is supposed to be contingent on having reliable data; for example, knowledge about the data relevance is important as it influence how to use the trend results in decision making.

12.3.2 Methodological Challenges: Robustness

Robustness is another issue not systematically taken into consideration in the current approach. Robustness analyses show the extent to which the results are stable and consistent under small variations in the underlying population data. The robustness will, amongst other factors, be dependent on the sensitivity to important conditions and assumptions and on what it takes for the conclusions to be changed. Such information is not systematically reflected in the current approach to trend detection.

To obtain appropriate information about robustness when detecting trends, different aspects need to be considered in more detail. We will also return to these in the Sections 12.4 and 12.5, but we give an outline of relevant aspects related to robustness below.

From the example in Section 12.2, no trend was detected, as the observed FF in 2014 was within the calculated 90% prediction interval. In addition, no information on how sensitive the conclusion was to changes in the observed FF was given by the existing method. Through a simple robustness analysis, we find that the number of failures needs to be more than 11% higher than the observed number of failures in 2014 to conclude the existence of a negative trend. This means that, by adding just one test failure, we would change the conclusions to a negative trend. To conclude the existence of a positive trend, the number of failures needs to be 67% less than observed. Such numbers show that we are closer to concluding that there is a negative trend a positive one. The same information is also available from Figure 12.1, as the observed FF for

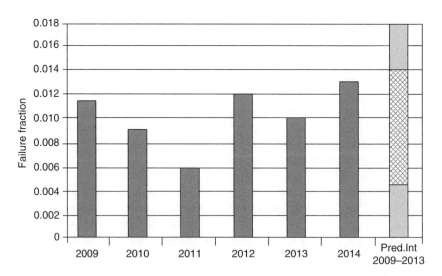

Figure 12.1 Observed failure fraction in the period 2009–2014 and calculated prediction interval.

2014 is closer to the upper grey area in the prediction interval than to the lower grey area. Any concrete information about what it takes to alter the conclusion is, however, not given in the figure.

Additionally, extreme values from a small segment of the data population may cloud an otherwise interesting picture. For instance, experience has shown that averaging barrier test data from a large population of installations, such as in the example from Section 12.2, could lead one plant or part of the plant to "skew" or "dominate" the conclusions. Test data could come from different parts of the plant from one year to the next. One relevant robustness analysis could thus be to run the analysis without the data from the plant with the most extreme data. Previous studies in Heide and Vinnem (2008) have illustrated this point in more detail.

The current method calculates the average value, regardless of the observed variation in the historical data and the number of observed years, as long as:

- there is fulfilment of the general requirement of having reliable, relevant data from a preceding time period that is viewed as a good description of the situation for the future period of interest
- the assumptions about the probability distributions used are reasonable, although this is not always the case; for example, by focusing on a shorter or longer period instead, one may be able to "manipulate" the FF values and produce different, and perhaps more preferred, conclusions.

From a robustness perspective, the current method does not in general account for robustness due to large yearly deviations in the observed values. Therefore, in practical settings, it could be useful to adopt a more formal procedure for the assessment of robustness.

12.4 A Semi-quantitative Approach for Assessment of Risk Trends

The approach for detecting risk trends in the Norwegian oil and gas industry is presented in this section. Compared to the method in the "old" approach described in Section 12.1, an adjustment is suggested to better cover the analytical issues described in previous sections. While the trend analysis method described in Section 12.2 is mainly quantitative, the "new" and extended approach consists of both quantitative and qualitative elements. The approach for deciding upon trends is carried out in accordance with the following five steps:

1) Evaluation and visualisation of risk trends (as in the current trend detection method)
2) Evaluation of the background knowledge (strength-of-knowledge)
3) Evaluation of robustness

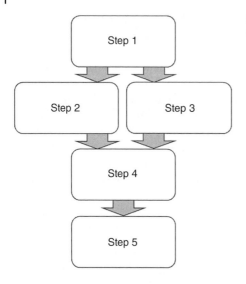

Figure 12.2 Illustration of the semi-quantitative approach.

4) Combining the above steps 1–3: mapping and presenting the results
5) Discussion and conclusion

Figure 12.2 shows how the different steps are structured. The overall structure of the extended approach is inspired by Wiencke *et al.* (2006), Abrahamsen *et al.* (2015), and Abrahamsen and Selvik (2013). Details about each step of the extended approach are described below.

Step 1. Evaluation and visualisation of risk trends The evaluation of trends and visualisation, as in the current approach, applies the analysis method described in Section 12.2 and will not be further explained in this section.

Step 2. Evaluation of background knowledge For the assessment of background knowledge, a main objective is to clarify the soundness of different knowledge aspects, such as by studying the assumptions made in the analysis. We propose using classification of the knowledge strength based on three categories: strong, medium and poor. To ensure consistency in the classification process, there is a need for some guidelines. Table 12.2 shows suggested guidelines, which are based on conditions defined in Flage and Aven (2009) and Selvik and Aven (2011). See also Aven (2014, p. 103).

Step 3. Evaluation of robustness In the same way as for the strength-of-knowledge, we propose using a qualitative classification based on three categories of robustness: high, moderate, and weak. To ensure consistency in the classification process, there is a need for a guideline. We define the three categories of robustness as shown below:

- *High robustness:* Very large changes in the indicator values are needed to change the conclusion achieved in the trend analysis; that is, there is low

Table 12.2 Guideline for categorisation of strength-of-knowledge.

Strength of knowledge	Criteria
Strong	All of the following conditions whenever relevant are met: • The assumptions made are seen as very reasonable. • A large amount of reliable and relevant data/information is available. • Relevant experts are involved in the assessments. • There is broad agreement among the experts. • The phenomena involved are well understood; the models used are known to give predictions with the required accuracy.
Poor	One or more of the following conditions is true: • The assumptions made represent strong simplifications. • Data/information are/is non-existent or highly unreliable/irrelevant. • There is a lack of relevant expertise within the assessment team. • There is strong disagreement among the experts (or within the assessment team). • The phenomena involved are poorly understood; models are non-existent or known/believed to give poor predictions.
Medium	Cases in between are classified as having a medium strength-of-knowledge.

sensitivity. The robustness is not significant if the values are such that the contribution of one single failure is sufficient to change the conclusions.

- *Weak robustness:* Relatively small changes in the indicator values are needed to change the conclusion achieved in the trend analysis; that is, there is high sensitivity. Essentially, if any change in the indicator values would lead to a different conclusion, then the robustness is weak.
- *Moderate robustness:* Conditions between high and weak robustness.

Step 4. Combining Steps 1–3: Mapping and presenting the results The results from Step 1 may still be visualised as in Figure 12.1, where a bar chart diagram is used to present the results from the current trend detection method. In addition, to supplement these results, Steps 2 and 3 could be visualised by combining the strength-of-knowledge evaluation and robustness evaluation into a matrix, as shown in Figure 12.3. This is a simplified 3×3 matrix, with strength of knowledge on one axis and robustness on the other.

Step 5. Discussion and conclusion The presentation of results in Step 4 must be seen in relation to the objective of the analysis and to how the results will be used. A discussion is essential to cover issues where the presented results may be interpreted in different ways. For example, if there is weak robustness, the discussion should cover the possible impacts on the conclusion.

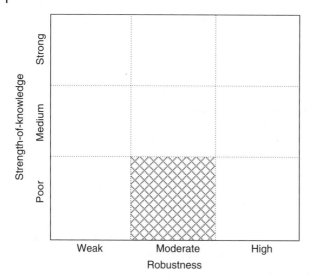

Figure 12.3 Visualisation of results from Steps 2 and 3.

It is also recommended that the main assumptions, and especially those that are sensitive, are included in the discussion of results. Issues related to the quality of the data, including the amount of available data, should also be discussed, before any conclusions are drawn. As part of this discussion, it may be reasonable to reflect on the data period, and thus the population, selected. In a narrowly mechanical approach, one would restrict focus to last year's observed FF with the calculated 90% prediction interval, as described in Section 12.2. The conclusion could, however, change, if one pays attention to the situation for different periods. Having a larger period normally makes the analysis less sensitive to fluctuations in the data. That, partly, is why it is important to apply a "triangulation approach" that covers a broader perspective. The conclusion should not be based on just one indicator value. It may be possible to produce some guidelines on how to understand and use different combinations of strength-of-knowledge and robustness for decision-making purposes. However, it could be argued that this would reduce flexibility, as it would to some extent limit the analysts' discussion. A preferred alternative could be just to present the output produced in Step 4 and add a relevant discussion suited to the decision makers. The decision makers could then use the results as one of many inputs in the decision-making process, as in the "triangulation approach". On the other hand, it may provide greater insight, if we indicate some guidelines. Firstly, if the robustness is "weak", we should not use the indicator to draw distinct conclusions about trends, unless the strength of knowledge is "strong". The same may apply if the robustness is "moderate", but this will need to be decided according to the actual context; sometimes it may be sufficient that strength of knowledge is "moderate". If the robustness is "Significant", we may draw conclusions about trends, as long as the strength of knowledge is better than "poor".

12.5 Example: Application of the Extended Approach

To illustrate the practical implications of the extended approach, we return to the PSV example given in Section 12.2, where risk trend analysis of PSV is performed based on the FF indicator. Information on each step of the suggested method is given in the following:

12.5.1 Step 1: Evaluation and Visualisation of Risk Trends

A main activity within this step is to select the appropriate performance indicators, such as the FF indicator that we used for the PSV example. As a key performance indicator in the RNNP project, FF is considered highly relevant to the example. The selection should reflect the fact that there should be sufficient data available to apply the risk trend method, which is a criterion that is satisfied by the data used to calculate the FF. As a general rule, more than one risk performance indicator should normally be selected. For simplicity, we focus on only one indicator in the following.

The evaluation of trends for the barrier test indicator PSV, as in the current approach, is already described in Section 12.2 and so will not be further explained in this section.

The only additional aspect required in this presentation is to consider who the decision makers are in the example. The decision makers may be:

- personnel in PSA, making decisions about next year's focus in their supervisory activities
- plant operator management, making decisions about next year's allocation of resources for maintenance of PSVs.

12.5.2 Steps 2 and 3: Evaluation of Background Knowledge and Robustness

For the PSV example, the FF indicator can be viewed as well understood, and there is often quite a large reliable dataset available. However, the underlying assumptions when interpreting this indicator may not be that reasonable. As previously mentioned, the test data may come from different parts of the plant, not operating under comparable circumstances: one PSV might be used on a gas segment and another might be used on an oil segment, which is often associated with higher failure rates. As described in PSA (2014), a more thorough test regime would be necessary in order to have the PSV (that is, the barrier element) under control as required in the regulations.

Further, the tests that are performed, as summarised in Table 12.1, do not cover other requirements such as functionality and vulnerability. Information is not provided on how many test results are found close to the test pressure acceptance criterion. One could imagine that several tests are passed, which, with some different operator or personnel, would have failed. Similarly, if it takes a long time to perform the test, this could indicate that the test pressure acceptance criterion is not met at first but later checked as "ok". Additionally, one may find that the incentive for performing the test is not consistent, and there may be situations leading to manipulation of the PSV before the test or the reporting of a re-test if the first test is negative. It may be important to summarise and communicate knowledge about these issues to those making the decision on the PSV risk trend.

On a more positive note, PSVs typically have quite standardised test intervals compared to other barrier elements, although the error definitions for PSV tests are not standardised between the operators. This means that one may find considerable differences when going into detail and comparing tests from different operators. Knowledge about this issue may be of relevance when drawing conclusions from the trend analysis.

To perform the FF calculations, several assumptions are made, many of which are considered necessary if the collected data are to be used. For example, making judgements regarding which personnel follow the test procedures in a less strict manner, and thus could give higher uncertainties related to their test results, would not in practice be a manageable task.

Based on the above information, we evaluate the strength of knowledge to be poor. Other plants may have a more homogeneous population of PSVs, meaning that there will be situations where the background knowledge will be better than in this example.

In respect of the evaluation of robustness, by using the proposed criteria for robustness outlined in Section 12.4, one would be led to conclude that the indicator robustness is high. As previously noted, it would only take one more test failure in 2014 to exceed the prediction interval. However, the observed variation and the fact that there is quite a large dataset available should be considered. Further, there are a lot of values of the number of failures which will not imply any change of conclusion: the values, 4, 5, 6, 7, 8. Since a change of conclusions will only occur with the extreme values 3 (or less) and 10 (or more), we conclude that in this case the robustness is not "Weak". It is more appropriate to assign a "Moderate" score to the robustness.

12.5.3 Step 4: Mapping and Presenting the Results

The results based on the analysis of the PSV FF are presented in Figure 12.4. The results achieved from the trend analysis method are shown in the bar chart to the left (same as Figure 12.1), while the results from Steps 2 and 3 are given in the matrix to the right (same as Figure 12.3).

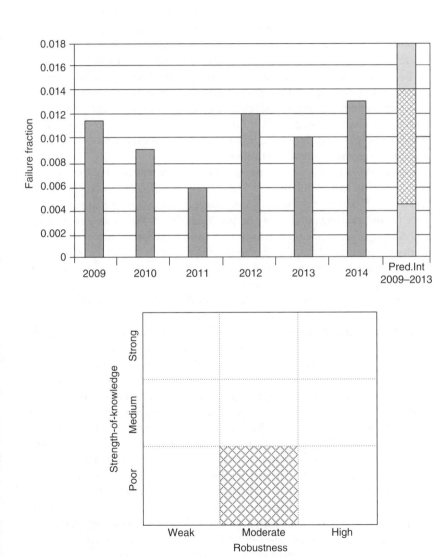

Figure 12.4 Visualisation of the results.

The results produced are supplemented with an interpretation guide, such as that for the categorisation used in the individual evaluations, so that it is clear how to read them.

12.5.4   Step 5: Discussion and Conclusion

Next, the results from the analyses summarised in Figure 12.4 are documented and reported. They are then applicable for different purposes, including, for example, decision-making purposes. The trend analysis results should also be communicated in a way that provides a broader risk trend picture compared with the traditional method. For example, decision makers should be informed of the results along with all the relevant information produced from both the trend analysis and the assessment of background knowledge and robustness; see discussion in Section 12.4. Although the reporting may produce a clear trend picture, it is considered the task of the decision maker to draw conclusions suitable to the application studied.

The situation may also be that the decision maker was involved in the process of analysing and evaluating the trends. In many situations, it is considered a key success factor that those with a mandate to make the decisions also contribute to and take ownership of the process. Nevertheless, we see it as the responsibility of the decision maker to ensure an appropriate use of the results from the analysis, and to evaluate whether the quality of the analysis is acceptable. As indicated above, the decision makers may, for example, be plant operator management or PSA management.

The decision makers should, for example, evaluate the indicators selected for the analysis and assess whether these are appropriate. In a sense, this makes the approach somewhat dynamic, as there may be room for adjustment through the "triangulation within the indicators". As an example, with reference to onshore plants, a set of generic weighted incident indicators was not used due to the great differences between the plants. As we have illustrated, it is challenging to express the risk trends. Therefore, it might be useful to develop some plant-specific weights for the incident indicators. When the offshore weights were developed (see Section 12.1), they were based on data from a considerable number of different installations. Therefore, the workload in developing onshore weights might not be a lot greater than for the offshore weights, and such an approach might, in combination with the extended approach described, contribute to a more useful risk picture. On the other hand, a main purpose of the RNNP project was to be better able to suggest new risk-reducing measures at an industry level and not particularly at a plant level. The individual weights might thus not aid this objective and not be selected for the analysis, since the onshore plants vary so much. This is most appropriate for PSA decision makers.

A main issue is that the decision-making should not be a mechanical process. This is achieved by adopting the "triangulation framework" described by Vinnem *et al.* (2006). Hence, the results presented above provide only part of the full risk picture; the decision makers (PSA or plant management) will also be able to communicate back to the analysis team any specific issues, such as regarding the assumptions used, which should be further clarified or investigated.

12.6 Conclusions

In this chapter, a semi-quantitative approach for how to assess and detect risk trends in the Norwegian oil and gas industry has been proposed. The approach is based on the framework described in Vinnem *et al.* (2006) and the risk trend method described in Kvaløy and Aven (2005). While the approach is closely based on the traditional method used for the RNNP project, there are some principal differences in the form of additional evaluations. The main differences are that, in the approach proposed, assessments of issues reflecting both background knowledge and robustness are explicitly incorporated. In this way, the new approach is able to better inform decision making related to risk trends than the traditional method.

Although the proposed approach is closely linked to the Norwegian oil and gas industry, it is in no way restricted to that industry. The basic principles should also be applicable to other industries performing trend analysis. The main point, which adds value beyond the "old" method, is that the approach should also capture robustness and a wider uncertainty description, where background knowledge issues are adequately taken into consideration.

Acknowledgements

The authors are grateful to Alireza Gelyani for his contributions to the paper titled "An improved method to express risk level and detect trends in risks in the Norwegian petroleum industry"(Abrahamsen *et al.*, 2014), which was the starting point for this book chapter.

The work has been partly funded by the Norwegian Research Council as a part of the Petromaks 2 program (grant number 228335/E30). The support is gratefully acknowledged.

References

Abrahamsen, E.B., Heide, B., Vinnem, J.E., and Gelyani A.M. (2014) An improved method to express risk level and detect trends in risks in the Norwegian petroleum industry. In: Gelyani, A.M. *Contributions to Risk Management – Safety, Economics & Uncertainty Treatment in Risk-informed*

Decision-making. PhD thesis No. 236. University of Stavanger, Faculty of Science and Technology.

Abrahamsen, E.B., Pettersen, K.A., Aven, T., Kaufmann, M., and Rosqvist, T. (2015) A framework for selection of strategy for management of security measures. *Journal of Risk Research*, 20(3), 404–417.

Abrahamsen, E.B. and Selvik, J.T. (2013) A framework for selection of inspection intervals for well barriers. In: Safety, reliability and risk analysis – beyond the horizon: *Proceedings of the European Safety and Reliability Conference, ESREL 2013*, Amsterdam, Netherlands, 29 September–2 October 2013. CRC Press. ISBN 978-1-138-00123-7.

Aven, T. (2014) *Risk, Surprises and Black Swans. Fundamental Ideas and Concepts in Risk Assessment and Risk Management*. Routledge Taylor and Francis Group.

Flage, R. and Aven, T. (2009) Expressing and communicating uncertainty in relation to quantitative risk analysis. *Reliability and Risk Analysis: Theory & Applications*, 2(13). 9–18.

Heide, B. and Vinnem, J.E. (2008) Trends in major hazard risks for the Norwegian offshore petroleum industry. In Heide, B., *Monitoring Major Hazard Risk for Industrial Sectors*. PhD thesis, University of Stavanger, no. 66. 2009.

Heide, K.B., Vinnem, J.E., and Aven, T. (2007) Methods to monitor risk for onshore petroleum plants. In: *Proceedings of the ESREL 2007 Conference*, Stavanger, Norway.

Kvaløy, J.T. and Aven, T. (2005) An alternative approach to trend analysis in accident data. *Reliability Engineering & System Safety*, 90(1), 75–82.

PSA – Petroleum Safety Authority Norway. (2014) Trends in risk level summary report 2013. http://www.psa.no/summary-report-2013/category912.html. (Accessed: 07 December 2016).

PSA – Petroleum Safety Authority Norway. (2016) RNNP 2015 summary report. http://www.psa.no/summary-report-2015/category1194.html. (Accessed: 07 December 2016).

Røed, W. and Aven, T. (2009) Bayesian approaches for detecting significant deterioration. *Reliability Engineering & System Safety*, 94, 604–610.

Selvik, J.T. and Abrahamsen, E.B. (2015) A review of safety valve reliability using failure fraction information. In: *Safety and Reliability of Complex Engineered Systems – Proceedings of the ESREL 2015 Conference*. CRC Press – Taylor & Francis Group.

Selvik, J.T. and Aven, T. (2011). A framework for reliability and risk centered maintenance. *Reliability Engineering & System Safety*, 96(2), 324–331.

Vinnem, J.E., Aven, T., Husebø, T., Seljelid, J., and Tveit, O.J. (2006) Major hazard risk indicators for monitoring of trends in the Norwegian offshore petroleum sector. *Reliability Engineering & System Safety*, 91, 778–791.

Wiencke, H.S., Aven, T., and Hagen, J. (2006) A framework for selection of methodology for risk and vulnerability assessments of infrastructures depending on information and communication technology. In: *Proceedings of the ESREL 2006 Conference*. Estoril, Portugal.

13

Knowledge Engineering at a Risk-informed Regulatory Agency: Challenges and Suggestions

Nathan Siu and Kevin Coyne

Office of Nuclear Regulatory Research, US Nuclear Regulatory Commission, Washington, DC

Acronyms and Abbreviations

ACRS	Advisory Committee on Reactor Safeguards (NRC)
ADAMS	Agencywide Document Access and Management System (NRC)
AERB	Atomic Energy Regulatory Board (India)
ANS	American Nuclear Society
ASME	American Society of Mechanical Engineers
ASP	accident sequence precursor
CCDP	conditional core damage probability
CDF	core damage frequency
CDP	core damage probability
CFR	US Code of Federal Regulations
CSN	Consejo de Seguridad Nuclear (Spain)
EDG	emergency diesel generator
IAEA	International Atomic Energy Agency
ICA 2.2	IBM Content Analytics Version 2.2
IBM	International Business Machines
INES	International Nuclear and Radiological Event Scale
IPE	Individual Plant Examination
IPEEE	Individual Plant Examination of External Events
IPSN	Institut de Protection et de Sûreté Nucléaire (France)
KE	knowledge engineering
LAR	license amendment request
LER	licensee event report
LHSI	low head safety injection
LOOP	loss of offsite power

Knowledge in Risk Assessment and Management, First Edition. Edited by Terje Aven and Enrico Zio.
© 2018 John Wiley & Sons Ltd. Published 2018 by John Wiley & Sons Ltd.

NRC   US Nuclear Regulatory Commission
NUREG   designator for reports issued by the NRC
NUREG/CR   designator for contractor-developed reports issued by the NRC
OCR   optical character recognition
PRA   probabilistic risk assessment
SECY   designator for NRC staff papers addressed to the Commission
SME   subject matter expert
SPAR   Standardized Plant Analysis Risk
SRM   Staff Requirements Memorandum (NRC)

The US Nuclear Regulatory Commission, as a risk-informed agency, is increasingly using multidisciplinary, multifaceted, and technically specialized information to support regulatory decision making. Ongoing knowledge engineering developments that may help agency staff identify, access, and assimilate relevant information in an increasingly voluminous, broad, and deep information base are promising. Further developments aimed at improving day-to-day tools used by the staff should consider short-term activities to improve database infrastructure and current search tools, as well as longer-term activities aimed at developing improved technologies to extract information from documents.

13.1 Introduction

On the evening of 27 December 1999, storm winds caused a loss of offsite power (LOOP) for Units 2 and 4 of the Le Blayais nuclear power plant in France (IPSN 2000; IAEA 2000; Gorbatchev *et al.* 2000; Vial *et al.* 2005). Shortly afterwards, a combination of a rising tide, a storm surge, and wind-driven waves led to the overtopping of a protective dyke and flooding of the site. Floodwaters entered a number of plant buildings through unsealed cable and pipe penetrations and led to, among other things, the failure of one train of essential service water for Unit 1 and the inoperability of low head safety injection (LHSI) pumps and containment spray pumps for Units 1 and 2. The flooding also led to falling trees and blocked roads, thereby preventing access to the site for a number of hours. The event was classified as an "incident" (Level 2) on the International Atomic Energy Agency's (IAEA) International Nuclear and Radiological Event Scale (INES).

Le Blayais provided an empirical indicator of the potential risk significance of beyond design basis external floods. Moreover, the event involved multiple concurrent hazards, affected multiple units, led to complications in plant operator response, and blocked access to the site. These are characteristics that are now widely recognized as important contributors to the March 2011 Fukushima Daiichi reactor accidents, and also as challenges to existing probabilistic risk assessment (PRA) methods, models, tools, and data (for example, Siu *et al.* 2013). However, neither Le Blayais, nor the tsunami-induced flooding of the Madras plant in 2004 (AERB 2005), nor the flood-debris clogging of service water at the Cruas plant in 2009 (Dupuy *et al.* 2014), initiated much activity in the general PRA community. It took the Fukushima accidents, bolstered by compelling images of the US Fort Calhoun nuclear power plant site surrounded by floodwaters in June 2011 (for example, see Sulzberger and Wald 2011), to spur broad reconsideration of the risks associated with external flooding and other extreme non-seismic hazards.

The US Nuclear Regulatory Commission (NRC), an agency which regulates commercial nuclear power plants and other uses of nuclear materials, for example those used in nuclear medicine, through licensing, inspection, and enforcement of its requirements is continually striving to increase its use of risk information in decision making (for example, see Apostolakis *et al.* 2012 and Siu *et al.* 2016a). As such, it makes extensive use of the results and insights generated by nuclear power plant PRAs. Oftentimes, the PRA-generated information is used directly (for example, as described in Regulatory Guide 1.174 (NRC 1998)). Other times, as in the case of the seminal WASH-1400 study (NRC 1975) the later NUREG-1150 study (NRC 1990), and the NRC's ongoing study for the Vogtle plant (Kuritzky *et al.* 2013), the PRA information is used to improve the agency's understanding of risk, thereby providing a context for other decisions. Clearly, it is important for the PRA models – as supported by standards (for example, ASME/ANS 2009) and associated guidance (for example, NRC 2009) – to adequately reflect the technical community's state-of-knowledge regarding potential scenarios (including underlying phenomena), consequences, and likelihoods relevant to the decision at hand. The Le Blayais example illustrates one important risk-related knowledge management challenge: ensuring that PRA method developers and analysts are cognizant of notable operational events (including those occurring in other countries) and their potential risk significance. More generally, the challenge is to ensure the PRA community's cognizance of potentially relevant information from a broad variety of sources, including experiments and analytical studies, in addition to operational experience.

Given a specific knowledge management challenge, a variety of direct, non-technical solutions can usually be identified. For instance, considering the Le Blayais example, solutions could include institutionalizing interactions between groups responsible for analyzing operational experience and those responsible for performing PRAs, or adding PRA standards requirements addressing explicit consideration of international operational events. However, for more general situations, recognizing the enormous (and growing) volume of information potentially relevant to a PRA (which, in the case of nuclear power plants and other complex technical systems is a multi-scale and multi-disciplinary enterprise), it is of interest to explore the capabilities and desirability of advanced knowledge engineering (KE) tools and techniques. To what extent can these tools and techniques help more efficiently and effectively identify, access, and assess information needed to develop or review PRA models, and to use model results and insights in support of risk-informed decision making.

The objective of this article is to discuss this question from the perspective of staff who:

- are charged with providing risk information to others, including decision makers
- rely heavily on the NRC and public information systems to perform their work.

Section 13.2 identifies a number of important risk-related KE challenges. Section 13.3 discusses a number of areas where KE advances might help address these challenges. Section 13.4 provides a brief overview of a recent, small-scale exploratory project aimed at developing a better understanding of the current capabilities of a particular technology (content analytics). Finally, Section 13.5 provides a number of conclusions and suggestions.

13.2   Risk-related KE Challenges from a User's Perspective

The NRC, as with any organization that deals with large volumes of information, has a number of information technology systems and associated activities aimed at:

- electronically capturing information important for the agency's decision-making efforts
- making the captured information accessible to the staff.

In addition to the NRC's official recordkeeping system (the Agencywide Document Access and Management System – ADAMS – https://www.nrc.gov/reading-rm/adams.html), staff can access information through a variety of tools, including the agency's website and staff-created sites used to share information. Staff can employ a variety of standard and NRC-specific search tools (for example, those included in ADAMS) and other aids (for example, hyperlinks, file structures, citations and reference lists, tables of content and indices) to find relevant documents (for example, text files, spreadsheets, databases, images, computer codes, and models) and specific pieces of information in these documents.

As illustrated in Section 13.4 and discussed further in Siu *et al.* (2016b), current databases and tools are quite effective and efficient. However, users are naturally interested in improvements that will enhance their ability to find, access, review, and assess potentially relevant information. The KE challenges in making improvements range from the simple to complex. There are three general challenges involved:

- expanding and improving the electronic database (for example, digitizing more legacy documents, improving the accuracy of digitization)
- improving search tools and aids, including guidance for users, to increase the likelihood that the search process finds desired information while reducing the number of undesired ("false positive") results
- providing capabilities to automatically derive explicit information from implicit information (for example, by mimicking the ability of subject matter experts (SMEs) to develop insights from a number of documents).

Regarding the third general challenge, Le Blayais provides an example: an SME reviewing the event description and plant-siting documents (documents that provide the technical basis for the geographic positioning of a nuclear power plant) for other nuclear power plants can readily infer that beyond design basis external floods can be risk-significant for other nuclear power plants.

These general challenges are clearly not unique to the risk arena; significant development efforts are underway in the commercial information technology sector, and a number of products are already available, as discussed in the following section. However, from the perspective of a risk information user, the challenges are modulated (and probably amplified) by the special characteristics of PRA, which influence the search for and analysis of supporting information. These characteristics include the multidisciplinary nature of PRA, the need for a systems viewpoint, the diversity and implicitness of information sources, and the continuing relevance of legacy documents (Siu *et al.* 2016b). As an example of associated challenges, the multidisciplinary aspect implies that KE solution development may require a wide range of SMEs (for example, to provide suitable word/phrase associations and search heuristics). This, in turn, implies the need to ensure the efficient use of numerous and diverse experts.

Other PRA characteristics that are particularly applicable to nuclear power plant and analogous applications and can pose special KE challenges include the complexity of problems addressed, the rarity of events and scenarios of concern, the importance of plant-specific design and operational details, and the large uncertainties associated with models and results.

It should also be noted that some of the special characteristics of risk information may affect the effectiveness and efficiency of KE solutions being developed for other communities. For example, analytics-based approaches that rely solely upon the number of times a search query finds a document with matching text (the number of search "hits") may miss situations in which a single document contains information on a rare event of interest, and may place undue emphasis on facts provided by multiple documents that are actually based on the same underlying information.

13.3 The Promise of Advancing Technology

One useful approach for meeting the general challenges discussed in the preceding section involves enlisting additional knowledge from SMEs to organize and make sense of the risk information stored in current databases. Three core technologies for automating this process are natural language processing, content analytics, and formal methods.

13.3.1 Natural Language Processing

Figure 13.1 is an excerpt from Gorbatchev *et al.* (2000), which provides a portion of the description of the 1999 Le Blayais flooding event. The meaning of the excerpt is clear to human readers familiar with the underlying terminology and concepts. However, with an automated system, challenges arise due to ambiguity, context dependence, implicitness, and non-uniqueness. For example, the text indicates that the Train A service water pumps were "lost", while other (LHSI and containment spray) pumps were "considered completely unavailable". Should an automated system supporting the use of risk information consider these effects synonymous? If so, under what circumstances? Table 13.1 provides additional examples of natural language challenges associated with the excerpt.

The excerpt also illustrates another challenge to natural language processing algorithms: widely separated text. In this figure, the text referring to the "cells" containing the LHSI and containment spray pumps is several text passages away from the introductory text indicating that the discussion concerns

---

"Of the facilities which were flooded in Units 1 *and* 2 *(Illustrations* 10 *and* 11), *the following should be noted:*

- *the rooms containing the essential service water pumps. The essential service water system of each unit comprises four pumps on two independent trains (A and B); each pump is capable of providing the entire throughput required. In Unit* 1, *the essential service water system pumps of Train A were lost as a result of immersion of their motors;*
- *some utility galleries, particularly those running in the vicinity of the fuel building linking the pump house to the platform;*
- *some rooms containing outgoing electrical feeders. The presence of water in these rooms indirectly led to the unavailability of certain electrical switchboards;*
- *the bottom of the fuel building of Units* 1 *and* 2 *containing the cells of the two LHSI pumps and the two containment spray system pumps. The nuclear operator considered that the pumps were completely unavailable. The systems to which these pumps belong are the engineered safety systems of the installation which are designed mainly to compensate for breaks in the primary system.*

Illustration 12 *illustrates the roles of the aforementioned systems. The essential service water system operates during normal operation of the units to cool the reactor auxiliaries and when the reactor is shut down to cool the decay heat removal system during accident situations in order to remove the decay heat by heat exchange in the containment spray system heat exchangers. "*

Figure 13.1 Summary description of 1999 Blayais flood (Gorbatchev *et al.* 2000).

Table 13.1 Examples of natural language challenges for automated processing arising in Le Blayais excerpt.

Challenge type	Example phrase	Challenge for KE tool
Ambiguity (multiple meanings for the same word or phrase)	"pumps of Train A were lost"	Determining that "lost" means "failed" (as opposed to its many other possible meanings, such as "missing" or "bewildered").
Context dependence (meaning depends on other factors, including document type, purpose, structure, and surrounding text)	"essential service water pumps"	Recognizing that "essential" is part of the name of the system (as opposed to being a descriptor; consider the possibility of narrative references to "non-essential service water pumps").
Implicitness (meaning is not stated directly, and must be inferred from other facts in document)	"the rooms containing the essential service water pumps"	Recognizing that these rooms were flooded, as implied by the preceding "the following should be noted".
Non-uniqueness (multiple ways of making a statement with the same meaning)	"The essential service water system of each unit comprises four pumps on two independent trains (A and B)"	Extracting information on system configuration from multiple possible alternatives (say, using different words, such as "...has four pumps in two separate trains..." or different grammatical constructions, such as "There are four pumps in the essential service water system, arranged in independent trains A and B").

flooding. It is easy for human readers to infer that the cells were flooded, but it is not simple for algorithms relying on proximity measures (for example, the number of words separating phrases). Figure 13.2, which provides highlighted excerpts from NUREG/CR-6738 (Nowlen *et al.* 2001) addressing a 1975 fire at the Browns Ferry nuclear power plant, provides another example. In this case, the Page A3-1 statement that the following event descriptions generally apply to Unit 1 is necessary to determine that the Page A3-5 statement (that the reactor was scrammed at 00:31) applies to Unit 1.

The highlighted text in Figure 13.2 shows a further challenge: the potential need to deal with flawed data. Due to the particular optical character recognition (OCR) software used to create the digitized version of NUREG/CR-6738, the digitized text available to search tools does not recognize the structure implied by the document graphics. Thus, for example, the highlighted text for the Page A3-6 entry is literally stored as "At 1:00 pm Unit 2 control room

From Page A3-1:

Whether an event from the chain of events is typically included in a fire PRA is discussed where deemed appropriate. Lessons that may be gleaned from a specific event in the context of fire PRA are also provided. Unless otherwise noted, the event descriptions refer to events impacting Unit 1.

Time (rel. to ignition) (hr:min)	Event Description (Note 1)	Fire PRA Implications
Prior to the incident	The power cables for two 480 VAC boards from opposite safety trains were routed during construction, erroneously, inside the same cable tray. (Regulatory Guide 1.75 which was in effect at the time disallows this practice.)	In a fire PRA, error in routing of cables is not taken into consideration. The actual discovery of such incidents are known to the authors. No other such a construction error is rare. No other such incidents are known to the authors. Therefore, the assumption used in fire PRAs should generally be considered as acceptable.

From Page A3-5:

00:31	At 12:51pm, operators manually scrammed the reactor from 704 MWe power level.	It is not entirely clear why operators delayed the scram for 15 minutes after learning of the fire. In a fire PRA a scram immediately upon a report of an unsuppressed CSR fire would typically be assumed.

From Page A3-6:

--	On the Unit 2 control panel, operators noticed malfunctions on ECCS panel 9-3 and feedwater panel. Unit 2 RB fans were switched to low by the operators.	Typical fire PRAs consider the impact of a fire only on a single unit, even if that fire occurs in a common or shared plant area. In this case, the second unit also experienced some difficulties and was shut down. Simultaneous demand for multi-unit shutdown may introduce unique equipment demands that may not be covered by current fire PRAs.
00:40	At 1:00pm Unit 2 control room operators observed several annunciations regarding DC power and that one reactor protection M-G set had tripped. They proceeded to scram the Unit 2 reactor and initiate shutdown cooling. Unit 2 operator confirmed that all rods inserted.	

Figure 13.2 Excerpts from analysis of 1975 Browns Ferry Fire (Nowlen *et al.* 2001).

operators demand for multi-unit shutdown may introduce [line break] observed several annunciations..." Aside from being nonsensical, the fragmentation of the actual phrase "may introduce unique equipment demands" potentially masks a key message from the document.

Within the information technology industry, advances continue in improving the access to and use of information. One of the most widely publicized activities was highlighted on 14 January 2011, when a computer system called Watson, developed by IBM, defeated two human experts on the television quiz show *Jeopardy!* (Markoff 2011). In addition to addressing complexities associated with natural language processing, the Watson project demonstrated the ability of computer technology, including the technology currently available and the technology developed specifically for the project, to address challenges associated with the volume, breadth, form, and trustworthiness of potentially relevant information. However, the Watson project, which was large and sustained (the project started in 2005 and involved a core team of about 20 researchers; Ferrucci *et al.* 2010), was a focused research activity with a relatively narrow problem domain.

Work is ongoing in many organizations to apply the technologies demonstrated by Watson, including the content analytics technology discussed in Section 13.4, to a variety of practical problems (Keim 2015). The relatively free-form query interface supported by common search engines and the widespread deployment and use of voice-activated virtual assistants provide additional demonstrations of the significant progress that has been made in understanding natural language queries and responding in kind.

13.3.2 Content Analytics

In the information technology world, where increasing amounts of resources are being spent to make better use of large (and ever-increasing) amounts of unstructured information, "content analytics" tools – software tools that use approaches such as natural language queries, trend analysis, contextual discovery, and predictive analytics to identify patterns and trends across an unstructured database (for example, text) – are being developed to, among other things, help users improve their searches and enhance their "discovery" activities (activities to develop insights through exploration of databases). As further discussed in Section 13.4, such tools use software routines to convert unstructured data (typically free text) into structured data (for example, terms with assigned characteristics), make that data readily accessible to user queries, and provide means (quantitative and qualitative) of characterizing query results.

13.3.3 Formal Methods

A third line of technology development that may be helpful to the NRC's risk-informed activities concerns the use of so-called "formal methods". Formal methods, which are well known in the computer science field, involve the development of mathematical specifications for hardware and software systems, and are intended to support the development and verification of such systems.

The PRA community has long recognized that logically equivalent (or nearly equivalent) models can take many different visual forms. (This recognition is exemplified by the resolution of the "large event tree/small fault tree" versus "small event tree/large fault tree" debate in the early days of PRA, later discussions on the merits of event sequence diagrams versus event trees, and current work on the automated development of binary decision diagram models.) A formal modeling approach could help suitably trained reviewers understand the essential aspects of the model despite these different forms.

A second potential benefit is that a formal modeling approach can put the PRA model being reviewed and external benchmarks (for example, models of similar systems in other PRAs and relevant operational experience) into a common format, thereby helping a reviewer to identify key similarities and differences.

The Open PSA initiative discussed by Epstein and Rauzy (2013), which is aimed at providing a standardized modeling language for PRAs, is a promising technology for NRC staff, who often need to function as model reviewers rather than developers. Friedlhuber *et al.* (2015) present a model comparison methodology, and Meléndez Asensio and Santos (2015) present review-oriented applications developed and considered for Consejo de Seguridad Nuclear (CSN, the Spanish regulatory authority). Both works are based on this technology. Although not further discussed in our article, it seems clear that formal methods could be very useful for the NRC's risk-related applications.

13.4   A Recent Exploration

In order to provide an indication of the status and potential value of commercially available tools benefitting from advances in natural language processing and document content analysis, the NRC has performed a feasibility study to explore the application of advanced KE tools and techniques to support PRA activities. This internally funded study, which was initiated in 2014 and completed in 2016, was conducted as a scoping study aimed at the planning of future KE-related activities.

The following discussion provides a summary of the project. Additional details can be found in Siu *et al.* (2016b).

13.4.1   Project Objectives and Scope

The overall objective of the project was to determine whether additional agency effort to develop production-level KE tools aimed at supporting risk-informed applications could be worthwhile. As a scoping study, the project employed the following limitations:

- The evaluation was limited to the consideration of content analytics tools.
- The evaluation was performed using a particular tool, IBM Content Analytics Version 2.2 (ICA 2.2), which was available to the NRC staff. This tool was judged by the authors to be representative of the broad set of commercially available content analytics tools.

The documents selected to provide the search space for ICA 2.2 were limited to the document types shown in Table 13.2. This document set, called a "corpus", was finalized in late 2015. It included over 330 000 documents,

Table 13.2 Project corpus contents.

Description	Notes
Publicly available documents from the NRC's ADAMS main library	Includes NRC staff (NUREG) and contractor (NUREG/CR) reports, staff papers to the commission (SECY papers) and commission staff requirements memoranda (SRMs), license amendment requests (LARs), and new reactor design control documents.
Final safety analysis reports (FSARs)	Provide terminology and design-related information useful for event analysis.
Documentation for NRC standardized plant analysis risk (SPAR) models	Provides design-related information useful for event analysis (for example, the size of the system involved) and PRA results that can be compared with licensee/applicant results.
Immediate notifications	Documents notifying the NRC of events submitted per the requirements of 10 CFR 50.72.
Licensee event reports (LERs)	Documents notifying the NRC of events submitted per the requirements of 10 CFR 50.73.
Inspection reports	Staff reports from the NRC's reactor oversight process (1999–present).
Individual plant examinations (IPEs)	Licensee submittals in response to Generic Letter 88–20.
Individual plant examinations of external events (IPEEEs)	Licensee submittals in response to Generic Letter 88–20, Supplement 4.
Advisory committee on reactor safeguards (ACRS) letter reports	1985–present.
ACRS meeting transcripts	1999–present (subcommittee as well as full committee).

representing a combination of selected documents from the ADAMS library (which, at the time of the project, contained around two million documents, of which roughly half were publicly available) and a number of other documents.

ICA 2.2 consists of a number of major software components, including the following (Zhu *et al.* 2011):

- "Crawlers", which go through the documents in the corpus and extract document content
- Document processors, which convert the unstructured text data generated by the crawlers into structured data using rules provided by text analytic "annotators" (including standard annotators to do such things as identify the document language, perform a linguistics analysis, and identify text patterns using user-supplied rules, as well as any additional custom annotators)

- An indexer, which prepares an optimized index of the processed document content (called a "text analytics collection", or "collection" for short) suitable for high-speed text mining and analysis
- A text mining application, which provides the user interface that enables an analyst to search the corpus.

ICA 2.2 is a general product that can be customized to address the needs of specific problems. This customization process requires:

- that software engineers configure the tool (for example, to control how a crawler uses system resources and when it should be run) and develop desired annotators
- that SMEs work with the software engineers to collaboratively define the search problem of interest and ensure efficient tool development.

From an end-user perspective, most of the work performed by the software engineers is "behind the scenes". For example, the SME generally does not construct or perform a detailed review of the annotators produced by the software engineers, but uses a customized text mining application, also produced by the software engineers, which provides a number of tools supporting user searches and discovery.

The principal tools are "facets", different subject-oriented collections of keywords that provide different views of the corpus data, and their associated searches. For example, a facet intended to provide a view of operational events involving multiple units could be constructed from sets of keywords capturing important aspects of such events (for example, extent of effect, causes, coupling mechanisms, near misses). A search hit involving one of these keywords would indicate that the identified document addresses one of these aspects and is therefore potentially relevant to an analysis of multi-unit events. A significant portion of the SME effort in developing the customized ICA 2.2 tool is involved in developing "facets" for a particular use case that help identify relevant documents without an excessive number of false positives.

Other ICA 2.2 features help filter search results and support the development of statistics (for example, matching document counts, frequencies of and trends in search phrase occurrences, and correlations between pairs of search phrase occurrences) and the visual identification of relationships between facets.

13.4.2 Overall Approach

The work involved the performance of three case studies ("use cases") is summarized in Table 13.3: the identification and characterization of operational events involving multiple reactor units; the determination of current core damage frequency (CDF) estimates developed in licensee PRAs; and a general exploration of a wide set of documents to identify potentially interesting

Table 13.3 Project use cases.

No.	Description	Notes
1	Search for multi-unit events	Supports characterization of past events involving multiple units at a site. This characterization could identify events that may need to be addressed in a site-wide PRA model.
2	Characterization of current licensee PRA results	Supports decision makers' understanding of current risk levels and contributors. This activity addresses a common question raised by managers and external stakeholders.
E	Exploration of corpus	Uses ICA 2.2 in a discovery/exploration mode. This use case supports the project's evaluation of the tool when used in a non-direct search mode.

risk-relevant topics for more detailed investigation. The first two use cases employed the ICA 2.2 tool in a traditional search mode to address the typical staff task of searching for answers to highly specific questions. The last employed the ICA 2.2 tool in a more general, discovery-oriented mode.

For each use case, the ability of ICA 2.2 to effectively and efficiently meet staff needs was assessed and compared with the capabilities of other tools currently available to the staff. All use cases involved an iterative search process in which the user provided an initial search query, reviewed results, refined the query, and so forth until either the desired results were achieved or the effort was terminated. Thus ICA 2.2 should be viewed as human-in-the-loop tools, rather than fully automatic answer generators, as is the case with IBM's Watson.

The following section discusses the motivation, approach, and results for use case 1. Information on the other two use cases can be found in Siu, *et al.* (2016b).

13.4.3   Use Case 1

As argued by Fleming (2005) and illustrated by the March 2011 reactor accidents at the Fukushima Daiichi nuclear power plant, events involving multiple reactor units at a single site can be important contributors to site risk. There are numerous technical challenges in assessing these contributions. NRC/RES is currently engaged in a full-scope Level 3 PRA study intended to address all relevant site radiological sources (including the spent fuel pool and dry cask storage), internal and external initiating event hazards, and modes of operation for a two-unit Westinghouse four-loop pressurized water reactor station with a large, dry containment (NRC 2011; Kuritzky *et al.* 2013). The technical approach for addressing multi-unit (and, more generally, multisource) events is described in broad terms in the project's Technical Analysis Approach Plan (NRC 2013). To inform the modeling of such events, it is a good idea to review

NRC FORM 366 (7-2001)

U.S. NUCLEAR REGULATORY COMMISSION

LICENSEE EVENT REPORT (LER)

(See reverse for required number of digits/characters for each block)

APPROVED BY OMB NO. 3150-0104 EXPIRES 6-30-2001

Estimated burden per response to comply with this mandatory information collection request: 50 hours. Reported lessons learned are incorporated into the licensing process and fed back to industry. Send comments regarding burden estimate to the Records Management Branch (T-6 E6), U.S. Nuclear Regulatory Commission, Washington, DC 20555-0001, or by internet e-mail to bjs1@nrc.gov, and to the Desk Officer, Office of Information and Regulatory Affairs, NEOB-10202 (3150-0104), Office of Management and Budget, Washington, DC 20503. If a means used to impose information collection does not display a currently valid OMB control number, the NRC may not conduct or sponsor, and a person is not required to respond to, the information collection.

FACILITY NAME (1)	DOCKET NUMBER (2)	PAGE (3)
Peach Bottom Atomic Power Station, Unit 2	05000 277	1 OF 4

TITLE (4)

Loss of Offsite Power Source Results in Specified System Actuation and Safety System Functional Failure.

EVENT DATE (5)			LER NUMBER (6)			REPORT DATE (7)			OTHER FACILITIES INVOLVED (8)	
MO	DAY	YEAR	YEAR	SEQUENTIAL NUMBER	REV NO	MO	DAY	YEAR	FACILITY NAME Unit 3	DOCKET NUMBER 05000 278
06	18	01	01	0 0 1	00	08	17	01	FACILITY NAME	DOCKET NUMBER

OPERATING MODE (9)	1
POWER LEVEL (10)	100

THIS REPORT IS SUBMITTED PURSUANT TO THE REQUIREMENTS OF 10 CFR §: (Check all that apply) (11)

	20.2201(b)		20.2203(a)(3)(ii)		50.73(a)(2)(ii)(B)		50.73(a)(2)(ix)(A)
	20.2201(d)		20.2203(a)(4)		50.73(a)(2)(iii)		50.73(a)(2)(x)
	20.2203(a)(1)		50.36(c)(1)(i)(A)	x	50.73(a)(2)(iv)(A)		73.71(a)(4)
	20.2203(a)(2)(i)		50.36(c)(1)(ii)(A)		50.73(a)(2)(v)(A)		73.71(a)(5) OTHER Specify in Abstract below or in NRC Form 366A
	20.2203(a)(2)(ii)		50.36(c)(2)		50.73(a)(2)(v)(B)		
	20.2203(a)(2)(iii)		50.46(a)(3)(ii)		50.73(a)(2)(v)(C)		
	20.2203(a)(2)(iv)		50.73(a)(2)(i)(A)	x	50.73(a)(2)(v)(D)		
	20.2203(a)(2)(v)		50.73(a)(2)(i)(B)	x	50.73(a)(2)(vii)		
	20.2203(a)(2)(vi)		50.73(a)(2)(i)(C)		50.73(a)(2)(viii)(A)		
	20.2203(a)(3)(i)		50.73(a)(2)(ii)(A)		50.73(a)(2)(viii)(B)		

Figure 13.3 Excerpt from example LER for a multi-unit event.

past operational events to provide an indication of the likelihood and impact of these events, and of their salient features.

However, such a review, although straightforward in principle, can be extremely labor-intensive. The NRC receives thousands of licensee event reports (LERs) each year. These contain both structured and unstructured data; Figure 13.3 reproduces the first page of an example LER. Publicly available aids such as LERSearch (https://lersearch.inl.gov/LERSearchCriteria.aspx), search tools provided by the ADAMS system, and general search aids (for example, indices for pdf files created using programs such as Adobe Acrobat) are helpful but are not tailored to address the multi-unit problem, and (in the case of LERSearch) do not provide access to a number of non-LER-related documents that might be useful.

13.4.3.1 Use Case 1 Objective and Scope

The specific objective of this use case was to evaluate the effectiveness and efficiency of ICA 2.2 in helping users identify and characterize past US operational events involving multiple reactors. The use case scope limitations were as follows:

- The project corpus was limited to the document types shown in Table 13.2.
- The focus was on events involving an "initiating event": an event that perturbs the steady-state operation of a nuclear power plant and could lead to an undesired plant condition (Drouin *et al.* 2013) at one or more units at a single site. The search did not exclude but was not aimed at identifying degraded

conditions that could affect the response of multiple units at a site during an accident, or at identifying events/conditions affecting multiple sites.

- The events were characterized in terms of the event date, site involved, event extent, and event cause.

13.4.3.2   Use Case 1 Technical Challenges

On the surface, it might seem that a search for multi-unit initiating events should be straightforward. After all, surely a human analyst, upon reading an event summary, can readily determine whether that event involved initiating events at multiple units or not. However, there are an enormous number of event reports to review: the project's corpus contains nearly 55 000 LERs covering the period 1980–2014. Furthermore, although determining whether an event involved multiple units is straightforward (see the highlighted text in Figure 13.3), the event descriptions often must be read carefully to determine whether the event involved an initiating event or a degraded condition: a situation that weakened the plant but did not actually involve an accident.

Computer tools, at least in principle, are well suited for addressing large numbers of documents. However, at least for text-based tools such as ICA 2.2, there are significant challenges in recognizing the significance of graphical elements (for example, box lines around text to provide special emphasis) in an arbitrary document; taking advantage of the highlighted field in Figure 13.3 requires a non-trivial custom programming effort. Another challenge arises from the natural language used to describe events. As an example, Table 13.4 provides a sample of multi-unit events identified as precursors by the NRC's Accident Sequence Precursor (ASP) Program. According to SECY-15-0124 (NRC 2015), which provides the status and results of the ASP program as of 2015, a nuclear power plant accident precursor is defined as an event with a conditional core damage probability or a change in core damage probability greater than or equal to 1×10^{-6}.

The last column in the table contains key phrases from the associated LERs indicating that the event involved initiating events at multiple units. Not only are the phrases non-standardized, sometimes the effects on different units are described in different places in the LER. Additional challenges to software tools include those discussed in Section 13.5.1 (for example, flawed digitized data).

13.4.3.3   Use Case 1 Approach

The general approach for this use case employed the following steps:

- Specify the search problem.
- Develop a project-specific, customized search application using ICA 2.2.
- Test and refine the customized application.
- Exercise the application to identify and retrieve documents containing the information sought, and compare with alternate approaches.

Table 13.4 Example multi-unit precursor events with indicative phrases.

Date	Site	Type	LER(s)	Indicative phrase(s)
22 June 1982	Quad Cities	LOOP	254/82–012	*Separated text, requires inference:* "Unit Two reactor tripped" AND "Due to the degraded mode of the Unit One emergency AC power system, a Generating Station Emergency Plan Unusual Event was declared." *Could also infer from:* "Unit 1/2 Diesel Generator tripped."
11 August 1983	Salem	LOOP	272/83–033, 272/83–034	*Direct statements:* "Both Salem units tripped," "Salem Units 1 and 2 Reactor Trips."
26 July 1984	Susquehanna	Station blackout during test	388/84–013	*Separated text, requires inference:* "Unit 2 operating" AND "This resulted in a scram" AND "Unit 1 entered an LCO."
17 May 1985	Turkey Point	LOOP	251/85–011	*Direct statement:* "An Unusual Event was declared for both Units 3 and 4."
23 July 1987	Calvert Cliffs	LOOP	317/87–012	*Direct statement:* "Resulting in both reactors tripping on loss of load."
20 March 1990	Vogtle	LOOP	424/90–006, 425/90–002	*Direct statement:* "Tripped Unit 1 RAT A and Unit 2 RAT B." *Could also infer from:* Unit 1 LER (424/90–006) "Further description of the Unit 2 response to this event is provided in LER 50-425/1990-002" OR Unit 2 LER (425/90-002) "See Licensee Event Report 50-424/1990-006 for a discussion of the resulting effect on Unit 1."

The use-case team comprised three SMEs and two software engineers. Two of the SMEs had pre-project experience performing manual searches of LERs for multi-unit events and conditions, and helped the software engineers develop the use-case-specific facets for the customized search application (constructed using ICA 2.2). The third SME, who had no formal experience searching for multi-unit events and was not involved in the development of the customized application, conducted the final demonstration as a blind test.

The Step 4 analysis was performed in two phases to exercise the customized search application in two different usage modes: informed search (in which very specific information is known about the target documents) and basic search (in which only general information is known about the target documents). In all cases, the demonstration was limited to events involving initiating events. This greatly reduced the number of LERs to be reviewed. (For example, of the 392 multi-unit LERs identified by Schroer and Modarres (2013) for the period 2000–2011, the large majority do not involve initiating events.)

Phase 1 – Informed Search involved searches of the corpus to find specific LERs for multi-unit events, was performed in two stages. The first stage, which helped the SME that was conducting the final demonstration to become better acquainted with the use-case-specific facets of the customized search application, was aimed at finding the LERs for a 2011 dual-unit LOOP at the North Anna nuclear power plant (caused by an earthquake) and a 2011 three-unit LOOP at the Browns Ferry plant (caused by a tornado). The search process involved performing an initial search using selected facets and individual keywords. Progressive refinements of the search query, sometimes using additional user-supplied keywords to supplement the built-in keywords, eventually resulted in a manageable number of hits. At this point, a quick review of contextual text supplied by ICA2.2 along with each search hit, or of the target documents, was usually sufficient to determine whether the hits represented the desired search results. The second stage involved a search of the corpus for the LERs for all of the multi-unit initiating events judged to be accident precursors by the NRC's ASP program. (There were 27 such events from 1969–2015). This stage used a user-constructed search query building on the keywords included in the customized search application, and taking advantage of the ICA 2.2 interface compatibility with standard word processors, which facilitated the construction of complex queries.

Phase 2 – Basic Search involved two separate searches for multi-unit initiating events that exercised the customized search application in a more exploratory mode; that is, without prior knowledge regarding which specific events involved multiple units. The first search focused on the LERs in the project corpus. The second search focused on finding ASP-related SECY papers referring to multi-unit initiating events. The search was only aimed at identifying relevant SECY papers; the papers themselves typically provided the LER numbers for the events.

13.4.3.4 Use Case 1 Results

The general results of use case 1 are provided below. Additional details are provided in Siu *et al.* (2016b).

With respect to multi-unit event identification, when provided with highly discriminating information (for example, unique characteristics, such as the occurrence of an earthquake or tornado, or specific event identifiers, such as LER number), the customized search application enabled effective and efficient searches. The search results were as complete as could be expected (search misses were caused by missing documents in the corpus rather than application deficiencies) and resulted in very few false positives. The application was easy to use and provided rapid responses (often within a few seconds) to queries.

When provided with less specific information, the searches were less successful; they only identified a small number of relevant events and also identified a fair number of false positives. Improved keyword lists better reflecting the variety of key terms used in the LERs would probably help, but more advanced programming (for example, to draw inferences across widely separated text) is likely necessary to ensure that the searches are effective and efficient. Such additional effort was not judged to be necessary for the purposes of this feasibility study.

With respect to multi-unit event characterization, the customized search application provided a number of aids (principally highlighted contextual text) that helped users identify event characteristics of interest (for example, event date, facility name, and event extent). However, these aids were not helpful for all LERs; document download and review remained the surest approach to collecting the desired information. In this light, the primary value of the application was in identifying the best documents to download and review.

Two other tools tested for their ability to help identify and characterize multi-unit LERs were LERSearch (https://lersearch.inl.gov/Entry.aspx) and the pdf library search capabilities provided by Adobe Acrobat. LERSearch also proved extremely effective and efficient for simple searches. However, as compared with the customized search application, its advanced query capabilities proved somewhat less powerful, its search space was restricted to LERs, and it lacked the ability to save searches. This last point becomes especially important when refining a search query, and when performing multiple searches.

Adobe Acrobat searches of the library of LERs used in this project were slower than those of the customized search application or LERSearch and were less flexible, and the contextual text provided with search results was less helpful.

13.4.4 Scoping Study Conclusions and Commentary

13.4.4.1 Conclusions

Based upon the results of the three use cases identified in Table 13.3, we observe the following:

- The customized search application developed from ICA 2.2 was generally effective and efficient in identifying target documents of interest to the use cases. In the one test situation in which the tool was not effective (a basic, uninformed search for LERs involving multi-unit events), additional refinements (particularly updating the tool facets) would likely improve its performance.
- The application proved capable of supporting more open-ended explorations of the database that led to potentially interesting insights and suggested avenues for further exploration.
- The human-in-the-loop, stepwise search approach underlying ICA 2.2 was comfortable to use, at least for the corpus and use cases tested. Feedback from queries was quick (typically on the order of a few seconds) and informative, and document downloads (when more detailed information was needed) were also quick.
- The initial development and subsequent refinement of a useful application required extensive interactions between the SMEs and the software engineers to ensure mutual understanding of the technical problem(s) targeted by the tool, examples of a successful search, and the objectives and capabilities of the tool.
- Although the customized application was developed only to support this project's technology evaluation, it appears to be capable of assisting staff interested in extracting PRA-relevant lessons from operational experience documents.
  - As compared with LERSearch (the current staff tool of choice), the ICA 2.2 interface provided additional capabilities (for example, supporting the development of complex searches, the saving of searches, and the rapid screening of search results through contextual text). The ICA 2.2 tool also provided access to potentially useful documents beyond LERs.
  - As compared with more general ADAMS-based tools, the reduced size and pre-indexing of the project corpus led to significantly more rapid searches.
- Further work, perhaps requiring major programming effort or even technology development, could significantly increase the application's power and ease of use. This includes work to take advantage of data structures in technical documents, including document sections, structures within text passages (for example, subordinate clauses), and tables.

13.4.4.2 Additional Observations

The following observations, derived from the experiences of the scoping project, should be useful when developing future KE solutions:

- In general, problems with database documents (for example, due to errors in the documents, OCR faults, or faulty document profiling) can hinder text-based searches by any tool. In many cases, the keywords of interest occur multiple times within a document, so database problems may not significantly affect search results. However, cases can arise (for example, when searching for a document with a specific identifier) in which such problems are critical. If it is important that the search identify all documents matching a specific query, considerable effort may be needed to ensure that potential errors in the documents are identified and handled by the tool.

- The willingness of users to pursue searches (or explorations) using any tool depends on, among other things, the time required to obtain informative feedback for each query. To help ensure rapid yet helpful feedback, it may be useful to:
  – focus applications on problems that can be addressed with a smaller corpus
  – provide users with tips for developing queries that generate quicker responses.

- For ICA 2.2 and similar tools, document download and review is an integral part of the search process. Download by hyperlink is straightforward. However, the review portion can be resource-intensive. For use case 1, the review was aided by the title and summary sections of LERs. For use case 2, the review was aided by reports that provided standardized tables of CDF information in standard document sections. Thus, although ICA 2.2 has been developed to deal with unstructured data, the overall search process benefits from structured data.

13.4.4.3 Commentary: On Oracles Versus Aides

At the beginning of the project, encouraged by the implications of the IBM Watson *Jeopardy!* demonstration and the natural language capabilities of personal assistant software, the project SMEs hoped that ICA 2.2 would be able to provide direct answers to such natural language questions as "What are some key multi-unit events worth further examination?" (use case 1) or "What is the CDF for Plant X?" (use case 2). As the project progressed, it became clear that ICA 2.2 is not targeted at this kind of problem.

First, ICA 2.2 is largely intended to support database exploration. When employed in a direct question/answer mode, it can generate applications that produce informative intermediate results (for example, which LERs involving multiple units are referenced in ASP SECY papers) and potentially useful statistics (for example, how many documents include references to total CDF). However, in general, the user must review contextual text or review linked documents to answer a posed question. Furthermore, given the natural language variations in source documents (for example, see Table 13.4 and Figure 13.3), significant effort (well beyond that employed in this technology evaluation project) is necessary to ensure that the search results are reasonably complete (without including an excessive number of false positives).

Second, and related to the point above, ICA 2.2 is designed as a human-in-the-loop tool. Thus, in search mode, the tool does not function as an oracle that provides final answers to a user's questions. Rather, it acts as an aide, providing information that suggests, as the search progresses, the next steps a user might take to refine a search, and then hyperlinks that help the user download and review documents that might contain the answers.

Due to the limited scope of this project, we did not generate any empirical data relevant to the current effectiveness and efficiency of commercial, off-the-shelf software to (after appropriate customization) directly answer questions of the sort underlying use cases 1 and 2. However, given the complexities revealed in the two use cases, it appears likely that the development of an industrial grade, fully automated solution will require considerable SME and software engineer involvement. Moreover, by not involving the SME as an integral part of the actual search process, such a solution:

- may not take full advantage of:
  - SME skills, for example recognizing words and numbers despite faulty OCR or faulty entry of metadata – titles, authors, dates, and so on – characterizing documents stored in databases, recognizing the data relationships implied by a tabular structure
  - SME knowledge, for example, to recognize apparent conflicts between documents.
- may generate results not fully trusted by the SME
- will minimize the learning benefits associated with formulating and refining a search, including learning from efforts to develop a search strategy, lessons from "failed" searches, and useful information and insights from intermediate search results.

In addition to the fully automated ("oracle") versus human-in-the-loop ("aide") issue, KE solution developers need to consider whether the emphasis is on:

- providing a partner – collaborating with the user to build knowledge or even alerting them when items of interest, such as the Blayais event, arise – or a servant that only responds to requests
- supporting open-ended exploration or answering specific factual questions
- developing broad base understanding by encouraging user "play" or answering immediate, task-oriented needs.

A notional representation of how current technologies appear to be approaching these considerations is shown in Figure 13.4.

For such organizations as the NRC, near-term efforts are likely to be aimed at highly focused and pragmatic developments. However, it is important to recognize that a broad staff knowledge base is important for flexible and agile agency operations, and non-traditional knowledge management approaches (with associated KE solutions) may be helpful in developing such breadth.

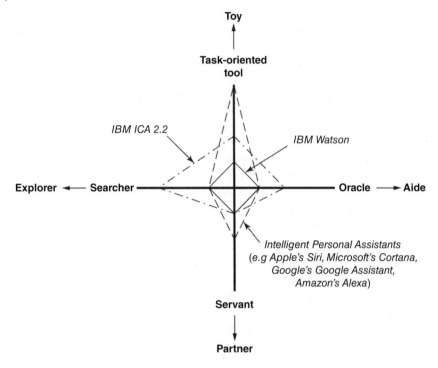

Figure 13.4 Notional representation of different KE solutions.

13.5 Conclusions and Suggestions for Future Developments

In this article, we have shown the following:

- The NRC uses information to support risk-informed decision making in a wide variety of applications. The breadth of applications and the inherent breadth of considerations involved in risk-informed decision making imply a wide variety of informational needs.
- The special characteristics of risk information, including the information supporting PRAs and the information resulting from PRAs, pose special challenges to KE activities supporting the creation, management, retrieval, and use of risk information.
- Advanced KE technologies are evolving to support the growing needs of organizations relying on massive amounts of unstructured information. Currently available commercial tools based on these technologies are sufficiently capable of supplementing tools used by NRC staff in risk-relevant activities.

- Additional efforts from the user and developer communities are likely to result in improved tools for the staff:
  - In the near term, useful work could involve improving the electronic database (for example, through the digitization of legacy documents and the correction of faulty digitized records) and the development of more efficient and effective query structures (for example, facets in the case of ICA 2.2) for targeted staff tasks (for example, those represented by use cases 1 and 2). The organizational resources and commitment required for such work should not be underestimated.
  - Somewhat longer-term work, which would require significant programming effort, at least in the case of ICA 2.2, could involve the development of software tools that can take advantage of internal document structures (for example, document sections, structures within text passages, and tables).
  - In the long term, (i) tools that combine implicit information ("connecting the dots" between declarations) and (ii) "watchdog" applications, alerting users of new noteworthy information about, for example, potential accident precursors (as in our Le Blayais example) could be valuable as a way to provide explicit risk information.

It is important to recognize that there are many communities actively engaged in improving the access to and use of information. These include communities concerned with artificial intelligence and expert systems, natural language processing, analytics, "big data," library science, and education, as well as KM. Involving these communities in future discussions regarding risk information will not only help avoid unnecessary duplication of effort, it will also add a breadth of views that could improve the tools provided to users.

Finally, it is also important to recognize that KE solutions are only part of the knowledge management toolbox. There are many non-technical approaches for enhancing staff awareness of and access to important information. The prioritization of activities to develop and implement improved KE technology will need to consider the full range of potentially viable approaches for addressing staff needs.

Acknowledgements

The authors gratefully acknowledge project support provided by M. Tobin, S. Dennis, P. Appignani, G. Young, S. Raimist, and K. Bojja; the information provided by G. Georgescu, C. Pfefferkorn, and A. D'Agostino; the helpful comments provided by E. Zio; and the editing support provided by C. Siu.

References

Note: ADAMS document accession numbers (starting with the designator "ML") can be used to obtain the associated documents from the NRC ADAMS Public Documents System (see http://www.nrc.gov/reading-rm/adams.html). Similarly, NRC reports (with the NUREG designator) can be obtained from the NRC website (see http://www.nrc.gov/reading-rm/doc-collections/).

AERB (2005) AERB Annual report for the year 2004–2005. Atomic Energy Regulatory Board, Mumbai, India.

Apostolakis, G., Lui, C., Cunningham, M., Pangburn, G., and Reckley, W. (2012) A proposed risk management regulatory framework. *NUREG-2150*, US Nuclear Regulatory Commission, Washington, DC, USA.

ASME/ANS (2009) Standard for Level 1/large early release frequency probabilistic risk assessment for nuclear power plant applications. ASME/ANS RA-Sa-2009, Addendum A to RA-S-2008, ASME, New York, NY, American Nuclear Society, La Grange Park, Illinois.

Drouin, M., Gonzalez, M., Herrick, S., *et al.* (2013) Glossary of risk-related terms in support of risk-informed decisionmaking. *NUREG-2122*, US Nuclear Regulatory Commission, Washington, DC, USA.

Dupuy, P., Georgescu, G., and Corenwinder, F. (2014) Treatment of the loss of ultimate heat sink initiating events in the IRSN Level 1 PSA. NEA/CSNI/R(2014)9, Probabilistic Safety Assessment (PSA) of Natural External Hazards Including Earthquakes: *Workshop Proceedings, Prague, Czech Republic, June 17–20, 2013*, Nuclear Energy Agency, Boulogne-Billancourt, France.

Epstein, W. and Rauzy, A. (2013) New developments in Open PSA. In: *Proceedings of ANS PSA 2013 International Topical Meeting on Probabilistic Safety Assessment and Analysis*, Columbia, SC, September 22–26.

Ferrucci, D., Brown, E., Chu-Carroll, J., *et al.* (2010) Building Watson: an overview of the DeepQA Project. *AI Magazine*, 31(3), 59–79.

Fleming, K. (2005) On the issue of integrated risk – a PRA practitioner's perspective. *Proceedings of ANS. International Topical Meeting on Probabilistic Safety Analysis* (PSA'05), San Francisco, CA, September 11–15.

Friedlhuber, T., Hibti, M., and Rauzy, A. (2015) A method to compare PSA models in a modular PSA. In: *Proceedings of ANS PSA 2015 International Topical Meeting on Probabilistic Safety Assessment and Analysis*, Sun Valley, ID, April 26–30.

Gorbatchev, A., Mattéi, J.M, Rebour, V., and Vial, E. (2000) Report on flooding of Le Blayais power plant on 27 December 1999. *Proceedings of EUROSAFE 2000, Cologne, Germany, November 6–7*, Gesellschaft für Anlagen- und Reaktorsicherheit (GRS) Gmbh, Cologne, Germany.

IAEA (2000) Measures to strengthen international co-operation in nuclear, radiation and waste safety including nuclear safety review for the year 1999.

IAEA General Conference, International Atomic Energy Agency, Vienna, Austria.

IPSN (2000) Rapport sur l'inondation du site du Blayais. Institut de Protection et de Sûreté Nucléaire, Fontenay-aux-Roses, France.

Keim, B. (2015) IBM's Dr. Watson will see you...someday. *IEEE Spectrum*, 29 May 2015.

Kuritzky, A., Siu, N., Coyne, K., Hudson, D., and Stutzke, M. (2013) L3PRA: Updating NRC's Level 3 PRA insights and capabilities. *Proceedings IAEA Technical Meeting on Level 3 Probabilistic Safety Assessment, Vienna, Austria, July 2–6, 2012*, International Atomic Energy Agency, Vienna, Austria. (ADAMS ML12173A092)

Markoff, J. (2011) Computer wins on "Jeopardy!": trivial, it's not. *New York Times*, 16 February.

Meléndez Asensio, E. and Santos, R.H. (2015) Use of PSA model XML standard formats for V&V. In: *Proceedings of ANS PSA 2015 International Topical Meeting on Probabilistic Safety Assessment and Analysis*, Sun Valley, ID, April 26–30.

Nowlen, S.P., Kazarians, M. and Wyant, F. (2001) Risk methods insights gained from fire incidents. NUREG/CR-6738, US Nuclear Regulatory Commission, Washington, DC, USA.

NRC (1975) Reactor safety study: An assessment of accident risks in U.S. commercial nuclear power plants. WASH-1400 (NUREG-75/014), US Nuclear Regulatory Commission, Washington, DC, USA.

NRC (1990) Severe accident risks: An assessment for five U.S. nuclear power plants. NUREG-1150, US Nuclear Regulatory Commission, Washington, DC, USA.

NRC (1998) An approach for using probabilistic risk assessment in risk-informed decisions on plant-specific changes to the licensing basis. Regulatory Guide RG 1.174, US Nuclear Regulatory Commission, Washington, DC, USA.

NRC (2009) An approach for determining the technical adequacy of probabilistic risk assessment results for risk-informed activities. Regulatory Guide RG 1.200 Rev. 2, US Nuclear Regulatory Commission, Washington, DC, USA.

NRC (2011) Options for proceeding with future Level 3 probabilistic risk assessment (PRA) activities. SECY-11–0089, US Nuclear Regulatory Commission, Washington, DC, USA. (ADAMS ML11090A039)

NRC (2013) Technical analysis approach plan for Level 3 PRA project, Rev 0b. US Nuclear Regulatory Commission, Washington, DC, USA. (ADAMS ML13296A064)

NRC (2015) Status of the accident sequence precursor program and the standardized plant analysis risk models. *SECY-15–0124*, US Nuclear Regulatory Commission, Washington, DC, USA. (ADAMS ML15187A434)

Schroer, S. and Modarres, M. (2013) An event classification schema for evaluating site risk in a multi-unit nuclear power plant probabilistic risk assessment. *Reliability Engineering & System Safety*, 117, 40–51.

Siu, N., Marksberry, D., Cooper, S., Coyne, K., and Stutzke, M. (2013) PSA technology challenges revealed by the Great East Japan Earthquake. *Proceedings of PSAM Topical Conference in Light of the Fukushima Dai-Ichi Accident, Tokyo, Japan, April 15–17.* (ADAMS ML13038A203)

Siu, N., Stutzke, M., Dennis, S., and Harrison, D. (2016a) Probabilistic risk assessment and regulatory decisionmaking: Some frequently asked questions. NUREG-2201, US Nuclear Regulatory Commission, Washington, DC, USA.

Siu, N., Dennis, S., and Tobin, M. (2016b) Advanced knowledge engineering tools to support risk-informed decision making: Final report. US Nuclear Regulatory Commission, Washington, DC, USA. (ADAMS ML16355A373)

Sulzberger, A.G. and Wald, M.L. (2011) Flooding brings worries over two nuclear plants. *New York Times*, 20 June.

Vial, E., Rebour, V., and Perrin, B. (2005) Severe storm resulting in partial plant flooding in "Le Blayais" nuclear power plant. In: *Proceedings of International Workshop on External Flooding Hazards at Nuclear Power Plant Sites* (jointly organized by Atomic Energy Regulatory Board of India, Nuclear Power Corporation of India, Ltd., and International Atomic Energy Agency), Kalpakkam, Tamil Nadu, India, August 29 – September 2.

Zhu, W.-D., Iwai, A., Leyba, T., *et al.* (2011) IBM content analytics version 2.2: Discovering actionable insight from your content, (2nd edn). International Business Machines Corporation.

Index

Knowledge in Risk Assessment and Management, First Edition. Edited by Terje Aven and Enrico Zio.
© 2018 John Wiley & Sons Ltd. Published 2018 by John Wiley & Sons Ltd.